The Fifties Spiritual Marketplace

The Fifties Spiritual Marketplace

American Religion in a Decade of Conflict

ROBERT S. ELLWOOD

RUTGERS UNIVERSITY PRESS
New Brunswick, New Jersey

Library of Congress Cataloging-in-Publication Data

Ellwood, Robert S., 1933–
    The fifties spiritual marketplace: American religion in a decade
of conflict / Robert S. Ellwood.
        p.   cm.
    Includes bibliographical references and index.
    ISBN 0-8135-2345-1. — ISBN 0-8135-2346-X (pbk.)
    1. United States—Religion—1945–1960.   2. United States—Church
history—20th century. I. Title.
BL2525.E426 1997
200'.973'09045—dc20   96-9044
                                                                         CIP

British Cataloging-in-Publication information available

Manufactured in the United States of America

Contents

Preface

THIS VOLUME represents a continuation of a study of U.S. religion in the mid–twentieth century begun with *The Sixties Spiritual Awakening*. Working backward from that tumultuous decade, my intention is now to look at the previous ten years. The Fifties have often been considered a sort of baseline for all the subsequent twists and turns of religion and society generally in the United States, as though they represented a "normalcy" against which everything else can be judged. Nothing could be further from the truth; like most immediate postwar eras, they combined yearning for normalcy with the effects of profound dislocations. No less distorted is the view of many, no doubt enhanced by the memories of those millions of baby-boom Americans who had reasonably happy Fifties childhoods, that those were generally tranquil, secure days. Such was not likely the view of their parents, who knew what was going on.

Religion was, however, also very much going on in the Fifties. I propose to look at religion in its own terms, and in terms of its reaction to the great events and issues of the day. If not the decade many seem to have imagined it to have been, it was an unusual and fascinating time.

This book owes much to the unfailing support and good advice I have received from readers and staff of Rutgers University Press. I would particularly like to express my appreciation to my editor, Martha Heller, whose encouragement and insight have been invaluable, and to Professor Philip Hammond, who read and critiqued the manuscript. I have also received much of great importance from colleagues on the faculty of the School of Religion of the University of Southern California, especially Professor Donald E. Miller, who have read portions of the manuscript and provided excellent assistance.

The chapter epigraphs are passages that seemed appropriate to me from the Revised Standard Version of the Bible, whose publication was a major Fifties religious event.

The Fifties Spiritual Marketplace

Introduction: Foundations of the Fifties

Again, the kingdom of heaven is like a net which was
thrown into the sea and gathered fish of every kind.
—MATT. 13:47 *RSV*

Little Church on the Prairie

IN 1957, fresh out of divinity school, I became pastor of an Episcopal church in a small town in Nebraska. This parish was probably one of very few in that predominantly eastern and upscale denomination to have a preponderance of real midwestern dirt farmers among its members. Like many churches on the Great Plains it had nineteenth-century immigrant roots; in this case the core remained the progeny and relations by marriage of three families who had come over from England to settle on the land nearly a hundred years before and wanted something resembling a proper Anglican village church. Their numbers were augmented by a sprinkling of upwardly mobile converts, and a few strayed Episcopalians from back east.

Though only a pale reflection of the celebrated suburban ecclesiastical powerhouses of the decade, this church in the late Fifties possessed some characteristics of the decade's religious life. I recall young families and innumerable children crowding Sunday school, vacation church school, picnics, and potluck suppers. Many of the leading men, the fathers of those children, were veterans of the great and good war that had ended only twelve years before.

It was a fine time to go to church. According to Gallup polls, the highest historical level of church attendance, about 47 percent of the U.S. population on an average Sunday, was reached in 1955 and 1958. While these figures, like most such poll findings, are probably on the high side, I remember thinking that about half the congregation was usually there on the typical Sunday.

It was also a good time to build. During my tenure the church put up a new parish hall that cost, with the help of much volunteer labor, only some

$6,500; it was a tiny part of the $935 million that went into new church construction across the nation in 1959, up from $26 million in 1945 and from $409 million in 1950. The high point was, in fact, 1959; new construction fell to $358 million in 1960 as the calendar turned to a very different sort of decade for religion.

Everyone in the church looked and dressed very conventionally for the times: hats and heels for the women, coats and ties, short hair, and a clean shave on the males. Young people were the most clean shaven of all. The exception came when the town celebrated its centennial and, as a token of nostalgia for pioneer days, the men (though not high school and college students) grew beards. A hundred years before, this town had not been far from the route of the great overland migrations, with their covered wagons and straining oxen, and their cargo of hopeful young families who sang around the campfires of an evening. (The 1950s were the scene of another vast internal migration of hardly less dimension and consequence, the movement of young families from small rural towns like mine, and from the inner cities, to burgeoning suburbs where a new way of life and constellation of attitudes was being forged, including new religious styles. But enough remained behind in the Fifties to keep the church going.)

Many families of the 1950s had more disposable income than ever before and were busy buying dishwashers, television sets with big antennae to while away their evenings, and new cars every year. Some well-off people would take long trips over the expanding freeways each summer or even travel to Europe, which was still cheap.

Not everyone prospered in the Fifties. The church was situated only a block from a main east-west highway and a major transcontinental railroad. Hardly a week passed without some out-of-work wanderer, or old-fashioned hobo, stopping by for help. I learned soon enough that some were authentic and some were con artists and tried to do the best I could in each case. Out in the country, on the back roads, one could find families still scarred by Thirties-style grinding poverty. They had married too young, and there was too much hard work. When I came calling I met women with wide tired eyes, silent hard-bitten men, and little girls in dirty flour-sack dresses. Sometimes I could not avoid suspecting after-hours violence and abuse toward wife and children.

Like Garrison Keillor's Lake Wobegon, Nebraska had its share of bachelor farmers. Some were homosexual, some drank, some just worked hard and then sat and stared into space of an evening. Once in a while one would get up on some dark subzero winter morning and go out and shoot himself behind the barn.

I recall only a handful of women who worked outside the home, usually as teachers or nurses, or in government offices like the county clerk's or the farm bureau. Most working women were divorced or widowed, what would today be called single parents, and despite the extended families that were still functional in that part of the country, their lives were not easy. A few women labored alongside their husbands in a family business or, more commonly in this parish, on a family farm. Their lives were also hard, for gender division of labor was taken for granted, and a woman had to do all the woman's work, plus whatever she could behind the counter or in the barnyard.

But most town women were simply wives and mothers, and the more prosperous farmers prided themselves on freeing their mates from all but these roles. That also afforded women a certain level of free time for service to church and community, and there was seldom any shortage of volunteers to serve on the altar guild, teach Sunday school, sing in the choir, serve as den mothers for the church's Cub Scout pack, and maintain a variety of worthy community organizations from PTA to the local Red Cross chapter.

Again, this state of affairs was basically seen to be as it should be, even as ordained by God. The ideal, expressed by *McCall's* magazine in 1954, was articulated in the famous word *togetherness.*[1] The nuclear, not extended, family seemed best to embody the dream. This family was to be a single functioning unit, with the husband out in the working world earning its bread, and the wife maintaining the home front. She was to support her partner materially through her unpaid labor and emotionally through her appreciation and encouragement—as well as her social activity—in every way she could.

As David Halberstam has put it, "A family was a single perfect universe—instead of a complicated, fragile mechanism of conflicting political and emotional pulls. Families portrayed in women's magazines exhibited no conflicts or contradictions or unfulfilled ambitions."[2] For a wife to have a separate career with competitive demands would, obviously, quite undermine that "perfect universe." (Even a wife who was noncompetitive but less than perfectly suited for the role could mean difficulty. William H. Whyte, Jr., in a 1952 *Life* article, "The Wife Problem," noted that the wife—whether she is a good conversationalist, puts people at ease, and "loves her husband's job"—is accounted an important factor when corporations pick their executives.)[3]

That new feature of Fifties homes, the "family room," where husband, wife, and growing children could gather in the evening or, among the sophisticated, for the cocktail hour, to watch television and possibly share adventures of the day, seemed to bespeak the togetherness-alone-with-the-nuclear-family vision. And it was ultimately the responsibility of the wife to make it work, or so the women's magazines seemed to say.

My parish probably did not take all this quite as seriously as did the new suburban tracts around Omaha and other cities. Very small towns with vital kinship networks have their own rhythms that are longer and slower than those of the national magazines, as well as their own styles of evil. But the young wives read those magazines, and they inevitably fulfilled youthful Fifties ideals by presenting themselves slimmer, better dressed, better coiffured, and less active outside the home than their mothers.

The new nuclear, "perfect universe" family could be fun. I remember housewives, with their houses and husbands and children in order, well placed in a well-defined world, who seemed happier than a good many women (or men) I have known since. The happiness of the happy growing families sparkles in my fondest memories of the decade. I do recall the occasional searching look, as though trying to find something just outside the line of vision, in the eyes of some Fifties wives. But most seemed to accept their world as it was and find joy in it—things were a lot better, we convinced ourselves, than anywhere else in the world, or than they used to be before and during the war.

So far as politics went, the parish contained active Republicans and Democrats alike, and this was occasion for good-natured joshing. But there were limits beyond which it was dangerous to go. When I publicly supported a Quaker pacifist on the faculty of the University of Nebraska whom a local McCarthy (also a prominent Episcopalian) in the state legislature was trying to get fired, I received both support and censure, but this was obviously a very serious, very tricky matter about which nobody smiled.

Virtually everyone in the Platte Valley was properly anticommunist and generally took it for granted that the postwar United States represented the highest pinnacle of human civilization. Yet unlike some Fifties Americans we didn't worry too much about "The Bomb." Nebraskans are nothing if not survivors, at that time having the longest life expectancy in the nation despite the highest suicide rate, and we calculated that if the great cities east and west of us were taken out, we would keep on farming.

Services in my church were conventional; Scripture was read from the King James version. (I once ordered a shipment of the new Revised Standard Version from New York for use in classes. Those Bibles eventually arrived in our tiny Nebraska town, wrapped and the box stuffed with pages of the *Daily Worker*. That would certainly have confirmed the suspicions of some heartlanders about New York, the National Council of Churches, and its new Bible. But I said nothing locally.)

On the denominational level, the push in the Fifties was toward smooth organizational life, a sort of institutional equivalent of family togetherness. We had regional conferences for men, women, and young people (it sometimes seemed that, except for the Sunday morning service, nearly all church activities were segregated these three ways); we had clergy gatherings wherein we did flow charts analyzing the dynamics of meetings, and group encounters in which we heard from one another what sort of impressions we made—sophisticated techniques that could have been designed to wear down the genteel eccentricity for which a goodly portion of the Episcopal clergy, like their Church of England forebears, has long been famous. Fifties clergy tended to be conventional, well-organized, businesslike men who knew the value of real estate and how to emcee a dinner, though they had their crotchets, as became apparent if the prospect of ordaining women ever came up in a clerical conversation.

But at the time it seemed we were doing something right, for the church was growing much faster in those days than in the time of the kindly, dithery, birdwatching or Greek-muttering parson of old. In the Fifties, the Episcopal Church rose from 2.5 to 3.1 million members. Other denominations fared comparably: the Presbyterians went from 2.3 to 3.1 million, the Methodists from 8.9 to 9.8 million, the Southern Baptists from 7 to 9.4 million. In the Fifties, church membership nationwide grew at a faster rate than the national population, from 57 percent of the U.S. population in 1950 to 63.3 percent in 1959.

I knew, of course, of spiritual alternatives, and even of a spiritual "underground" to the religious world of which I was at the moment very much an above-ground part. In the early Fifties, when I was an undergraduate at the University of Colorado, some friends and I would get a thrill by going into Denver to a dark, Left Bankish espresso shop allegedly run by satanists. In that same city, I once heard a bearded cultist called Krishna Venta who claimed to have piloted the spaceship that brought the first humans to earth from Venus eighteen million years ago. One of my parishioners said that a flying saucer had landed in the barnyard of her mother's farm.

People of this generation were well aware of Jack Kerouac, Gary Snyder, Alan Watts, and the Beats. They were part of our fantasy world, whether we did anything about it or not. We loved to think about being "on the road," hitchhiking or in souped-up V-8s, traveling the endless highways of the vast nation. Being pious, I imagined a new kind of itinerant Christian saint, maybe a Fifties Franciscan, who would wander about like Kerouac's Beats, but spread the faith at the same time. While in seminary I saw Kerouac's famous underground film, *Pull My Daisy*, in which a group of Beats ask plaintive questions of a bishop of the Liberal Catholic Church, a tiny theosophically oriented denomination I was eventually to join. In my Nebraska parish, an elderly dowager, one of the largest donors, confided to me that she loved to read theosophical books, a small collection of which had been given years before to the local Carnegie Library. I got to know some Quakers who resided in the same town, and who as members of a traditional peace church exercised a quiet but healthy skepticism toward much of the national mood in those cold-war years.

All in all, I would say that my personal vantage point on the religious Fifties—only one of countless possible vantages, of course—lay within the mainline at a time that was the apotheosis of mainline U.S. religion, but furtively looking out in all directions: backward, forward, sideways. Perhaps that is a perspective from which to begin this quest for the Fifties spiritual landscape. The Fifties were a potent spiritual marketplace in which the traditional denominations were highly competitive, the nostalgia for normalcy working in their favor. But the religion boom coexisted with tension between Catholics and Protestants, and between "highbrow" theology and "lowbrow" popular faith. There was also a spiritual underground represented by the Beats and many others.

All of this was set against a distinctive Fifties cultural milieu dominated by the immense fact of the recently ended Second World War, and what it meant for the United States: a new postwar affluence, a young and rapidly growing population, a typical postwar exaltation of breeding and family togetherness plus a half-covert perpetuation of wartime male bonding, the great internal migration to the suburbs, a typical postwar interest in traditional and religious values, and the shadow cast by the United States's new postwar status as a world power in conflict with communism and the other world power, the Soviet Union. It was indeed an American high: high confidence and pride, high responsibility, high wariness and anxiety all somehow coexisted, just as the desire for, and belief in, normalization somehow located itself alongside a world role and militarization that had thoroughly changed the shape and meaning of the United States, it seemed permanently.

The present study plays on all of these themes, finding them embedded in the great issues of Fifties religion: church growth, religion in higher education, civil rights, religious response to major events from Korea and McCarthyism to Sputnik and Little Rock. In the remainder of this introductory chapter, I briefly preview and explain certain basic ideas against which the concrete workings of Fifties religion in the United States can be set.

The Marketplace and the Fifties

I would first like to propose that U.S. religion in the 1950s can effectively be conceptualized with the help of the supply side paradigm for religious participation advanced by Stephen Warner, Rodney Stark, Roger Finke, Laurence Iannoccone, and others.[4] The crux of this "new paradigm" is the obvious but often under-regarded realization that organized religion thrives in the United States in an open-market system.

In Europe, a town as small as the one in which my Fifties parish was located—2,400 souls plus a rural area—would be overwhelmingly likely to boast only one real church, doubtless a noble edifice on the central square, perhaps many hundreds of years old, Catholic, Anglican, Protestant, or Orthodox depending on the dominant religious culture. In more tolerant countries, there might be two or three hole-and-corner chapels somewhere for the minority of dissidents, as well as a Jewish synagogue. If the small town was unlucky enough to be located in one of the places, from Ireland to Bosnia, where two major churches or faiths were set up altar against altar, that would be cause for anything from constant bitter antagonism to genocidal bloodshed.

My town, however, had perhaps a dozen churches of all sizes and shapes— all the mainline denominations, with their well-known ethnic roots, together with a clutch of small but dynamic fundamentalist/ Pentecostal groups. These churches may have had some varying respectability ratings, though that was not as conspicuous on the Great Plains as in certain eastern cities. By and large they were all considered more or less equally legitimate and collectively responsible for the spiritual and moral well-being of the community. It was the U.S. denominational society in action; few of those to whom it seemed so natural realized how strange and unlikely such an arrangement would appear in most of the religious world.

The U.S. religious consumer did not demand that such a goodly variety of faiths and churches be available even in a town of a couple thousand. The variety was simply there, for well-known historical reasons: disestablishment, the frontier, immigration, even the fine public libraries, which produced at least one crypto-theosophist out on the prairies, and another woman I knew who, having read Vedanta-type literature, proudly claimed to be the only Hindu in Nebraska.

In these terms, the religious boom of the 1950s, it seems to me, can be understood first of all as a supply-side phenomenon. Availability of religion in plenteous diversity was not the only reason, of course. Immediate postwar periods in the United States have traditionally been good years for religion; one thinks of the revivals after the Revolution and of piety and church building after the Civil War. They are certainly related to another reason for postwar religious booms—a booming birthrate. But supply was better supplied in the Fifties than ever before, as Catholics, Jews, and evangelicals moved into high visibility and into the mainstream, and unprecedented prosperity meant that all denominations could put up the parish halls and skyline sanctuaries about which they had long dreamed. Though consumers essentially responded to availability rather than themselves demanding rampant pluralism, they had the means and the interest in the Fifties to answer enthusiastically—and contrary to stereotypes, sometimes with more than adequate interest and devotion.

Rodney Stark and Laurence Iannoccone are surely right in insisting that modern American religion cannot be dismissed, as it was by some European observers in the Fifties and since, as somehow more "cultural" and less "spiritual" than monopoly-based religion in traditional or modern Europe. Despite much religious fatuousness and foolishness in the Fifties, one cannot so easily slight the spirituality of a Thomas Merton or the impressive popular interest in the theology of such persons as Karl Barth, Reinhold Niebuhr, or Paul Tillich, or the stereotype-shattering emergence of Martin Luther King, Jr., at the end of the decade. Nor can one overlook the imposingly higher levels of religious attendance in the United States over Europe. By all commonsense criteria, one might have expected the opposite claim, that U.S. religion was more vital than European. (But a British observer like Bryan Wilson asserted in 1960 that "religious attendance is itself a secular value in America," American Fifties faith being no more than "culture religion," as though even that decade's high levels of churchgoing were only a paradoxical and perverse form of secularization! As we have noted, a cultural disposition toward religion in general is stronger in the United States than in some comparable societies, and perhaps there is less antagonism toward religion in general even on the part of the nonreligious. But this hardly seems to amount to secularism.)[5]

A second theme relevant to the Fifties, developed particularly in Roger Finke and Rodney Stark's *Churching of America, 1776–1990*, is that religions in the United States flourish best under conditions of "medium tension" with the environment. In a free market, for consumers to feel a religion is worth investing in at all, it must offer some degree of apparent authenticity and seriousness represented by its standing in relative contrast to the values of nonreligious society. Too much tension, like that of a "withdrawal" sect or cult, will draw only a few devotees; on the other hand, an extremely "low-demand" church will generate laxity if not contempt.

Throughout U.S. religious history low-demand, establishment religions have been challenged by new movements competing with them from a position of greater tension, only to become themselves after two or three generations religions at ease with society and the target of new threats. So was the colonial "establishment" of Episcopalians, Congregationalists, and Presbyterians devastated by circuit-riding Methodists and Baptists on the frontier, themselves to be later displaced on the edge by Holiness and Pentecostal movements, and they in turn by the new evangelicals and charismatics of the late twentieth century.

Just as it was not always "culture religion," Fifties religion was not always low demand, and the Fifties do not necessarily represent a disconfirmation of the medium-tension thesis. The growing and increasingly prominent Roman Catholicism of the decade was virtually by definition in a state of medium tension with traditionally Protestant America, and furthermore continued to make conspicuous demands on its adherents, from weekly mass to fish on Friday. Protestant churches, influenced by neoorthodoxy, could be reasonably demanding theologically, and even the stereotypical suburban superchurch with all its spiritual/social activities could be demanding in terms of time and participation.

Fifties Demographics

So it was that in the decade of the Fifties, religion was, and was perceived to be, in a pronounced upswing. The market was good. Religious institutions were growing substantially year by year in numbers, wealth, and real estate; seminaries and novitiates were full; the influence of religion on people's thoughts and lives was considered to be increasing. Polls said that 99 percent of Americans believed in God, best-seller lists were crowded with religion titles, a radio series like Edward R. Murrow's *This I Believe* reached thirty-nine million people a week in the early Fifties and eventually became a newspaper column. Magazines joined in; in 1954 *Good Housekeeping* ran a sequence of articles called "I Remember a Church," and *Life* did a Christmas double issue in 1955 entirely on Christianity.[6]

A 1954 article on Henry P. Van Dusen, dean of Union Theological Seminary, remarked that twenty-five years ago traditional Christianity seemed to be winding down in U.S. life, giving way to Sigmund Freud and John Dewey, but now church membership had grown by 70 percent in a generation, twice the rate of the general population, and best-seller lists were crowded with religion books.[7] Although this article was oriented toward Protestantism, it might have added that few denominations were growing as fast as Roman Catholicism, and the seminaries, monasteries, and convents of that faith were bursting with eager aspirants.

The increase was supported by demographics. The U.S. population grew from 150 million in 1950 to 180 million in 1960, the largest increase in a single decade in history. Not surprisingly, that increase was supported by a marriage explosion. In 1940, 31 percent of the adult population was single; in 1950, 23 percent and in 1960, 21 percent. The Fifties saw the lowest median age for marriage in the century, 24.3 for males and 21.5 for females (in 1990 it was back up to 26.1 and 23.9), and a divorce rate that had leveled off to one in ten marriages. Each woman who came of age in the Fifties bore 3.2 children. They were getting a better education than ever before too. In 1945 just 25 percent of adults were high school graduates, and only 5 percent had graduated from college. Those numbers shot up after the war as returning veterans took advantage of the GI Bill, and their baby-boom children were to get even more schooling, school construction being a major Fifties and early Sixties industry, from elementary to university. (An ultimate upshot would be the famous Sixties generation gap.) Children and schools were all parts of Fifties togetherness, though that ideal would begin to unravel in the late Fifties as the first baby boomers hit the teens.

These are important considerations. The fortunes of religion often rise and fall with the birthrate. More specifically, it is rightly claimed that people tend to go to church during their prime child-bearing years, and that religiosity (as measured by church attendance) is a function of family size. Religion assists parents in socializing their children, provides a site for family activities (togetherness!), and is generally deemed a safe environment for raising children.

Here is an interesting and relevant example of one consequence of these realities. Insofar as the labels "liberal" versus "moderate" Protestant indicate low versus medium demand, figures suggest that the former can produce quick growth but less staying power than the latter. During the 1950s, liberal Protestant churches grew at a more rapid rate than those of moderate Protestants but also declined more rapidly.[8] Wade Clark Roof and William McKinney in *American Mainline Religion* argue that one reason for the decline of liberal Protestantism is simply that the women in these churches, typically more affluent than other religiodemographic groups, tend to have fewer children than do women in conservative churches.[9] There may be a multiplying effect to all this: given the lower birthrates of liberal and mainline churches, they do less programming for youth, therefore do a poor job of retaining youth as they move into adulthood, and finally attract fewer families in their neighborhoods with growing families. All this means mainline churches sadly fallen, as many are, from their golden age in the Fifties.

However, in the early Fifties virtually all denominations grew, the Roman Catholics most dramatically of all, their numbers up by nearly 25 percent from 1950 to 1955. While of course one cannot gauge the profoundest depths of religious life through statistics, the overwhelming evidence is that religion in the United States in the 1950s was very much alive both spiritually and culturally, perhaps as much or more than in any other modern society anywhere—for that matter, more than in many ancient or medieval societies. But also as with the medieval church, Fifties faith was found in two strata, the folk religion of the masses and the elite version held by the monks and professors.

Highbrow and Lowbrow Religion

Let us look again at the way the religious upsurge took place on two distinct levels, the intellectual and the popular. William Lee Miller put the situation like this in 1954:

One remarkable thing about the interest in religion among intellectuals is how separate it is from the revival in popular culture. The
interest in Kafka and Kierkegaard, in Berdyaev, Maritain and religious
existentialism, appears to bear little relation to the revival of religious
interest in the broad mass of the people. One is struck by the lack of
interest in the popular revival among the theologians, and the lack of
intellectual leadership in the popular revival. There is no figure like a
Jonathan Edwards of the Great Awakening, or a Walter
Rauschenbusch of the Social Gospel period, who is at once a popular
and a theological leader. Those who are most read and discussed
among the intellectuals—Kafka and Kierkegaard, Tillich and
Niebuhr—tend to be symbols of incomprehensibility and intellectual
pretense to the popular religionists.[10]

And one might add that the intellectuals, including Miller, scarcely hid
their disdain for the popular religion of the day, making sport of its sentimen-
tality and inconsistency, its convenient infatuation with capitalism and
"Americanism," and above all its emphasis on personal happiness and success
rather than the larger theological issues. But each level had its own market,
and the supply-side overall result was religion for almost everyone.

The Fifties were a time when intellectuals were taken seriously as a class,
whether one liked them or not. Culture mavens talked of "highbrows," "eggheads," and "U accents," and the eggheads among the pious had their own
cults. Intellectuals, theologians, and "serious" writers characteristically held
to some thoroughgoing, internally consistent system of thought in which everything fell into place: neoorthodoxy for Protestants; neo-Thomism for
Catholics; existentialism, Freudianism, or Marxism for secularists.

As we shall see, other contenders were stirring under the surface—
Vedanta, Buddhism, new types of Christian liberalism like the "secular theology" of the next decade. But neoorthodoxy, neo-Thomism, and existentialism
were dominant among intellectuals of various sects during most of the Fifties.
At Union Theological Seminary in New York during its Fifties heyday, when
this bastion of Reinhold Niebuhr and neoorthodoxy was the hub of
Protestantism's intellectual wing, the most radical men were the most orthodox (in the neoorthodox sense). Alluding to the current theologians' fashionable pessimism about human nature, *Time* reported that "sin is back in
fashion."[11]

Turning to popular religion, its aspirations are well evoked by the great
religious bestsellers that marked the early Fifties particularly: Norman Vincent
Peale, *The Power of Positive Thinking* (1952); Catherine Marshall, *A Man Called
Peter* (1951); Dale Evans Rogers, *Angel Unaware* (1953) and *My Spiritual
Diary* (1955); Thomas B. Costain, *The Silver Chalice* (1952); Fulton Sheen,

Peace of Soul (1949); Billy Graham, *Peace with God* (1953); James Bishop, *The Day Christ Died* (1950), and Fulton Oursler, *The Greatest Story Ever Told* (1949), *The Greatest Book Ever Written* (1951), and *The Greatest Faith Ever Known* (1953).

Add to these the glorious religious movies of the decade, such as *Quo Vadis* (1951; at $7 million, presented as the most expensive movie ever made); *David and Bathsheba* (1950); *Ben Hur* (1959); *The Robe* and *Salome* (1954); and of course the most magnificent of them all, the Cecil B. DeMille/ Charlton Heston version of *The Ten Commandments* (1956). These cinematic spectaculars were carefully designed to offend no one of any faith, except perhaps pagans or skeptics. The epics of the silver screen mixed pageantry, debauchery, heroism, blood, and pious attitude with a theatrical eye and a generous hand. Religious Hollywood, like any good marketer, created a market while meeting it.

What the popular books and the flicks have in common is a focus on some single, simple, sure key to peace and power (faith, prayer, the image of Christ), transmitted by accessible stories and images (Peale's famous anecdotes, the life of Peter Marshall, vivid biblical scenes) uncluttered by critical issues (the truth of the Bible was not argued but assumed). Ordinary people wanted products whose basic principles were easy to understand, user friendly and troublefree, whether in home appliances or faiths. Lack of logical consistency there might be; Theodore A. Gill, reviewing *My Spiritual Diary* in the *Christian Century*, pointed out that Dale Evans Rogers offered "a very riot of religiousness. Every professedly Christian manifestation is hymned with equal enthusiasm. This disciple of Billy Graham rejoices in the gospel of Norman Vincent Peale and joins the Episcopal church . . . she decries theological disagreement and then summons us to a bristlingly theological statement on Christ."[12]

But the more important point is how popular religion works in an open market. It first directly addresses the raw inner yearnings of the individual, juxtaposes religion and those needs in an easily understandable way, and provides a striking image or technique that ameliorates them by making religion the answer—the point of popular religion being not coherent wisdom or meaning so much as power. In all this it was unlike elite religion, which tended to view one's raw inner yearnings as sinful—selfish or materialistic. Elite religion subordinates religion as a source of power to the need for consistent theological systems and universal judgments—which were, of course, sources of power for theologians. In popular religion it was the other way around, consistency running a poor second to spiritual utility in the rational-choice table of desiderata.

Popular religion was epitomized above all by three vendors—one Roman Catholic, one liberal Protestant, and one evangelical Protestant—Fulton

Sheen, Norman Vincent Peale, and Billy Graham respectively. Their faith was characterized by feeling, pragmatism, and attachment to powerful evocative images. Its emphasis was on meeting personal needs, and the message was therefore aimed directly at the individual hearer or reader. The religious intellectuals like Niebuhr or Tillich talked about "man"; the populists talked about "you." The words *you and your* are employed over and over. Peale's advertisements asked, "*Are* you *missing the life of success?*" Sheen's customary opener was "Thank you for inviting me into your home." Billy Graham ended a sermon in his 1958 San Francisco crusade with this characteristic appeal: "This is your moment with God; it may never come again just like this. You need Christ. You need to come to the Cross. You need the courage and strength God can give you. I am inviting you to do something about it now. I am inviting you to come forward and give your heart to Jesus Christ. You come."[13]

What were the personal needs this religion of "you" met? First, they spoke to one's yearning for personal peace. Rabbi Joshua Lieb's *Peace of Mind* (1946), Fulton Sheen's *Peace of Soul* (1949), and Billy Graham's *Peace with God* (1953) were three significant and popular titles.

Next, and even more important, they responded to one's quest for power, above all power over one's life in a new world that seemed baffling and full of stunning opportunities at the same time. Personal power, in turn, would inevitably lead to happiness and success, and was generally promised as the sure result of a technique, way, or secret that you could easily acquire and practice. These keys to happiness and success were retailed in such works as Peale's famous *Power of Positive Thinking* (1952), Sheen's *Way to Happiness* (1954), and Graham's *Secret of Happiness* (1955). (As in the successive "peace" books, one senses the big three and their cohorts continually striving, consciously or unconsciously, to top one another.)

Needless to say, religious intellectuals carped at what they perceived to be the subordination of religion to personal yearnings and strivings, making prayer no more than a means to peace and power, and even God no more than copilot as one flew upward toward greater and greater heights of success. No religious critique of such goals as becoming a top salesperson or business executive, or of the products conveyed on the way to the top, was suggested by the religious populists.

This was certainly not, in the eyes of the intellectuals, what Kierkegaard or Barth meant by faith. Nor did it embody any of the serious social-justice concerns of a Rauschenbusch or a Niebuhr. To the elite the popular cults seemed like the sort of sorcery that puts spiritual power at the service of the ego. It was religious marketing in the crassest sense, whether in Peale's Manhattan temple or on the televised sawdust trail with Billy Graham.

A mediating word may be in order, however. In retrospect, one is distressed by the lack of mutual understanding on the part of the two camps, by the snobbism of the one and the defiant shallowness of the other. Indeed it is tragic that no figure was large enough to bridge the two worlds, no Edwards, John Wesley, or even a younger Harry Fosdick. At the same time, it may be pointed out that helping individuals of whatever station in life in hours of anguish, or of need for healing and personal betterment, even by means of the occasional personal miracle, is a function of religion going back at least to the Gospels, and not always an ignoble one. At some point, religion needs to be effectively personalized.

The Individual versus Mass Society

An important theme in both popular and highbrow intellectual life in the Fifties was the issue of the individual versus the crowd. The former was valued, but somewhere out there, in the form of other-directed pressures, of big institutions and big government, worst of all in the collectivism of the Marxist world, lurked the individual's nemesis, alert to destroy one's freedom and swallow one up. People have no doubt always been much concerned with the boundary lines between themselves and the institutions of their societies, but the issue was cast into especially sharp relief in the Fifties, no doubt because of the apparent power of the opposing pole, whether it presented itself as Communism or Madison Avenue or the Orwellian bureaucratic state or the impersonal new world being made by assembly-line industries and even newer technologies. On the state side, much of this was new in the experience of most Americans, a product of the New Deal and the wartime mobilization of resources through rationing, price controls, and postwar benefits like subsidized veterans' education. Scholars talked of ominous predictions concerning bureaucratization by fathers of sociology like Emile Durkheim and Max Weber. More voguish reactions ranged from existentialism to rightist diatribes against collectivism to religious responses.

The "you" emphasis in popular religion, though it flowed smoothly into family togetherness and national-scale Americanism, really had the same starting point as the existentialism popular early in the decade among intellectuals. From Søren Kierkegaard to more recent figures like Karl Jaspers, Martin Heidegger, or Jean-Paul Sartre, the common feature of their philosophies was its commencement with the subjectivity of the individual, which first of all simply finds itself thrown into this oft alien world, where it must define itself against all the impersonal abstractions of metaphysical world-systems and bureaucratic societies alike.

So it was that Fifties people, activated by the fashionable existentialist image of the heroic rebel on the one hand, and by the terrible fascination of mass society on the other, saw as a dominant theme of their era the individual against the organization and the mass. They read books like David Riesman's *Lonely Crowd* and William H. Whyte, Jr.'s *Organization Man*. But this was an extraordinarily confusing, double-binding kind of conflict. It seemed if you won it one way, you lost it another.

Although no doubt only the intellectuals articulated the issue in the explicit manner of Riesman, Whyte, or the existentialists, in a real sense everyday people felt the tension of mass versus individual as much as anyone, and they were as confused by it. They jumped from one side to another, now asserting freedom and then demanding conformity, without fear of contradiction. One part of the problem was that both poles were stereotyped abstractions. Another was the way that the cold war, though conceptualized as freedom versus communism, required conformity of belief and life-style on behalf of that struggle for freedom. Closer to everyday life, the new big government and corporation-based economy demanded organization-man behavior and values and rewarded them well, while even in their mass-circulated advertisements harping on the values of an older, and idealized, individualist America. And where does good togetherness end and the evils of collectivism begin? Simply at the limits of the nuclear family? In that case, where would the much-touted and much-imposed Americanism become the dreaded individuality-crushing mass society? The conundrums were ones the churches were ill prepared to sort out.

Religion was ambivalent because it was itself caught between the two poles, like everyone else saying one thing but doing another. What did religion really want, the ideal of the loving community or of the solitary saintly or prophetic individual? Individual faith and freedom or a godly nation? Power to succeed in the organization or to criticize it? Positive thinking, the contemplative revival, evangelicalism, and neoorthodoxy all spoke in terms of individual initiative and response to God and the world. It was fashionable for Christian intellectuals, usually more or less under the influence of existentialism, to emphasize the individualizing power of faith, its power to liberate the individual from the mass. Religious existentialists from Karl Barth to Nicholas Berdyaev emphasized that true religion is not conformity but freedom, attained through a radically deep subjective decision that asserts the authenticity of the self as surely as it does God; to choose God is to affirm the freedom of the choosing self. Billy Graham made the same point in the rally, and so did Catholics like Thomas Merton as they elected the confining freedom of the cloister.

Yet the burgeoning suburban churches hardly seemed highly distinct from the organization, and even seemingly individualistic movements from conversion to contemplation appeared predicated on some other-directed definition of truth or reality. The fact is the Fifties confronted religion with massively new and important sociological realities—the suburb, the expanding white-collar world, the new mass higher education, not to mention new tensions from race to cold war—that despite all the howls of the existentialists and the anti–mass man social critics were undoubtedly irreversible. But people were only painfully learning to live in them, and the churches were only grudgingly finding theologically helpful and positive ways to talk about the new city and its culture. (The next decade was to bring book titles like Gibson Winter's *New Creation as Metropolis* and Harvey Cox's *Secular City*.)

Fifties religion, then, had to contend with fast-breeding young families, large-scale internal migration, the spiritual paradoxes of a new affluence, and the psychic paradoxes of a society that experienced itself as both triumphant and under siege, and that seemed to value both conformism and an abstract ideal of liberty. All that meant that mainstream Fifties religion was family oriented, very conscious of the cold war, and inwardly traditionalist while trying to adapt institutionally to the needs of a rapidly growing and changing society. Yet though its values were communal, from family on up, its messages most often did not speak to society as such, in the prophetic manner of social activists, but to the individual, to "you." Its pulpit messages could be almost schizophrenic in their capacity to jump from words of warm uncritical endorsement of accepted values to words of judgment, but the objects of both tended to be more the individual than the structures of society.

In order to put Fifties religion into perspective, it may be worthwhile to glance for a moment at the next decade, the Sixties, to see what happened then to the Fifties marketplace. In that tumultuous decade, though religious diversity increased, from the consumer point of view supplies became somewhat unreliable. Any market-wise retailer knows that remodeling or rearranging the shop floor and changing brands is very tricky from the point of view of maintaining customer loyalty. Some will like it, but others may never come back. Rapid and traumatic changes at the local level in the nature of post–Vatican II Roman Catholic, and liberal to mainstream Protestant religion—new liturgies, guitars, speaking in tongues, inflammatory political stances—shook confidence in standard brands and produced associations, even in the established outlets, unsettling to some consumers. At the same time, new vendors seemed to be moving into the market and confusing it, even though some of their products, such as meditation or psychedelic drugs, were hard to understand as religion in conventional U.S. terms. Attendance dropped from 47 percent to 40 percent. Only evangelicalism held steady.

Religion was no doubt of better quality in the Sixties than before from the suppliers' standpoint, but it was also less familiar than that of the Fifties to the consumer. For the supply side to produce a high level of participation, products must be not only abundant and in good variety, but also recognizable as what they are labeled to be in the eyes of the consumer. Secularization, for example, was an idea held by many suppliers to describe the current situation, and so secular theology was widely proffered in the belief that was where the market was. But not all consumers believed secularity was what religion should be selling. It may have sounded like General Motors saying, "It's true we sell cars, but we know you don't really believe in travel anymore, so we'll sell you a kind of car for staying home in."

This kind of mix-up often happened to supply-side religion in the Sixties. To some the reshuffling may have been hopeful, to others disturbing, but in almost every case it laid the foundation for deep-level religious restructuring, more on the conceptual and practical than the institutional levels. Fifties consumers wanted and got lots of religion—fifty-seven varieties—but in familiar forms.

Some might even say all from the same conglomerate, the religious equivalent of Heinz. The master template was U.S. religion itself, in Will Herberg's sense that it was American to have a religion, and it didn't matter what it was—so long as it was within the respectable, culturally acceptable Protestant-Catholic-Jewish orbit. Not all Fifties Americans would agree, however, that it made no difference what faith it was. Religious conflicts could be pronounced: Catholic versus Protestant, "high" versus "low" culture, mainstream versus underground, liberal versus evangelical. The early years of the decade saw not only McCarthyism and Korea, but also a midcentury nadir in Catholic-Protestant relations, strained by bitter altercations on questions like parochial schools and public funding, birth control issues, an ambassador to the Vatican, and Catholic ties to repressive regimes in Spain and Colombia. All this was augmented by Catholic doubts as to whether Protestants—especially the hegemonic liberal Anglo-Protestants—were sufficiently anticommunist. At the crux of the trouble was the pugnacious figure of Francis Cardinal Spellman, symbol of his church's rapidly growing numbers, wealth, political power, and social conservatism; the differences were crystallized in his much-publicized quarrel with Eleanor Roosevelt in 1949. On the other hand, some liberal religionists were gradually becoming more socially active—against McCarthy, for example, or for integration—while other of the faithful remain quietist or veered toward the conservative movement.

Venues for such contests as these were institutionally provided and present before the Fifties demand, in the shape of Catholic and Protestant churches of all stripes, together with Jewish temples and other institutions, or in position-oriented books and magazines. But the concrete conflictive and activist phenomena emerged in the complex interaction of supply and demand. Thus, supply in one venue might competitively stimulate demand in another. The Fifties growth of the retreat movement among Protestants was certainly ultimately influenced by publicity surrounding Thomas Merton and Zen.

Religious demand was further created by a sense of immense social and economic change in the postwar world. The extent to which the experience of World War II shaped the deep structures of U.S. consciousness, religious and otherwise, in the Fifties, and indeed for several postwar decades, can hardly be overestimated. Michael S. Sherry, in his book *In the Shadow of War*, has brilliantly shown how war and militarization has reshaped every aspect of American life since that great war—politics, economics, culture, social values—making America a profoundly different nation.[14] The military and defense industries became the primary means of social welfare, income distribution, and economic stimulus. On deeper levels, the wartime imperatives of dualistic thinking and orientation toward total victory have shaped the thinking even of those opposed to war: an "us" versus "them" mentality has informed discourse, including religious discourse, and the language has incorporated expressions like "war" on drugs or crime, "operation" this or that. In a nation at war, hot or cold, it was not surprising that religion sometimes had the appearance of a national chaplaincy.

Cautions are in order, however. Some histories of the cold war and its culture have suggested that the religion of the Fifties revival was largely nationalistic, a spiritual chaplaincy to the republic's world mission. Certainly much can be adduced to suggest this view; the quotes and examples would be nearly endless. Yet I hope this study may show the total to be not quite so monochrome. The demographics of the revival lay in the postwar baby boom and internal migration, not the cold war. The conflict with the Soviet bloc and its home-court devolutions like McCarthy's were not assessed in the same way or given the same emphasis by all mainstream religious leaders. Finally, other genuinely deep and historically important developments only indirectly related to the cold war were afoot in the religious world as well, such as Catholic-Protestant tensions and the burgeoning civil-rights movement of Martin Luther King, Jr. Yet the cold war created much of the impetus to deal with them, and much of the rhetoric by which they were approached: "If we're going to beat the Russians, we have to overcome our differences," or "We've got to resolve race at home" were arguments just as puissant as those that claimed all those problems were communist inspired.

Such times were good yet scary—hopeful, if an atomic Armageddon did not destroy everything first. The war and the cold war had imposed seriousness about values. What were perceived to be traditional values were especially well positioned, since fascism and communism were modern innovations, and ill-begotten ones at that. Yet things were moving too fast for true conservatism to work, much as some might have hoped or thought otherwise. The booming baby population, migrations, suburbanization, and rapid acceleration of education meant that the new postwar world could not and was not going to be merely traditional. How could race be the same after Montgomery and Little Rock, or education stress traditional Americanism and the weeding out of subversives more than cutting-edge science after *Sputnik I*? The whole situation called for some way to prioritize values; given the U.S. supply-side presence and good image of religion, religion would be the means of choice for doing that. Sherry rightly indicated that the postwar revival affirmed the value of religion more than of any particular form, making religion in general synonymous with nationalism.[15] But the predominant priorities of U.S. religion would themselves make a corresponding shift as the decade advanced.

Underground Religion

The supply-side model of U.S. religion, based on economic models, interprets the Fifties well. But alongside the official economy of a society is likely also to be an underground economy, as there certainly was in the Fifties and is today. The secular underground economy is characterized by the use of barter or cash rather than credit, by dependence on friendship and relational networks, by not paying taxes, and above all by nonappearance in the regular economic reports. Was there such an underground spiritual economy in the Fifties? Indeed there was, ranging from Beats to UFOnauts, from monks to mythologists. We will be paying particular attention to a few exemplary undergrounders: A. J. Muste, Thomas Merton, George Adamski, Jack Kerouac, Alan Watts, Aldous Huxley, Joseph Campbell, Billy Hargis.

What connecting themes can be found among those spiritual dissenters who, whether to right or left, up or down, veered significantly from togetherness and the Fifties mainstream? Was it really that they were more Fifties than anyone else, joining with the existentialists to take more seriously than most the admonition to be inner rather than other directed, and to reject the comforts of mass society? If so, they would only look dissident but would really simply be living what the social critics talked. If they stood out, it would only be to show up the hypocrisy of a society that talked about freedom but had little tolerance for its practice. Not a few dissidents viewed their experience in this light, and certainly in important ways it is a valid interpretation. But the concept must be examined carefully.

First we need to note that individual versus mass society may not be quite the right way to describe the tension underlying the rebel's role. However much one may be a rebel or a recluse, these are still social roles, acted out in full awareness of society even in reaction against it. And more often than not these reactions are enacted amongst a phalanx of fellow believers, with whom an alternative bonding is established.

The rebel will soon enough find himself or herself in a coterie of political radicals, or avant-garde poets, and this resocialization completes and reifies the process of rebellion. A thought is not complete till it forms a sentence, a rebel till he finds his clan. When the insurrection is religious, it must end in some kind of underground church. For religion even at its most radical does not create radical individualism so much as alternative communities or bondings. I propose that three kinds of bonding obtained among the Fifties spiritual underground, in varying degrees but all at odds with some significant area of bonding by the mainstream.

1. Male bonding as over against the dominant nuclear family. This was a feature of the Beats, as we shall see; but, even if not expressed in quite the same way, it was also obviously a characteristic of the monastery and of male devotion to causes, whether on the right or the left, that compellingly transcended family.
2. Bonding around the ideal of religion as the inner-directed following of an interiorized myth or mystical experience leading to individuation, rather than as the upholder of the consensual values of society. In the deepest sense, all religion may entail identification with a myth, but myths can be either the normative icon or the myth of the rebel. This is one reason Carl Jung, Joseph Campbell, and "mystics" like Alan Watts or Aldous Huxley or even the UFO contactees were important to the underground; they were purveyors of the alternative myths and pathways to spiritual experience. Even the rebel is not likely to be truly alone religiously; he simply bonds with other rebels.
3. Bonding around exotic rather than normative religious symbols. Where religions come from tells much about their social role, culturally conforming or countercultural. But even conventional religions can come up with new and exotic symbols, as were Thomas Merton's Trappists for most Americans. There was also Zen, Vedanta, and the rest of it.

Here is a comment by William Whyte about troubled Fifties communitarians: "They sense that by their immersion in the group they are frustrating other urges, yet they feel that responding to the group is a moral duty—and so they continue, hesitant and unsure, imprisoned in brotherhood."[16]

A few were prepared, with a band of brothers and sisters, to try to make an escape from that prison.

Historical Structure of the Fifties

Despite our tendency to think of the Fifties, as we do so many decades, in terms of single stereotypes, there was change and development as the decade advanced. J. Ronald Oakley has divided the Fifties into three periods: the Age of Fear and Suspicion, 1950–1952; the Good Years, 1953–1956; and a time of heightening anxiety he called Trouble in God's Country, 1957–1961.[17] We will follow the same periodization, though with different titles.

The first period obviously corresponds with McCarthyism and Korea, and also with the founding of the National Council of Churches and the strongest surges of the religion upswing. The second began with by the inauguration of President Eisenhower and the ending of the Korean War and was capped by the censure of Senator McCarthy by the Senate in December of 1954, and by the Supreme Court decision against segregation earlier that year. This was a time of relatively lessening tensions abroad, but of new struggles at home, for all these events produced vehement religious response; those middecade years also saw the continuing growth both of mainline churches and of spiritual alternatives.

The third period featured renewed anxiety as *Sputnik I* raised new worry about competition with the Soviet Union, and at home army-enforced integration in Little Rock brought long-simmering racial tensions to a boil. (Sydney Ahlstrom called the 1957 Little Rock episode "probably the most important religio-ethical event of the decade.") On a more positive side, the election of John XXIII as pope in 1958, and the upcoming Vatican Council for which he issued a call in January of 1959, caused a dramatically changed climate for Catholic-Protestant relations. But at the same time, observers were already talking about the postwar religious revival in the past tense. This is where we shall end.

The Years of Dark and Dreaming, Part I
1950–1952

We looked for peace, but no good came;
For a time of healing, but behold, terror.
— JER. 14:19 RSV

The Storm and the Rock

W<small>HAT WAS</small> religious America like in 1950?

First some background. To pilfer words said of another time and place, it was the best and worst of times. The good side was that it was a time of youth, of babies, of growth—growth of the economy, the population, the cities, the suburbs, the young families, the churches. Most Americans had more money than ever before. They were spending it on cars, houses, and everything that went with them, and they had something left over for the expanding budgets of churches and synagogues. The bad side was that all this seemed threatened by dark clouds gathering on the horizon, perhaps building into stormheads, and already raising foul winds of accusation and mistrust around the land.

The year began with President Harry Truman's announcement of H-bomb production January 31. That was followed by the opening speech of Senator Joseph McCarthy's anticommunist crusade on February 9. In midyear came war in Korea, and disaster there by year's end. But first the good news.

In the early Fifties new homes were being built at a rate of over a hundred thousand a month, largely in the new suburbs, and churches were springing up along with them. The population was increasing at over two million new Americans a year, most of them the early fruits of the celebrated postwar baby boom. Although in 1949 membership in all faiths had grown by a record 2,426,723, when the reports were in early in 1950, Roman Catholics had increased by over a million in one year for the first time, and for the first time membership in Jewish congregations hit the five million mark. In the years following, churches grew even faster, from 86,830,000 members or 57 percent of the population in 1950 (already up from 52 percent in 1944) to 94,842,000 or 59.5 percent in 1953. Those families, and the institutions ministering to them, felt free, prosperous, and (apart from atomic and cold-war traumas) hopeful about the future.

In a sense it was hard for a church not to be successful in 1950. The people were there, and a general spiritual hunger was in the air, together with a yearning for supportive communities. From the supply side, religion was presented in fundamentally consumer-friendly, nonthreatening ways, though with sufficient demands on people's time, energy, and life-style to make faith appear serious. The religious appetite was evidenced in growing churches, in burgeoning seminary enrollments, and in best-seller lists, which included not only *The Power of Positive Thinking* (1952) but also, a little earlier, Thomas Merton's *The Seven Storey Mountain* (1948).

As Merton's book reminds us, what impresses one about the religion and spirituality boom of the early Fifties is, first, that it could be demanding—it is not that easy, after all, to be a Trappist monk even vicariously—and, second, that the spiritual boomers had little conscious desire for innovation. What fascinated readers of Merton's auto-saga was surely not only the all-too-modern intellectual and sensual struggles of his youth, but also the refuge he found in a monastic tradition that reminded jaded readers of a silent kingdom of faith and discipline still flourishing without change in the backcountry of a world whose stellar minds thought they had long since left medievalism behind—a kingdom that seemed more and more relevant with each passing year as the crises of modernity became more and more ominous.

In a world threatened by too much change and innovation, in which too much had happened and was still happening, and in which too many modern ideas seemed discredited if not disastrous, the religious mind assumed that truth was already there, in traditions that went well back into the past; the challenge was not to remake them but to bring them whole into the contemporary world, hard parts and all. Some outward repackaging for the benefit of Main Street, or the gray-flannel world of Madison Avenue, was acceptable, but the basic product was to be a standard brand. A church that kept that in mind, while at the same time offering a good Sunday school and choir, could hardly fail.

As for the socialization, for the new families moving in their millions to the new suburbs, religious institutions were good places to meet and mix and find support. In any period, church membership and attendance are usually high among families with young children. A substantial and growing part of the religious population were Roman Catholics, and their families were still large and churchgoing. Routine religion was envisioned as part of normalcy, and after the upheavals and terrors of war one wants nothing so much as normalcy, with all its familiar symbols.

Wars are typically followed by marriages and babies, as minds shift from the glories and terrors of far-flung fronts to that other dimension of life. Not that the strange climes are entirely forgotten by those who were there, and readapting to home and hearth may call for a few private adjustments of conscience. Late Forties and early Fifties musicals and movies, like *South Pacific* and *Roman Holiday*, no doubt reflected the experience of countless GIs as they seemed to suggest subliminally that while a brief romantic fling in some exotic setting is all right—maybe even somewhat healthy—it must be soon subordinated to the more serious obligations of marriage, family, and social role. This was a perspective that, of course, most churches were pleased to reinforce.

The United States in 1950 desired religious institutions to do what they had always done, and do it well, for a grimmer reason too. The country, which rightly saw itself as very fortunate in so many ways, was also under threat as never before. The Broadways and Main Streets, the Levittowns and surviving country centers, were islands in a worldwide storm. For, contrary to all hope in 1945, the struggle between light and dark was not over. The present conflict was cold war rather than hot, but it was real. A new foe had arisen in the East, some said even more cruel and devious, and even more at odds with all that was fair, than the former tyrants of Berlin and Tokyo.

Moreover, far more than the others, the enemy had extended the shadow of its evil and its might even into the heartland of the United States, the last redoubt and best hope of those who stood free against it. For even there were those who had softened to the enemy's blandishments or taken its silver, and some such secret traitors allegedly were high in the counsels of the White House. The walls of the final fortress still held, but across the sea the enemy was on the move as nation after nation fell, it seemed with relentless regularity, before the red onslaught: most of Eastern Europe in 1945, Czechoslovakia in 1948, vast China in 1949, now Korea—and once taken none escaped its prison in those days. The world of 1950 was one in which the enemy was advancing implacably, victory upon victory, as though nothing could stop it, with the last battle perhaps at hand. That was the picture emerging in 1950 out of the evening news and *Life* magazine pictures, and it was framed by much political and pulpit rhetoric.

In this montage the church more than anything else was not Peter's fishing bark sailing toward new shores, not a vine extending exploratory tendrils toward the light, but a rock. It was supposed to be a bulwark unchanging, sure, well armed. The day was dark, all agreed, and the onrushing night full of foes. A 1951 survey of the younger generation by *Time* found them generally grave, fatalistic, expecting to do military service in Korea or some such place and maybe die, some anticipating an atomic holocaust sooner or later.[1] One had plans, but one knew they were tentative. The Silent Generation, as it was often called, was silent not only out of reaction against Thirties radicalism, not only because the ideological stakes were so high that debate about them appeared unseemly, but also because it was the first generation to have a reasonable secular expectation that it might be the last—or at least that a good many of its members might not last more than a few years longer. The awesome face of death can be an effective silencer.

The tense and anxious tone of 1950, the pessimism despite all that was good, the way people talked about World War III as though it were a sure thing, only the date uncertain—and its virtual arrival, or so it seemed, in Korea during the terrible last week of June of that year—need to be fully grasped if one is to understand the sometimes bizarre events and attitudes of those times. Perhaps, one thought, even the two climactic wars the century had already seen, and the cold war as well, were but preliminaries to an impending ultimate armed conflict between light and darkness, God and his emboldened adversary. In that day of Armageddon what one would hope for above all else from the church would not be new ideas but a final and secure redoubt, against which even the gates of hell could not prevail.

Unfortunately for that hope, what the church of 1950 offered was not one but several redoubts, not all in full accord with one another as to what the final recourse of the free human spirit ought to be. To be sure, major parts of the fissiparous world of Protestantism were moving magisterially toward unity of spirit, concertized in the World Council of Churches, formed in 1948, and in late 1950 in the National Council of Churches in the United States. But on one flank of those cooperating churches was ranged the evangelical Protestant world, now energized by the dynamic revival preaching of Billy Graham; and on the other flank, the conservative, monolithic Roman Catholic church of Pius XII and Francis Cardinal Spellman, an ecclesiastical empire now attaining unprecedented heights of numerical, political, and economic strength in the United States.

But in a broader sense this panorama of piety only strengthened the church in supply-side terms as it girded up its several loins for battle—and expansion. The temper of the times, however, was to emphasize that there could be only one truth, whatever it was. Therefore division was perceived only negatively. The strengths of pluralism in a free-market, rational-choice religious world remained as yet unseen and unappreciated. Instead the Catholicism of the Knights of Columbus ads had its one truth; the tracts of evangelicals their opposing single truth; even the liberals of the day, ever ready to skirmish with the pope or revisit the bitter liberal-fundamentalist battles of the Twenties, were no less self-assured in their righteousness. The one-truth mood also suited the harsh dogmatism of the triumphalist communism that those divided armies of the spirit sought to combat.

Chapter 1

Events: Korea, Catholics, Protestants, and Anticommunism

Let us begin at the beginning of the decade. It was early in the year 1950 that Senator Joseph McCarthy, whose name will, as McCarthyism, forever indicate the temper of those times, first tantalized hearers with his famous but elusive and ever changing lists. McCarthy and McCarthyism are important to the religious history of the Fifties for three reasons. First, religion-based argument for and against what he represented was a staple of religious discourse, articulated in books, innumerable impassioned journal articles and editorials, and no doubt countless sermons. Second, the relations of McCarthyism to the nation's religious contours, notably its firm base in the senator's own Roman Catholicism and a little later in evangelical Protestantism, cannot be overlooked. Third, on another level of analysis, McCarthyism can be seen as a bid to create what can only be considered an anticommunist state church, complete with unquestioned dogmas and rites of exorcism.

Here is how it started. On February 9, in Wheeling, West Virginia, at a commemoration of Lincoln's birthday, Joseph McCarthy said, "While I cannot take the time to name all the men in the State Department who have been named as members of the Communist Party and members of a spy ring I have here in my hand a list of 205 that were known to the Secretary of State as being members of the Communist Party and who nevertheless are still working and shaping the policy of the State Department."

That was the essence of McCarthyism. The numbers varied from speech to speech, the names (whether in State or in universities or wherever) were not always forthcoming and even when they were did not hold up well to rigorous investigation, but the charges put the senator's own name on everyone's lips. One of his most famous attacks, for example, was that against Owen Lattimore, the prominent Asian scholar of Johns Hopkins University, who during the war had been President Roosevelt's personal political advisor to Chiang Kai-shek. Lattimore was fingered by the senator in March 1950, in McCarthyism's first round, and after long and painful hearings was formally declared by the Senate Internal Security Subcommittee to be a "conscious articulate instrument of the Soviet conspiracy," so great was the need for a scapegoat for the "loss" of China. The hearings had climaxed in testimony by Louis Budenz, former editor of the Communist *Daily Worker* and now fervent Catholic anticommunist. Critics of McCarthyism suspected that the Catholic Budenz was just as capable of manipulating the truth for ideological ends as the Communist journalist had been, but he became a conservative hero of the hour. Later investigations have indicated that Lattimore, though a liberal, was no communist or participant in any plot and was beyond doubt an innocent victim of McCarthyism.[1]

Perhaps the majority of those named at the congressional level, however, had in fact been communists or communist sympathizers at some point in their lives, generally during the "Red Decade," the Thirties, but almost none were ever proven to have engaged in treasonous or other illegal activity. Membership in the Party was, after all, legal. Many "took the Fifth" in congressional hearings, the Bill of Rights amendment protecting one from being compelled to testify against oneself. Nonetheless, in the hysteria of the times, they were hounded, interrogated, fired, and blacklisted, and so effectively debarred from government, teaching, or industrial jobs (including particularly the movie and entertainment industries) from Washington to Hollywood. The hue and cry may have been mild as such repression goes in world history; only two persons were executed (the Rosenbergs), and only a few dozen imprisoned. But countless names were tarnished and careers destroyed, some for a decade or two, some until death, and a strange unwholesome atmosphere seemed to hang over the land.

The gale rose with remarkable rapidity and fury. McCarthy knew how to inflame a crowd, how to create an atmosphere of fearful excitement and a sense—never far beneath the surface for many hinterland Americans—that something was terribly wrong in Washington. Too many of McCarthy's fellow Republicans, famished for power after nearly two decades of Roosevelt and Truman, seized on the Wisconsin senator's demagogic claims in hopes of a hot election issue, defending and even elaborating the McCarthy mythos. Despite the rationale of a need for unity against an alien foe, the result was to polarize the country in a way it had not been for some time, certainly more than it had been in the war years

Responses were quick to come in from the religious community. One early

major mention was in a *Christian Century* editorial of April 5, "The Cultivation of Fear." On April 12 the *Christian Century* noted that "Washington has
permitted itself to be obsessed for weeks by Senator McCarthy" and commented that politics are "degenerating into the art of producing and exploit-
ing fears" of Communism and of nuclear annihilation. It can only lead, we
are told, to phobias and mass neurosis. Just as it overcomes fear of death, the
Christian faith must show the way beyond these fears as well, the editorial
insisted. This will be done not by denying the reality of what is feared. Communism and the atomic bomb, the two great current dreads, will best be managed by those who triumph over fear rather than exploit it. Christians must
show another way to respond to those modern terrors.[2]

But alongside those lofty sentiments, the liberal Protestant journal brought
in another consideration typical of the time. In the April 5 article it was suggested that the senator's campaign was instigated by Father Edmund A. Walsh,
SJ, founder and dean since 1919 of the famous School of Foreign Service at
Georgetown University in Washington, who had reportedly "pointed to a
communist-hunt as an issue which would do most for him in his campaign
for re-election." David Halberstam much later spoke more allusively of
McCarthy as "an Irish Catholic, who had been urged to take up the issue by
an official at Georgetown University."[3]

The matter is more fully developed by John Cooney in his biography of
Francis Cardinal Spellman. Cooney presents the widely repeated story that
on January 7, 1950, McCarthy had dined at the Colony Restaurant in Washington with Walsh and a couple of other prominent individuals. McCarthy
mentioned that he needed an issue that would help get him reelected. A few
possibilities were floated, including the St. Lawrence Seaway and a large-scale
pension plan for the aged, but they were thought not sufficiently inflammatory.

Then allegedly Walsh came up with the solution. The Jesuit had long
had an interest in Russia and, in his sophisticated and worldly-wise way, was
firmly anticommunist. The next year he was to publish a grim account of the
enemy entitled *Total Empire*.[4] Now, according to the legend, he suggested that
McCarthy seize on the question of communist infiltration in the United
States.[5]

Donald Crosby, after thoroughly investigating the matter, has found much
reason to doubt that Colony Restaurant story. The suggestion would have been,
he believes, very much out of character for Father Walsh, and this version of
McCarthyism's origin seems to have ultimately started in a March 14, 1950,
column by Drew Pearson in the *Washington Post*. Pearson was not always
known for scrupulous accuracy, and no other primary testimony to the alleged
event is known to exist. The Colony myth-narrative might be seen as urban
folklore voicing the mysterious but intimate connection many sensed must

exist between McCarthyism and U.S. Catholicism, even though Pearson added that when McCarthy then began his campaign Walsh was "not happy at the outcome" of his advice.[6]

Still, much of McCarthy's rapid success derived from the enthusiastic support he received in the Catholic press. Periodicals like *Ave Maria*, *Catholic World*, *Our Sunday Visitor*, the *Brooklyn Tablet*, and other diocesan papers hymned the Wisconsin Republican's campaign with unqualified praise. Over the past five years they had run story after distressing story of the persecution of Catholicism in its East European strongholds and fertile mission fields like China. In the face of this catastrophe of earthshaking dimensions for the faith and its people, the United States, the adopted homeland of millions of Catholics, but one dominated by Protestants and secularized liberals, had allegedly done nothing. The large Catholic minority was profoundly distressed in the face of such laxity; as Donald Crosby has pointed out, at that time both liberal and conservative Catholics "were passionately, even obsessively, opposed to communism, profoundly convinced that it represented the greatest of all possible dangers to both church and Republic."[7]

Someone, somewhere, must be to blame. Now one of their own was striking back, leveling charges and naming, or preparing to name, names. The church and its innocent peoples, Catholics had been told over and over, were besieged throughout the world by communists, and communism's diabolical force as often as not gained its entry by devious means and was doing so here. Indeed, the extent to which these Catholic media were obsessed with the communist issue in 1950 strikes one turning through their bound volumes forty-five years later as remarkable, even though one knows anticommunism was top Vatican policy under Pius XII, and a matter of ethnic and even family importance, as well as religious faith, to countless Americans. Scarcely an issue of any Catholic periodical for the general reader appears without major articles on the persecution of the faith under godless Marxist oppressors from Hungary to Haiphong, together with sizzling commentary on the "betrayal" of those places by Washington; it is also intimated that networks of such "traitors" are still at large and operative in the federal government.

One important icon of this passion was Dr. Tom Dooley, Catholic and sometime student at Notre Dame, whose work as a navy doctor in Haiphong treating Vietnamese refugees from communism, and later as a "jungle doctor" in Laos, was widely reported. Books by Dooley like *Deliver Us from Evil* presented in very explicit detail communist atrocities he claimed to have seen.[8] Though questioned by some observers, Dooley's accounts, from an exotic frontline part of the world soon to be the site of epic conflict between the two sides, were widely used by Catholic and government publicists to promote anticommunism. *Deliver Us from Evil*, confirming as it did the dualistic if not

Manichaean view of the world in which most Catholics of the time believed, and wanted to believe, met with a powerful response. As James Fisher put it, "The book served both to confirm and reshape the ferocious anticommunism which had unified their community—across ethnic lines, for a change—since the end of the Second World War. The contents of the book heightened the religious experience of many."[9] In a characteristic Fifties way, the homosexuality that had been the real reason for Dooley's sudden resignation from the navy in 1956 was well concealed, as were other controversial aspects of his career, and there were those who saw in him a candidate for sainthood. The battle of total good and evil needs total heroes.[10]

The middlebrow Catholic magazine *The Sign*, in a relatively moderate piece but one that seemed ready to put the burden of proof on McCarthy's critics, noted that "on July 4, 1950, there is genuine worry in the hearts of many an American . . . deep-seated worry about the extent to which betrayal from within penetrated the various branches of government."[11]

To be sure, not all Catholics were pro-McCarthy, and though all serious Catholics were staunchly anticommunist, not all adhered to the rest of the conservative agenda. Despite increasingly strident conservatism on the part of many priests and bishops, and younger assimilated families moving into the suburbs, the Catholic vote was still reasonably safe for labor- and New Deal–oriented Democrats, especially in the old ethnic neighborhoods. The majority of Catholics in Congress, mostly Democrats of that stripe, agonized over the Catholic aspect of the issue but eventually lined up with their party to oppose McCarthy and voted for his censure; some, such as Dennis Chavez of New Mexico and Eugene McCarthy of Minnesota, outspokenly condemned the Wisconsin Republican. Liberal Catholic periodicals like *Commonweal* and (until 1954) the Jesuit magazine *America* came out swinging against him. McCarthy was attacked by some members of the hierarchy, such as Bishop Matthew Ready and Monsignor George Higgins of the National Catholic Welfare Conference, and the prolabor Cardinal Mooney of Detroit was thought to be negative on him.

Early in 1950 *America* called McCarthy's charges "pretty irresponsible," although it acknowledged that "there is sufficient smoke in the ruinous collapse of our policy in China to justify Congress in looking for the fire."[12] The highbrow *Commonweal* was skeptical, and published a curious article called "The Lost Liberals," whose author, Doris Grumbach, evoked nostalgia for the "Red decade" when, at Columbia the same time as Thomas Merton, she read a few radical books by authors like Stephen Spender and Max Eastman and occasionally even put their exciting ideas for social change into practice: "I remember how cold and hostile the New York waterfront dawn was morning after morning during the dock strike of 1938 as we few sleepy-eyed Juniors assembled behind the coffee tables set out on the street corners and served the striking longshoremen." Yet communism as such was not at issue. Even a figure as well-known to the bohemia of those earlier years as the social activist convert and leader of the Catholic Worker movement, Dorothy Day (whose autobiography, The Long Loneliness, was published in 1952), though to outward appearances far to the left of the church's political center of gravity, was fervently anticommunist. She liked to call herself a radical Catholic, not a liberal Catholic—believing that by being "fools for Christ" and uncompromisingly true to the social demands of their own faith Catholics could do better anything the communists could do.[13]

The most outstanding Catholic critic of McCarthyism was Bishop Bernard Sheil, auxiliary bishop of Chicago, widely known as founder of the Catholic Youth Organization, and a leading liberal in the church. In a speech to the United Auto Workers-Congress of Industrial Organizations, he condemned the senator's tactics: "It is not enough to say that someone is anticommunist to win my support. As I remember, one of the noisiest anti-Communists of recent history was a man named Adolf Hitler." Spellman and many others, however, were furious. Many felt it was this courageous stand that caused Sheil to "resign" his post as director general of the CYO he had founded nine months later, though Donald Crosby doubts there was a direct relation.[14]

In November 1951, at the height of the McCarthy frenzy, the annual conference of Catholic bishops issued an enigmatic statement on political morality that ended, "Dishonesty, slander, detraction, and defamation of character are as truly transgressions of God's commandments when resorted to by men in political life as they are for all other men." Debate quickly emerged as to whether the prelates had McCarthy in mind; his enemies assumed they did.[15]

Donald Crosby has concluded, after careful study of public-opinion polls, election returns, letters to the editor by Catholics, and other indicators, that Catholics did not overwhelmingly support McCarthy in the ways sometimes assumed, but like other Americans were deeply divided over the issue. He was more strongly supported by some Catholic ethnic groups (Irish more vocally than Italian, German, or Polish Catholics) and by Catholics in some geographic areas (New York and Boston) than others, but McCarthy did not substantially change Catholic voting patterns more than did major demographic changes going on at the time. He holds that all in all Catholic approval and disapproval of the Catholic senator over the years of his activity did not differ extremely from the attitudes of other Americans.

Nonetheless something was going on. Major Protestant and Jewish organizations did not support McCarthy the way the leadership and much of the rank and file of the Knights of Columbus or the Catholic War Veterans obviously did, though they carefully avoided official endorsements; nor did they hold the large and enthusiastic anticommunist rallies of these Catholic groups. The controversial lawmaker did not receive public favor from Protestant or Jewish leaders or journals in a way that suggested he held a place in their hearts comparable to the place he clearly had in the hearts of Spellman, Cardinal McIntyre of Los Angeles, and many other leading Catholics, or in their papers. When Catholics did stand with the Wisconsin crusader, the backing could engage deeply felt emotions among a people tired of feeling second class in their adopted land, their patriotism questioned and their voice excluded from the highest levels of decision. One can well imagine an Irish trucker from Boston's Back Bay considering that if Harvard, the Brahmins, and the frosty liberal Protestants of the city's other culture despised McCarthy as they obviously did, that was sufficient reason to cheer him on. The fervor of pro-McCarthy Catholic opinion, as reflected in innumerable rallies, letters to editors, columns, and comments, was awesome.

A bitter editorial in *The Sign* during the presidential election (and McCarthy-ridden) year 1952 gives insight into such Catholic attitudes of the early Fifties. Called "A Paper Democracy," the editorial declares,

> A Catholic in the United States cannot realistically consider the
> United States a democracy. To him it is a Protestant aristocracy where
> Catholics are accorded little more than a half-share of the common
> rights. The United States is a place where a Catholic can be president
> *theoretically*, but not *actually*. . . . It is a place where heroic fighters for
> human rights—Stepinatz and Mindszenty—are smeared by Protestant
> spokesmen to make sure that no credit comes to the Catholic Church
> because of them. . . . The Catholic sees Protestants as the great group
> which stands in the way of full democratic development. They have
> no patience with a democracy which would grant equal rights to
> Catholics.[16]

Even Catholics who did not feel McCarthy was the right answer could probably relate to the anguish here represented, and one can understand how the feeling might be transferred by some to McCarthyism. This was moreover a time when Catholic voices like this one met their adversarial counterparts in numerous Protestant journals that attacked church-sponsored bingo, the Vatican ambassador, or federal or state aid to parochial schools. Catholic-Protestant relations in the United States were icy, only marginally better than those between Catholics and communists.

This world was clearly ready for McCarthy, and here he was. Now finally someone on the right side—a good Irish Catholic, at that—was prepared to stand up to the church's critics and give the hypocrites a bit of their own medicine. Many clerical and other supporters were not in a mood to care what anyone else thought. Speaking in Europe, where McCarthyism was widely considered a sort of American madness, Spellman was bold enough to say on October 23, 1953, "Congressional inquiries into Communist activities in the United States are not the result of mad legislative whim. There are strong reasons for these inquiries and we thank God that they have begun while there is still time to do something about it. . . . If American prestige is going to suffer in Europe because of this understandable desire we have to keep our society immune from Communist subversion, then it seems more a reflection of European standards of honor and patriotism rather than ours."[17]

Spellman remained loyal to McCarthy even after the senator's popularity fell dramatically in 1954 with the army hearings, and the Wisconsin lawmaker had become more of a liability than an asset to the archbishop. By then, well-publicized non-Catholic critics, including Senator Ralph Flanders and the dean of the Episcopal Cathedral of St. John the Divine in New York, James Pike, had publicly associated the senator's unsavory career with Catholic support, thus exacerbating Catholic-Protestant tensions. For it was becoming apparent that the core of McCarthy's die-hard believers were in the Roman Catholic community, their zeal fanned by its more conservative periodicals and prelates; the Protestant press, like the mainstream national papers generally, was rapidly falling away if it had ever given him the benefit of the doubt.

But while Spellman was aware that some of McCarthy's charges were unfair, he seemed to need the senator's abrasive passion as a prop for his own fervently anticommunist worldview and appeared to believe that cause important enough to justify the means used. He became an intimate friend of McCarthy, even personally arranging for him to adopt a child from a Catholic foundling home under his jurisdiction.

We must not, however, overlook the number of Protestants, notably the sort of midwestern conservative Republicans who took as daily scripture the fulminations of the Protestant Colonel Robert McCormick's *Chicago Tribune*, who were sympathetic to McCarthy. Probably as many Protestants as Catholics liked what McCarthy was doing, or felt it just and necessary, if their mainstream leaders were not as conspicuously behind him. It was another story with certain evangelical and fundamentalist Protestants. Donald Crosby, in fact, holds that McCarthyism amounted to a turning point in the history of U.S. Protestant fundamentalism, which heretofore had been characterized by vehement anti-Catholicism. But now right-wing fundamentalists like Carl McIntyre found themselves supporting the Catholic McCarthy, willing to overlook his wrong theology for the sake of his right politics—a political and social-issues alliance of conservatives in both faiths that was to carry over into such crusades as those against abortion or for prayer in schools.[18] If I have emphasized the Catholic factor in his support, it is because that emphasis affords a particular aperture into the religious situation in 1950, when U.S. Catholicism was undergoing a process of redefinition, and when Catholicism, because of its international character and its new level of power in the United States, was in special relationship to the cold-war anxiety of the country as a whole. In the words of the historian James Fisher, "One thing which can be said for certain (that could definitely not be said with respect to other Christian denominations) is that no one in the American church of the 1940s and early 1950s believed it was possible to be at once a Catholic and a Communist, socialist, or self-styled Marxist of any flavor."[19]

Korea

After the McCarthy opening came seven days at the end of June and the first of July 1950 that seemed to confirm and trump in spades the pervasive anxiety everyone felt about communism and the cold war. The Korean crisis hit suddenly and hard. North Korean troops invaded South Korea on June 25. The United Nations immediately authorized a police-action response under the command of General Douglas MacArthur, manned mostly by U.S. troops. For a week or so people waited in a daze, numbly wondering whether the next newscast would announce Soviet intervention and World War III, which would undoubtedly be nuclear. It was only as July wore on that the public began to realize the Russians, though not the Americans, would stay out. But when apocalypses are moving over the horizon, religions are sure to look skyward—in a free market, though, not with a single eye.

On July 15, 1950, the General Committee of the World Council of Churches, meeting in Toronto, defended the U.N. action in Korea as a necessary police action and commended the United States for undertaking it on behalf of the world. Pastor Martin Niemöller and Reinhold Niebuhr supported the majority, though two pacifist members dissented. Niemöller, noted for his courageous stand against Hitler, said, "We in Germany do not think of what is happening in Korea as war, but police action against armed violence in defiance of authority."

But Fred Haslam, a Canadian Quaker, responded, "A world organization speaking for Christ should not make such a statement as this. I doubt whether this action in Korea can rightly be called a police action."

Back in Nebraska, the mother of a young man who had been in the army in Korea told me, "Truman can call it a police action, but for the boys there, it was a war."

Editorially the *Christian Century* supported the police work, representing it as a U.N. action, a beginning of the internationalist future of which one-world idealists had long dreamed. A common police action carried out by the family of nations seemed a great step forward in international affairs, and the

Century proposed putting U.S. foreign policy in Asia entirely in the hands of the United Nations.

The pacifist A. J. Muste of the Fellowship of Reconciliation was not buy-ing it. In a letter to the *Century*, he pointed out that turning U.S. Asian af-fairs over to the international body would truly entail a "virtual revolution in American foreign policy," and he doubted the Truman administration was ready to do any such thing. Second, he indicated that if this meant the United Nations, including Russia, that scenario would first require the resolution of the global conflict between the two great powers; if it meant the United Na-tions without Russia, it would simply mean a perpetuation of the East-West struggle under the U.N. label—which in effect was what the Korean War was. On July 25 a group of seventy-five pacifists, including Muste, issued a state-ment maintaining that the Korean situation was simply "a phase of the glo-bal power struggle conflict between Russia and the United States."

The *Century* replied with a stinging editorial,

> Mr. Muste is right in his characterization. We are talking about a revolution in our foreign policy. He is wrong in his assessment of what has happened. The revolution has already started! Our contention is that the road to peace is to be found by pressing forward in the direction pointed by the decisions which have been made since the beginning of the Korean crisis. It is to expand a role which the United Nations has already assumed and to which we are already committed.
>
> It is true that the American people and their government have as yet only dimly recognized where this is going to lead. *But we are on our way!* We are moving into new territory which must be explored under conditions of extreme peril. But a beginning has been made, and there can be no turning back. Retreat is precisely what a group of 75 pacifists, of whom Mr. Muste was one, proposed in a statement issued on July 25. They refuse to recognize that the relation of the United Nations to the Korean situation has any significance. . . . They urge that "the United States withdraw from the conflict and itself take the initiative in seeking a peaceful solution and developing a Gandhian nonviolent means for resistance to aggression and tyranny." If there is any better formula than that for wrecking the United Nations, strengthening isolationism, turning the world over to a galloping communist advance and bringing on atomic war. it has not come to our attention.[20]

The tension and, for this liberal magazine, immoderate tone one senses in the editorial position was endemic to 1950, a season of high-strung feel-ings and virulent anticommunism that Korea only raised to even higher pitch. (The editorial also indicates the acceptance of the credibility and virtue of

Korea, Catholics, Protestants, and Anticommunism

37

the official U.S. position the in 1950 was granted by all but those as radicalized as Muste and his group—a position that, older and wiser, the *Century* like many others would question more and more over the years, especially with regard to Vietnam in the next decade.)

On the home front, late 1950 and 1951 increasingly reflected a jittery, anxious society given to explosive outbursts of frenzy against communism, progressive education, and the like, all based more on demonology than on facts. Respected school superintendents were fired in Pasadena, Denver, and elsewhere. Clearly, anticommunism as a quasi-religious state church was moving in, bringing with it religious rather than merely political ways of thinking.

Even in the liberal religious press, skepticism about communism and peace was common. A 1950 article by Robert Root, "All in the Name of Peace," expressed thoroughgoing skepticism of a current Soviet "Peace Offensive" based on the Stockholm Peace Petition. Patriarch Alexei of Moscow had given it his "whole-hearted support," and called on other Orthodox to join the cause, but Root considered such so-called peace "a Soviet propaganda tool."[21] On this score he was doubtless right, since beyond question the Russian church was firmly under the control of the Kremlin at the time, above all in its foreign relations.

The war went through its own vicissitudes, which provide a background to the religious history of the times. The northern invaders were initially successful, pushing the South Koreans and their U.S./U.N. supporters into an enclave around the southern port of Pusan. Then the Allies were relieved by the last great example of MacArthur's military genius, the Inchon landing of September 15, and drove north, reaching the Yalu River on the Chinese border by November 20.

China then sent troops across the border; MacArthur, in his " no substitute for victory" mood, responded with an ill-prepared, politically dangerous, and apparently unauthorized offensive northward against them on November 24. This venture was disastrously mauled by the new foe. On November 26, as delegates gathered in Cleveland to form the National Council of Churches, a Chinese counteroffensive overwhelmed the hero of the Philippines. The Allies were once again in full retreat down the peninsula ahead of up to a million communist troops, and there was talk of a Dunkirklike disaster in the making. Seoul fell once again to the communists on January 4, 1951. Although the enemy offensive was halted on January 15, and Seoul recaptured for the second time by U.N. forces on March 14, the drive did not again go north and the front was eventually stabilized the next year, not far from the original thirty-eighth parallel separating North and South Korea.

This was the crisis that led up to the dismissal of MacArthur by Truman on April 11, 1951. The much-laureled general's blatant insubordination made that a necessary as well as a courageous move on the part of the commander-in-chief. But it was a touchstone event for a generation of anticommunists, and a political negative for Truman. Constrained, limited war, however necessary, would bring no shouts from the crowd such as MacArthur received on his triumphal, rather than disgraced, return. World War II, with its events of now mythic proportions, still hung in the near background, and it was difficult to make gestures that seemed out of harmony with its wide stage, and its tableau of heroes and villains.

The Cold War at Home

The early Fifties were the Antarctic years of the cold war, and to most Americans it seemed only prudent common sense that anticommunism should take precedence over virtually any other policy consideration at home and abroad. Sometimes, however, the requisite means at home assumed shapes less reminiscent of politics than of the dark side of religion—heresy hunts, witch hunts, and the expulsion of pollutants. That sort of religious anticommunism as a total worldview, a kind of state church often called "Americanism," was finally to decline. But it is worth looking for a moment at the vision behind it at its early-Fifties peak.

Americanism took for granted, first of all, that communism was by no means only a political, military, or economic challenge, but also a spiritual one that threatened the deepest foundations of human life, the relation of soul to Ultimate Reality. In that sense it was indeed a parallel to invasions of demons or attacks through witchcraft. The ideal America was unified spiritually, a righteous and God-fearing nation, giving expression to belief in God with one voice and concurring that in this cohesion would be powerful; those few who broke unanimity must be expelled like witches, for the good of the community as a whole.

Anticommunism struck paydirt in both outsider wings of U.S. Christianity, first the Roman Catholic and later the evangelical. Both flanks were passionately anticommunist, and both challenged the supposed political and theological liberalism of the mainstream center, though for the moment that flexible middle was rapidly turning to Barthian neoorthodoxy. More profoundly, the flanks challenged the hegemony of the class the center presumably represented: the long-dominant Anglo-American elite associated with the Ivy League universities and their ilk, with the mainline Anglo-Protestant denominations, and with the levers of ultimate power on Wall Street and in Washington. On anticommunism the evangelicals and Roman Catholics were generally clean, and the most-publicized culprits were elite Protestants. Evangelical and Catholic anticommunist rhetoric was several decibels louder than that of the mainline churches, and the outsiders pounced with glee on charges by the likes of Senator Joseph McCarthy or Whittaker Chambers and Representative Richard Nixon (all of "outsider" background) that the striped-pants establishment was riddled with communists.

In 1950 religion was part of a very important concept, the "American Way of Life," a unique way seen as threatened, both from without and from within. But just as the way could be defined in liberal or conservative terms, one could choose a correspondingly different response to the threat.

To all, the United States was unique. It was relatively wealthy in a world of want. Other places were wracked by poverty that was the dismal product of war and imperialism, both professedly hated by Americans, and by laggard development. In 1950 virtually half the world's wealth was in or on its way to the United States, where 5 percent of the world's population lived. America was held to be different also because it was founded on values far nobler than those of the corrupt, cynical Old World with its kings and dictators, not to mention its alien ideologies. There was, however, much U.S. sympathy in those years for the subjects of European colonialism then struggling for independence: India, Indonesia, a little later Africa. If all went well, those lands might become new outposts of what the United States stood for.

At the same time, the Fifties had been bequeathed a religious consciousness shaped by the tensions and archetypes of the Thirties and Forties, when good and evil—whether workers versus Wall Street, colonialized peoples versus imperialists, or Allies versus Axis—had appeared polarized into almost Manichaean dualisms. It was hard to let go of the dualistic pattern, especially when fresh candidates for the requisite two sides were so obviously at hand. Now in the Fifties, for all the comfortable fellowship of the new suburban homes and churches, with their overflowing nurseries, in a red sky somewhere behind them whirled images of titanic conflict, of the children of light battling the children of darkness, of whispered intrigue in the corridors of power, of simple but heroic peoples laboring under oppression and awaiting liberation.

That was the conservative version of the vision. In order to implement that vision, its visionaries saw to it that loyalty boards were established in government departments and elsewhere to screen the political predilections of employees. Vigilantes, often religious—such as those of a group called the American Council of Christian Laymen—put out slick, well-financed booklets with titles like "How Red Is the Federal Council of Churches?" and eagerly joined the hunt for commies and "comsymps" on an amateur basis. The fight was carried to numerous school boards, unions, industries, and of course government bureaucracies. Sometimes the hunt for pollutants took forms that can only seem bizarre to the later reader. In 1950 Monogram Pictures in Hollywood shelved a projected film on the life of Hiawatha; the American Indian made immortal by Longfellow was instrumental in ending the fighting among some tribes and organizing the famous Five Nations, something like a Native American equivalent of the United Nations. The Monogram moguls decided that such a picture might play into the hands of communist propaganda, since the Reds also talked about peace and used the United Nations to try to subvert U.S. sovereignty. However grotesque, the anti-Red binge was less than amusing to the thousands of church, academic, entertainment, library, and government workers who found themselves its targets. Not a few reputations and careers were ruined, not seldom on the grounds of hearsay and innuendo alone. But the witch-hunt way of affirming U.S. uniqueness did not go unchallenged in religious circles, even though the premises were taken for granted. A chastened but pro–free speech version of the liberal vision remained throughout 1950 in churches as in politics.

According to Samuel A. Stouffer's 1954 survey, *Communism, Conformity, and Civil Liberties*, most Americans felt that an admitted communist should not be allowed to speak in their community (though county party chairpeople, both Democrat and Republican, did), and should be fired if a teacher; the respondents were more lenient in the case of communists in less sensitive jobs.[22]

In 1952 such views were tested in court in Fairmont, West Virginia. Dr. Luella Raab Mundel, recently dismissed head of the art department at Fairmont State College, was suing Thelma Brand Loudin, vice president of the state board of education, for $100,000 for falsely labeling her a "security risk" and "an atheist," thereby causing her to lose her job. The atheism charge immediately illuminates the close relation of anticommunist fervor with religious ideology.

The president of the college, Dr. George Hand, testified that he had asked the FBI to check on the former charge and that he himself had checked on the atheism, with the result that he had asked the board to reappoint Professor Mundel with an increase in pay. But the board ignored that recommendation and voted to discharge her. The security-risk charge seems to have stemmed from a local American Legion seminar in which Mundel had asked a few questions implying she did not agree with the claims of the speaker, an "ex-communist," that U.S. colleges were full of communists, that communists and liberals were pretty much the same, and that ordinary citizens were qualified to identify and report communists among their acquaintances and coworkers.

Senator Matthew Neely of West Virginia, doubtless with political as well as ideological prospects in mind, served as counsel for Loudin, and, as *Commonweal* magazine indicated, the courtroom took on a Bible-cum-circus atmosphere perhaps not seen since the famous confrontation between Clarence Darrow and William Jennings Bryan in the Tennessee "Monkey Trial" nearly thirty years earlier. Senator Neely began by calling for "teachers without any high-faluting ideas about not being able to prove there isn't a God—teachers who believe the old-fashioned American way that our forefathers handed down from the time the barefoot soldiers of Washington stained the snows of Valley Forge with their precious blood. I'm for these teachers." He then added, "I'm not for teachers tainted with foreignisms."[23]

In cross-examination, the senator asked Mundel such questions as, "Have you ever admitted there is a God?" to which she made such ingenious replies as, "Yes, I have. I will admit there is a God if you will accept Webster's definition that a God is something that man worships. I worship truth. I worship Christian ethics and the teachings of Christ and I wish they'd be applied more often."

Counsel then challenged her with Webster's definition of an atheist, and so on for several hours. Finally Mundel broke down weeping and had to be excused. At that point Senator Neely informed the judge that he intended to make his interrogation "as pitiless and as thorough as I can. It is my duty to my client and my country." Mundel was unable to appear in court the next day; the doctor who treated her said that she was out of money and had not eaten for several days. Friends said she was also talking of suicide. The judge and the senator went to her home to complete the examination there.

The following Sunday, the Sunday after Christmas, the priest of the Episcopal church in Fairmont, Graham Luckenbill, referred to the trial as "a farce" and averred that it "smacks loudly of all the bad traits of the Inquisition and the Crucifixion." After these remarks were reported next day in the Fairmont *Times*, Neely asked the court to declare a mistrial on the grounds that Father Luckenbill's statements could not help but prejudice a jury. The judge, always very obliging to the senator, did so, and the case ended on that note of ambiguity.

Mundel's supporters declared a moral victory, however, claiming that Neely ended the "farce" knowing that public opinion was rising against him.[24] (The elderly, rough-hewn and rough-tongued Democrat from West Virginia, Matthew Neely, supporter of the colorful mineworkers' unionizer John L. Lewis and other blue-collar causes, would better have left religion and quasi-religion entirely alone. In 1955 he got in trouble for a remark in a speech to the United Auto Workers in Detroit disparaging President Eisenhower's churchgoing and his having never joined a church before becoming president. Senator Neely received a mountain of unfavorable mail on that matter suggesting his remarks were tasteless and out of bounds; he was wounded by the letter writers' intensity.)[25]

The Mundel case, one among many, makes eloquently clear the religious overtones of early Fifties anticommunism: the parallels to the heresy hunting and demonology of the Inquisition or the witch hunts; the assumption that "security risk" and "atheist" went together, and that, correspondingly, a good American was a believer in God; and finally, the resultant view—undoubtedly unconstitutional—that a teacher or other public employee could be put to a religious test concerning belief in God, and fired if she or he failed it.[26]

But there were other religious perspectives. In an editorial, "Fighting Fire with Gasoline," the *Christian Century* opposed blacklisting and other forms of extreme anticommunism that jeopardize civil rights, yet also was at pains to emphasize its own opposition to communism, pointing out that no independent religious journalism like its own exists in communist countries.[27] The account of the Fairmont case, in which Graham Luckenbill who stood in the prophetic rather than the culture-religion tradition of faith, was presented, with obvious sympathy for Mundel, in *Commonweal*. This Catholic periodical of liberal perspective was much at odds with the official line in the days of Pius XII and Cardinal Spellman. Moreover, some churchly sympathy for change at home and abroad continued in 1950. Many ministers and members molded by the rather different social atmosphere of the Thirties remained in pulpits and pews, some not fully comprehending why the world now appeared so dark and dangerous to a new and ostensibly more fortunate generation.

For example, the Methodist Women's Society for Christian Service, meeting in Cleveland in 1950 at the same time as McCarthy's initial charges, had as its theme "Christian Faith for a World in Revolution." An accompanying editorial in the Methodist *Christian Advocate* pointed out that the revolution was not only political but was also going on in families, with their breakdown as self-sufficient units and their integration in larger communities. This revolution was said to be in full swing in the new nuclear-family suburban churches as they supplanted, for their young couples, traditional back-home parishes that probably relied on extended clans as their core. (The most far-reaching revolutions are those that overtake conservative people without their fully realizing it.) There was also, Methodists were told, a revolution in national and international life. "The old traditions of the nation-state are tottering, and old ideas of an unyielding national sovereignty are losing out," as indicated by the United Nations and economic cooperation. The United States was the great "have" nation, but through foreign aid and the Marshall Plan, it was about to give others a chance to buy what Americans could not use; all this was revolutionary.[28]

One instinctively senses, however, that these Methodist revolutionaries did not mean by "revolution" what the communists meant, or what the New Left would mean a decade later; theirs was a benign social-gospel usage carried over from the days when sympathetic encouragement of ongoing radical change under the banner of progress was a mark of the forward-looking Christian, days when it was the church's business to keep up with change and Christianize it.

Yet those days were gone. After McCarthy, even the *Christian Advocate* would publish occasional opinion pieces, not to mention rabidly alarmed letters to the editor, opposing the church's alleged liberalism and internationalism at the top. The new nationalism of the cold war and extreme anticommunism soon made its impact in Methodism as elsewhere, especially with the advent of the Korean War only a couple of months after the "World in Revolution" study. Nonetheless, two ways of looking at the world could be seen vying with each other in the mainstream churches of 1950.

Taking the old line was another anti–cold warrior, the Reverend G. S. Nichols of Collegiate Methodist Church in Ames, Iowa, the home of Iowa State College (now University). There, from the heart of midwestern Methodism, this outspoken but popular pacifist maintained a free pulpit. Despite some complaints and heckling, his church sponsored controversially interracial student cooperatives during the depression, dialogue between conscientious objectors and fighters during the war, and free debates on military conscription during the cold war. Students flocked to Collegiate Methodist, drawn by the vital atmosphere and sense of being on the religious cutting edge. Dr. Nichols, a powerful preacher, was supported by a large majority of his parishioners in these and other ventures.[29]

The battle was joined, prophet against prophet and priest against priest. It was still in a real sense an open market. Although the tone of such meetings and periodicals of Methodism and of other "cooperative" denominations was still often social gospel, that Christian style was now challenged by the conservative, vociferously anticommunist rhetoric from the flanks as well as increasingly from aroused backbiters within their own sanctuaries. But the liberals and moderates were regrouping.

The National Council of Churches

The National Council of Churches was formed at the end of November 1950 in Cleveland, literally under a cloud—snow paralyzed the city on Lake Erie as delegates gathered from twenty-nine denominations representing thirty-one million members. The Ohio community, according to the December 13 *Christian Century*, was reportedly "like a bombed-out city"—stores did not open, cars were buried, and on Sunday "there were more empty churches in Cleveland than at any time in its history." As grim as the weather came the tidings from Korea, which prevented hoped-for appearances in Cleveland by President Harry Truman or Secretary of State Dean Acheson. The communist offensive had begun, and the military situation on the Asian peninsula was darkening by the hour.

Nonetheless, the establishment of the National Council of Churches was auspicious for the Fifties. The council was officially inaugurated on November 29, when in a solemn service representatives of the cooperating denominations came forward one by one to sign the document as the name of their church was called. By and large, this body presented a moral voice on a high level. It institutionalized two longstanding trends in Protestantism, the ecumenical movement already reified in the World Council of Churches, and the already mentioned division of Protestantism between the cooperative mainstream and the others, mainly evangelicals.

Henry Knox Sherrill, presiding bishop of the Episcopal Church and first president of the new National Council of Churches, was featured on the cover of *Time*, March 26, 1951. The story presents this dignified, snowy-haired prelate as a stable, unruffled churchman with a kindly manner and a knack for administration who had risen to the top via tours of duty in the most proper of Bostonian parishes. He was chosen bishop of Massachusetts and then presiding bishop, despite his insistence that he would really rather be doing ordinary pastoral work among all sorts and conditions of persons. Bishop Sherrill was a great and large-hearted man by no means limited by his personal background. In the darkest hours of McCarthyist hysteria and the Korean War, his clear vision and steady hand were undoubtedly what his church and the cooperative churches needed. Yet he somehow also personifies the mainline Protestantism of his day, both at its best, and as it was ultimately connected to a class and geographical base.

The *Time* cover story concluded by pointing to widespread evidence in the United States of renewed interest in the Christian life. Young men were going to seminaries and joining religious orders in unprecedented numbers, religious books were on the bestseller lists, and church membership was growing. But, *Time* further warned, a new anti-Christian force was rising in the world, moving against religion's very basis, belief in God and the spiritual significance of humanity. "This will probably lead to a moment of crisis within the next ten to fifteen years," readers were warned. It was in this atmosphere that Fifties religious life existed.[30]

Actions of the NCC over its first two years, the Sherrill years, suggest its range of interest. The organization had sponsored resettlement of fifty-two thousand displaced persons and shipped eleven million pounds of food overseas. In an evangelism program, it had sent 175 preachers to military bases, and 250 to college campuses. It provided a voice for opposition to a U.S. ambassador at the Vatican and sponsored the publication of the Revised Standard Version of the Bible. At its 1952 meeting, Methodist bishop William C. Martin of Dallas was elected to succeed Henry Knox Sherrill as president of the NCC. John Foster Dulles, the secretary of state designate after Dwight Eisenhower's election to the White House that fall, spoke to the delegates, urging a "dynamic faith" to combat the fanatic devotion of communists to their cause.[31]

Protestantism in the Early Fifties

For a sense of what 1950 Protestant churches were doing at the grass-roots level, the *Christian Century*'s 1950 "Great Churches" series provides an invaluable picture. A fine example of the suburbanization of religion is Mount Olivet Augustana Lutheran church of Minneapolis, the first congregation in the series. An archetypal example of the rapidly growing, white middle-class suburban parish, Mount Olivet was generously endowed with young couples and their lively children, which is one's premier image of a successful 1950s church. Not all successful parishes of the time were like that, as the series makes clear by including rural and "Old First" downtown churches as well as suburban dynamos— though even this explicitly Protestant selection does not include any African American, not to mention Roman Catholic or Eastern Orthodox, churches.

Mount Olivet had grown from 331 members in 1938 to over 5,000 in 1950. The phenomenal increase was apparently due to a fortunate combination of demographics and doing well what a church ought to do, not to any gimmicks or special plans. The church was well situated in a new white-collar section said to have the highest education level in the city. It was full of rising young families enjoying an average annual income of $3,600 and living in houses worth from $12,000 to $15,000.

The dedicated and popular pastor, Reuben K. Youngdahl, over six feet tall, had worked his way through seminary by playing part-time professional basketball. That Augustana was a Swedish Lutheran denomination and that this was Minnesota undoubtedly helped (though no more than half the 1950 membership was Augustana in background), and it no doubt also helped that the pastor's brother, Luther Youngdahl, was Republican governor of the state. But the Reverend Reuben Youngdahl worked hard. His three Sunday morning services offered dignified Lutheran liturgies and well-crafted biblical sermons without special effects or personality cult. After a full day in the office and in such public activities as service on the Mayor's Committee on Human Relations or the Minneapolis Society for the Blind, Youngdahl spent from five o'clock to eight o'clock each evening making fifteen-minute calls on members and prospective members, and after that he and his wife hosted receptions in their home for thirty to fifty church people on three nights a week.[32]

And churches in 1950 continued to germinate and grow. According to the

The Lutheran of April 26, in those years a new church of the United Lutheran denomination came into existence every two weeks. Here is an example of supply-side church formation. Martin Luther Evangelical Lutheran Church, Milwaukee, was formally organized on Palm Sunday, April 2. The effort had begun in August 1949, when the Home Missions Board of the regional synod sponsored a canvass of 1,400 residences in the West Bluemond Road area. It turned up some four thousand souls: 44 percent Roman Catholic, 30 percent Lutheran, 26 percent other denominations in background. But of them, 31 percent were currently members of no church. These persons were naturally targeted; of the 110 members received at the inaugural service, only 24 were active members of another congregation before joining Martin Luther church. Of the new members, 64 had previously been Lutherans of some type and 46 were former non-Lutherans, ranging from Roman Catholics to secularists.[33]

Churches in the South were strictly segregated. In 1950 the Alabama Supreme Court upheld the conviction of Glen H. Taylor, U.S. senator from Idaho and Henry A. Wallace's vice presidential candidate on the 1948 Progressive Party ticket. During the campaign, Taylor had attempted to enter a Baptist church in Birmingham, where he was to speak at a Southern Negro Youth Congress, via the "colored" door. When he was directed by police to the white entrance, he tried again to force his way through the entry his black audience would be required to use, allegedly calling the officers of the law "vile names" in the process. Taylor was arrested and convicted of disorderly conduct; he appealed, but the state supreme court sustained the judgment and upheld the right of churches to establish separate entries for the two races.

Churches had many styles and emphases. First Community Church of Columbus, Ohio, was an independent parish of Congregationalist background that presented itself, in the phrase of its pastor, Dr. Roy A. Burkhart, as a "full-guidance church." This meant that it specialized in giving its members an exceptional amount of counseling and personal contact, often couched more in the idiom of psychiatry than of traditional religion. Indeed, Karl Menninger, the well-known psychiatrist, commented that "the inspiring First Community Church, Columbus, is providing the best example of organized mental hygiene that I know of or have ever seen." The parish made extensive use of the psychological tests, or personality inventories, so popular in the Fifties, especially in connection with young people and in premarital counseling, and kept an eye out for any "sign of deviation or abnormality in any direction."[34] While undoubtedly successful and helpful in many instances, First Community also appears a salient example of that side of the Fifties preoccupied with psychology, normality, and mental hygiene; the yearning for religion-tinged guidance was also tapped by Norman Vincent Peale, touter of healthy-minded "positive thinking" and founder of *Guideposts* magazine.

Successful churches in 1950 ranged from Peale's Marble Collegiate Church in New York, with its message about positive thinking, to another example in the *Christian Century* series, Bellevue Baptist in Memphis, where stem-winding sermons were preached against evolution as readily as against booze. But most of the growing early-Fifties churches and synagogues were probably like Mount Olivet—they stayed away from anything that smacked of the highly experimental or extreme. They did religion in accordance with their tradition and did it very well, making concessions only to the young and mobile population's implicit demand for socialization as well as worship in church, and for practical psychology as well as theology.

Protestantism was having a successful decade. But it was divided, not only between intellectual and popular forms of expression, but also between its longstanding liberal and evangelical wings. By liberal Christians I mean those who believe that the gospel must be communicated in ways that are compatible with the worldview of the age, including its best science, philosophy, and critical scholarship; it is not the letter but the spirit that counts, and it can and should continually be put in new bottles. Evangelicals, on the other hand, say that the gospel can only be communicated in its own terms, since it must stand above the spirit of every age; while preachers may use contextual references for homiletic purposes, the authority and language of Scripture must be taken very seriously, and serious matters like incarnation and redemption presented only as they are in the revealed Word.

The mainstream liberal denominations tended to be those with historical roots in colonial America. They were largely places of prayer for white northern Europeans, especially those British-descended Protestants who still, in the Fifties, had some characteristics of an elite class with a special role as power brokers and ultimate custodians of the U.S. heritage. Not surprisingly, this class and its churches had close ties to major elite educational institutions like Harvard, Yale, Chicago, and their respective theological schools. Though not limited to them, as my Great Plains congregation shows, these denominations ministered to the spiritual requirements of the well-educated, eastern-based establishment that continued (though more and more tenuously owing to increasing Catholic, Jewish, and southern/ western participation) to dominate government, business, and the academy in the Fifties. They constituted the cooperative denominations that, in 1950, formed the National Council of Churches.

Those thirty-one million Christians, however, were only about half of the nation's Protestants. A small number, such as the Unitarians and Universalists, were too liberal for the NCC with its Trinitarian profession of faith. But most stay outers were evangelicals, ranging from flamboyant Southern Baptists to sobersided conservative Calvinists and Lutherans, who dissented perhaps for reasons as much of temperament and style as of creed. Unlike the cooperatives, evangelicals were likely to harbor some alienation from the Ivy League and the Wasp establishment, and they were strongest among those races, classes, and sections of the country most likely to feel so estranged. Conversely, mainline cooperators were likely to look upon the evangelicals with undisguised condescension. Presbyterian stated clerk Eugene Carson Blake, while president of the National Council of Churches in 1959, remarked on the "cultural crudities" of evangelical "sects" and urged his ecumenical colleagues to help Christian conservatives overcome their "theological isolation and personal provincialism."[35]

Billy Graham and the Evangelicals

In the fall of 1949, in a seven-week crusade in Los Angeles in which he preached to more than 300,000 and won some six thousands decisions for Christ, the intense young evangelist Billy Graham first attracted nationwide attention. The next January he successfully visited Boston and went on to even greater achievement for Christ in his home country, the Carolinas. His bursting onto the national and world stages was thus essentially a Fifties phenomenon.

Commentators noted his hand-painted ties, his stylish suits, and his extravagant claims: "America has only three or four more years at the most and then it will all be over and we will fall as Rome fell and Germany fell."[36] When it came to attacking the satanic evils of communism, he was outdone by no one. But not all outsiders to his tradition understood what preaching was and meant to evangelicals, particularly to Baptists, among whom it is like a work of art, a sacrament, even a theophany, experienced for its own sake and in its own terms as it washes like the Holy Spirit over the heart and informs the rational mind. Some hyperbole in preachers, as in salespeople or symbolist painters, is expected and discounted. But the fervor and the evident sincerity behind those same extravagant words communicate their own message about the revival power of the Spirit. Truly great preachers must convey, also by almost subliminal signs, several things outside the literal meanings of spoken words. Two are that they are both contemporary and uncompromised. Hence Billy's voguish neckties and apocalyptic rhetoric.

When all this together swept to the forefront of national consciousness, it seemed to those in evangelicalism or drawn toward it the rushing wind of a new day of Pentecost. And so it was, for surely in Billy Graham the billows of the evangelical renewal that rose in America in the latter decades of the twentieth century were beginning to stir. All the signs were there: countercultural message, cultural conformity in such media as sharp dress and the latest communications technology, thorough up-to-date personnel mobilization, conservative politics, mass audiences, rhetoric directed to the individual. In short, the language of the old message in modern packaging, an ideal and very successful supply-side presentation of religion. (Or not quite the old message, for I have been convinced by Marshall McLuhan that the medium is at least part of the message, and I am not completely sure that an evangelical message communicated with space-age technology and business-school organization does not in some subtle way differ from frontier preaching, though the theology may be the same.)

Other signs of an evangelical awakening appeared, as yet little noticed by the mainstream save as curiosities. Some were indeed as face-to-face and unprogrammed as any of yore. For example, at Graham's own alma mater, evangelical Wheaton College in Illinois, a spontaneous revival occurred early in 1950. During a semiannual evangelistic week, students were asked to give testimonials. On Wednesday evening, February 8, they started with ten student testifiers; more and more came forward to accuse themselves of sin in a spontaneous revival. It went on for no less than thirty-nine hours, when the president of the college finally stopped the spiritual marathon for fear of "notoriety." Many students declared this event the start of a revival that would "sweep the nation."[37]

In Graham's own rallies, planning was important. A Lutheran pastor in Columbia, South Carolina, reported that before the forty thousand gathered in the University of South Carolina stadium in 1950 a well-organized campaign had put out advance publicity. Prayer meetings were held at the block level, and also in stores and office buildings. The pastor, Wynn Boliek, found the revivalist's preaching to be sincere, straightforward, but with an emphasis on fear, as for example the predictions that five years from now, none of us might be here. At the end, Graham called for hands. Those who responded went to prayer rooms accompanied by well-trained "personal workers." The new converts filled out decision cards with the name of their church preference. In his own conversations, Boliek found a mixed situation among those who signed decision cards. Some did so to get rid of a persistent worker; some young people put up their hands and went to the prayer rooms just to check out what was going on, or because of friends, or on impulse. Some churches gained a few members, some lost. But at least, he concluded, people *were* talking about religion during the campaign.[38]

Billy Graham preached the following year in Seattle. A careful study by Arthur Lester Frederick of the effects of this 1951 evangelistic effort found, first, that the Graham campaign began its preparatory work in the city more than a year beforehand. Strenuous efforts were made to secure the support of the city's churches and religious organizations. The National Association of

Evangelicals brought most of their member churches into the effort, but the Council of Churches declined to cooperate officially, leaving the decision to individual parishes. In the end, about one-third of the city's churches cooperated.

Some 40,000 attended the rallies. Of those, about 6,000 signed decision cards, of which 3,349 were forwarded to churches within the city of Seattle itself. (The other decisions presumably were by visitors from outside the city.) Of those, 1,598 or 48 percent were by people having a previous connection with the church receiving the card. In the end, 534 new members were received by Seattle churches as a result of the campaign. The total money raised by the crusade was $190,651.36. Local expenses, including the salaries of Graham and his team while in Seattle, came to $123,651.69; $67,268.67 went to Graham's national organization.

Of course, figures alone do not tell the story of an activity like this. Many who did not make a decision on the spot may have been strengthened in a faith they already possessed, or prepared for a longer-term conversion process. Certainly the city was made more conscious of religion. But the reactions of 186 ministers who responded to a follow-up survey three months later were mixed; a little over half said results of the campaign were good (30 percent) or fair (20 percent); a little under half (40 percent) saw it as negligible or detrimental in effect. Respondents saw good in the consciousness it had raised and the follow-up; bad were too much "scare" preaching, a narrow and divisive view of Christianity, and weakening of denominational loyalties.[39]

Another part of the story is that mainline clergy like Boliek and Frederick were prepared to visit the Graham activities and write about them virtually in the manner of anthropologists venturing among the natives of some distant island. The difference in tone between the two Protestant religious worlds, the liberal and evangelical, was of such dimensions. Perhaps as much as anything the great gulf between the two realms is found in attitude toward religious experience. In mainline denominations, including such theologically traditional but state-church background denominations as the Lutheran, intense feeling is not essential to church commitment and indeed is not seldom a difficult subject in conversation. On the other hand, in evangelicalism such feeling is not only acceptable but a definite mark of Christian maturity. To overgeneralize: liberals can't talk about personal religious experience without embarrassment; evangelicals believe one should talk about nothing more freely.

Graham's Fifties message was something like the cold war internalized. He portrayed a world sharply divided between good and evil, in which the most important thing a person could do was to make the right choice about which side to be on. He was often taken to task by liberals for naiveté (as when he described heaven as 1,600 miles long, wide, and high), for superpatriotism and association with politicians like Richard Nixon. While in subsequent years he has shown an admirable capacity for growth in wisdom and spiritual stature and has learned like the psalmist not to put his trust in princes, the essential message has remained the same.

Personal conversion is the foundation of Christian experience for Graham, and all else must stem from it. This fitted the Fifties need for ways to affirm the responsible self over against mass society, and at the same time to find ways of assimilation into a cause larger and greater than oneself. But no one—unless it be God—asked or even expected someone like Billy Graham suddenly to burst onto the U.S. religious scene as he did about 1950. Thus he was one of the main supply-side channels in U.S. life, adding his own flavorsome gospel to the medley.

Billy Graham was controversial, and so was evangelicalism. He continued through the decade to spend himself in the work to which he was convinced his Lord had called him, and converts continued to come forward—though perhaps not in as great numbers as those who saw only pictures of crowded stadia supposed. Undoubtedly, though, he marked something far more difficult to quantify, but even more important than numbers, for the future of evangelicalism: a rising confidence, a sense of the deep tides of the Spirit flowing in the right direction, of victory here, or at the last day, within sight.

Interreligious Fights and Margins of Tolerance

Now, let us turn to conflicts between the two great U.S. faiths, Protestantism and Roman Catholicism. The world of 1950 was one of visions in epic conflict—a legacy of the ideological Thirties combined with the warlike energies raised in the Forties. "Freedom" versus "communism" was not the only conflict at home and abroad. The much older religious cold war between Catholic and Protestant was still a part of the scene.

Indeed, the Fifties were a time of heightened tension between Protestants and Catholics in the United States, climaxing in the Catholic-president issue at the very end of the decade. The appointment of an ambassador to the Vatican and government aid to parochial schools were hotly disputed topics. The dismal state of Catholic-Protestant relations in the early Fifties remained an important, almost the dominant, issue in U.S. religious news in those years.

The January 4, 1950, issue of the liberal Protestant *Christian Century*, the opening issue of the decade, called for the retirement of Myron Taylor as "personal representative at the Vatican of the President of the United States," and urging that no successor be named. "Vatican Embassy Must End!" a later headline screamed.

The Vatican ambassador issue was a very serious one. Protestants saw it as an affront, feeling that it gave one church a level of official recognition not afforded any other. A deep mistrust of Roman Catholic political activity, both at home and abroad, was also involved along with traditional Protestant American anti-Catholicism.

The background to the controversy that must be understood is pre–Vatican II Roman Catholicism, when church teaching (reversed at that council) legitimated government support for that faith and state suppression of "error." Such policies were still actively pursued in the Fifties in such countries as Spain, Portugal, and certain Latin American nations (Colombia was especially controversial), and they made Protestants very uneasy.

Even the working alliance between the world's two great anticommunist forces, the United States and the Vatican (an important justification of the ambassadorship), made the spiritual children of Martin Luther uneasy. An editorial in the next issue of the *Century*, January 11, "Is the Cold War a Holy War?" considered whether U.S. foreign policy was not "being manipulated by the astute diplomat now on St. Peter's throne," Pius XII, who was perhaps using our simplistic anticommunism to help him build up a "Catholic Western Europe."

The contemporary reader is immediately dragged into the pre–Vatican II world of frosty Catholic-Protestant relations, when the Vatican was, or was perceived to be from the outside, thoroughly secretive, autocratic, and deeply involved in both U.S. and world politics, not unlikely in sinister ways. Ecumenical ideals had yet to take hold between the two great wings of Western Christendom; in the Fifties not only was the *Christian Century* continually eying Rome suspiciously, but the religion and letters pages of the newsmagazines were marred by tomcatlike spats between ministers and monsignors over such issues as which church had taken the most converts from the other.

At the same time, the April 12 issue of the *Christian Century* contained a review of Henry Morton Robinson's novel *The Cardinal*, a popular work of the time that many took to reflect the career of Francis Spellman, the powerful archbishop of New York who had become a cardinal in 1946. Even more significantly, Robinson's story reflected an image of Roman Catholicism that would, despite controversy, hover in the background of Fifties religiosity: of a supremely powerful, confident organization with immense depths of wisdom and experience that, a few flawed individuals notwithstanding, was fundamentally on the side of everything good in Western civilization, and that possessed the might and subtle skill to save it. Compared to the fractious Protestant denominations, it was an express train alongside a fleet of buggies pulled by unruly steeds.

The novel's principal character, a priest destined to become a cardinal, was beaten by Klannish Protestant bigots while on a trip through the South. All the Catholic characters, on the other hand, including Vatican functionaries high and low, have pure hearts and good intentions beneath sometimes difficult exteriors. The Protestant reviewer, W. E. Garrison, labeled it "propaganda—but good." Rating its literary merits as "respectable but not remarkable," he reflected the edgy and suspicious attitudes of Protestants to Roman Catholics by adding gratuitously, "I thought better of it than did the reviewer in *Commonweal*, who ridiculed the story as a sequence of melodramatic improbabilities, perhaps with the thought that it would do more good for the Catholic cause if the Catholic press did not appear to be too enthusiastic about it."[40] (The review in the Jesuit *America* also found the novel a bit problematic, discussing earnestly its portrayal of human foibles in priests—however mild they may be by worldly standards—but finally concluding, rightly, that Robinson's ability to paint Catholic clerics as occasionally less than perfect meant that "the Church in the United States is growing in stature."[41] If nothing else, this unsophisticated yet somehow unforgettable novel (I still remember reading it back then) presented the idealized image Catholics, still a little unsure of their place in American life but seemingly very sure of their faith's authority, wanted to reinforce in themselves and if possible share with Protestants.

Both a symptom and a cause of anxiety, Catholic-Protestant relations were the subjects of books by Paul Blanshard. His 1951 work, *Communism, Democracy, and Catholic Power*, following on the heels of his well-known *American Freedom and Catholic Power*,[42] provocatively explored parallels between the modi operandi of the two great centers of centralized, ideologically based power, the Kremlin and its mortal enemy, the Vatican. Understandably, loud cries of bigotry were heard from the Catholic side, as well as urgent claims that Blanshard's facts, or their interpretation, were wrong. The liberal periodical *The Nation* was removed from public-school libraries in New York City following its publication of a series of articles by Blanshard in 1947 and 1948, characterized in 1950 by the Jesuit publication *America* as "cheap anti-Catholic propaganda." The editors of the latter magazine argued that banning *The Nation* was not a suppression of legitimate free speech because such material represented a religious point of view and so its availability under the auspices of the city's educational facilities violated separation of church and state; denominational and other publications representing particular religious perspectives were usually not carried by public-school libraries either.[43]

To be sure, Blanshard focused mainly on the political and institutional workings of his bête noire and showed little sense of Catholicism's religious and spiritual dimensions. Someone like Thomas Merton was totally outside his angle of vision. It must be fully acknowledged, too, that however authoritarian the Roman church was, its works of mercy certainly outweighed its negatives, and it did not deal in human suffering on the scale recorded in other books of the day, like Robert A. Vogeler's *I Was Stalin's Prisoner*, or Nicholas Prychodko's *One of the Fifteen Million*.[44] One must never forget what communism *was* in the early Fifties.

Yet as many of the more sensitive and responsible religious leaders were aware, in the years 1950–1952 interreligious relations in the United States were at a low ebb. Professor John J. Kane of Notre Dame wrote at this time of a "shifting in the direction of conflict" between the faiths. As a Catholic looking across the great divide, he reported that in the first half of 1939 the liberal Protestant *Christian Century* had contained fifteen articles criticizing Catholics; ten years later, in the first half of 1949, the count had risen to forty-two.[45] Fault undoubtedly lay on both sides. U.S. Catholicism, reforged by a complex mixture of cold-war passions, traditional insecurity, and new confidence wrought by growing wealth, numbers, and assimilation, was capable of appearing abrasively cocky and power grabbing. Spellman's talents in these directions did much to sow resentment. On the other hand, Protestants, despite their continuing high status, were also insecure in their divisions, their increasingly precarious preeminence, and even, in a world calling for the sword of the Spirit, their lack of Roman-type discipline. In compensation they too often fell into the attitudes of anti-Catholic nativism, squabbling with Catholics over such issues as bingo and liquor, as well as schools and the ambassadorship.

Fortunately, usable Fifties styles of thought and feeling were available to counter those rising tensions. U.S. religions were often defined as "ways of life," a concept that fitted well into the larger notion of an "American way of life." Will Herberg, in *Protestant, Catholic, Jew*, wrote of the United States as integrally a tradition made up of traditions, congenial to growing calls for "tolerance" between equal but different communities.[46] The idea of religious ways of life seemed also to suggest families and communities, merging into the warm feelings evoked by important words like *togetherness* and *heritage*. Spearheading such a perspective, *Look* published a series from 1952 to 1955 on the main U.S. faiths, with titles like "What Is an Episcopalian?" "What Is a Methodist?" "What Is a Jew?" "What Is a Catholic?"[47] Three or four years later Prentice-Hall presented a series of books in the same vein, retaining some of the same authors, with "way of life" titles: *The Episcopalian Way of Life*; *The Methodist Way of Life*; *The Jewish Way of Life*, and others.[48] Certainly there were damage-control aspects to these projects, but they also were undoubtedly supported by a latent American pride in the nation's rich spiritual diversity.

Other books affirming the Jewish tradition, which was growing in stature and confidence in postwar America, appeared as well. One of the most impressive was *Jews: Their History, Culture, and Religion*, two volumes edited by Louis Finkelstein containing thirty-five monographs by various authorities on all aspects of the Jewish tradition.[49]

Some in the burgeoning conservative counterattack of course found little to admire in this newfound ocean of tolerance, pluralism, and common U.S. values. One was the high-church Episcopalian Bernard Iddings Bell, who in *Crowd Culture: An Examination of the American Way of Life* saw nothing out there but lowest-common-denominator values imparted by the pressure of the "crowd," and who argued for a reversion to separatism through public funding of denominational schools for each religion (including schools for the secularists and atheists), so that the values of each could be preserved and inculcated in their plenitude.[50] It was a characteristic high-church conservative's reaction to postwar America: half snobbishness, half unpalatable home truths, and all quite unrealistic as a serious proposal.

The Assumption and Roman Catholicism in 1950

Pope Pius XII declared 1950 a Holy Year, a "Year of Pardon" when the faithful could obtain special plenary indulgences (full remission of the punishment in purgatory for sins) by making a pilgrimage to Rome and there performing certain religious rites. More than that, a Holy Year is also, for Catholics, an occasion to celebrate faith and reaffirm loyalty to Rome and the Holy See. It was an auspicious year for such a festival of faith, not only a round midcentury year but also a moment when the church could commemorate its recent passage through the terrible war years; rededicate itself for its current struggle to the death against an implacable foe, as its battle against communism was then almost universally seen to be; and rejoice in its growth and growing prestige in some parts of the world, including the United States.

At the beginning of the year Pope Pius XII ritually opened the Holy Door at St. Peter's, which had been closed since a jubilee in 1933 commemorating the nineteen hundredth anniversary of the crucifixion. According to *Newsweek*, the pontiff "seemed pale, gray, and tired with his 73 years," but the job was done and the year of plenary indulgence begun. The magazine could not refrain from adding that the year of pardon "marked a special opportunity for the Catholic Church to strengthen itself in its fight against atheistic Communism."[51]

The Holy Year also led to some unseemliness in the capitalist camp; conflicts between airlines over rights to charter flights bearing pilgrims to the Eternal City waxed bitter, and ended in a lawsuit between Pan Am and TWA.[52]

The climax of the Holy Year was the proclamation of the bodily Assumption of the Blessed Virgin Mary as a dogma of the church by Pope Pius XII

on All Saints' Day, November 1, 1950. In essence, the dogma stated that after the Mother of Jesus's "dormition" or "falling asleep," her physical body was
taken into heaven, where it was reunited with her soul; popular belief went
on to affirm that she was thereupon crowned Queen of Heaven, becoming
Co-Redemptrix and Mediatrix of all grace.

Since this doctrine had long been universally taught and celebrated with
a feast day on August 15 in the Roman Catholic church, its formal advance-
ment to the status of infallible dogma—a truth that must be believed by all
the faithful without mental reservation—made no great difference to the practical religious life of most Catholics. Indeed, an informal check of periodicals
from around the time of the proclamation leads to the surprising observation
that more of a fuss about the Assumption was made in Protestant and secular
journals in 1950 than in many Catholic ones. It was the sons of the Reformation—and a few bold Catholic theologians—who argued that the doctrine
lacked clear support in Scripture or even early church tradition. It was they
also who raised the inevitable questions of what it really meant psychologically, what it signified for the future of Catholicism and the ecumenical movement, and—unavoidably in 1950—why was it proclaimed now, and was this
seemingly recondite exercise of ecclesiastical authority somehow related to the
church's cold-war struggle against communism?

The definition of the Assumption was a symbolic climax of several trends
within Roman Catholicism that were no doubt enhanced at the time by the
struggle with communism, but that had been underway since the Counter Reformation and the post–medieval church's need to demarcate itself rigorously
in doctrinal and institutional terms against an increasingly alien world. One
was the growth of centralized papal authority. The definition of the Assumption was in fact the first and thus far only use of papal infallibility, in the strict
sense of a formal pronouncement on faith or morals spoken ex cathedra by
the supreme pontiff, since that infallibility was itself formally defined by the
First Vatican Council in 1870. It was a climax of what has been called the
"Pian Age" in modern Roman Catholicism, an era stretching from Pius IX,
he of the "Syllabus of Errors," the loss of "temporal power," and Vatican I,
through Pius X of the antimodernism campaign to Pius XI and Pius XII, the
two popes who were most forced to contend with the new totalitarianisms of
left and right. In this age the church set its face firmly against what it considered the apostasy of a bloody and troubled world. Against the spirit of the
secular age it kept firmly to papal authority, strict uniformity in doctrine and
worship, burgeoning Marian piety, and Thomistic philosophy. Little time was
given to ecumenicity, and little tolerance was shown deviants from orthodoxy
within or without the papal church. Most conspicuous of all to many was simply the Pian Age presumption, profoundly reassuring to some and no less irri-

tating to others, that the Roman church was a "perfect institution," and one that held precisely stated and correct answers to all important human issues. (How different was the Catholic flavor to be in only a dozen years, in the reign of John XXIII and with Vatican II in session!)

A few within the church, chiefly theologians from northern Europe, were unconvinced of the advisability of defining the Assumption as infallible dogma. With them in mind, in August 1950 Pius XII issued the encyclical *Humani Generis*, reaffirming papal authority as the definitive word on doctrine. Theologians have freedom in undecided issues, so long as they are prepared to accept the judgment of the church when it is made; when Rome has spoken, argument ends. This was the peak year of papal absolutism. A little more subtly, the definition also represented a climax of the Aristotelian Thomism promoted in those years as the church's favored philosophical foundation for theological thought, for the cosmology and the concept of bodily substance and soul implicit in the dogma derive from Thomas Aquinas's scholastic categories.[53]

The dogma of the Assumption was also a decisive advance in a movement toward more and more exalted Marian piety and doctrine, accompanied by the great series of modern apparitions of the Virgin that, with church approbation, had become major pilgrimage sites and centers of devotion: La Salette, Lourdes, Fatima. Alongside them had come the 1854 definition by Pope Pius IX of the dogma of the Immaculate Conception of the Blessed Virgin Mary (not to be confused, as it often is, with the virgin birth of Christ) and mounting expectation that the next step would be definition of the Assumption as a dogma, and after that the proclamation of still greater Marian "privileges," as yet undefined as dogma, especially her role as Co-Redemptrix and Mediatrix.

The type of theological thinking that supported the dogma of the Assumption stressed the coredemptive role of Mary in her union with the sufferings of Christ, and her mystical identity with the church as the mystical body of Christ. Therefore a Marian parallel to the resurrection of Christ, and a Marian prototype of the resurrection of all the faithful on the last day, was congruous. (As St. Alphonso Liguori had written a couple of centuries before, "What Christ has by nature, Mary has by grace.") A key word was convergence; theologians claimed that the convergence of all previously accepted doctrines concerning Mary, her immaculate conception, eminent sanctity, divine maternity, perpetual virginity, and coredemptive office together lead to a role so special as to amount to "metaphysical necessity" and "virtual revelation" on behalf of a dogma of admittedly weak scriptural and historical warrant, but long since sanctioned by the "universal belief of the church."[54]

But while Protestants complained that these "new" dogmas showed that the pope's church was not really unchanging after all, Catholics tended to see them as rather new landmarks in the timeless spiritual struggle. Moreover, in the atmosphere of 1950, it was common to regard the Immaculate Conception and the Assumption as not only theologically important doctrines, but also as tools in the great battle the church has been fighting for two hundred years against the Enlightenment and its fruits. We are told that Mary, in light of these doctrines, says that "man" is stricken by sin but can be reached by grace; the Enlightenment and its modern offspring, Marxism, believe in neither, so without God those who credence the hollow promises of that stream of thought end in materialism, worship of the state, and negation of the spiritual. Referring to the Enlightenment and Marxism, and to both the Immaculate Conception and the Assumption of the Blessed Virgin Mary, *Time* pronounced that "the Marian dogma challenged this *non credo* of the age— with an asserting that man is sinful but touched by God, that the greatest mysteries are beyond science, that the supernatural and the spiritual are real."[55]

Above all, the definition was a fitting climax to a Holy Year celebrated amidst a world struggle so apocalyptic as virtually to call for such signs in heaven. In its exaltation of a doctrine incomprehensible to dialectical materialism, and a view of human nature as interactive with the divinity the Marxists denied, this declaration appeared a fitting challenge to that other system claiming universal authority, and a total view of human nature and needs.

The importance afforded the Assumption and its proclamation that midcentury year thus manifests something of the religious mindset of 1950, and something of the Roman church's isolated, ingrown, rigid, yet also militant, challenging, and provocative position at that time. The views of outside commentators are hardly less revealing of the temper of that religious historical moment. The eminent analytic psychologist Carl G. Jung had written of the profound significance for the human psyche of completing a Quaternity by exalting female flesh into the highest heavens, otherwise reserved to the male flesh of the ascended Jesus and the spiritual but putatively male remainder of the Blessed Trinity. The great seriousness with which such lofty symbological matters were discussed by a non-Catholic prophet of the times like Jung, who called the declaration of the Assumption "the most important religious event since the Reformation," seems to characterize one facet of the introspective, intrapsychic intellectual world of 1950.[56]

On the other hand, Protestants were seriously unimpressed. An editorial in the *Christian Century* condemned the definition as putting the church "in opposition to all the canons of historical scholarship as that discipline is today understood." Making such a doctrine a matter of "faith" would only drive away from Christianity those with "the best mental training our times afford." Therefore, this journal added bitterly, the definition will only aid those in the Kremlin and elsewhere who seek reason to attack religion. The importance of a continuing Protestant witness was underscored by this bizarre development in another great wing of Christendom.[57]

True or false, the papal definition of the dogma of the bodily Assumption of the Blessed Virgin Mary to heaven, and the surrounding discussion of its philosophical, psychological, and political ramifications, now seems very much to belong to the year and the world of its happening, 1950. In the middle of that Holy Year came the sudden news of war in Korea, and the week the world might have ended. The high point of the solemnities in Rome, the All Saints' Day declaration ex cathedra of the "new dogma," like the inauguration of the National Council of Churches across the Atlantic only a month later, came when all seemed risky and dark in that brutal conflict on the other side of the planet, and World War III might have commenced at any hour.

Here are some other facets of early Fifties Roman Catholicism. The premier issue of *Time* for the decade, January 2, 1950, in addition to the story of the ceremonies by which Pope Pius XII inaugurated the 1950 Holy Year, contained an article about a San Francisco husband and wife who were ending their marriage, in accordance with certain Roman Catholic canonical provisions, to become respectively a monk and nun. Immediately we are confronted with two characteristics of Fifties religion journalism: the newsworthiness of Roman Catholicism, and the burgeoning popularity of religious orders and of the contemplative life generally.

Roman Catholicism, once an immigrant church in a nation that considered itself staunchly and foundationally Protestant, was expanding rapidly in postwar America. A May 24, 1954, *Newsweek* cover story on Cardinal Spellman and "his fast-growing church" noted that all Catholic figures for the fifteen years since 1939 were up: membership by 50 percent, from around twenty to thirty million; numbers of converts, clergy, and especially seminarians up even more. The parochial school system was thriving; in the Los Angeles archdiocese, sixty-four new schools had been opened over a two-year period. A 1955 *Time* article on women's religious orders emphasized their tremendous growth; there were now three times the number of nuns in the United States as in 1900, and twice the number of men in orders.[58] Much of this growth was postwar, not a small part of it sparked by the surprising popularity of Thomas Merton's chronicle of his pilgrimage to a very strict monastery, *The Seven Storey Mountain.*[59]

There were divisions in Fifties Catholicism, most conspicuously over Senator McCarthy. As we have seen, Bernard Sheil, auxiliary bishop of Chicago, harshly criticized McCarthy's methods, while Cardinal Spellman befriended him and, behind the scenes, apparently saw to it that Sheil was punished. No doubt this conflict was merely symptomatic of a deeper tension: between the church's immigrant, proletarian, Democratic roots in the United States and its postwar assimilation into the middle class and the mainstream combined with the fervent anticommunism it espoused in the Pius XII, cold-war era. That rightward tilt suited not only the authoritarian mentality and political alliances of some of its leadership, but also the shifting mood of many upwardly mobile Catholics, who not seldom switched from Democrat to Republican as they moved from the old urban ethnic neighborhoods to spacious new suburban addresses.

However, compared to the earthquakes of the decade to come, the Fifties Roman Catholic church, with its unvarying Latin liturgy and its vast ranks of obedient bishops, priests, monks, and nuns who seemed to act as one, appeared almost supernaturally united, consistent, and unchanging, with an answer for everything. Certainly that was the image it wished to project, and one that was widely accepted even by its enemies in the heyday of Spellman and Pius XII.

As a "perfect society" the church had no need to change and was the one solid rock in a world of conflict and uncertainty. It stood for eternal absolutes from the Eternal City, unflinchingly in opposition to the relativisms of the modern world and the false dogmas of communism. The highly disciplined, black-and-white parochial school education of Catholics of that era, together with the insecurities of their U.S. status, makes that picture of the world understandable. Hardly less was the boundary-defining role of Catholic higher education.[60] It was an age of a dramatically dualistic, almost Manichaean, picture of the church as fortress and army embattled against the world, the flesh, and the devil, in a conflict that amounted to nothing less than light against darkness, of faith in the transcendent against black materialism. The great war was reflected in struggles—aided by the sacraments—against sin within and, helped by the church's infallible voice, against error without. The 1953 *Time* story on Pius XII spoke of the pontiff as a "man of reality, for he is one of the world's leading spiritual fighters against Communism."

Fulton Sheen and American Catholicism

The best-known popular Roman Catholic figure in the Fifties was Fulton Sheen (1895–1979), a philosopher at Catholic University who became a popular radio and later television personality. As a youth Sheen had been a brilliant student who received degrees and high honors at CU and the Louvain in Belgium. He then taught at Catholic University until 1950, at the same time producing a steady stream of neo-Thomistic books and articles. Sheen was known as a powerful teacher whose charismatic presence and well-modulated voice suggested a larger sphere. As early as 1930 he began the

Catholic Hour radio series on NBC, as well as his famous courses of instruction for converts to Catholicism.[61]

In 1952, shortly after his best-selling *Peace of Soul* (1949) had appeared, and after he had been made an auxiliary bishop of New York in 1951, Sheen made his TV debut with his show "Life Is Worth Living." His dramatic presence, enhanced by striking deep-set eyes, purple episcopal robes with magenta cape and skullcap, distinct diction, and perfect sense of timing, quickly brought him more than two million viewers. Sheen well embodied the dogmatic, still combative, but newly confident and maturing Catholicism of the era. He vigorously attacked the twin "materialistic" evils of Marxism and Freudianism, but also aimed arrows at "post-Christian" U.S. society and tempered his onslaughts with warmly devotional and even humorous moments. He considered that fascism and communism were "cut from the same cloth."[62] His stable of well-known converts, ranging from Louis Budenz, former managing editor of the *Daily Worker*, to Claire Booth Luce and Henry Ford II, though presented in a way that might seem ostentatious today, conveyed as did Sheen himself a Fifties image of Catholicism as a unique church that was constant, sophisticated, authoritative, intellectually respectable, and capable of attracting troubled souls with good minds, and that was now maturing into a solid, co-equal place in the U.S. religious landscape. It wanted, eagerly and desperately, to be as authentically American as it was, in its own eyes, the most authentically and authoritatively Christian church.

Though Fulton Sheen was not as conservative socially or politically as his theological and anticommunist positions might have suggested, he can be thought of preeminently as a spokesperson for a Catholic version of the "American Way of Life" so celebrated in the decade. He did this in several ways. Through his collection of converts, he showed that persons of all sorts of American backgrounds could find their way into the church. In his own person he demonstrated that an educated and informed Catholic could hold his own with anyone intellectually. Finally, what could be more mainstream American than employing the new medium of television that was saturating cities and town across the land? Catholics were arriving.

There was a distance to go, but the ground was being covered. A comparison of the reported religious affiliation of individuals listed in *Who's Who* reveals that in 1950–1951 the colonial Protestant establishment continued to dominate this inventory of the supposedly most distinguished Americans, with 23.1 percent Episcopalians, 18.4 percent Presbyterians, and 8.8 percent Congregationalists. In 1992–1993 those figures were down to 18 percent, 13.2 percent and 3.2 percent respectively. In 1950–1951 listed Roman Catholics were only 8.4 percent and Jews 2.5 percent; in 1992–1993 those figures had risen to 23.1 percent and 12.3 percent.[63]

What about ordinary parishes of the pope's church at the same time he was busying himself in Rome with Holy Year and the Assumption? The best study is Joseph Fichter's *Southern Parish*, based on a sociological survey of a New Orleans Roman Catholic church about the same time.[64] Fichter, himself a priest trained as a sociologist, found that while attendance at mass and other services was relatively high, theological views tended to be more liberal, and social views of Catholics in this then-segregated southern city more conservative, than official church teaching. Of his respondents, 24 percent did not believe in damnation, and 36 percent denied a personal devil; on the other hand 47 percent would not send their children to a racially mixed Catholic kindergarten, and even more were opposed to racially integrated parishes. But only 24 percent disapproved of *religiously* mixed marriages. In the event of war between the United States and Russia, 70 percent of men would have approved of dropping an atomic bomb on Moscow, while 57 percent of women disapproved. In sum, Fichter's findings indicated that despite the cold war, the religion boom, and the new conservatism, in the pews of this church, and undoubtedly many others of many denominations, thinking was far from unanimous.

Chapter 2

Ideas: UFOs, Existentialists, and Double Lives

Iᴛ ᴡᴀѕ ᴀ time of double lives and of a book only God could review. The great issue of 1950 (after Korea) was communist infiltration of U.S. institutions, beginning (but not ending) with the government in Washington. Infiltration or "subversion" was itself a religious issue in a fundamental sense, though that also was not always stated. Why? First, because the world drama that lay behind it was of such mythic, not to say apocalyptic, character that it is hard to see it as other than at heart a struggle for the souls of men. Second, because the principal anticommunists involved, sensing such matters were soul sized, used religious-sounding language and presented themselves as religious persons; if ex-communists, they were often converts to Catholicism or, in one case to be studied in a moment, Quakerism. Third, because religious institutions and journals were quickly drawn into the bitter and divisive acrimony the issue spawned, generating countless sermons, editorials, and resolutions on all sides. As we have seen, sometimes the ideological vitriol masked class, regional, ethnic, and religious antagonisms as well.

Several highly publicized cases that involved espionage on behalf of the Soviet Union by U.S. communists hit the headlines in the early Fifties, each pushing to a still higher pitch the hysteria about communists and spies. The physicist Klaus Fuchs—German-born, a communist in 1932, anti-Nazi emigré to Britain, worker on the atomic bomb at Los Alamos, then prominent in British atomic energy research—was arrested and convicted in Britain in 1950 for passing information to Moscow since 1943. In the United States Julius and Ethel Rosenberg were also arrested in 1950, on the basis of connections uncovered through the Fuchs case. They were tried and convicted and, after several appeals and an unsuccessful worldwide campaign for mercy, executed for espionage June 19, 1953.[1] In March of 1950, Judith Coplon, an ebullient Justice Department employee, and Valentin Gubitchev, a Russian U.N. official, were found guilty of conspiracy and attempted espionage, in a colorful case involving an apparent love affair between the pair and a wild car chase a year earlier that led up to their arrest.

A very important episode in the infiltration issue that straddles the opening of the decade involved Alger Hiss, Whittaker Chambers, and Richard Nixon, among others. For reasons that will soon be apparent, this is the case with the most important religious ramifications. In 1948 hearings were held before the House Un-American Activities Committee (HUAC) over allegations concerning Hiss. Hiss was head of the Carnegie Endowment, a former State Department official who had been present at Yalta and the founding of the United Nations, an elegant product of the establishment and the Ivy League. Whittaker Chambers accused him of being a communist, and a member of a communist group at State in the late Thirties that was involved in spying for the Soviet Union. Chambers was a senior writer at *Time* magazine, and a person of tortured background. His childhood home had been ravaged by suicides and his father's alcoholism; he had himself been a communist between 1925 and 1938 and claimed to have then known Hiss in the same capacity. By 1948 he was a militant and, by his own account, deeply religious anticommunist.

At first the debonair Hiss held his own in the hearings, denying he had ever known Chambers. But as Chambers continued testifying against him, and the case was relentlessly pursued by the young congressman Richard Nixon of California—who did not conceal his distaste for Hiss's aristocratic snobbery—the defendant began to waver. Though the alleged espionage was never proved in court, it became evident to most observers that Hiss was evading the truth on some important matters, including his Thirties close acquaintance with Chambers. The former State Department official was, after one jury deadlocked, retried and eventually convicted of perjury on two counts: denying that he had known Chambers, and denying passing documents to Chambers. He served forty-four months of a five-year sentence beginning March 21, 1951.

The dramatic Hiss/Chambers/Nixon hearings were a watershed in U.S. public life, almost comparable to what the Dreyfus case meant for France. They quickly became far more than a set of charges, proven or unproven, about a single person. The contrast between the onetime friends, now adversaries, was dramatic enough. Here was the tight, controlled, quintessentially eastern establishment Hiss; there the short, squat, raffish, nervously smiling yet tormented figure of Chambers, who though well educated and highly intelligent somehow never shed the aura of his bitter and impoverished upbringing. Soon it became not only Hiss, but the whole New Deal and its era that was on trial; and not only the New Deal, but an entire class of privileged liberal intellectuals who allegedly ran it.

The maverick conservative Peter Viereck, writing in *Commonweal* in 1950, proposed that Hiss was probably guilty but was far more interested in him as a symbol of his times and of everything the "Babbitt Junior" of the present disliked, from the New Deal to "all modern art and all experimental poetry." "Today every word against Hiss awakens certain half-conscious memories [among certain intellectuals] . . . long-suppressed, semi-treasonable, semi-idealistic day-dreams about Russia in that early era of Writers Congresses and Leagues Against War and Fascism," when they "stripteased with revolution for the thrill of feeling progressive and unbourgeois."[2]

Finally, the case was two U.S. moods toward the world set against each other. One, personified by Hiss, was cosmopolitan, internationalist, activist, not averse on principle to foreign ideologies or to holding that one had an obligation to the good of the world as well as one's own country—the much reviled "one-worldism" so recently associated with Wendell Wilkie and Henry Wallace. The other, visible in Chambers and Nixon, was that of the nativist, of the instinctive America Firster, of those to whom outside influences suggested invading bacilli, above all when ideological and labeled communist.

The ramifications in the religious world of this affair are interesting and significant. One is the Quaker theme. Curiously, that tiny denomination was very well represented in the hearings. Nixon was, or at least had been raised, a Quaker; Chambers had become a Quaker in the course of his spiritual journey out of communism; and Hiss, though himself a lukewarm Episcopalian, was married to a Quaker attender and activist, Priscilla (herself accused of retyping some of the purloined documents in question, though never brought to trial), and had been a speaker at Quaker summer peace institutes and a member of American Friends Service Committee units, and had given the commencement address at Haverford College in 1947, entitled "The Prospects for Peace."[3] Important names at the Hiss trials included Noel and Herta Field, Quakers of good family who became communist activists in the Thirties, who allegedly were involved in the same network doing "secret work" for the cause as Hiss and Chambers, and who moved permanently behind the Iron Curtain at the onset of the trial, perhaps so they would not have to testify. The principal in the parallel spy case, Klaus Fuchs, was the son of a prominent Quaker worker in Germany.

These are perhaps only odd coincidences but may have some symbolic significance. The Society of Friends is known for its use of silence in worship, its nonsacramentalism, its pacifism, and its deep roots in the American colonial experience and in the radical tradition from abolition to gender equality. A basic Quaker self-image is of the righteous, "different" witness, who whether through dress or in prison stands outside the stream in service to the Inner Light and a more just world, like the early Friends. They are the sort of Christians who take the Sermon on the Mount and not offering incense to Caesar seriously, and who might be prepared to see peacemaking and the ordeals of those who hunger and thirst after righteousness better represented in an overseas paradise than at home.

Yet there is also a small-town, Republican side to Quakerism—the Quakerism of Herbert Hoover and Richard Nixon—more imbued with the homespun Friendly virtues of frugality and honesty than concerned about challenging authority and demonstrating in the streets.[4] In respect of its two sides Quakerism is like a miniature of spiritual America, and these disparate sides came together in the HUAC hearings.

Indeed, in the religious news of the early Fifties one comes across a surprising number of references to Quaker personalities, quite apart from those involved in the Hiss/Chambers case—A. J. Muste, Rufus Jones, Douglas Steere, Elton Trueblood—men who were not at all the same, but who were the remaining custodians of a heritage in American life at once radical and establishment.[5] In the supercharged atmosphere of the early Fifties those two legacies of the U.S. tradition were hard to square in any other context. One gets a sense that many thoughtful and disturbed people felt the Quakers might have something special to offer those anxious days if one could get a fix on it. They were, by and large, not quite elite, not quite cold warriors, and not communist either. How did they do it? But then the image began to change, and Quaker influence faded a little in proportion to others, as the generation of people like Muste, Jones, Steere, and Trueblood passed.

Of still more religious significance, there is the fruit of the hearings in the form of Whittaker Chambers's eight-hundred-page autobiographical bestseller, *Witness*, published in 1952. Then as now, one senses that something tremendously important, as a human as well as a social document, lies buried in this tormented, engrossing epic of this lost, searching, and sometimes finding life of a brilliant man from nowhere. One feels also that it casts an interesting retrospective light on the New Deal milieu and the Thirties ideological fascination with the left, in the process almost incidentally telling some of the truth about Hiss. For that was a time when the left—a culture as much as a political position—was regarded by many, including many religionists, as the social/political embodiment of pure and idealistic love. But that was then, and now was now.

Chambers had written *Time*'s twenty-fifth anniversary issue's feature on Reinhold Niebuhr of March 8, 1948, the magazine's first cover story on a theologian and an important milestone in making that "Christian realist" the gray eminence of U.S. theology in the cold-war era. Chambers was undoubtedly speaking of himself as well as Niebuhr when he wrote, in *Time*'s then telegraphic style:

> Against the easy conscience, Dr. Niebuhr asserted: man is by the nature of his creation sinful; at the height of man's perfection there is always the possibility of evil. Against easy optimism, he asserted that life is inevitably tragic. Says Niebuhr: "Mankind is living in a Lenten age."
>
> Dr. Niebuhr was one liberal Protestant who had indeed heard the Voice out of the whirlwind. It spoke the thought of three God-tormented men: Russian Novelist Fyodor Dostoevsky, Danish Theologian Søren Kierkegaard and Swiss Theologian Karl Barth. . . .
>
> Against liberalism's social optimism (progress by reform) and the social optimism of the revolutionary left (progress by force), Dostoevsky asserted the eternal necessity of the soul to be itself. . . .
>
> Kierkegaard too was obsessed with "the ultimate potentialities of the human soul." And like the great Russian, the great Dane was haunted by the tragic sense of life whose full implications only the presentiments of religious faith could grasp.
>
> Karl Barth, too, heard the Voice from the whirlwind. . . . It also caused him 1) to doubt that the will of God was being fulfilled by man's good works, or could be; 2) to reexamine the Bible where, to his surprise (since he, too, had been an optimist) he discovered that most of the principal characters shared his new pessimism about human nature.[6]

This is vintage religion for the anxious, existentialist years around 1950 and offers an excellent prelude to Chambers's *Witness*. That book is far more than the usual sort of profitably published act of repentance and polemic by an ex-communist, of which there were many in those years. Chambers was clearly a voracious reader, a real thinker and an anguished soul, and—though he may not have gotten everything straight—not a deliberate prevaricator. Undoubtedly the author makes many telling critiques of communist and other leftist illusions about God, sin, totalitarianism, and human nature as he wends his way out of communism and into his Quaker meeting. He does so with no mean show of intellectual prowess, dilating along the way on George Fox, Kierkegaard, Dostoevsky, Barth, and Niebuhr

Yet his book has not, in fact, become the spiritual classic, the twentieth-century Augustinian *Confessions*, that it perhaps might have been. Its flaws mainly lie around Chambers's inveterate tendency to extremism and to self-dramatization. In reading of his deprived and miserable childhood one can easily grasp reasons for those apparent needs. But they are there. He undoubt-edly overpaints the real influence of communism in U.S. life. He much too crudely lumps with communism, in the manner of other demagogues on the right, all New Dealism and socialism, even as communists are quick to label everyone to their own right fascists. The well-known short path of the con-vert from one authoritarian system to apostle of an equally absolute contra position is all too apparent. Chambers himself put it plainly enough: "My need was to be a practicing Christian in the same sense that I had been a practic-ing Communist." Critics have identified exaggerations and misstatements that enhanced Chambers's vindictiveness toward various "enemies."[7]

Yet *Witness* has passages of remarkable power and awareness and in any case is an essential document of the spiritual state of the nation in the early Fifties. Note the way Chambers portrays the struggle with communism as a religious battle between two utterly opposed Gods—in the early Fifties, far from a unique theme. Pulpits across the country promoted the ongoing reli-gion boom with the message that "it takes a faith to fight a faith." But Cham-bers, on the basis both of his own experience in the dragon's den and of his literary craft, put it memorably.

> Communists are that part of mankind which has recovered the power
> to live or die—to bear witness—for its faith. And it is a simple,
> rational faith that inspires men to live or die for it.
>   It is not new. It is, in fact, man's second oldest faith. Its promise
> was whispered in the first days of the Creation under the Tree of the
> Knowledge of Good and Evil: " Ye shall be as gods." It is the great
> alternative faith of mankind. Like all great faiths, its force derives
> from a simple vision. Other ages have had great visions. They have
> always been different versions of the same vision: the vision of God
> and man's relationship to God. The Communist vision is the vision of
> Man without God.[8]

Beside this awesome clash of ultimate creeds, the impulse for radical so-cial justice, which as Chambers and others acknowledged had led them, and even some devoutly religious persons, toward sympathy for communism in the Thirties, is now but a faint and plaintive cry. True, there is a once-burned quality about Chambers, and not he alone in the early Fifties, as he gave up the social progressivism of the left in favor of the apparently profounder search-light of existentialism and neoorthodoxy. The shattering discovery Chambers, like many others, had made, and finally had to come to terms with was that though communism drew idealistic people through its call for world commu-nity and social justice, it demanded in particular cases acts that were utterly contrary to these and many other virtues, including basic honesty about one's life; as a communist one lived a double life. One lied, spied, and if ordered to do so killed or let die for the cause, and then one changed hats and lived a "normal" life the rest of the time.

The famous ex-communist Elizabeth Bentley, writing in *The Sign*, claimed, "Communism would never have gained a foothold in this country had it not appealed primarily to the idealism of the young." She told of appalling child-hood observations in McKeesport, Pennsylvania, after World War I. It was a city "ugly, dirty, noisy, overcast with heavy smoke—in brief, the typical in-dustrial town at its worst. It was suffering from intolerable social conditions, wages had been slashed mercilessly, people were starving or barely making ends meet (the preceding year a steel workers' strike had been starved out), most of the people were too busy with their own affairs to bother with others. Mill workers were of 57 varieties of foreigners and they were treated like dirt by any who felt they could get away with it." In this dreadful situation, her mother set an activist example as a volunteer social worker.

From McKeesport, Bentley went to Vassar, where she met other students who were concerned about such conditions, who were interested in the Rus-sian "experiment" and ready for radical action. A study trip to Mussolini's Italy in 1933 had embittered her against fascism. From then on, in the late Thir-ties, she moved into the communist orbit. The communists "seemed to be act-ing as my mother had taught me good Christians should"—that is, solicitous for their neighbor's welfare. She came to believe the communists had the an-swer to the question of why suffering and injustice—and she believed one should put into practice what one believed. Only later was she disillusioned to learn how much the means entailed lying and totalitarian practices, and how much the Party was controlled by the Kremlin.[9] (Even so, she seemed at the time of her Fifties repentance to have no alternative concrete solutions to offer for the injustices that had prompted her leftward move.)

Klaus Fuchs, the atom-bomb spy, in sober retrospect reportedly called his communist mind "controlled schizophrenia," saying, "In the course of this work I began naturally to form bonds of personal friendship and I had to conceal from them my inner thoughts. I used my Marxist philosophy to establish in my mind two separate compartments."[10] Supposedly these were "revolution-ary" means to the idealist end. But they expeditiously moved the moral focus from community and social justice to means, which then quickly became an issue of faith. For it seemed what means one would permit oneself depended upon what master one served.

Thus the early Fifties were an age of faith, and the issue was less how, or whether, the world could be made better than in whose Name it would be done. Typical of the times, it is not the voices of the unfree or of those crushed under the wheel of history that we hear, but those of the philosophers and theologians talking of freedom and history and, of course, atheism and God. Yet it was the trauma of Stalin's 1936–1938 purge and judicial murder of old communist loyalists that set Chambers on his inward course away from the Party; he began to question whether any murder, even that of the czar and his family, could be justified by whatever justice (without freedom) communism brought to however many millions. The agonies of faith and doubt were internal, in the serpentine muscles of his own mind and soul, and had more to do with the absolute questions than with practical problems of land and bread. But they were demigods capable of commanding their own oblations and in the end led him to give up his very well paying position at *Time* to testify freely and fully against his former comrade.

In the end, one must agree with Paul Hutchinson, who in reviewing *Witness* in the *Christian Century* on June 11, 1952, remarked that in taking up the task he found himself thinking, "Only God knows enough to review this book."

God, Man, and the Conservative Mind

The conservative reaction of the Fifties was no doubt to be expected. Most immediate postwar eras have been drenched in a conservative mood, as returning warriors want nothing more than normalcy and retain the idealized version of their homeland that was part of their battlefield armor. The reformist impulse to make it live up to the idealization—as, for example, in the U.S. civil-rights movement—is typically a few steps behind.

The early Fifties, however, saw not only a general conservative swing, exemplified in the 1952 election of Eisenhower, but also the emergence of a conservative intellectual movement. This movement is of some importance to our quest for Fifties spirituality, for it interacted profoundly with religion. It drew from religious sources, cast issues in religious terms, and shaped the religious lives of millions. We have already hinted at some of its theological contours in noting the fashionableness of "sin." Notable religious figures mingled their anticommunism with a preoccupation less with the achievement of social justice than with the reasons why it can never be done perfectly by such imperfect instruments as humans, and can become an idolatrous illusion. Not all those who said such things were conservatives in the political sense; Reinhold Niebuhr remained a Democrat and cold-war liberal.

But the new conservatives were, like him, strongly anticommunist and professed a passionate love of limited government, individual freedom, and capitalism. Not a few of them based their views on Christianity as they understood it, not overlooking the skepticism about human schemes allegedly built into the concept of fallen human nature. One, the Episcopal clergyman

Bernard Iddings Bell, claimed that "exaggerated optimism about man" is "the chief cause of our decay," and another, the political scientist Peter Viereck, defined conservatism as "the political secularization of the doctrine of original sin."[11]

Original sin was topical in the early Fifties. Sermons were more at home with Adam's pride than with utopian hope. Many of that generation of conservatives in America were, like Viereck, refugees from Nazi or communist totalitarianism in Europe; their credentials included firsthand experience of such forcing houses of human perfection; they knew the worst could come of the best-laid human plans. They had seen those particular futures, and they didn't work.

One such voice was the one-time refugee from Nazism Eric Voegelin, whose 1952 book *The New Science of Politics* was the basis of an intriguing *Time* article (see chapter 3). Voegelin considered all efforts to transcend the "normal" ebb and flow of history, in which all human creations are imperfect and go out of being as readily as they manifest, to be "gnosticism"—the attempted use of secret historical laws and forces to construct an irreversible and superior reality. Gnosticism embraced a vast array of historical predictions and endeavors, from the "age of the spirit" of the medieval Joachim of Flora to the Puritan "kingdom of the saints" to progressivism, fascism, and communism. The modern "gnostics" who fabricated such disastrous fantasies were living in illusory worlds of "dreams"; unfortunately they can seduce others who ought to know better into the same ruinous unreality.

Here is a sample of Voegelin's rhetoric, from a discussion of the Puritan "saints": "The Saint is a Gnostic who will not leave the transfiguration of the world to the grace of God beyond history but will do the work of God himself, right here and now, in history"—a presumption that will end in nothing less than communism. For today "the Gnostic politicians have put the Soviet army on the Elbe, surrendered China to the Communists, at the same time demilitarized Germany and Japan, and in addition demobilized our own army. . . . These polities were pursued as a matter of principle, on the basis of Gnostic dream assumptions about the nature of man, about a mysterious evolution of mankind toward peace and world order, about the possibility of establishing an international order in the abstract without relation to the structure of the field of existential forces, about armies being the cause of war and not the forces and constellations which build them and set them into motion."[12] This is very much in the spirit of the new early-Fifties conservatism, very much in reaction against "modern" belief in progress and human perfectability; accusatory, quasi-spiritual in language and flavor.

A number of people were writing in a conservative vein in those years: Viereck, Bell, Voegelin, Eric Hoffer, Karl Popper, Friedrich Hayek, James

Burnham, William F. Buckley, Jr., L. Brent Bozell, and Russell Kirk, among others. They did not take identical positions, and intellectually often they seemed cumulatively little more than a cult. Nonetheless they were the forward edge of a mind swing that was to deeply influence America for the next generation.

In terms of the theme of our study, Fifties intellectual conservatism was supply-side religion only insofar as it was medium demand: it enjoyed the frisson of countering the conventional social-gospel liberalism of many mainline churches and eminent divinity schools, while remaining "safe" in that it echoed the practical anticommunist conservatism of the flanks and strengthened their free-market appeal with an intellectual tone. The new conservatives tried, not too convincingly, to present themselves as a persecuted sect and part of the spiritual underground, with all the rebel excitement pertaining thereto. They seemed to support the existentialists in their defense of the individual against "mass man"—whether conservatism really meant metaphysical individualism or something less ultimate in practice may be debated. To further confuse the matter of appearances, the new conservatives, unlike the older Bible Belt or country-club varieties, tried to link themselves with high-culture religion through their European connections and their references to heavyweight intellectuals. At the same time they ended up in favor of political values attractive to Main Street and, at least so far as all-important anticommunism was concerned, to ethnic/Catholic-dominated union halls.

Conservatism, like *liberalism*, is one of those words whose meaning one thinks one knows until a precise definition is called for. What is it exactly that conservatives want to conserve? Certainly not everything from the past equally. The conservative movement was divided—at some points, torn apart—into two wings: the individualist or libertarian, and the traditionalist. The former, whose most vociferous advocate was the former communist Frank Meyer, but which also included the followers of the "Objectivist" Ayn Rand and some conservative politicians like Barry Goldwater, was basically in the tradition of the nineteenth-century Whig or "classical" liberalism. Philosophical followers of Jeremy Bentham and John Stuart Mill, libertarian conservatives' primary commitment was to the free-enterprise capitalism of Manchesterian economics, limited government, and individual freedom as understood by that legacy. They were not, by and large, religious in the sense the traditionalists were; some, taking freedom of thought as seriously as freedom from the state, were skeptics.

Very different were the traditionalist conservatives, whose supreme opus was Russell Kirk's *Conservative Mind*, and whose ranks included to some extent William Buckley and his brother-in-law the conservative Catholic L. Trent Bozell. This Tory-style conservatism, drawn from the thought of Edmund

Burke, emphasized an organic, nonegalitarian view of society, rejection of relativism, and affirmation of traditional moral values, imposed by state authority if need be. These conservatives were definitely religious, seeing God and church as bulwarks of the kind of social order they wanted. Kirk began his study with a list of "six canons of conservative thought":

— Belief that a "divine intent" rules society and individual conscience, imposing eternal, nonnegotiable rights and duties on persons.
— "Affections for the proliferating variety and mystery of traditional life, as distinguished from the narrowing uniformity and egalitarianism and utilitarian aims of most radical systems." One senses that this attractive quality had a particular appeal for Kirk, perhaps justifying the harsher constraints of some of the other canons.
— Acknowledging that civilized society requires orders and classes.
— Holding that the right of private property is inseparable from freedom.
— "Faith in prescription [a Burkean term for the customary ways of the past] and distrust of 'sophistries and calculators.'"[13]
— "Recognition that change and reform are not identical."

Kirk then essays a study of conservative thinkers in his mold, beginning with Edmund Burke, the greatest of them all, admiring especially Burke's traditionalist view of society as a contract between the generations. He proceeds to John Adams and John Randolph, who together with John Calhoun were speakers for antebellum southern conservatism. He quotes with some approval a line of Randolph, that slaveholding planter and fanatic enemy of corruption, that "Ishmael of politics": "I am an aristocrat: I love liberty, I hate equality."[14] Kirk clearly has in the back, or more likely the forefront, of his mind a much beloved image of a happy rural society, in which a grave but kindly lord, maintaining all the old laws and usages, smiles paternally as his villagers cheerfully bring in his harvest, offer thanksgiving for it in church, and celebrate with traditional fair and country dance.

But, as Kirk and others of his faction were quite aware, all this was inconsistent with the values of the individualist, free-enterprise camp. Traditionalists deplored nothing so much as the anomic "mass man," free of traditional, organic social loyalties or connections, whom they saw all around, and they acknowledged that the industrial revolution and the concomitant Benthamite, Millsian individualism and laissez-faire economics had produced this modern monstrosity. Kirk rejected "rationalistic, atomistic capitalism and utilitarianism," together with their modern products, the "soulless corporation"

and the "dreary industrial city."[15] Scorning the Enlightenment worship of individual "reason," the traditionalist found in Bentham, Cobden, and Utilitarianism the source of most of the ills of the modern world and, for good
measure, the ultimate root of Marxism.

Other traditionalists pointed out that the Whiggish emphasis on free
choice actually makes virtue more difficult than does a traditional society that
readily admits divine law and inculcates it. L. Brent Bozell, a chief advocate
of this position, said the purpose of politics was not to promote freedom of
choice but "to establish temporal conditions conducive to human virtue—that
is, to build a Christian civilization."[16] Bozell insisted that even a free market,
though he approved of it, was not the highest good; the quest for virtue is
more important than the quest for freedom, and a good society is better than
a free society. To this the individualists strongly objected; Bozell's conservative Catholic good society sounded too much like theocratic authoritarianism,
in which some would have the power to impose their version of God's will
on others.

Nonetheless, conservatives of both camps held some common beliefs. First
and foremost was anticommunism; though for somewhat different reasons, both
individualists and traditionalists saw Marxism and the Party as baleful to their
core values. Second, the right to private property, and the acceptance of differences of income and status within society, were important to both, though
individualists might have seen them chiefly as fruits of free enterprise, traditionalists in more feudal terms. Most importantly, both knew what they wanted
in practical, contemporary U.S. political terms: strong anticommunism in foreign policy, removal of communist sympathizers in government at home, rejection of "liberal," New Deal–type legislation.

To be sure, McCarthy was a problem in this program. The new conservatives liked to think of themselves as refined gentlemen of the old school, and
much about the badgering, often drunken senator was distasteful. They knew
that many of his charges were absurd. Yet they had to recognize that he had
done more than anyone else in the early Fifties to rally sentiment for anticommunism. Wrangling with their consciences to find ways to support, or at
least avoid condemning, the abrasive embarrassment, they came up with statements like this by Buckley and Bozell, in a book they coauthored, *McCarthy
and His Enemies:* "The members of a society must share certain values if that
society is to cohere. . . . A hard and indelible fact of freedom is that a conformity of sorts is always dominant . . . the freeman's principal concern is that it
shall be a conformity that honors the values he esteems rather than those he
rejects." The real point about McCarthyism, they said, was that it was part of
a process of establishing conformity on the communist issue, a way by which
the American people were showing that they had examined and "emphati-

cally rejected" communism; in this respect it was "rallying around an ortho-doxy."[17]

That was not the only orthodoxy. A look at the religious connections of the new conservatism of the early Fifties shows how much it differed in social background from the old conservatism of Republicans and of many southern Democrats, from William McKinley to Robert Taft. Those conservatives were fundamentally rural, Anglo-American, midwestern or southern, and Protes-tant, though of course there were links to Wall Street where it counted. It was mostly an instinctive or pocketbook conservatism, ghostly pale in the area of ideas. The new conservatism, by contrast, was conspicuously Roman Catho-lic or Anglo-Catholic, urban, academic, heavily salted with European émigrés, and self-consciously intellectual.[18] It is important to understand that in the early Fifties both Catholics and conservatives were definitely outsiders to the U.S. intellectual world, comfortably ensconced as it was in Protestant-dominated and fashionably liberal Ivy League universities and their outsta-tions across the land. That outsider status accounted for the conservatives' initial lack of serious recognition, but also, no doubt, for a certain rebel appeal.

Such was the case with an audacious—but much discussed and much sold—book of 1951, William F. Buckley, Jr.'s *God and Man at Yale*. On the basis of his undergraduate years at that distinguished university, 1946 to 1950, the brash young man wrote a scathing indictment of his alma mater, claim-ing that prominent professors ridiculed religion and advanced atheism, that even the Religion Department faculty tested anemic on commitment to the truth of what they taught, and moreover that instruction in other departments like Economics and Political Science was imbued with liberalism if not "col-lectivism" and opposed to individualism and free enterprise.

Buckley stirred up a hornet's nest, largely among Yale students, faculty, and alumni, but I can remember it being read and discussed even at the small college in western Nebraska I was then attending. Most of the response was critical, but the book was nonetheless read. Protestants criticized Buckley for "concealing" (that is, never mentioning) that he was a Roman Catholic, and then they declared that as a Catholic he could never understand religion at a school with a Protestant heritage like Yale. A little more surprisingly, *God and Man* was generally panned in the Catholic press as well, largely on the grounds that Buckley's economic views were so extremely "individualist" as to be at odds with the great papal encyclicals on social justice. *The Sign* pointed out that some of the texts he condemned were also used at Catholic University, said that "the popes have been of Yale's viewpoint" on major issues, and even accused Buckley of holding "Nazi views."[19] One suspects that Roman Catho-lics with *gravitas* were not yet ready to confront the Ivy League head-on, that they would have preferred young Buckley to have taken what he could from

Yale and kept his mouth shut, or better yet gone to a good Catholic school and come out with his head in the right place.

Nothing daunted, Buckley went ahead to establish a major intellectual conservative periodical, the *National Review*, in 1955.

As in many other of its observations—and perhaps this helps explain its influence—*God and Man* was at least prescient in its suggestion of tension between the views on religion of many undergraduates and their professors, who had quite likely been among the campus atheists of the more skeptical Thirties. Religion was coming back as an intellectual force on campuses in the early Fifties. Niebuhr was popular among intellectuals, C. S. Lewis among students and college chaplains.

Reaching out to the new faithful, most of the new conservatives (borrowing from such thinkers and more explicitly from conservative writers like B. I. Bell) contended that God finally justified their position since conservatism was in tune with the divine order. What ultimately discredited communism, and its socialist and other "statist" forerunners, was the Christian understanding of human nature, including original sin. Buckley put it forcefully enough in the foreword to *God and Man at Yale*: "I myself believe that the duel between Christianity and atheism is the most important in the world. I further believe that the struggle between individualism and collectivism is the same struggle reproduced on another level."[20]

Probably written in 1950—Buckley claimed later they were actually proposed and penned by his intellectual mentor at Yale, Willmoore Kendall—those much quoted and discussed words sum up that ominous midcentury year, when everything seemed starkly plain and polarized, and it was, paradoxically, the evil forces who believed too much in human goodness, and the good guys who believed in evil and so in limits and in the control of the present by the reputed wisdom of the past. By whatever means one can, countless denizens of the early Fifties believed, some passionately, one must engage oneself in this struggle between God and atheism and their respective political surrogates.

The intellectual conservative revival of the early Fifties undoubtedly contained serious problems of definition and consistency. It was clear enough what conservatives were against: communism, and also the Roosevelt New Deal and Truman Fair Deal. They were against evils labeled by such terms as *statism* and *collectivism*. But it was not entirely clear what those monstrosities included. Were Social Security and the minimum wage, which most Americans favored, necessarily the first steps on the road to statist ruin? What about the draft, passively accepted in the Fifties, but in the next decade to be denounced as an egregious example of statism? In my own view (and I think the view of Peter Viereck, who was in the end to break with most new conservatives and support Adlai Stevenson for president), the New Deal could well be taken as representing Burkean reformism at its best, correcting what needed to be corrected pragmatically and in limited ways, without changing the system or breaking the generational continuity of society. There are those who still argue that, far from being some sort of revolution, in the desperate days of 1933 Roosevelt and the New Deal kept this country from turning to a communist or fascist panacea. I suspect that Burkeanism has worked better in the United States all along than Edmund Burke's more fervent disciples give it credit for—though Burke himself, who supported the American revolution, might have been pleased but not too surprised.

In the Fifties and Sixties, one might have thought the conservative affirmation of individual freedom and opposition to collectivism would have led conservatives to support Martin Luther King and the civil-rights movement against state-imposed Jim Crow laws. But if one so thought, one would have thought wrong, despite the retroactive support for that one-time "dangerous radical" even by professed conservatives of the Nineties. It is not clear that the Fifties conservatives, who touted Russell Kirk's beloved Randolph of Virginia as well as Christian values, would have even brought themselves to oppose slavery at the time, not to mention voting rights for women. Individual freedom seemed to apply chiefly to white males. As they seemed impotent before Jim Crow and McCarthyism, so they could not decide whether they really supported corporate capitalism (which largely paid their expenses), despite its responsibility for "mass man" and its odd parallels to the "state capitalism" of communism—both powerful self-perpetuating bureaucracies beyond the effective control of most of those whose lives they most affected—or whether they resided in a traditionalist Tory dreamworld, replete with godly bishops and Sir Walter Scott castles.

But the new conservatives are important. Even if sometimes muddled themselves, they have raised arguments that have helped define issues essential to the contemporary world.

A similar mood supported the popularity of T. S. Eliot in the eyes and ears of the early Fifties literary set and its churchly auxiliaries. The great U.S. expatriate poet's Anglo-Catholicism, classicism, and elegies for the spiritual sureties of old suited well the antimodernism of the new traditionalists, and his ability to express the same in chic, urbane language consorted well with their aspirations to sophisticated piety. Eliot's verse play, *The Cocktail Party*, published in 1950, was much read, performed, and discussed that year.

Based on the *Alcestis* of Euripides, this drama opens to a set of witty, modern people at a cocktail party, then a very modish, up-to-date form of socialization, who are engaged in the usual sort of facile, empty conversation. It eventually becomes apparent that various conventional infidelities and a marriage failure have occurred among members of the group, but of a sort easily forgiven among people like these, who claim not to believe in sin. Nonetheless some of them are unaccountably seized by guilt. Having recourse to the modern surrogate for the priest, a psychiatrist, they are told by that uncommonly wise therapist they can choose one of two ways to proceed, both worthy and both needed in the world. One is the good living of ordinary life, the other is an extraordinary way so rare its true nature "is unknown," and so it "requires faith—the kind of faith that issues from despair"—which makes it sound properly existentialist. One of the protagonists, Celia, took the second way, became a missionary sister, and soon underwent a horrible martyrdom by means of crucifixion near an ant hill. The atrocity was committed by rebellious heathen on a far-off island under British colonial rule, and there are characteristic Fifties hints of "foreign agitators, stirring up trouble." This event was part of the remainder of the clique's chatter at another cocktail party two years later.[21]

This work surely has lasting merit but is also very highbrow 1950: the studied and refined religiosity, the uneasy affluence, the almost fashionable prattle (cf. existentialism) about the emptiness of modern life, the yearning to be rescued from all that—or to think about being rescued—in a dramatic manner affirming individual choice and commitment (cf. existentialism again), which confirmed that the world still offered interesting extremes of goodness and evil. One Catholic commentator described the play's burden as "salvation within the tensions of modern city existence," a special concern of the era.[22] Fifties people enjoyed their new affluent urban or suburban life, excitingly fresh to many of them, but still felt guilty in some part of their hearts about giving up rural roots and the presumed solid pieties for the temptations and shallow glamor that went with the city's bright lights and cocktail parties; they were not yet up to Harvey Cox's *Secular City*, published in the next decade, with its argument that many features of urban existence are really closer to godliness than those of the agrarian past.

In 1952 the screenplay of Eliot's rather different *Murder in the Cathedral* was published with stills from the film, reminding the world again in magnificent verse and stately symbolist acting of that contest between worldly and spiritual kinds of power.[23] In this play the archetypal conflict was incarnated in the persons of Henry II and his archbishop of Canterbury, Thomas Becket, but no doubt many would also have thought of more recent enactments of the same drama in the fascist and communist worlds and perhaps closer to home. As is well known, Becket, stabbed by a knight at his own altar, became a martyr to the impetuousness of the ruler; high office and a mitre had made the prelate more loyal to the pope's laws than to his royal former friend.

But one reviewer was impertinent enough to point out that the struggle between kingly tyrant and soon-to-be-sainted cleric was simply the escalation of a dispute over nothing more than title to a fairly unimportant piece of property, which the unyielding archbishop considered to have been settled in church courts.[24] No great point of faith or morals was involved. Some lesson about the tendency of traditionalists to magnify the past, and of power to blind and then destroy politicians and ecclesiastics alike, ought to have been drawn from the drama. In hindsight, there were those in 1952 who might have profited from such instruction. What little of the kinds of power that shook the world from Moscow, Washington, or Rome in that year still remains in the forms it had then!

Eminent Protestants

The Fifties were a golden age of prominent Protestant leaders, men (the word is used advisedly) of strong character and individuality who had been tested in the toils of depression and war, and who came into their own amidst the ripening spiritual harvest of the midcentury decade. Many have been or will be mentioned in the course of this book: G. Bromley Oxnam, Henry Knox Sherrill, Paul Tillich, C. S. Lewis, Emil Brunner, H. Richard Niebuhr, Liston Pope. Here are three in profile.

REINHOLD NIEBUHR

The most prominent establishment Protestant theologian of the day, Reinhold Niebuhr, served as a neoorthodox counterpoint to the anxious optimism of the decade. As we have seen, *Time* had presented him on the cover of its twenty-fifth-anniversary issue, March 8, 1948, entitling the article "Faith for a Lenten Age," and prominently featuring Niebuhr's saying, "Man's story is not a success story." Written by the soon-to-be celebrated ex-communist and nemesis of Alger Hiss, Whittaker Chambers, this account put the Union Theological Seminary prophet in the tradition of Kierkegaard, Dostoevsky, and Barth, Christian pessimists who had doubted the fashionable social optimism of their day, anticipating that progress would occur as much in the works of evil as of good. (Up front in the news sections, the same issue of *Time* that immortalized Reinhold Niebuhr's pessimism reported the final communist capture of Czechoslovakia, predicted that China would probably fall within a year, and held the fates of Italy and Greece uncertain.)

For Niebuhr knew that humanity was by nature sinful yet also possessed spirit that stood outside nature and was able to know its sin. Hence humans must control their sinfulness but will do so effectively only by means that take sin's full dimensions seriously, especially its capacity to enter precisely at the moment when perfection is thought to have been reached. Yet Niebuhr

believed one must do what one can for justice. He was himself a liberal activist in politics but opposed what he considered the false absolutes of pacifism
and Marxism.

His most influential Fifties book was *The Irony of American History* (1952),
essentially a theology of the cold war for cold warriors who needed a spiritually sophisticated rationale for doing what they believed they had to do, uncongenial to their finer sensibilities as it might be. In the anticommunist
conflict the United States was engaged in a struggle against "a demonic religiopolitical creed" that rested on the false premise that it was possible "to take
the leap from the realm of necessity to the realm of freedom," and so escape
the ambiguity of the human situation.[25]

But the U.S. position in this titanic war for the world was full of ironies.
The primary one seemed to be that of the American "illusions of innocency"
(35), based on the idea that in the United States a society free of the abuses
of the old world was created, versus the guilty use we must make of our power,
which has come to us in part because of that innocence, in part because of
progressive losses of innocence.

American innocence was not entirely an illusion, but it had become the
mother of guilt, for "power cannot be wielded without guilt, since it is never
transcendent over interest." Yet the guilt must be borne, for "disavowal of the
responsibilities of power can involve an individual or nation in even more
grievous guilt" (37). Thus, in high irony, the "innocent" nation found itself
responsible for holding back communism and possessing, in the atomic bomb,
the greatest weapon ever known. The ironies go on: we must act in world history though thinking of our nation as (up to now) somehow exempt from it,
and we must exercise power we would not have if we were as innocent as we
thought. Still, loss of innocence cannot be avoided. "The free world must cover
itself with guilt in order to ward off the peril of communism" (4). Guilt there
will be, for we must disabuse ourselves of the illusion "that any measure taken
in a good cause must be unequivocally virtuous" (5). But it must be done.

Neoorthodoxy's emphasis on human sinfulness undergirded the "Christian realism" (23) by which theologians like Reinhold Niebuhr justified the
nation's cold-war role. Real evil was out there, and Christians must not shrink
from the burden of opposing it by the fallen but still God-sanctioned means
of legitimate state authority, including use of the sword. The faithful must be
realist enough to recognize that, in a sinful world, moral responsibility sometimes entails painful choices among varying degrees of evil. Niebuhr had no
doubt that communism, being totalitarian, was worse than the worst of the
capitalist world since the latter still contained some roots of the "open society" in which change is possible.

Niebuhr's Christian realism was one of the underpinnings of a generation that was to bring the nation Vietnam, though in another irony Niebuhr himself came to oppose that war. But one will never fully understand the Fifties—or the next decade, when America's implacable "innocence" and worldly "realism" were pitted against each other as never before or since—without reading *The Irony of American History*.

KARL BARTH

Although he did not visit the United States until 1962, the famous Swiss theologian Karl Barth, the founding father of neoorthodoxy, was the ghost behind the gospel as presented by his earnest disciples in a thousand U.S. pulpits of the early Fifties. Barth emphasized the complete otherness of God from humankind. He rejected any idea that God can be known through reason or nature ("natural theology"), one of the standbys of traditional liberalism. Chastened by the horrors of the First World War, which had made such a mockery of the previous century's belief in progress and natural virtue, he no less rejected the often cognate idea of innate human goodness. Sinful humanity instead can know God only by "straight down" revelation, delivered through Word and sacrament. Barth's doctrine was important for religious opposition to the Nazi regime in Germany; he strongly castigated its idolatry of race and nation and declared that Christians must worship and obey God alone.

As a Fifties figure, albeit a distant, half-legendary one often mediated through Niebuhr and various stellar young U.S. theologians who had been privileged to study with him in his Basel redoubt, Barth was important to religion in this country. His astringent neoorthodoxy, though it may have reached many in the pews only in watery form, was a lofty presence that stood in contrast to the spiritual self-indulgence of much of the religion boom.

But in the Fifties Barth himself puzzled Niebuhr and many of his disciples, especially in cold-war America, by his refusal to condemn the present communist regimes with the same thunder he had delivered against the Nazis. Possibly to undercut the use of his system as cold-war theology, the great utterer of "Nein!" to all such attempts instead claimed that communism posed a far different problem to Christianity than Nazism. The latter was a temptation to adulterate the pure gospel with another one, that of race and culture, as espoused by the "German Christians." But communism presented no temptation, since it frankly opposed all religion. Therefore Christians need not denounce it, but be content to demonstrate the validity of the alternative by their own concrete social and moral action.

In his book *Against the Stream*, Barth published a response to a letter by Emil Brunner taking him to task for his refusal to condemn communism theologically. Barth said, "For I cannot admit it is the duty of Christians or of the church to give theological backing to what every citizen can, with much shaking of the head, read in his daily paper and what is so admirably expressed by Mr. Truman and by the Pope."[26]

In other words, the way of life of people in the Soviet empire was so obviously undesirable, and denounced on so many sides, that it was unnecessary—and indeed would be almost insulting—for the church to tell people the same thing they have been hearing from all sorts of leaders, or could see on their own. Let them decide for themselves, and let the churches in communist countries come to the best terms they can with their governments, without second-guessing by those not in that situation.

In "The Church between East and West" published in the same volume, Barth took a rather avuncular stance toward the United States and Russia, saying that they were both children of old Europe who in different ways have run away from their mother to become giant rivals. That conflict is not our concern as Christians. It is not genuine, or necessary, or interesting, being just a power conflict; Christians can only warn against the worst, a third world war, and otherwise can do no more than emulate Barth's own Switzerland, which amid titanic struggles around it strives only to maintain its neutrality and freedom.[27]

In response to this unexpected stance in the midst of the cold war, *Newsweek* said of the book, "Summing up: Passages [in it] will justly make an American reader's temperature rise, but the point of view, held by many Europeans, is worth a look."[28]

In answer to Barth's refusal to condemn communist tyranny, Niebuhr was typically curt and cutting: "The whole performance prompts revulsion against every pretension to derive detailed political judgments from ultimate theological positions. When a man lacks ordinary common sense in reacting against evil, no amount of theological sophistication will help him."[29]

From a later perspective, one can only acknowledge a kind of Christian realism all his own in Barth's refusal to jump into the high-decibel ideological polarization of so many others, especially in the East and West camps. At the same time, it must be regretted he was unwilling to say anything as a moralist distinguishing the totalitarian Stalinism of the time, with its purges, gulags, and planned famines, not to mention its idolatry of state and Party, from the West, which for all its faults still sometimes retained the capacity to value human rights and engage in democratic self-correction.

One gets a sense that, his theological brilliance notwithstanding, the human Barth was peculiarly unable to look beyond the perspective natural to his native German-speaking middle-European milieu. Nazism was morally and theologically serious because it struck in the very heart of that world; the cold war instead involved Europe's overgrown children out over the horizons, and in this situation the serious problem for Barth was how those caught in the middle can survive their rampages. (A little later we will look at A. J. Muste's cutting rebuttal, as a pacifist, of Niebuhr and Christian realism, and also at his clear-eyed assessment, as a former Marxist, of the communism of his day.)

NORMAN VINCENT PEALE

On the popular religion side, the major liberal figure is Norman Vincent Peale, the great advocate of positive thinking. The label "liberal" may be somewhat misleading, since he was anything but that on political and social issues and showed little interest in the shibboleths of academic liberal theology. Yet Peale, born in 1898, came out of midwestern Methodism and Boston University at a time when the denomination was breaking loose from old-fashioned evangelicalism, and his upbeat, anecdotal preaching style—surely an example of putting the gospel in the jargon of the day, though that of the boardroom rather than the classroom—reflects populist religious liberalism. Peale's translation of the gospel into such terminology as "confidence-concepts," "faith-attitudes," and "spirit-lifters," not to mention his insistence that Christianity was an "exact science" offering formulae that could produce "proven," "guaranteed" results, can be seen in the same light.

It was not critical liberalism, but certainly not sawdust-trail evangelicalism either. Peale was active in mainline religious federations such as the Protestant Council of New York and the National Council of Churches, as was his wife, Ruth, and both were stung by the severe criticism he received from colleagues in those bodies. Yet it must be acknowledged that his Protestantism was not what that tradition meant to many others. Peale's fundamental message, repeated over and over again with the help of countless anecdotes and slogans, was really very simple. It is well expressed in the title of one of his books, *You Can If You Think You Can*. This is positive thinking: setting goals, believing you can accomplish them, not giving way to the "mental drainage" of gloomy, defeatist thoughts.

Clearly something in the Fifties atmosphere resonated to the Pealean evangel. His *Power of Positive Thinking* remained on the bestseller list for more than three years, and crowds overflowed his Marble Collegiate Church in Manhattan every Sunday. Millions read his *Guideposts* magazine and his newspaper column. Perhaps the best assessment that can be made is that, on the one hand, his simple upbeat message and homey, anecdotal preaching style tapped into a nostalgia on the part of many, often newly urbanized or suburbanized, for the optimism and solid verities they imagined informed the old-fashioned American small town; on the other hand, the legitimation of high business-world goals and success ministered to the inner hopes of the many caught up in the dazzling but ambivalent new world of Fifties affluence. Peale's political world was staunchly conservative Republican; he seemed to have little sense of the realities of life for laborers, minorities, and others out-side the realm of the religion-inspired businesspeople with whom he connected so well. More than once he had to withdraw his endorsement in embarrass-ment from causes that he had naively assumed were merely conservative, but that turned out to occupy the verges of anti-Semitic, anti-Catholic, or crypto-fascist terrain.[30] Yet Peale meant well and was an essential spiritual founda-tion of the Fifties. Both he and Reinhold Niebuhr, though coming from very different directions, provided spiritual legitimation for the cold war and the Fifties "American Way of Life."

The Existentialist Posture

The dominant intellectual strand in the early Fifties, at least according to the mass media and the popular pundits, was existentialism. It was a powerful vogue among students, artists, bohemians, and religionists as well as creden-tialed philosophers.

Indeed, James Collins, pointing to articles on that intellectual enthusi-asm in newsstand journals like *Life*, *Mademoiselle*, and the *New York Times Magazine*, and the popularity of novels and plays by the likes of Albert Camus and Jean-Paul Sartre, stated of the existentialist draw that "since the heyday of William James' lectures to teachers' associations and Henri Bergson's talks before Parisian high society, philosophy has not found itself so squarely planted in the marketplace, so gifted with the power to move people."[31]

Like the later beatniks and hippies, public existentialists became quickly identified with dress, beards, and life-styles as much as with ideology, much to the pleasure of the school's young devotees and the scandal of their elders. But even a definition of this popular vogue is elusive; the "ism" meant a num-ber of things, perhaps something different to every self-proclaimed existen-tialist. A basic proposition was that one finds oneself existing in a universe that is absurd, yet one also possesses absolute freedom to make choices, al-though there are no rational criteria for these choices. Through one's choices, which must be expressed in act and way of life as well as idea, one freely de-termines one's nature, thereby moving from mere existence to essence.

Together with this, existentialism placed much emphasis on the themes of anxiety and alienation. The existentialist posture, as well articulated in po-etry and novels as in academic prose, naturally appealed to those who had survived the terrible war, who wanted to make a new world but were disillu-sioned with all ideologies, including the neoconservative ideologies popular in some quarters and the rationalism that had too often been pressed into ideo-logical service.

In Europe existentialism was a late Forties and early Fifties vogue; throngs of self-declared existentialists crowded the bohemian quarters of Paris with their unkempt hair and costumes featuring black and berets. *Newsweek*, in describing the labors of a heroic young Dutch Augustinian priest, Engelmund Balm, found only the most graphic writing suitable as it detailed his special mission to enter darkest Paris and "mingle with the bearded, long-haired, and tartan-shirted *Existentialistes* who loiter empty-eyed and empty-stomached in St. Germain-de-Près *caves* or sprawl on zinc-topped tables in the Café de Mabillon. Dressed as one of them, Father Balm was to play cards with them, discussing their theory of the absurdity of life."[32] These discussions lasted long into the night and were occasionally fruitful.

Nothing quite like this hit the United States until the arrival of the beatniks in Greenwich Village and North Beach in the middle of the decade. One is happy to be able to report that it also produced a suitable ecclesiastical response, in the form of the Bread and Wine Mission established in San Francisco's North Beach by the Reverend Pierre Delattre, a Congregationalist, in 1958. Delattre, like Balm acculturating himself to the milieu, featured food, wine, plays, music, group therapy, Saturday-night poetry readings, and all-night bull sessions. But there were no formal services except a bread, wine, and cheese agape (the "love feast" of the early Christians) on Sunday.[33]

Two kinds of existentialism were generally distinguished: the naturalist type, associated with Jean-Paul Sartre, which saw the universe as so absurd as to lack even a God; and the Christian, traced back to Søren Kierkegaard in the nineteenth century and now revived in a sometimes uneasy alliance with the neoorthodox theology of Karl Barth, Emil Brunner, and others. Barthianism, sometimes called "crisis theology" when its existentialist face was emphasized, stressed the divine-human encounter as a moment of free response through a "leap of faith" to the Word of God. The Word cannot be comprehended by the rational faculties of the human mind, twisted as they are by sin, and can only be seized upon in the entirely different way of sheer faith. The act of faith is the equivalent of existential choice, for it can only be made freely, since the "rational" arguments for and against God more or less balance each other off, and one is left with making the dread final decision alone, without props. In this respect the existentialists are right, crisis theology said, for we can only find the fallen cosmos around us absurd to any reason of which we are capable, and we are plagued with a radical freedom which can only locate its answer and fulfillment in the freedom of God, for anything less would be exchanging freedom for slavery.

Charles Clayton Morrison, pointing toward that which existentialism and neoorthodoxy hold in common, defined it as "the doctrine that the apprehension of and response to the Christian gospel rests ultimately upon faith and not upon rational proof." He added that "the static liberalism of our time is more or less baffled by this new element in theological thinking and strongly inclined to regard it as plain dogma and so under the liberal ban. I hope to show that such a view is itself illiberal."[34]

The new kind of existentialist-faith Christianity had the courage, Morrison thought, to probe deeper into the nature of reality than those under the "dictatorship of human reason as it operates in science and philosophy." No less an icon of liberalism than John Dewey himself said that reason can operate only *within* the process of existence. It cannot transcend the process to operate upon it, that is, to see it from outside. But Christian existentialism is not the Sartrean kind, in which "the universe is self-existent and cannot tell us why it exists or why man exists," and in which one finds nothing but nothingness upon nothingness the deeper one probes. It is rather a Kierkegaardian probe to find response and meaning. An answer is to be expected since the probing consciousness is itself part of the universe. But because of the direct rather than discursive nature of the probe, it is faith—not reason—that casts the light at those depths.

Not all religionists were favorably impressed with existentialism. As early as 1946, Pope Pius XII, in an address to a convention of philosophers in Rome, called existentialism a "filosofia del disastro" that antagonized reason and reduced religion to volunteerism. He called instead for Thomism, the "philosophia perennis" that put reason and will, humanity and God, all in their proper place. James Collins, in *The Existentialists*, also argued in favor of Thomism as the best answer to what the existentialist thinkers were groping toward.[35]

But Nicolas Berdyaev, among the most profound of existentialist Christians, put the favorable case this way: "In opposition to Schleiermacher and many others it must be stated that religion is not a 'sense of dependence' . . . but, on the contrary, a sense of independence. If God does not exist, man is a being wholly dependent on nature or society, on the world or the state. If God exists, man is a spiritually independent being; and his relation to God is to be defined as freedom."[36]

This dream of true independence fitted in well, of course, with that near obsession of the intellectual Fifties, the fear of "mass society." That was a paradoxical phobia, for it had to be set alongside the decade's equal devotion to conformity and dread of any hint of "deviance" or "abnormality." But the aversion to the "mass" and to "dehumanization" was thought necessary to individualism, capitalism, and anticommunism, at least theoretically. On another level, aversion to the masses made common cause with the elitism of intellectuals, artists, and critics of the world that was being created by television and suburban tract houses. The existentialists pointed with anguish and horror to the humdrum repetitious life of a ticket taker or assembly-line worker, reduced to a function and a uniform or blue collar. They cried out against the crushing force of mass opinion, now enhanced by new media.

The existentialists' position in the world of the Forties and Fifties may have been basically reactive, and as such they received the decades' stock answers, from Thomism to its disdain for conspicuous nonconformists. In their own countercontempt of "mass man" and all his works, the existentialists, like other Fifties elite critics, dehumanized the masses just as they believed the masses had dehumanized themselves. In the United States, not a few of those Fifties disparagers of the new television, automobile, and suburban tract-house culture almost callously overlooked the way that same culture was opening new horizons to the sons and daughters of rural and blue-collar stock far beyond those of their depression-era parents with grade school educations. If not perfect, the Fifties felt far better to most people than what they had known before. (In turn, however, some of their own sons and daughters would rebel against the Fifties in the Sixties.)

But the existentialists, like their Beat cousins, presented a colorful counterpoint to Fifties drabness. At their best, they recalled to overly conditioned minds the importance of personal choice and personal responsibilities in values. They produced unforgettable art, literature, and theology; all in all—if the term is construed fairly broadly—probably most of what was produced in the fifties in those areas that is still living and challenging intellectually is existentialist inspired.

Notes from Underground

Here are a few personalities especially prominent in the early Fifties who represent a counterpoint to the stereotype, at least, of Fifties religion. They are not totally alien to it, for their impact came from whatever dialogue they could establish with above-ground religion, and that required some common territory. But like the prophets, or in some cases pseudoprophets, of old, they looked at things from another angle than the commonality.

THOMAS MERTON

A good example is Thomas Merton (1915–1968), often called the most famous monk in America. He was born in France of New Zealand/U.S. artist parents and spent a rather chaotic childhood in several countries before entering Columbia University in the late Thirties. He vividly describes the atmosphere of a great cosmopolitan university of that era, with all its noisy political factions, mostly leftist, and its opportunities for spiritual seekers, in his celebrated autobiography, *The Seven Storey Mountain*.[37] Amidst that carnival of options for the soul, he became a Roman Catholic, and then in

December of 1941, just after Pearl Harbor, entered Gethsemani Abbey in Kentucky, a house of the Cistercians of the Strict Observance, or Trappists.

From that grim December until his sudden death in December 1968, Merton, like Catholic monks and nuns of the Fifties and Sixties generally, went through several lives in one. When he entered the monastery, Merton undoubtedly believed he would never see the world outside its walls again, much less die of electrocution from a faulty electric fan in a place as remote and exotic as Bangkok, where he was attending a conference with Buddhist monks. When Merton entered Gethsemani, life there was hard, lived in silence, often cold and hungry, centering around long services in Latin; by 1968, although still ascetic by worldly standards, the monks were rather less regimented and more outgoing.

But, for all the hardships, Merton remembered his early years in the monastery as "Edenic." These years included 1948, when *The Seven Storey Mountain* amazed his publishers by making the bestseller list, selling 600,000 copies in its first edition. In 1949 a splendid book on the inner life, *Seeds of Contemplation*, appeared, as did *The Waters of Siloe*, a history of the Cistercians which, coming on the heels of *The Seven Storey Mountain*, sold remarkably well for the story of an otherwise little-known monastic order.[38] In 1949 Merton was also ordained priest.

His experience with the enclosed life extended into the early Fifties and is well recorded in his diaries, published as *The Sign of Jonas*. An entry for December 23, 1949: "The sun shines in a very happy room this morning, in which a monk is where he belongs, in silence, with angels, his hand and eye moved by the loving God in deep tranquility. The watch ticks: but perhaps there is after all no such thing as time." And again, June, the Octave of Corpus Christi, 1952:

> The Lord God is present where the new day shines in the moisture on the young grasses. The Lord God is present where the small wildflowers are known to Him alone. The Lord God passes suddenly, in the wind, at the moment when night ebbs into the ground. He Who is infinitely great has given His children a share in his own innocence. His alone is the gentlest of loves: Whose pure flame respects all things.
>
> God, Who owns all things, leaves them all to themselves.[39]

In some ways Merton in the early Fifties was a model of the "old church," as it has sometimes been called from the post-Vatican II perspective. The ascetic discipline of his life was the chaste, rule-following self-discipline incumbent on all Catholics writ large. For a few years around 1950, like most Catholics he seems to have accepted the cold-war perspective on the world, understandably in view of his sources of information and the realities of the outside world.[40] *The Waters of Siloe* describes in harrowing detail the persecution of Trappists by "Reds" during the Spanish civil war, and by communists in China—positions different from his own sympathies in the Thirties, and his pacifism on Vietnam in the Sixties.[41] The radical social criticism of the next decade, and the interest in non-Christian religions, had not yet appeared in very explicit form.

(But in *The Sign of Jonas* Merton does include a journal entry for Nov. 16, 1949, stating, "I think I shall ask permission to write to a Hindu who wrote me a letter about Patanjali's yoga, and who is in Simla. I shall ask him to send me some books. A chemist who has been helping us with some paint jobs turned out to have been a postulant in a Zen Buddhist monastery in Hawaii and he spoke to the community about it in Chapter."[42] More signs of the spiritual underground in those years; it was even establishing invisible networks.)

In general, however, Merton in the early Fifties was nonpolitical and adventurous in only limited ways, such as in gaining new freedom for himself and other monks to walk about the monastery grounds. He was concerned chiefly with laying deeply the foundation of spirituality by which he, as a monk, could best be of service to the world: as an observer who saw all the more clearly because he was disengaged, and all the more compassionately because he was caught up in divine love. At the time all this was mainly expressed in properly orthodox sermons.

Thus, writing in *Commonweal* in 1950, Merton remarked that "a life without asceticism is a life of illusion, unreality, and unhappiness," though one should honor the things of creation.[43] In the midst of rapidly growing early-Fifties affluence, a compensatory call to the cloister, or at least to an inwardly ascetic life in the world, had some appeal for sensitive souls. A few years later, the French Catholic Jean Canu wrote, "The strictest rules seem not to repel but to attract vocations, as we see, for instance, in the United States, with the extraordinary multiplication of Cistercian monasteries." In 1940, he said, there were three Trappist houses in the United States; between 1944 and 1956 nine others appeared. (Indeed this was the case; Trappist monasteries received more novices than they knew what to do with. In the prologue to *The Sign of Jonas*, Merton mentions Gethsemani Abbey growing from 70 to 270, adding with a touch of sarcasm, "Thus two hundred and seventy lovers of silence and solitude are all packed into a building that was built for seventy."[44] A huge circus tent had to be set up on the grounds to house them. Trappist silence and solitude was in the air as the ultimate refuge and challenge; I remember a young man even in my small town in western Nebraska who wanted to join the Trappists in 1951.) In no small part, Canu adds correctly, this was all due to Thomas Merton, "one of the new ascetics," who has written of the "formidable existentialist silence of God," and of "the monk, man of silence and solitude," who "seems precisely the opposite of the American and modern man in general."[45]

Another book of this period by the prolific Merton was *The Ascent to Truth*, an introduction to Christian mysticism based on the teachings of St. John of the Cross. While unexceptional in its intellectual background, it was written elegantly and with a particular eye on the needs, and likely delusions, of Merton's contemporaries. A reviewer in the *New York Herald Tribune* mentioned not only the appeal of asceticism to those surfeited with affluence, but also the perennial call of faith in times of anxiety and impending doom. "With the threat of a negative destiny hanging over society, people turn instinctively toward religion, and Father Merton expects a wave of false mysticism. As an antidote to that anticipated wave he has written this book." This is the kind of presence Merton was in the early Fifties as he expounded true mysticism solidly based on the Catholic faith, but woven into soft and eloquent webs of words.[46]

A. J. MUSTE

The grand old man of U.S. pacifism, a conspicuous presence on the fringes of the Fifties, is well portrayed in this anecdote by Milton Mayer.

> It was a Sunday morning, in the summer of 1940, on the shore of one of the Finger Lakes in upper New York, and [Quaker] silent worship was going on. A man stood up, a long stringy man about six feet high that you'd say had been disjointed and reassembled. He had a big sloping forehead wrinkled like the back of his pants knees, a big nose, big ears set at 45 degrees, a nice wide mouth, and a nice mop of brown and gray hair. You couldn't say how old he was; he had the seasoned skin of country men; it doesn't change much.
> "If I can't love Hitler," he said, "I can't love at all."
> Then he sat down.[47]

This was Abraham Johannes Muste. Born in the Netherlands in 1885, he was brought to the U.S. as a child. He became a minister in the Reformed Church in 1909 but left it as his theology became more liberal, taking a Congregational parish in Newtonville, Massachusetts, in 1914. He was forced to leave that pastorate after the United States entered the war, for by then he was outspokenly a pacifist as well as a liberal. He then joined the Society of Friends (Quakers) in Providence, Rhode Island, where he was provided with a home and expenses in exchange for some speaking and pastoral work. Muste soon became involved in labor action as well and was arrested and beaten on the picket line of a strike in Lawrence, Massachusetts. After the war he worked briefly for the Amalgamated Textile Workers, then became a teacher at Brookwood Labor College in Katonah, New York, a training school for labor leaders.

During the 1920s and early 1930s Muste threw himself wholeheartedly into the labor struggle, becoming relatively inactive religiously and moving more and more to the left politically. Though never a communist, he knew and worked with a number of persons in the Communist Party and other groups on the far left. For a time he supported the use of violence in revolution, and in 1934 he became a spokesperson for the Trotskyite Workers Party—which brought him much vilification from the "Stalinist" communists.

Muste quickly became disillusioned by the infighting and cynical tactics that were so much a matter of course in that world. Nonetheless, in 1936 he traveled to Europe, where he attended conferences and spent a week talking with Trotsky himself at the latter's home in Norway. But on the way back, visiting Paris with his family, he dropped into the famous church of St. Sulpice on the Left Bank. His account, cited in Nat Hentoff's *Peace Agitator:*

> St. Sulpice seemed very much cluttered with statues. In addition, repair work was going on and there was a good deal of scaffolding, especially near the altar. Yet somehow, almost from the moment I came into the sanctuary, a deep and what I can only describe as a singing peace came over me. . . . The sudden *new* sensation was one of a deepened, a fathomless peace, and of the spirit hearing what I suppose people are trying to describe when they use the stuffy and banal phrase, "the music of the spheres." The Bible has worthier words when it speaks of the time "when the morning stars sang together." I seated myself on a bench and looked toward the altar and the cross. I felt, "This is where you belong, in the church, not outside it." (97–98)

Immediately Muste split with the Trotskyites and became again active in the Fellowship of Reconciliation, as he had been much earlier before his radical leftward move. Founded in 1914, this group (which will be mentioned later in connection with Reinhold Niebuhr and Joseph Matthews) is a religiously based pacifist organization that sponsors lectures, seminars, publications, and some demonstrations on behalf of the pacifist cause; it has also been active in race and labor relations. Muste became executive secretary of FOR in 1940, a job that was exactly right for him and that he retained for the rest of his career.

It is remarkable the extent to which the activist Sixties of civil rights and the antiwar movement were really a product of the Fellowship of Reconciliation during the days of Muste's vigorous leadership. He was in a real sense the grandfather and godfather of the Sixties. He and his group pioneered the styles of Gandhian, nonviolent protest—including civil disobedience—that worked well in those times. Leaders of the civil-rights movement who were active in FOR in their formative years include Martin Luther King, Jr., James Farmer, Bayard Rustin, and James Lawson.

Muste was himself an activist in the less promising decade of the Fifties. He declined to pay federal taxes, since a large part of that revenue went to military purposes. It was not until 1960, however, that he was charged with owing $1,165 in back taxes for 1948–1952, plus penalties for fraud. The case allowed Muste and his supporters a platform, although not all pacifists felt that nonpayment of taxes was an appropriate gesture. In the end, Muste both won and lost; he had to make up the back taxes, but the charge of fraud was dismissed since the court was convinced he had acted in good faith. He paid, feeling that the point had been made. One supporter said, "It's another example of how A. J. 'leads' the movement, and it also illustrates how he can draw attention to our point of view. When a man as respected as A. J. refuses to pay taxes, it's like Jeremiah walking down the street naked. People stop, look, and listen" (129).

Muste visited India in December 1949 to attend a world pacifist meeting. This trip gave him an opportunity to study the political and spiritual situation in the newly independent land of his great mentor, M. K. Gandhi. A couple of perceptive and well-informed articles in the *Christian Century* were the result; in these pieces Muste was, at one and the same time, as radical as ever about social justice, trenchantly anticommunist, and as cultured a voice of the liberal Protestant establishment as ever wrote in that creditable journal. In "Nehru Walks a Thin Wire," Muste notes the prime minister's endeavor to avoid the exploitation of capitalism and the totalitarianism of communism. In this article and in "Neo-Gandhian India," he points to the "third way" of Gandhi's remaining disciples, particularly Vinoba Bhave. The latter made a practice of persuading landlords voluntarily to give up property to the poor; Muste spoke of him as "looting through love."[48]

In 1950 the "peace agitator," as Nat Hentoff called him, began stumping the country on behalf of unilateral disarmament. He was apparently the first prominent noncommunist to do so. In April 1950 he fasted for peace in Washington. In 1959, in the "Omaha Action," he got himself arrested for entering a missile base at Mead, Nebraska, spending nine days in a miserable prison. He handled planning and preliminary negotiations with governments on behalf of a Peace Walk from San Francisco to Moscow in 1960–1961, which covered six thousand miles and crossed six frontiers. Walkers left San Francisco December 1, 1960, arriving in the Soviet capital October 8, 1961, where they represented the first public challenge to Russian nuclear policy ever permitted. Activists considered this a significant breakthrough, and no doubt it was. It answered the frequent taunt, "Why don't you protest at the Kremlin as well as the Pentagon?" and it may well have been a first step toward 1989 as well as toward the great antiwar activities of the Sixties.

A. J. Muste, however, did not see the results, even in his own century, of his lifework for peace, though he undoubtedly took great satisfaction in the mid-Sixties successes of the civil-rights movement so heavily staffed by his docents. He died in 1967, in the midst of his final campaign, against the war in Vietnam.

GEORGE ADAMSKI AND THE FLYING-SAUCER ENTHUSIASM

On June 14, 1947, Kenneth Arnold, a businessman in a private plane, saw nine bright circular objects speeding around Mount Rainier. Before long reports of the shiny flying devices were coming in from across the country. They were capable of extraordinary maneuvers; three airmen died chasing the disks. Most of these "flying saucers" were round and flat like a Frisbee, but the UFOs (unidentified flying objects), as they were also called, could take the shape of cigars or ice cream cones as well. The air force and various learned authorities solemnly denied their existence, or at least that they were (as everyone was speculating) visitors from another world. But the lively accounts kept coming in. Perhaps they were surcease from the grimmer side of 1950. On April 17 of that year, *Newsweek* ran a light-hearted account of the "delusion," embellished by a photo of a madcap-looking young woman in a silly flying-saucer hat; the piece was stuck between dead-serious stories on McCarthy's charges against Owen Lattimore, and on the conviction of San Francisco labor leader Harry Bridges of perjury for denying his affiliation with the Communist Party.[49]

For some, flying saucers had their serious side too. Clearly, any suggestion that earth was being contacted by extraterrestials would have religious significance. The analytic psychologist C. G. Jung weighed in with a widely quoted essay claiming that archetypally the disks were "technological angels," the space-age equivalents of the descending angels, gods, and saviors of yore. Their present-day appearance was surely related to the anxiety and danger of the times.[50]

That was the message still others got from the saucers themselves. It was not long before persons began appearing to claim they had been contacted by the beings piloting the mysterious ships, in some cases traveling with them to the wondrous planets from which they had come. These "contactees" were invariably earthlings of obscure background who reported experiences virtually comparable to a shaman's initiation and marvelous flight, and who then often maintained contact with the saucerians through mediumship like that of Spiritualism. In the Fifties, the intruders from outer space were generally splendid, almost godlike beings, advanced millennia beyond earth, who—particularly

in light of the recent atomic explosions—were coming to warn this recalci-
trant planet to repent and mend its ways. The entire contactee phenomenon
can hardly be regarded as other than religious.

The best known of all the contactees was George Adamski (1891–1965).
Born in Poland and brought to the United States as an infant, Adamski pur-
sued various occupations in the western states, from being a painter at
Yellowstone to lecturing on occultism in California, where he founded the
Royal Order of Tibet in 1934 and acquired the title "professor." In the late
Forties Adamski took up residence on the slopes of Mt. Palomar, near the fa-
mous observatory, working in a hamburger stand and setting up a small obser-
vatory of his own, where he would entertain his students and visitors.

In this capacity he later claimed to have observed spacecraft overhead
from 1946 on, taking alleged photos of the objects, and lecturing on them
beginning in 1949. Then, on November 20, 1952, Adamski reportedly saw a
UFO land on the Mojave Desert. Approaching it, he met a man from Venus
(attractive, with long blond hair and high forehead), with whom he communicated in sign language. The meeting was described in *Flying Saucers Have
Landed*. Further encounters, including conversations, followed, to be recounted
in *Inside the Space Ships*. The teaching was basically that the other inhabit-
ants of our solar system are guided by "cosmic law"; by adhering to the same
we could create a perfect world here on earth.[51]

Like all new religions, UFOism combined signs and wonders in contemporary idiom with moral teaching attuned to the deep anxieties and dreams
of the day. In a world beset by McCarthyism and cold war, with nuclear disaster only a button away, it is not surprising that some hoped for wise guidance from better beings than we, and looked for better signs in the skies than
bombers and missiles.

All of the "underground" religious figures, in fact, have this in common.
Whether in the monastery, the peace march, or the UFO, they projected the
image of a way of life, a community, and a symbolic token of something radically other than the norms of the day. These three tokens, different as they
are, are all also other than the much-vaunted nuclear family with its togetherness, than the burgeoning economic world of affluence and gray-flannel suits,
and than the "realist" world of anticommunism and cold-war tensions. The
monastery, the protest community, and the interworldly fellowship with
saucerians were other communities than the togetherness family, and implied
quite different economic or political values than the conventional.

In a different way, those worlds were also challenged by existentialism,
and by books, through many of which one could quietly and vicariously, for a
few hours at a time, get away from the prison of togetherness.

Books of the Early Fifties

The Fifties were the last full decade in which books still reigned supreme, as they had since Gutenberg, as the great conveyors of all ideas and memories central to the cultural tradition. Television was a novelty. Movies were entertainment, or at best revelatory of popular rather than great-tradition culture. Music and art were important, of course, but to really understand them one had to read the books about them, just as in literature one had to read the poems and novels and then the critics.

In religion, this was no less true. It was a decade of important religious publishing ventures, of major editions, significant commentaries, and a few obliquely spiritual novels that may not have seemed religious on the surface.

Protestant Christianity asserted itself well in the early Fifties. The tone was confident—Protestantism was, after all, the dominant religion in the world's dominant power, and well aware of it—lacking the edgy over-assertiveness of some Catholic and other critics. At the same time, like the others it was looking to its roots and rediscovering its heritage through fresh takes on history. Examples are Roland Bainton's classic life of Martin Luther, *Here I Stand*, and Wilhelm Pauck's more scholarly *Heritage of the Reformation*. Another kind of landmark book was H. Richard Niebuhr's *Christ and Culture*, which has long endured as a study of different ways in which Christian societies have seen the relationship of their culture and the object of their worship: the Christ of culture, Christ against culture, Christ above culture, Christ and culture in paradox. Niebuhr ends by reviving as an ideal the nineteenth-century Anglican F. D. Maurice's vision, which he denominates Christ the transformer of culture. Maurice and Niebuhr presented a Christ capable of irradiating a culture as its center whether he is humanly known or not, and yet who is also capable of judging it—a model Niebuhr no doubt envisioned for Christian America in the Fifties.[52]

Just how important and yet also how difficult that achievement would be in the early Fifties was evident in the cold-war manifesto of his brother, Reinhold Niebuhr, *The Irony of American History*, already discussed. The United States was a country that could never forget the haunting person of Christ yet could never seem to quite get it right: full of Christ-against-culture sectarians and Christ-with-culture chauvinists, it needed to accept both its sinfulness and its historical mission, and to be less ready to preach than to hear the word of Christ come through its traditional culture yet also from above, as if from the mount.

Another tradition of Protestant theology was inaugurated with the publication in 1951 of the first volume of Paul Tillich's *Systematic Theology*.[53] Tillich was in the existentialist theology tradition, like the neoorthodox among whom the Niebuhrs were frequently counted, but with a good deal more of Plato and Meister Eckhart than of John Calvin and Kierkegaard in him. He was existentialist in the sense that he too began with humanity's asking questions of a seemingly absurd universe, but for him the questions did not lead to confrontation with the Word of a wholly other deity. Rather, Tillich's questing faith led to the expression of an ultimate concern, which because it has to do with reality leads anagogically to the ultimate reality, the Ground of Being—call it God. Certain points within conditioned reality, like Jesus, are particularly "transparent" to this Ground of Being. As the anxiety of the early Fifties gradually gave way to the "new optimism" (as William Hamilton was to call it) of the youthful Sixties, neoorthodoxy in its pure form was to decrease and Tillich was for a while to increase.

The most memorable stories of the early Fifties immediately confront us with the existentialist theme. One way or another, they portray an individual or small group standing against the world, or at least a culture. In J. D. Salinger's *Catcher in the Rye*, it is a boy observing with sardonic and increasingly cynical eye the values of the public-school culture and upper-class life into which he finds himself "thrown," as the existentialists might have said. Herman Wouk's *Caine Mutiny*, on the *New York Times* best-seller list for forty-eight weeks, set individual sense and military regulations against each other in wartime, when the stakes on both sides were unconscionably high. The grand old man of U.S. letters, Ernest Hemingway, wrote *The Old Man and the Sea*, the narrative of a single individual's struggle with the natural forces of the universe and the inevitable victory in defeat that unequal conflict entailed. Unlike the "popular" religious novels mentioned in chapter 1 (for example, Costain's *Silver Chalice* and Bishop's *The Day Christ Died*, both at the top of Fifties best-seller lists), which were characteristic of the bottom half of Fifties split-level culture, in an existentialist manner these books were religious without being religious; they did nothing but portray human nature mercilessly, and in such a way as to call for either God or despair, or so the numerous Fifties predicants who preached out of the latest fashionable novels read them.[54]

In 1950, Harry Overstreet's *Mature Mind*, a characteristic Fifties mental-hygiene treatise published in a year when there was much evidence of immature minds at work in the nation and the world, remained number one on the *New York Times* best-seller list for nine weeks. Immanuel Velikovsky's *Worlds in Collision*, an unexpected contender claiming that such ancient biblical prodigies as the parting of the Red Sea and the manna falling in the wilderness can be explained through catastrophic astronomical events—planets moving to new orbits and the like—held first place on the same list for eleven weeks. It so outraged conventional scientists that they seriously threatened to boycott the publisher, Doubleday, in a move toward academic McCarthyism hardly less disturbing than the bizarre theories of the emigré Russian Jew Velikovsky.[55]

But *Worlds in Collision* held its place on the *New York Times* best-seller list of, for example, October 1, 1950, alongside L. Ron Hubbard's *Dianetics*, the scripture of a brief psychological vogue that was to eventuate in the powerful and controversial Church of Scientology. It was joined on the same list, same day, by Overstreet's *Mature Mind*; Thor Heyerdahl's *Kon-Tiki*, on his journey across the South Pacific by raft; and Frank Scully's *Behind the Flying Saucers*, an early sensational account of crashed saucers in the Southwest, later revealed to represent a hoax perpetrated on Scully himself.

Then—same list, same day—came books that seemed to want more than anything else to recall in tranquility and near nostalgia the awful and awesome days of the previous two decades. *Anybody Can Do Anything*, by Betty MacDonald, author of the earlier best-seller *The Egg and I*, describes job hunting and job losing during the depression with her usual hilarious sparkle. Glamor and sentiment from those same years, different setting, was evoked by Marion Crawford, nanny of the British royal family, in *The Little Princesses*. *The Story of Ernie Pyle*, which was virtually also the story of World War II for many stateside readers, is told by his close friend, Lee Graham Miller. John Gunther's *Roosevelt in Retrospect* offered pleasant reminiscences more than solid history, as did Quentin James Reynold's *Courtroom*, a breezy biography of the famous lawyer and judge Samuel Leibowitz, and Jack Lait and Lee Mortimer's *Chicago Confidential*, a hack and hatchet job on the Windy City's nightlife and lowlife. Completing the list was Gayelord Hauser's *Look Younger, Live Longer*, full of tips like eat lots of yeast and yogurt. All together they paint an interesting portrait of the mind of the moment: nostalgic, doubting, sensation seeking, vicariously adventure loving, and somewhere else than in the United States of 1950. No histories of Korea or, quite yet, treatises on communism or by ex-communists.

The Fifties were also a golden age of monumental publishing ventures, and of these pride of place must go to the *Revised Standard Version of the Bible*, published under the auspices of the National Council of Churches in 1952, on the five-hundredth anniversary of the Gutenberg Bible.[56] Since then a number of modern-language versions of the Scriptures have appeared, but the RSV, as it was universally called, was the first widely used edition to employ thoroughly contemporary, though dignified, language, as well as to incorporate generally accepted results of modern scholarship on the level of textual variants and the precise meanings of words. To see and hear the hallowed text in current idiom rather than in the sonorous archaisms of the King James version was something of a shock; its use in Sunday-morning lections was controversial in many churches, including mine. Not a few Christians in the pews responded with enthusiasm for this new unlocking of the plain meaning behind the stained-glass language of old. But literati considered it insipid or vulgar, while fundamentalists were scandalized by what they regarded as the liberal tone of the new translation, including its alleged undermining of doctrines like the virgin birth (Is. 7:14, RSV: "Behold, a young woman [note: or *virgin*] shall conceive"; KJ: "Behold, a virgin shall conceive"). Those who harbored dark suspicions about the National Council generally found them confirmed in the "New Bible." While the RSV was in some ways in dialectic with the conservative—or, better, traditionalist—mood of religion in the early Fifties, it was a showpiece of the postwar era's release of powerful fresh religious energies, and on a deeper level was a pioneer effort in the tide of religious populism that was rising behind the prodigious church growth of the early Fifties and would crest in the Sixties and after.

Another token of that publishing boom of more interest to students, and definitely in line with the rediscover-the-sources academic zeitgeist, was *The Library of Christian Classics*, begun in 1953 and to be completed in twenty-six volumes. Edited by Protestant scholars and published by the Presbyterian-related Westminster Press, the series included great Christian texts from the Apostolic Fathers through the major Reformers. Parallel to it was a new Roman Catholic *Fathers of the Church* series that has now run to ninety volumes. From the Protestant camp came the twelve-volume *Interpreters Bible*, an invaluable aid to students and preachers that presented the biblical text in both King James and RSV translations, together with readable middle-of-the-road critical and homiletical commentary.[57]

Among the monumental series that seemed to proliferate in this era was the *Great Books of the Western World* in fifty-four volumes, edited out of the University of Chicago by Robert Maynard Hutchins with Mortimer Adler and published by the *Encyclopaedia Britannica*. Some seventy authors are presented, mostly in the form of complete works; nor are religious and philosophical issues ignored, as one would expect given the substantial input of the philosopher Mortimer Adler to the project. Major Western thinkers from the Greeks to the moderns are here, and Adler's intriguing four-volume Synopticon, part of the set, enables one to synthesize the thinking of the greats on topics from angels on. But Adler's biases are generally regarded as responsible for the astonishing fact that Christianity is represented entirely by Catholics, including two volumes of Thomas Aquinas, and by skeptics; Protestant thought is entirely overlooked, as Protestant reviewers complained at the time. Writers on the level of Montaigne, Rabelais, or Henry Fielding were considered worthy of admission to this Western canon, but not Martin Luther or John Calvin.[58]

The idea that a special sanctity hung over Western civilization was big in the Fifties. (I question the whole concept of a "Western" collection, favoring a world symposium of Great Books that would include the classics of all six of the inhabited continents on an equal footing.) Indeed, despite increasing evidence, from the Sixties moon flights and otherwise, that the world is round, the notion that it can be neatly divided into totally opposite "Eastern" and "Western" styles of civilization and religion still lingers today, engendering mostly prejudice and stereotypes.

As though to test that bias, a spate of publishing about Asian religion emerged in the early Fifties as well, clearly a part of the spiritual "minority report" associated with people like Aldous Huxley and Alan Watts, to be enacted by the Beats and with great exuberance in the Sixties counterculture. This report challenged the Jewish and Christian God's vaunted otherness, personality, and action in history. The other spiritualities, whether Buddhism, Daoism, or Vedanta Hinduism, looked instead toward knowing the timeless divine within, and in nature, through mystical experience. The distinguished novelist Christopher Isherwood, associated with the Vedanta Center of Southern California and like his fellow British expatriates Aldous Huxley and Alan Watts a California neomystic, edited *Vedanta for Modern Man*. Containing essays by Huxley, Watts, Gerald Heard, and such eminent Indians as Jawaharlal Nehru, Radhakrishnan, and Rabindranath Tagore, the book collectively sought like Merton to find (or rather, having found, to expound) a relevant tradition, but encountered it some three thousand miles east of Jerusalem. Another Vedantic work, Swami Akhilananda's *Mental Health and Hindu Psychology*, found at the depths of the psyche not the Freudian snakes of popular psychoanalysis but God.[59]

Daisetz T. Suzuki from Japan, the famous exponent of Zen Buddhism, was a popular lecturer, especially on college campuses, in the early Fifties. Many (though not Suzuki himself) thought there was a significant parallel between Zen and existentialism. Abetted by Alan Watts and the Beats as well as Suzuki's work, Zen would become a significant force in the mid to late Fifties. Suzuki's second collection of writings, *Essays in Zen Buddhism*, was published in 1952.[60]

Mohandas K. Gandhi was, posthumously, an important presence in early Fifties spiritual culture, a counterfoil to cold-war religion. While perhaps only A. J. Muste and other Fellowship of Reconciliation pacifists took him literally, many seemed to have an almost wistful yearning to know more about him and to sense his presence, if only vicariously on the printed page. Books about Gandhi kept coming out and selling, and the *Christian Century* in 1952 devoted a whole bibliographical article to Gandhiana. Among the interesting new titles were *The Wit and Wisdom of Gandhi*, by Homer A. Jack, Unitarian minister and a longtime aficionado and publicist of the Mahatma, as well as of Albert Schweitzer. There was also Louis Fischer's valuable and award-winning though almost too sympathetic biography, *The Life of Mahatma Gandhi*.[61]

Another frontier of conflict and interaction in the early Fifties lay between religion and Freudian psychoanalysis. To some, it appeared that nothing, not even communism, presented a profounder threat to faith than the new doctrine that made all sacred sentiments, however mystical and spiritual, reducible to childish projections and delusions: the "Father figure," the "oceanic consciousness." The challenge was only augmented by the Viennese doctor's well-known disdain for religion, suggested in the title of a book of his, *The Future of an Illusion*. Yet the Fifties were the heyday in the United States of psychoanalysis not only as the most prestigious (and most costly) form of therapy, but also as a constituent of popular culture. Everyone, it seemed, talked about rationalizations, Oedipus complexes, and their libidos.

Since this was also a golden age of religion, how were the two reconciled? Some people, of course, simply went to analysis on Wednesday and church on Sunday, or temple on the Sabbath. They were less interested in salvation than in happiness, willing to take whatever help they could in its pursuit. Then again, some on the religion side rejected Freudianism as downrightly as its true believers dismissed religion. But there were also those who tried to integrate insights from both realms. Of these, one of the most interesting efforts, if not the profoundest or the most famous, was that of R. S. Lee, an Anglican priest from Hong Kong of mixed Chinese and British descent, in *Freud and Christianity*. Lee provides an intriguing and quite uninhibited Freudian interpretation of numerous traditional Christian doctrines and symbols, many of which can best be understood in psychoanalytic terms such as sublimation and the Oedipus complex. Freud can now perform two functions for Christians, Lee said: he can explain the psychological basis of Christian doctrine and "in so far as psychoanalysis frees individual Christians from the thraldom of the unconscious motivation, it enables them to think and act more effectively in religious matters."[62] It can, in short, liberate them to act simply out of mature, genuine love, which was what the religion is supposed to be all about.

Conclusion: The Dark and the Dreaming

Not all early Fifties people wanted to get straight, however, so much as they wanted to dream their dreams and fight their demons. The early Fifties were a time of many dreams, most of them conflicting and some of them demon haunted: the mythical backdrop of the epic and victorious war; the dream of the new affluent suburban life-style; the visions that young couples with young children are always prone to have; the bitter Protestant-Catholic tensions and the happier dream of tolerance; liberal political scenarios in conflict with the rising conservative images; religious power-pictures like the Assumption and the Billy Graham experience of evangelical conversion; the togetherness family and the self-consciously alienated existentialist stance, plus the monastic option; the traditionalism of the Great Books and the Christian classics versus the futurism of the atomic (and automobile) age; and above all, the apocalyptic panorama of a planet in conflict between expanding communism and the free world.

It was also a religious time, for religion was involved in not a few of the visions and moreover offered ways to sort them out in terms of hierarchies of values. On some level, religion is the ideological management of dreams and visions, and in the early Fifties that was a capacity much needed. The United States has often been torn between two visions of religion and society—the Augustinian, which views the City of God as entirely apart from this world, and the role of the state as only to police the terrain so as to enable it to flourish privately in the hearts of those called to it; and the Platonic or Thomistic, which grants the state a positive role in enacting rules and enforcing behavior that will advance the cause of the saints, ultimately perhaps itself to become the Beloved Community. In their early Fifties forms, these visions veered between the Platonic anticommunist state and the Augustinian libertarian society. By the middle of the decade, the latter seemed in precarious lead, and the sacred community was reverting to the churches.

Shadows at High Noon, 1953–1956

Part II

"The LORD has set the sun in the heavens,
  but has said that he would dwell in thick darkness.
I have built thee an exalted house,
  a place for thee to dwell in for ever."
      —Solomon, at the dedication of the temple,
        1 KINGS 8:12–13 RSV

The Classic Fifties

THE YEARS 1953 to 1956 represented as much as any the Fifties of popular lore: fishtail automobiles; the hula hoop fad, introduced in 1954; Elvis, whose first big hit, "Heartbreak Hotel," was released in 1956; the daring new *Playboy* magazine, its first issue in fall 1953; and an increasingly affluent and youth-oriented culture. The jitters were diminishing, with the reassuring Dwight D. Eisenhower in the White House, the end of Korea and McCarthy in sight, and the spectre of nuclear apocalypse receding ever so slightly.

Church growth was continuing, and the return to religion remained a major theme. Church membership was claimed by 57 percent of the population in 1950, and 61 percent in 1955, with attendance, according to polls, reaching 49 percent of the population in December 1955, the highest on record before or since. (While I consider such self-reported poll figures on attendance to be considerably on the high side, they are useful for comparative purposes.) Religious songs were hitting big on Tin Pan Alley, as Patti Page urged sinners to "Cross over the Bridge," Kay Starr asked "Have You Talked to the Man Upstairs?" and Eddie Fisher declared that "My Friend Is the King of All Kings."[1] The year 1954 was "television's greatest," according to a 1994 book, and religion (despite the doubts of some TV executives) was part of its greatness, placing stellar names from Fulton Sheen to Billy Graham and Oral Roberts in the new living-room culture.[2]

The image of religious revival persisted. In a letter from the editor prefacing the issue of *Newsweek* that featured a cover story on Cardinal Spellman, publisher Theodore F. Mueller said, "More and more, in these troubled times, people are turning to religion for guidance and understanding," and mentioned a series of features on Billy Graham, Norman Vincent Peale, Christmas, and the like.[3] President Eisenhower's pastor, the Reverend Edward Elson, of Washington National Presbyterian church, said that Ike was leading "one of the great periods of religious renaissance."[4]

But what kind of religion was being revived by 1953?

For example, do we affirm nature, or not? A convoluted *Time* essay early in 1953 was based on Eric Voegelin's 1952 *New Science of Politics*, mentioned in the last chapter. This notable book of the day, though written "in somewhat technical language," was, according to *Time*, "an intellectual detective story, a quest through the history of Western thought for the culprits responsible for contemporary confusion." Most provocatively, it compared those whom Voegelin called "gnostics," who seek to rise above nature and find salvation through "hidden knowledge," with those prepared to serve the world through faith and works done in accordance with nature as it really is. Gnosticism "substitutes dreams for reason because it disregards the facts of the world that exists, misunderstands cause & effect, and has no luck in getting where it wants to get."[5] Thus, according to Voegelin and *Time*, gnosticism led to World War II and Russian armies in the middle of Europe, because thinkers and leaders influenced by it refused to see moral barbarism when it was there, preferring instead their dreams of how the world should be. According to Voegelin, the trouble begins with a "fallacious immanentization of the Christian eschaton." The gnostic elite fantasizes that by human effort based on "speculative knowledge" of that ultimate goal, their kind can create "a society that will come into being but have no end," an earthly paradise equal to God's.[6] Modern examples of the gnostic were Auguste Comte, Friedrich Nietzsche, and of course the communists, with their ideological credence that through understanding the secret laws of history and nature—those of dialectical materialism—human nature can be radically changed and perfected.

On the other side are those who recognize sin and the limitations of human nature, and for that reason are on the "good" side—the side of freedom, limited government, and a society unburdened by an imposed totalistic ideology. These include Reinhold Niebuhr, Mortimer Adler, and (needless to say) the Christians. They believe, *Time* assures us, in "progress" and the "American proposition," but not in human perfectibility. (The "American proposition" is never really defined, except negatively as something other than "gnostic" politics. We are told that because the American Revolution preceded the French, it was "relatively free of Gnostic influence." Apparently the difference is that the American republic was founded on a "natural" view of human nature and society that trusted individual freedom and allowed for sin, without professing any new or special knowledge about the subjects of nature or humanity.)

Regarded as period pieces, both the strained *Time* article and *The New Science of Politics* are of interest. Voegelin went so far as to define all modernity as gnosticism, a term that encompassed such diverse phenomena as progressivism, Marxism, psychoanalysis, fascism, and German National Socialism.[7] Later he clarified his position to the extent of revealing that modern persons who hold to "the gnostic attitude" share six characteristics: dissatisfaction with the world; confidence that the ills of the world stem from the way it is organized; surety that amelioration is possible; belief that the improvement must evolve historically; belief that humans can change the world; conviction that knowledge—gnosis—is the key to change.[8]

Revisited after the intense ideological passions of the day have waned a bit, the argument, like Voegelin's fascinating though tendentious book, seems rather forced and full of loose ends. One wonders, for example, exactly why the worldview of *Time*'s favorite orthodox Christian theologians, based on Christianity's quite extraordinary claims of special revelation, should be considered less "gnostic" than those of non-Christian modern thinkers. Perhaps one is right and the others wrong, but would the Apostles' Creed really appear more "natural" to the proverbial man from Mars than the *Communist Manifesto*? Both gnostic and naturalist themes have long lain side by side in U.S. culture. Herman Melville, well regarded in the Fifties, was a gnostic, not only by implication in *Moby Dick* but explicitly in his reading, his letters, and by way of several allusions; his pessimistic view that this world was wrongly made by a lesser god, and has ended up a mess in which outcasts should be most valorized, contrasts vividly with the sunny pantheistic naturalism of Ralph Waldo Emerson or Henry David Thoreau. But one could argue it was really the outcast Beats in the Fifties who saw the world as good in the tradition of the Transcendentalists they admired, and orthodox religiopolitical opinion that saw sin almost all the way up to the highest heaven and perceived their cold-war world in covertly gnostic or Manichaean terms.[9]

To be sure, as we have seen, Voegelin—whose position is a bit more complex than one would gather from the *Time* article—viewed the Puritans as prototypical gnostics. They were in fact "gnostic revolutionaries" set about to make the world a kingdom of the saints (145). But it was curiously out of Puritan culture that Melville and not a little of Niebuhr's cold-war sinful innocence had emerged. No small part of what Voegelin had to say, in his densely luminous way, about the Puritans might also have been directed toward early cold-war America. Maybe the sin-preoccupied neoorthodox theologians of those years, often Calvinist in intellectual heritage like the Puritans, worked both sides of the gnosticism-versus-nature street.

Nonetheless Voegelin's and *Time*'s definitions, together with the negative in which both cast what they call gnosticism, are quite revealing of 1952 and 1953. They display early, and heavy-handed, reaction against all of what had once been considered "modern" when that was a good word, even the progressivism once as American as the proverbial apple pie. Now, with enemies all around and sin rediscovered, it is something else, occultly linked to an ancient heresy.[10]

Thus the *Time* article revealed the desperate continuing effort of engaged pro-American intellectuals, like Niebuhr and others of Henry Luce's ideological and publishing empire, to find universal, even metaphysical, grounds for their cold-war position. The struggle was still, as in 1950, cast in a theological light. It was still the day when "it takes a faith to fight a faith," and it was possible to assume that the theological Christian worldview was foundational to the "free world." At the same time, as the Eisenhower era commenced, one sensed a slight opening toward pragmatism in the very claim that the "American proposition" entailed a recognition of human fallibility and demanded no more of human beings than what was possible in accordance with nature. That might suggest that the cold war was fading just a bit as an apocalyptic, war-in-heaven scenario, and becoming just a human problem to be solved by human means.

	Events: Bikini, the
Chapter 3	World Council, and
	the McCarthy Endgame

K<small>OREA WAS</small> a good place to test the perception that the cold war might be a manageable human problem. In early 1953, as it had been all through 1952, the Korean conflict had been essentially stalemated. Rather than ending in nuclear doomsday, as not a few anticipated in 1950, it had turned to tedium and mud. Now a new president promised a way out of the quagmire. All those who knew Ike expected his solution to be more pragmatic than apocalyptic.

The Christian camp, at least in its liberal wing, seemed increasingly to be looking at Korea as soluble, but to have few concrete ideas how to proceed; perhaps that was the message that, in the end, most effectively left the way open to pragmatists working within the limits of human nature. Around the time of Ike's inauguration, the *Christian Century* sent a letter to twenty-seven theologians and church leaders in the United States and Europe asking, "What can Christians contribute to peace in Korea?" Ten replied; of those, six declined to answer the question, saying they were too busy or did not know. None seemed to think there was any specifically Christian way out of the Korean mess itself, though a few had larger ideas reflecting longstanding positions.

Kirby Page, a pacifist since World War I, called for abandoning the arms race and diverting money spent for military purposes into "a stupendous program through the United Nations of technical assistance to increase the efficiency of agriculture and industry, worldwide sanitary and health measures, and comprehensive and adequate aid to education." But he never got to specifics on Korea. Reinhold Niebuhr characteristically said there is no "particularly Christian solution" for Korea. But he added there are "Christian resources"

we may need to avoid global conflict and "Christian resources will be necessary if we are to be modest enough, despite our power, to establish community with the free nations." Finally, "there seems to me also no way, without
the Christian faith, to bear the tremendous burdens which we have to bear
without certainty of historic success."[1]

Again the religious focus was on the big picture—but religion apparently
had no specific, concrete answer to Korea.

A further symposium appeared in the February 18 issue: "What Can Christians Contribute to Peace in Korea? A Symposium." This exchange consisted
of letters sent by less well-known but very earnest readers in response to the
earlier panel. All respondents favored forbearance; none favored "unleashing"
Chiang Kai-shek—a favorite remedy on the right—or blockading China. Otherwise they wavered between pacifistic idealism—sending support through such
agencies as the Church World Service, not "abandoning" Korea, and "going
the extra mile"—and a distasteful but perhaps helpful gesture like recognizing Red China.[2]

The war did end in a weary compromise, the boundary lines about where
they had been in 1950, with the signing of an armistice at Panmunjom on
July 19, 1953. Hostilities ended on July 27, and a massive exchange of prisoners commenced. South Korea's feisty and autocratic president, Syngman
Rhee, was loudly displeased, but his hands were tied by the unwillingness of
his more powerful ally to continue the conflict. Nearly everyone else, including most Americans, wanted nothing so much as to forget about Korea, which
they promptly did. "Chastened Nation Is Grateful for Truce," said the *Christian Century* in an editorial title.[3]

But the cold war carried on, and with it a war-based culture, economy,
and educational system in the United States. It was one of those changes so
pervasive it was hardly noticed, especially by those young people who were
most affected but who could hardly remember a time without war, hot or cold.
For many of them it was not really bad. Young men (not yet women) who
might otherwise not have had the opportunity for higher education could have
college paid by the Reserve Officer Training Corps (ROTC) or the GI bill;
they could receive advance training at government expense in fields like op-
tics or electronics as part of their army or navy service; if they did not stay in,
they could use the training and experience to good advantage in the job market, perhaps in the burgeoning and well-paying defense industries. In short,
debates over the moral issues involved in Korea, the cold war, and anticommunism skimmed the surface without touching a new U.S. way of life in which
people were more prosperous and better educated than ever before, but whose
prosperity, education, and values were profoundly intertwined with the cold
war.[4]

McCarthy: Decline and Fall

Amid cold-war questions, traumatizing reassessments, and benign life-style changes on the part of "innocent" Americans, Joseph McCarthy's anticommunist crusade continued, in some ways one of those political high dramas that actually mask more profound but quieter social changes on other levels. Here are some key events. On June 22, 1953 (just after the execution of the Rosenbergs on June 19) Joseph B. Matthews was signed on as chief investigator for McCarthy's committee. This individual's vita included credentials as a former Methodist missionary, a past Fellowship of Reconciliation executive, a one-time communist-front organizer, and now a fanatical anticommunist. McCarthy thought that the silver-haired, distinguished-looking Matthews would lend a sense of maturity to his staff definitely not conveyed by his cocky young lackeys, chief counsel Roy Cohn and investigator David Schine.[5]

But only days later reporters noticed an article Matthews had written for the July *American Mercury*, "Reds and Our Churches." Its opening sentence set the tone: "The largest single group supporting the Communist apparatus in the United States today is comprised of Protestant clergymen." This group was said to number "at least 7,000," and to have helped substantially to provide the party with "its agents, stooges, dupes, front men, and fellow-travelers."[6]

That was too much, and McCarthy faced a firestorm of protest, including open revolt on the part of the Democratic members of his own committee and blistering commentary in the Protestant press. On July 2 the Democrats on the Senate Investigations subcommittee denounced the article. The *Christian Century* editorialized that Matthews's essay was "its own best refutation. Its charges are venomous; its proofs puerile."[7] In true McCarthyite fashion, Matthews, while naming a number of names, had apparently counted everyone who had ever signed a petition or joined a group he considered communist-leaning; even so, he was able to produce less than seven hundred documented examples, most of them pacifists who signed such statements as the "Stockholm Peace Appeal," or concerned clergy who opposed the McCarren Immigration Act or otherwise questioned the rightist agenda.[8]

In March McCarthy's House colleague, Harold Velde of the House Un-American Activities Committee, had suggested investigating "subversive" influences among the clergy, and as we shall see received little but trouble in return.[9] McCarthy himself had always been careful to keep religion and religious figures out of his inquiries. The senator had apparently been unaware of Matthews's article, written several months before the appointment; now it put him in the extremely awkward position, as a member of the Catholic minority, of having to defend an irresponsible attack on the nation's largest religious grouping.

On July 7 McCarthy rejected Democratic calls for Matthews's resignation. But on July 9, after Republicans on the subcommittee engineered a face-saving compromise permitting McCarthy to hire and fire staff at will (which provoked a temporary Democratic walkout), Matthews's resignation was accepted. This was the same day that a board of the National Conference of Christians and Jews sent President Eisenhower a telegram signed by a minister, a priest, and a rabbi asking the president to condemn Matthews's article, and he had done so promptly. "Generalized and irresponsible attacks that sweepingly condemn the whole of any group of citizens," the president said, "are alien to America . . . when [they] condemn such a vast portion of the churches and clergy as to create doubt in the loyalty of all, the damage to our nation is multiplied."[10] Though he did not name Matthews, the reference was clear; it was the first time Ike had so pointedly and publicly rebuked McCarthy and his works. However, the senator had removed Matthews before knowing of Ike's statement.

Many Catholic periodicals, however, wanted to give Matthews at least the benefit of the doubt and criticized the Catholic signer of the telegram to Ike, Father John A. O'Brien, a philosophy professor from Notre Dame. Attacks on Father O'Brien stressed the failure of those who telegraphed the president to acknowledge that Matthews, near the end of his article, had conceded that "the great majority of the Protestant clergy are loyal." O'Brien responded on September 3 by issuing a statement declaring, "If the limitation had been placed next to the opening summary sentence where it belonged, the sweeping and shocking character of the charge would have been obviated and the misunderstanding avoided." As it was, with this sentence "buried under 4, 257 words and weirdly placed on the very last page, quite naturally the public regarded it as an attack on Protestant ministers as a whole."

O'Brien stated that he was happy to join in the defense of the Protestants, not as a matter of partisan politics but to support justice and truth. "A careful study of Mr. Matthews' charges," he said, "convinces me that most of them boil down to the simple fact that some ministers, like many other good people, unwittingly allowed themselves or their names to be used by ostensibly idealistic peace organizations which concealed communist aims. That's a far cry from 7,000 Protestant ministers consciously supporting the communist apparatus."[11]

A related article in the *Christian Century*, together with other information on Matthews, casts an interesting light on this episode. Matthews (1894–1966) as a young man had been a Methodist missionary in Java, but after a very short career of teaching and translating had been expelled by the East Indies' Dutch overlords for his sympathy toward Indonesian patriots opposing their rule. A gifted linguist, he then did graduate work in Hebrew and the Old Testament, teaching at Drew and at Scarritt College, a Methodist institution in Tennessee. In both settings Matthews got into various kinds of trouble for liberal views on the Bible and race, and his tenures were short; in Tennessee he was accused of hosting a mixed-race party.

The young radical then became a socialist and, in 1929, executive secretary of the Fellowship of Reconciliation. He also became the first head of the American League against War and Fascism, generally regarded as the most successful communist "front" in the United States. In December 1933 he was forced to leave the Christian pacifist FOR because of his sympathy for communism, and he was suspended by the Socialist Party in 1935 for the same reason. His views in those days appear to have been a mirror image of his later assertions. He "proved" in his McCarthyite days that the Protestant churches were riddled with supporters of communism; in 1935 he had coauthored a book, *Partners in Plunder*, which "proved" no less decisively that J. Pierpont Morgan owned the Episcopal church, Andrew Mellon the Presbyterians, and the Rockefellers the Baptists.[12] He was conspicuous at rallies and demonstrations for the left in which communists were also quite visibly involved in the early and middle Thirties, and he then broke his ties with the church.

The 180-degree turn in Matthews's attitude came after he took yet another position destined to end disastrously for him. In mid-1935 he became an executive for Consumer's Research, Inc., an organization that distributed information on innumerable products to consumers. There he had to face a strike of its employees. Despite pleas from such old associates as Norman Thomas, Matthews's labor sympathies dissolved when he found himself on the other side of the table; he was outraged by the strike, considered the union's demands unacceptable, allegedly refused to negotiate, and blamed the communists. The confrontation reached the point of angry picketing, stone throwing, broken windows, jailed strikers, and subsequent hunger strikes in prison.

Consumer's Research was virtually destroyed; many of its locked-out employees regrouped to form the successful Consumer's Reports, and Matthews moved on to testify, in 1938, before Martin Dies's House Un-American Activities Committee. For this body he named ninety-four alleged communist-front groups with which he had been associated. He was then hired as chief investigator by Dies; when he left the committee in 1945, he took with him numerous files and lists of names, together with important contacts among other disillusioned ex-communists. Reportedly the best such privately held file in the nation, Matthews's lists were to become invaluable resources for McCarthy in the Senate.[13] He may well have been feeding McCarthy with names and material since the start of the senator's crusade with the Wheeling speech of 1950.

Like Whittaker Chambers and many another Thirties communist or "comsymp," Matthews had now let anticommunism radicalize and devour him to the same degree the Party or its fronts once had. If communism left any truly poisonous legacy in U.S. life, it was its passion for extremist and duplicitous intrigue, for suspicion and anger and leading double lives, for considering the truth merely a tool to be used in the service of a greater cause, a tool that once released could be used as venomously against the left as for it, not seldom by the same person.

There was conspiratorial comradeship to be found in such circles, to be sure. The columnist Westbrook Pegler, another anticommunist often accused of irresponsibility or worse, spoke of Matthews fondly as a member of "our cell of Red-baiters," an informal group that, he said, often got together for a "small festive evening," during which Matthews, an amateur chef, would serve the rightist clique a gourmet meal.[14] But all his knowledge and all his friendships were not to save him, or his latest employer, from their own excesses. July 1953 was the first significant milestone in McCarthy's fall, and after that month Matthews had little prominence save in the most ultraright circles. In the 1960s his name appeared on the masthead of *American Opinion*, the mouthpiece of the John Birch Society.

A final note on the Matthews affair: the historian of McCarthyism, Donald Crosby, believes that, contrary to what one might have liked to think, despite the former Methodist's fall and the Catholic senator's humiliation, the decade's already precarious Catholic-Protestant relations were worsened by the imbroglio. The charges were seen as an attack on Protestant loyalty, and the "gloating" over them in which some pro-McCarthy Catholic periodicals unwisely indulged infuriated Protestants, including some conservative southern Democrats of that faith whose opinions shifted against the senator.[15] But though Protestants and Catholics found unity on the matter difficult, anticommunism continued to ride high in 1953.

The atmosphere of that summer of 1953 may be gauged from the declaration of Representative John Pillior, Republican from New York, on July 6 at the Hawaii statehood hearings raucously underway at the same time, that if the islands were admitted as a state, it was "a certainty its two senators would be Soviet agents"—an assumption presumably made in the wake of the recent sentencing of six Hawaiian communists in Honolulu. It was also the summer of the July truce in Korea, of Edmund Hillary and Norgay Tenzing's conquest of Mt. Everest, of the Soviet Union's H-bomb in August, and of articles on an unprecedented building boom in churches and home bomb shelters.

Communism and the Clergy

At virtually the same time, July 21–22, 1953, Methodist bishop G. Bromley Oxnam voluntarily confronted the House Un-American Activities Committee. The prominent liberal churchman, bishop of the Washington, D.C., area, had requested and obtained the opportunity to appear before the members of Congress who had over some seven years selectively released material that, in his words, was "prepared in a way capable of creating the impression that I have been and am sympathetic to communism and therefore subversive." Given the rare privilege of making a fifteen-minute opening statement, Oxnam sought redress for damages. He called on the committee to repent of "practices that jeopardize the rights of free men won after a thousand years of struggle for political and religious freedom" and demanded that one of its members, Donald L. Jackson of California, apologize on the floor of the House of Representatives for a March 17, 1953, speech in which he had accused the bishop of "serving God on Sunday and Communist fronts for the balance of the week over . . . a long period of time."

In denial of this accusation, Oxnam stated that he had been actively opposed to communism all his life. This opposition was affirmed, he said, whenever he recited the Apostles' Creed: "When I say I believe in God the Father Almighty, I strike at the fundamental error of Communism, which is atheism." He went on to say that he believed in Christ and a spiritual view of life, whereas communism rejects Christ and is based on materialism.

Both sides knew that this confrontation was being carefully watched, above all by churchpeople. The deluge of letters, the constant phone calls, the media presence, the overflow crowds striving to gain admission to the hearing room testified to that. Both sides were carefully prepared, Oxnam with briefcases full of documents. As a favor he was also permitted to have with him counsel in the person of Charles P. Parlin, a New York attorney.

Bishop Oxnam was taxed with a number of quotes from sermons and other addresses or writings produced over many years of an active ministerial life, often cited by his harassers with little regard for the context or occasion. When charged with taking positions compatible with the communist line, he responded with his reformist desire "to make the society impregnable to communist attack." The principal associational charge was in regard to his wartime membership in the Massachusetts Council of American-Soviet Friendship, and his having been invited to join it by an alleged communist. The Methodist bishop responded that he had resigned from this council in 1943, that at the time, when Russia was an ally, many prominent persons, including Secretary of State Cordell Hull, were also members, and that none other than General Dwight D. Eisenhower, now president, had once recommended the organization.

All through the hearing, which ground along until midnight the first day, neither the bishop nor the Republican majority on the committee, chaired by Harold Velde of Illinois, himself a Methodist, showed much give, although the Democrats increasingly asked questions helpful to Oxnam. The bishop maintained his stamina and showed himself well prepared with documentation to support his answers, but the committee was in no mood to recant or apologize. The best it would do was vote unanimously at the end that Oxnam was not affiliated with the Communist Party; it then divided on strict party lines, five to four, in favor of saying he had given aid and comfort to communism through association with communist-front organizations. By then, however, such votes in themselves meant little.

The Washington prelate kept his position and his dignity, and the hearings hurt the McCarthy cause as much as helped it. *Time* considered Oxnam clearly the winner.[16] The country was slowly making up its mind; the next year, with the aid of the far more disastrous McCarthy-Army hearings, it would turn moderately against the style of anticommunism McCarthy and Velde represented and restore a slim Democratic majority to both houses of Congress, though the HUAC would linger on into the Sixties.[17]

The J. B. Matthews and G. Bromley Oxnam affairs together inspired a hard-hitting but nuanced article on the situation by Reinhold Niebuhr, "Communism and the Clergy." He acknowledged that there may be a few "Stalinists" in the churches, but so few as to be insignificant. Most of those behind Matthews's "ridiculous charge" were pacifists, "many of whom (foolishly in my opinion) signed the 'Stockholm Peace Appeal.'" As for Oxnam, "no one who knows the bishop and has knowledge of his activities would accuse him of Communist sympathies. But he is undoubtedly a social 'liberal' and has been active in many social causes, some of which had Communists enlisted in them."

The great theologian's contempt for investigating committees is clear and complete, though he grants that he and others were once (read the Thirties, now being dredged up time and time again) too sympathetic to Marxism, which, "in its orthodox variety, makes for a monopoly of political and economic power which is dangerous to justice." Niebuhr went on to say, "Those of us who were critical of capitalism were in short too uncritical of the Marxist alternative, even when we rejected the Communist version of Marxism and espoused the democratic Marxism."

"The present writer," he added, "is ready to confess to his complicity in these errors, though he is quick to affirm that the Marxist errors do not make more true the ridiculous dogma of laissez faire."[18]

The surfacing of J. B. Matthews on McCarthy's committee must have brought back ironic memories to Niebuhr, a man by now well attuned to irony.

In 1933 Reinhold Niebuhr had been chair of the executive council of the Fellowship of Reconciliation when, after a bitter debate within the membership of FOR, that council voted eighteen to thirteen on December 16 to oust Matthews from his position as executive director, on the grounds of his affiliation with communist-front organizations that rejected Christian pacifism, and Matthews's own increasingly outspoken secularism and support for revolutionary violence in the struggle against capitalism.

Niebuhr himself had voted with the minority. Though he thought Matthews foolish, he did not entirely disagree with him on the question of violence, as was evident in his 1932 book, *Moral Man and Immoral Society*, which had already expressed his break with absolute pacifism. "My political convictions are on the side of [Matthews]," he had said once to Kirby Page, "but my personal friendships are on the other side, so I feel like a lonely soul." He felt he had no choice then but to resign from the FOR executive council, and the episode was perhaps a significant step in the move he had already begun away from pacifism and the extreme left.[19]

Niebuhr's involvement in these events, described in Richard Fox's *Reinhold Niebuhr: A Biography*, is an interesting and significant icon of how the Spirit moved in the United States in the Fifties. Niebuhr emerged from the war years a convinced "Christian realist." Still a social liberal, he was also staunchly anticommunist, sure that the Communist Party was simply an agency of the Soviet Union, itself a ruthless and expansive dictatorship no better than fascism. (Indeed, he had been known to say that because communism could appear less heinous than Nazism—with a gloss of idealism, without the crude racism of the Hitlerites—it was actually more dangerous because it made totalitarianism more seductive to well-meaning reformers [228–229].)

By 1949 Niebuhr's trenchant combination of idealism and political reality had attracted attention in the corridors of power, in large part because he had become the favorite theologian of the Luce publications. He served as an occasional State Department advisor and delegate to such bodies as UNESCO. However, when the Korean War commenced, Niebuhr opposed a large U.S. commitment, particularly resisting General Douglas MacArthur's desire to carry the battle to China.

This was not because he was averse to anticommunist wars as such, but because he believed that for the United States to became entangled in Korea would give a boost to the communists in Europe, perhaps even permitting a Russian invasion of the West. The "free world can live if we lose Asia," he said, speaking the language of the cold war as global chess game, and reflecting the Eurocentric myopia of most U.S. policymakers and public opinion at the time, "but we cannot live in security if Russia should come into possession of the economic and technical resources of Europe." It was Europe that must be defended at all costs; he was even prepared to give Taiwan to Red China, despite Chiang Kai-shek, in exchange for a compromise on Korea (241).

In late 1950 Niebuhr became an official consultant of the State Department, which necessitated an FBI "loyalty investigation" of the theologian that lasted through the next year. Besides that, in the frenzied atmosphere of 1951, the coldest of all cold-war years, packs of volunteer loyalty "experts" were more than willing to join the hunt. In the case of Niebuhr, despite his present positions, they found much to report. A group called the American Council of Christian Laymen alleged the eminent theologian had belonged to no less than twenty-four "God-hating, Un-American organizations." Many of the references were to forgotten connections from the Thirties. But even now the intellectuals' favorite anticommunist was taxed with chairing the Resettlement Campaign for Exiled Professionals, which brought displaced European intellectuals (in certain circles, a description virtually synonymous with leftists if not communist sympathizers) to the United States, and with wishing to "abandon" Chiang and Taiwan, sacred calves to many on the far right.

In response, Niebuhr veered to the right himself, expressing his anticommunism more and more vehemently, and emphasizing that the Resettlement Campaign was now engaged in rescuing persecuted anticommunist intellectuals from behind the Iron Curtain. By 1953 he supported executing the Rosenbergs: "Traitors are never ordinary criminals and the Rosenbergs are quite obviously fiercely loyal Communists."[20] The same year, in the wake of the Matthews accusations and the Oxnam hearings, he was excoriating the hypocrisy and weak-headedness of "fellow travelers" while at the same time condemning the stupidity, as he saw it, of the McCarthy-Velde HUAC investigations, whose scattershot attacks were doing as much harm as good by mixing the few real offenders in with numerous innocents, thereby discrediting the whole process.

His earlier *Christian Century* article, "Communism and the Clergy," was only a preview of one Niebuhr wrote for the masses in *Look*, published later in 1953. The latter essay had originally been intended as a profile of J. B. Matthews, based on Niebuhr's recollections of him in the radical days of the Thirties. It no doubt grew out of Niebuhr's worthy concern that the anticommunist cause, in which he honestly and deeply believed, should not be permitted to be usurped by the likes of McCarthy and Velde, whom he despised. There was, he was convinced, a legitimate liberal democratic case against Marxism and communism. It ought to be voiced by liberal clergy like himself alongside their democratic support of prolabor, social-justice causes, including many regarded as "leftist." But this stance had been confused and perverted by the very small number of clergy who were actually procommunist.

Thus the *Look* piece turned into a general discussion of Matthews's charge that seven thousand Protestant clergy had been influenced by "red propaganda." Niebuhr called Matthews "almost as dangerous to democracy in the anti-Communist phase of his career as he was in its Communist phase"—a remarkable statement in view of Niebuhr's support of Matthews at the time of the earlier phase. But Niebuhr, quite willing to flush out the real red offenders, went on to say that "Matthews, who is fairly unscrupulous in handling total figures, is reasonably accurate when he actually names names. He has identified with considerable accuracy the slightly more than a dozen fellow travelers in the churches." And Niebuhr proceeded to name the names in *Look*.[21]

One of those named, Guy Emery Shipler, editor of the *Churchman*, a liberal Episcopalian magazine, was understandably indignant, pointing out that both he and the periodical had been critical of communism and the Soviets since the Thirties, and demanding Niebuhr's evidence. Niebuhr weakly replied, as Matthews might have, that he had no time to dig out "specific evidence"; he said the charge was derived from "impressions" based on reading Shipler's magazine. Shipler pointed out that Niebuhr himself had been indicted on no better evidence in publications of such groups as the American Council of Christian Laymen. Finally, a year later, in the relatively more clement atmosphere of 1954, Niebuhr recanted and apologized to Shipler. He also repented of his support for the execution of the Rosenbergs.[22]

In January of 1953, Arthur Miller's play *The Crucible*, on Salem witch-hunting, had opened on Broadway. In March it won the Tony Award for best play of the year, and its topical relevance was widely noted.

As the sacred vision of the American mission faded slightly in practical terms, its theoretical affirmation reached new heights. Action to add the words "under God" to the Pledge of Allegiance was introduced into the House by Representative Louis C. Rabaut. This move was presented in *Time* directly underneath an article reporting that a judge in Hawaii had refused citizenship to a Pole, who had been imprisoned for five years by the Nazis and who had served in the U.S. Army, because he was an atheist and refused to say "So help me God" at the end of the oath of citizenship.[23]

On May 28 President Eisenhower signed the bill adding "under God" to the Pledge of Allegiance. In a July 4 editorial, the *Living Church* perceived the addition as "one more example of the renewed religious earnestness of our nation," not a "declaration of national righteousness." But that presumption had perhaps been rejected on a more serious level with the simultaneous rejection of McCarthyism.

Let me add a personal note to this account of mid-Fifties communism and the clergy in the United States. In the summer of 1956, while traveling and studying in England, I attended a service in Canterbury Cathedral in which the then notorious "Red Dean" of Canterbury, the Very Reverend Hewlett Johnson, was the minister and preacher. Already past eighty, this high cleric of the Church of England (not to be confused with the archbishop of Canterbury, the primate), with his flowing white hair, colorful vestments, and ecclesiastical dignity could have stepped out of Anthony Trollope's *Barchester Towers*. He chanted the ancient words of the liturgy in a clear silvery voice, backed by a well-scrubbed and sublimely English cathedral boys' choir.

But when he began the sermon, the dean's aged eyes flashed with true believer's fire. He commenced with a scathing account of the social evils perpetrated by capitalism in the West. Then with prophetic vision he looked east, and saw there a new social order being built that, though it disdained the name of Christ, was in fact doing Christ's work of justice and care far better than we. With fervor he described how this new faith, communism, was passionately held by millions who, despite a few "dark blots" in its past, shared its vision and knew how it had changed their lives for the better. He said that he was "personally convinced" that a synthesis of communism and Christianity was possible.[24]

I was aware that the undoubtedly gullible dean of Canterbury had few followers in commonsense England. Most leading churchpeople, including the archbishop, had publicly distanced themselves from his position. At the same time, coming from McCarthy-era America, I could not but be struck by the immense gulf between the two societies on how communism among the clergy was regarded. Here was a priest very openly and outspokenly a real communist or "comsymp" to a degree most of Matthews's targets were not, occupying a position of national prominence unequaled by the office of any of the harried divines in the United States. Yet the British, while generally disagreeing with the dean of Canterbury, seemed largely unperturbed by the spectacle, disinterested in mounting a witch-hunt and willing to let what was fatuous in his words speak for itself. People were generally content to regard him as just another pulpit eccentric. The Anglican church has enjoyed or endured more than a few clerical cranks over the centuries and has managed to survive them. My English friends expressed to me a rather pointed pride in the fact that, in their system, regardless of what one thought of Johnson's views, he retained "parson's freehold." (Still, the archbishop and other cathedral clergy repeatedly and publicly dissociated themselves from the dean's political views, and there were in fact strong calls from various quarters for his removal; in 1963, at eighty-eight, he was finally pushed into retirement.)

American Innocence and the World

The coronation of Queen Elizabeth on June 2, 1953, occasioned great interest in the United States, where millions listened in via radio and later watched the sacred drama on their black-and-white TVs. For many it seemed to raise wistful yearnings for a different sort of relation to the human symbols of state than the noisy, accusatory politics of the dominant power that summer. Some opined that the obsessive American regard at that time for such symbols of patriotism as the flag and such fateful abstractions as "Americanism" reflected the lack of a focal human symbol like the queen, grounded in long tradition.

Reinhold Niebuhr, remarking on the phenomenal U.S. interest in the event, called it "a tribute to the permanent power of poetry in politics in a nonpoetic technological age." He then made the rather more original observation that the interest was also a tribute *to* technology, which had made the coronation's transmission across the Atlantic possible.[25] Indeed much of the twentieth century, when modernism crested and with it the rationalized, unitary state, was also a high point for the symbolic, if not the political, value of constitutional monarchs or their surrogates in the dictator or the quasi-monarchical president. Modernism needed such symbols to cap its drives toward cultural and political unity, and its linear view of history culminating in present success; it has only been with the postmodern failure of such values that monarchy has fallen into the decline one now sees in Britain and elsewhere.

If Americans in this slightly incongruous case showed their love for a foreign nation, they were increasingly becoming aware that they themselves were not always loved. An article entitled "America the Unloved" noted in people overseas a rising penchant for "blaming all their troubles on something the U.S. has or hasn't done." It went on to observe that "the psychology behind their widespread lack of appreciation for our superlative qualities is familiar. Nobody loves a boss, even when he tries not to be bossy. Nobody loves a benefactor, even when he tries to keep all condescension out of his benefactions. . . . Americans should accept the fact of their present unpopularity, and not let politicians at home and abroad, who seek easy cheers by playing to the galley, stampede them into calling for a foreign policy based in emotion."[26] That was in 1953; the next year, events from Bikini to Guatemala were to present Americans with ears to hear some samples of the substance behind the complaints.

On April 29, 1953, the Grand Prix of the Cannes festival went to the French film *The Wages of Fear*, which was criticized by some Americans for anti-American overtones.

Americans could also look critically at foreign events, and not only when they involved communists. Paul Blanshard, the inveterate watchdog of

Catholic machinations, now turned his attention to Archbishop Gerald P. O'Hara of Atlanta-Savannah, who was presently also serving in the Vatican diplomatic corps as papal nuncio to the Irish Republic. Blanshard was in that highly Catholic country on a fact-finding mission, and the recently passed anticommunist McCarren Act, which called for loss of citizenship for Americans caught in the service of a foreign power, was on his mind. He put his question this way: "May an American serve as a Vatican diplomat in a foreign country and still retain American citizenship?" The Protestant visitor was resented by the Irish for his impertinence; some called for his expulsion from Ireland. But the Irish minister for foreign affairs, Frank Aiken, said of Blanshard's vendetta, "It is not worth noticing." The Vatican's response was to affirm that a nuncio does not represent a temporal state but the spiritual office of the pope; so a nuncio of U.S. citizenship is not in violation of the McCarren Act.[27] But Blanshard's irritating penchant for responding to the Roman See's anticommunism with "You're another!" once more made headlines.

On December 8, 1953, the Feast of the Immaculate Conception, Pius XII opened the 1954 Marian Year commemorating the hundredth anniversary of the proclamation of that dogma by Pius IX.

A Year of Events: 1954

Even though culturally 1954 may be considered one of the "classic" Fifties years, it was in fact a year of traumatic events that would cast shadows into the future, and there would be much religious commentary on them. Here are the four most important.

THE McCARTHY-ARMY HEARINGS

In 1954, Joseph McCarthy overreached himself. In October of 1953, he had started an investigation of the army, focusing on the Fort Monmouth Army Signal Corps Center in New Jersey. In January 1954, the senator went further, charging the promotion at Fort Kilmer of a supposedly leftist captain, Irving Peress. In the process, he viciously attacked the commanding officer, General Ralph Zwicker, a World War II combat hero, and for good measure the secretary of the army, Robert Stevens. The country was enflamed by these charges, and President Eisenhower, whose second home was the army, was enraged. His administration finally stood up to McCarthy, charging him with trying to blackmail the army. On April 22 a Senate subcommittee began to probe the affair—with an audience of some twenty million television viewers, who saw firsthand what a large number perceived as bullying tactics and unproved charges.

That final major act of the McCarthy drama, the McCarthy-Army hearings dominated the news most of the year, and as they ground on McCarthy's popularity perceptibly faded. Apart from holdout McCarthy loyalists like Cardinal Spellman, church leaders and religious publications were beginning to express open negativity toward the blundering anticommunist crusader. The two leading Roman Catholic intellectual periodicals unstintingly criticized their senatorial coreligionist. By May 14 *Commonweal* was commenting that the hearings had value only in that no one who had followed them could "continue to take McCarthy at his own valuation."[28] *America* condemned the investigative senator harshly on May 22 in its own widely publicized editorial. The Jesuit periodical presented the hearings as fundamentally a struggle between the legislative and executive branches of the U.S. government that did not bode well for the separation of powers. Referring to the deepening crisis in Southeast Asia—a real communist threat overshadowed in the news by McCarthy's alleged one—the editorial concluded, "If he [McCarthy] insists on his piecemeal and 'peaceful' overthrow of the presidency, he may do great harm to U.S. policy by his so far very successful diversionary tactics."[29]

It is indicative of the temper of the times, and in this case of many Roman Catholics in particular, that even as temperate an editorial as this should have received wide publicity and a vociferous response. A couple of weeks later *America* offered a second editorial that began like this:

> The Associated Press "shocked" a great many Catholic newspaper readers by its May 17 story on this review's editorial, "Peaceful Overthrow of the U.S. Presidency" (5/22). We regret we cannot acknowledge the letters of protest sent us by Senator McCarthy's admirers nor discuss the McCarthy issue over the telephone with the many Catholics who feel conscience-bound to set us—and Attorney General Brownell—right on the constitutional separation of powers. An uncritically pro-McCarthy diocesan weekly immediately complained about our editorial. It relayed to its readers the assurance that America "represents the thinking of a small minority of members of the Society of Jesus."

America regarded these criticisms as out of line. The magazine emphasized that it is intended to represent the thinking of neither a majority nor a minority of Jesuits, priests, Catholics, or anyone else, but only of the editorial board selected by the Jesuit order for that purpose, and given wide editorial freedom. It wished that more Catholic individuals and papers had a better regard for freedom of expression.[30]

All of this, however, masked a crisis going on behind the scenes at *America* and in the Jesuit order in America. The journal's anti-McCarthy stand had in fact offended many Catholic readers, including many Jesuits; reportedly there were houses of the Society of Jesus in which passions ran so deeply that discussion of McCarthy had to be forbidden. A shot was fired through the door of a Jesuit church in New York, and St. Patrick's Cathedral canceled its subscription to the magazine. After the May 22 editorial had been favorably and unfavorably publicized nationwide, on May 29 the superiors of the order in the United States suddenly ordered the periodical to say no more about McCarthy on the grounds that Jesuits should not engage in "disputes among Catholics," and moreover this directive was to be kept secret. The editor of *America*, Father Robert Hartnett, immediately protested this abrupt command, claiming that it would be impossible for such an injunction to be kept secret, and that it was contrary to the freedom of expression he thought he had been promised. A compromise was reached allowing that editorials on the controversial subject would be reviewed by all editors and would be published only when it was clearly for the "good of the Church" to do so.

So matters might have remained had not the Father General of the Jesuits in Rome, the Reverend John Baptist Janssens, entered the debate in June 1954 with an order that the magazine be completely silenced on the issue. From then forward nothing was said in *America* about McCarthy, and Father Hartnett, saying he was thoroughly "sick of the thing," resigned as editor the next year.[31]

Deviations such as those of *Commonweal* and *America* were not well received in Cardinal Spellman's office either. From his headquarters in New York came word that "the publication known as the *Commonweal* is conducted by Catholic laymen, and at times even carries articles by members of the clergy. This publication does not have an ecclesiastical approval. . . . It is unfortunate that the *Commonweal* is described as a 'Catholic' magazine, for . . . such is not the case."[32] (We have already noted that *America* was said to represent only "the thinking of a small minority of members of the Society of Jesus.")

But Roman Catholic auxiliary bishop Bernard Sheil of Chicago, as we have seen, proceeded to condemn McCarthy. The NCC protested against McCarthy. The Methodist *Christian Advocate* editorially quoted the Reverend Ralph Sockman, Methodism's best-known urban pastor, to the effect that "American common sense soon will lay the dust stirred up by demagogues, and by those who will find it profitable to play on people's fears and passions," demagoguery based partly on "faked evidence and phony statistics." The same periodical a little later ran an article by the lawyer who had counseled Methodist bishop G. Bromley Oxnam at his HUAC hearings, accusing his investigators of sloppy research and inadequate regard for the rights of the accused.[33]

The Eisenhower administration no longer hesitated to condemn the Wisconsin Republican and distance itself from him. In that atmosphere, the GOP was deeply divided. After the Democrats narrowly regained control of both houses of Congress in the fall elections, the Senate voted to censure McCarthy on December 2.

The Living Church, an Episcopal weekly of high-church leanings, and of no particular predisposition toward liberalism in either theology or politics, under the editorship of Peter Day in the 1950s offered some of the best editorials to be found anywhere in religion journalism. On the McCarthy-Army hearings it said in April:

> If there is any one place where a Congressman has the right and duty to investigate Communism, it is in the army. There is therefore something ironical about the fact that the public has become upset about the tactics of the junior Senator from Wisconsin only when he began to look into something strictly within the lines of his authority and responsibilities.
>
> The secret of the public upset is this—we have all known right along that witch-hunting tactics were not really security measures, but rather a grisly form of public entertainment. But we do not choose to have those on whom our lives and safety depend made the butt of the show. When investigation of communism really comes close to our security we want it done in an intelligent and skillful manner, not for emotional effect.[34]

With perceptions like this McCarthyism as a psychodrama of national purgation was largely finished, for when a liturgical mystery is seen for what it is, an act of theater and the manipulation of special effects, its days are numbered. With it went the brief lifespan of the early Fifties possibility that the United States would embrace anticommunism as a sort of national religion, a state church in the sense suggested by the West Virginia creedal interrogations, the purging of impurities, and the theologizing of the likes of Whittaker Chambers and even Reinhold Niebuhr, rather than just a matter of secular policy.

But another sacred drama was about to begin, one of a very different nature, which would be consummated in the Sixties.

THE SUPREME COURT DESEGREGATION DECISION

In *Brown v. Board of Education*, the Supreme Court on May 17 unanimously declared that racial segregation in itself violates the U.S. Constitution. The foundation was laid for what would prove to be a decade and a half of racial activism and change. Most religious periodicals supported or ignored the decision. As a token of the way some religious leaders even in the South were moving toward integration in anticipation of the decision, or independently of it, the Roman Catholic archbishop of San Antonio had forbidden segregation in Catholic schools on April 30, before the Supreme Court acted.

The Living Church in a May 30 editorial situated the Supreme Court decision nicely in the context of the times. The piece began with a characteristic evocation of a view of history, with a bow to what Time would have called the "American proposition": "The distinguishing principle of modern history is probably no great theological truth nor profound philosophical insight nor ringing political rallying-cry. Rather, it is probably a slow-growing and unspectacular development in world affairs expressed in the Declaration of Independence by the phrase, 'a decent respect to the opinion of mankind.'" In this light the Supreme Court had made its decision, and one not irrelevant to the world struggle, also never far from anyone's mind in 1954; the editorial later noted, "For many years Communism has been seeking to capture the conscience of mankind by an appeal to the solidarity of the human race; but now the situation is reversed, and it is America that stands for human solidarity while Communism seeks to inflame nationalistic and racial passions." The churches, we are told, had done much quietly to prepare for the great changes now to come, especially in the South, but a great deal of that story would not or could not be told, and that was just as well: "It is better for the Church to make history than to make news."[35]

Clergy were generally well-meaning but not entirely unanimous in their response. A later article in the Living Church presented reaction statements by bishops and other Episcopal leaders in the South. Most were supportive but laced their statements with cautions about the speed of implementation. Perhaps the most outspoken was by Bishop Girault M. Jones of Louisiana, who said what many no doubt felt: "The basic problem is not one of color but of culture." It was, that prelate said, a question of how to give "Negroes" rights without having to "lower the cultural environment in which our children live. If in some way we can have one without sacrificing the other, we shall have solved the problem."[36]

Even before the decision, the leading Methodist periodical had presented an article on how that denomination's extensive system of colleges and universities, some of them traditionally black, would meet the verdict should the Supreme Court rule against segregation. For some, racial change would take time; a major concern would be the impact on Methodist schools for "Negroes"; they want integration, but have special needs.[37] The Court decision was welcomed as in line with a series of Methodist statements; the church warned editorially against the dangers of expedients such as doing away with public schools, advocated by many diehards in the South. The church must lead—and realize there are many kinds of segregation besides those now outlawed, including some in the pews.[38]

THE H-BOMB

Although the first thermonuclear device had been tested at Eniwetok November 1, 1952, the blast of March 1, 1954, on Bikini atoll in the Marshall islands produced panic throughout the world. This was a bomb of unprecedented power, five times that of the 1952 device. It came after the first Soviet hydrogen-bomb test of August 1953, thus suggesting an arms race at the most destructive level imaginable.

Worse, there seemed reason to think that something had gone wrong, that the explosion had been even greater than anticipated. Both the November 1952 and the March 1954 tests had, in fact, at first been concealed and acknowledged by the Atomic Energy Commission only after letters home from servicemen had reported an extraordinary occurrence. In the latter case, in mid-March 1954 it was reported in the press that a marine corporal had written his mother in Cincinnati that something had shaken the island of Kwajalein where he was located, nearly two hundred miles from Bikini—and that then two destroyers had arrived bearing "natives of one of the Marshall islands suffering from various burns and radioactivity." Confronted with this disclosure, the AEC acknowledged "in the course of an atomic routine test in the Marshall Islands, 28 United States personnel and 236 residents were transported from neighboring atolls to Kwajalein island . . . the individuals were unexpectedly exposed to some radiation."[39]

Although the public was assured that this unfortunate happenstance was nothing to worry about, more was to come. A Japanese fishing vessel had been eighty miles outside the closed area around the blast site on that fateful March 1; on March 16 it reached home port with twenty-three crew members suffering from radiation burns, five seriously. The Japanese, who alone among the peoples of earth had already experienced the agony brought by atomic radiation, were in near hysteria. In the days following, other Japanese fishing ships, nine in all, came in radioactive from as far away as eight hundred miles beyond the epicenter. In Japan, as the sailors were rushed to hospitals, police and shoppers went on a wild quest to track down all the fish, now radioactive, unloaded off those contaminated boats. Fear rode in their wakes; insistent calls rose for an end to testing—calls quite ignored, of course, by those in high places.[40]

Parliamentary outrage, even terror, was expressed in several capitals. Prime Minister Churchill told the House of Commons, in a voice cracking with intensity, that the atomic worries "fill my mind out of all comparison with anything else," and in India Prime Minister Nehru called for a worldwide disarmament conference.[41] The fear was generated by belief that this weapon was no less than the ultimate instrument of mass destruction, from which there would be no escape. The H-bomb, it was widely believed, was capable of destroying all humanity and perhaps all life as the price of someone's "victory" in a war with only losers. The chair of the Atomic Energy Commission, Admiral Lewis Strauss, said himself that this latest weapon had five thousand times the explosive force of the Hiroshima A-bomb and could wipe out an entire metropolitan area up to a radius of fifty miles. Shelters were virtually useless; there was simply nowhere to run from the new agent of apocalypse.[42] Even so, cold warriors talked of the "availability" of still more upgraded products in the same line: the nitrogen bomb, the cobalt bomb . . .

But as the *Christian Century* put it, "This is the end of the line. The road runs no farther. The desperate race for atomic power has reached its ultimate goal. . . . We live in a nightmare world." To be sure, as the same article reminded us, President Eisenhower had assured Americans that their fears were unworthy of them, that the United States was "the greatest force that God had ever allowed to exist on his footstool," one that with the help of the new weapons can "lead this world to a peaceful and secure existence." Yet even the smiling chief executive had to observe that "the advances of science have outraced our social consciousness."[43]

It was untrue, as the *Living Church* alleged, that "revelations as to the awesome destructive possibilities of the hydrogen bomb have not, so far as we can discover, led to much comment in religious circles." But the Episcopal magazine is worth hearing out, whether one regards its perspective as the epitome of inanity, Christian wisdom, or both. Bikini, we are told, did not really change anything in the issue of Christian response to war and violence. For that matter, neither did the A-bomb nor the mass bombings of World War II. "The H-bomb raises no new moral problems, although the scope of the devastation it can inflict has a bearing on the moral question of the proportion of means to ends." Then the journal let fly an editorial bombshell of its own:

> Fundamentally, Christianity's answer to the H-bomb sounds so callous that we are almost reluctant to state it—the H-bomb simply does not matter. Civilization does not matter. The world does not matter.
>
> It is significant to note that the eccentric new Churches that spring up among the plain people of our country present their members with just such an interpretation of the fate of the world and purpose of life—and those are the fastest growing Churches in the country today.[44]

That position was, in fact, not too different from Reinhold Niebuhr's on the H-bomb. His "realism" led him to hold that the bomb was dangerous not because it was a thousand times more powerful than the weapon that had devastated Hiroshima, but because it might tempt nations to use it as a quick fix—and because it was tempting moralists toward pacifism. He was sure the bomb ought to be stockpiled, since the Russians would surely stockpile simi-lar weapons; the moral goal was "only to prevent its use and of course to pre-vent our subjugation." Niebuhr held essentially to the effective-deterrence philosophy of conducting the cold war, and any weapon that contributed to retributive credibility was as good as any other.[45]

As is often the case, however, popular culture—representing the people most likely to suffer the deadly or disfiguring effects of the new devices—saw the issues from perspectives that characteristically mythologized the matter more than they theologized or moralized it; and not seldom in religion, myth is closer to the heart than theology. In that mode of discourse, the bomb and its death rays became what everyone knew in their hearts they were: apoca-lyptic, Armageddon presences that indeed advanced the world several notches along a last-days scenario, putting us in marginal time or end time in which conventional rules might not hold and anything could happen.

Movies and science fiction like *The Blob, The Attack of the Crab Mon-sters,* and *Them!* made much of strange radiation effects. Genetic monstrosi-ties swarmed out of those grade-B flicks as if from a modern variant on the Book of Revelation. In the somewhat better *Invasion of the Body Snatchers* the main character suggested, though wrongly, that the victims' relentless desires could have been caused by radiation.[46] Nevil Shute's 1957 novel, *On the Beach,* and the 1959 film version, in which the last survivors of an atomic holocaust await death in Australia, actually kindled a cabinet discussion in Washing-ton. Those in power construed the influential work as "'Ban the Bomb' pro-paganda" and called on the Atomic Energy Commission to counter its message at home and abroad by claiming that it was "of science fiction and not of sci-ence fact." People must understand the reassuring truths that atomic war would not wipe out all life on earth and that they could do more after an attack than wait for death passively. But people knew the deep unease they felt in those outwardly peaceful and prosperous, inwardly dreadful years of the high Fifties; and nuclear fallout, the silent killer, focused those fears.

In the 1956 presidential campaign, Adlai Stevenson called for a halt to nuclear tests, speaking of "the danger of poisoning the atmosphere." President Eisenhower was reluctant to respond directly, but let Vice President Richard Nixon call this "catastrophic nonsense." The secretary of state, John Foster Dulles, added that the radiation hazard was as great "from wearing a wrist watch with a luminous dial" as from atomic testing. In response to attitudes like this, SANE, the National Committee for a Sane Nuclear Policy, was formed in 1957.[47]

Roman Catholic archbishop Patrick A. O'Boyle of Washington, D.C., re-flected the views of many thoughtful religionists: "The H-bomb is symbolic of the widespread perversion of values, of purposes and powers that find their most malignant form in the distortion of the human spirit. This process is found in the gradual exclusion of God from whole areas of human life, the refusal to submit to moral conscience and moral laws." The bomb, he continued, was shocking scientists into discovering "a sense of sin."[48]

DIENBIENPHU AND GUATEMALA

The cold war tended to grow hot in scattered remote and exotic places. In mid-1954, temperatures rose in two tropical arenas of conflict and produced two dramatic changes, one interpreted as a victory for the United States and the forces of freedom, the other as a defeat. Both were early gusts of storms to come in their parts of the world.

The first event was the fall of Dienbienphu in Indochina on May 7. This military disaster marked the effective end of France's long-contested colonial rule, giving the north part of Vietnam to the Viet Minh under Ho Chi Minh, uprooting Tom Dooley's Haiphong refugees. The noncommunist south, increasingly a United States client state, was left vulnerable to the pressures that led up to the Vietnam War in the next decade. The French effort to hang on, for which the United States had been footing some three-fourths of the bill, was fast fading into history.

Commonweal said, "We have, to put it simply, awakened again to the fact that the world is in an uproar, and that no amount of self-deception will permit us to live the life of 'normalcy' or win the cold war at a cut rate."[49] At this point there was little concern about Indochina except as a counter in the cold war, and among Catholics because of that church's traditional missionary interest in the tropical land. Secretary of State John Foster Dulles had his priorities straight. At the June diplomatic conference on Vietnam in Geneva, he declared flatly that the United States would not intervene.

That was not the case in regard to the second event, nearer to home, which occurred later that June. On its face this was a happier occasion for the United States and anticommunism. After the fact, Dulles proudly declared developments in the tiny, dirt-poor Central American republic of Guatemala to be "the biggest success in the last five years against Communism."[50] This was the Department of State's interpretation of a series of moves climaxing June 25, in which a military junta ousted leftist president Jacobo Arbenz Guzman of Guatemala.

As State and the U.S. press repeatedly emphasized, the Arbenz government had been guilty of human-rights violations in its crackdown on dissidents, particularly as extreme pressure against it from outside mounted in its final weeks, and a few known or suspected communists did have roles in that regime. The arrival in port of a notorious shipment of Soviet arms a few weeks earlier provided the excuse for the United States and its Guatemalan allies to act when they did.

The Arbenz regime also had been attempting much-needed reforms in a land of notorious worker exploitation and extremes of wealth and poverty. There is little doubt the coup was essentially engineered by the U.S. State Department on behalf of the United Fruit Company's profits, which Arbenz's land reforms and prolabor policies threatened, and by John Foster Dulles's obsession with a possible communist "beachhead" in the Western Hemisphere. United Fruit, with its banana plantations and transportation networks, set the standards for the impoverished republic's economic and social policies; recently it had been incensed by a strike of plantation workers for wages of $1.50 a day. Anyone who questioned the legitimacy of its $30 million investment in Guatemala, or its labor practices, was in the company's eyes and those of its spokespersons a "communist."

The response in the religious press to the Guatemala coup was significantly muted in those days before the traumas of Vietnam and Iran-Contra. Even the liberal journals, wishing to distance themselves from any taint of sympathy for communism, were slow to perceive fully the nature of the U.S. role, guided as it was by Dulles, son of a Presbyterian minister and a sturdy NCC churchman. Thus the *Christian Century* editorialized that the Russian arms shipment represented developments that "should be carefully watched." But, it added, so should U.S. countermoves, consisting of flying arms cargoes to Honduras and Nicaragua: "The truth is that both international communism and the United States are playing a dangerous game in fostering an armament race in Central America."[51]

Commentators wordily noted Arbenz's suspension of constitutional guarantees of press freedom and censorship of all outgoing news dispatches; but they observed also that, as abysmal land and labor conditions in Guatemala evidenced, not everything happening in that country could be attributed to a communist plot. The *Christian Century* claimed, "There is no question that the Communists have infiltrated the Guatemalan government and have had a leading part in determining its actions." But reform was fostered by the anger of workers against their failure to receive social justice, with much of the rage aimed at United Fruit. "That company's labor policies have improved greatly in the last few years, but it is still under fire for its sins of the past," and the same feelings of resentment toward the United States, the magazine acknowledged, could be found throughout Latin America.[52]

After the coup, liberal clergy could at best only utter the fatuous hope that the reforms would continue under the better auspices of Arbenz's successors. The *Christian Century* opined that now new problems for the United States were "more difficult than were the problems produced by the propensity of Arbenz to play footsie with the communists." If the radical government that had been overthrown was followed by a reactionary regime that reversed land

reforms, allowing United Fruit to resume domination and the old feudal landowners to return, "Latin America will say the United States did it."
Commonweal editorialized that the communists must be kept from power, but
liberal democratic reforms must continue under U.S. supervision.[53]

As it happened, Guatemala's new rulers displayed considerably less enthusiasm for land reform than for rounding up and shooting alleged supporters of Arbenz, a process that continued for weeks and included skirmishes
between the coup forces and the regular army. The country's new masters' continuation of democracy featured taking the vote away from the country's long-
suffering Indian peasants on the basis of their illiteracy, and their land reform
consisted of repossessing for the government or the landowners most of the
land that was being redistributed by Arbenz, on the grounds of the same peasants' inefficient farming methods.[54]

For some liberal but not communist observers in the religious community, Guatemala provided the first graphic illustration that America's cold-
war support of "freedom" could be highly selective, that realities on the ground
might not always be exactly as they were trumpeted in Washington, and that
Niebuhrian "realism" about such matters might entail some very distasteful
ironies indeed. The foundations of churchly anti–Vietnam War activism in
the Sixties, and against the Reagan administration's policies in Central
America in the Eighties, were quietly being laid. Korea, even support for France
in Indochina, could be tolerated when it was apparently a truly international
effort against ruthless invading or marauding Red armies, though the glow wore
quickly off those efforts too. But in Guatemala the struggle came to look more
and more like a war against peasants rather than commissars.

However, for most Americans in the United States, even in the liberal
churches, Guatemala was very much a sideshow, soon forgotten amid the real
preoccupations of the summer—the decline of McCarthy and the new world
of race relations created by the Supreme Court that hopeful spring. At best
Guatemala was seen as a pawn in the struggle against communism; the popular press reported not only the ruthlessness of the new regime under Costillo
Armas, but also the wealth Arbenz and his henchmen had taken into exile.
It was hard for most folks to know what to believe, or who the real good guys
were. And for churchpersons a grander and still more hopeful diversion would
arrive in August, far from Guatemala, on the shores of Lake Michigan.

The Hope of the World

The second assembly of the World Council of Churches convened in
Evanston, Illinois, in August 1954. Centering around the theme "Christ—
the Hope of the World," this ecumenical event attracted an amount of media

attention allegedly equaled only by that for the Republican convention of 1952. "Evanston '54" drew more reporters, according to the *Christian Century*, than the Democratic convention, the establishment of the United Nations in San Francisco, the coronation of Queen Elizabeth, the funeral of Stalin, the peace conference in Berlin and Geneva, all Roman Catholic events from the Holy Year to various Marian and Eucharistic congresses, the wars in Korea and Indochina, or the atomic tests in Nevada and the Pacific.[55]

What were they looking—and hoping—for? Much was made of the fact that this gathering represented no less than 168 million Christians. Though Roman Catholics, fundamentalist Protestants, and some Eastern Orthodox (such as the Russian Orthodox church) were absent, Evanston did represent a goodly number and moreover gave voice to the faiths of many of the era's most discussed preachers and theologians, not to mention those of the U.S. political and social establishments. They were the churches of presidents and Ivy League graduates, and in Europe of heroic struggles, not always successful, with Nazism or communism.

It was considered significant that this, the second assembly after the one at which the WCC was founded at Amsterdam in 1948, was being held in the United States. The country was, after all, the world's bulwark against forces of antireligious, totalitarian evil, and now a major world religious presence was being symbolically brought into alignment with it. Moreover, the United States was technologically the most advanced nation in the world; this worked to the advantage of the armies of journalists, radio interviewers, photographers, and television camera crews covering the event.

Countless photographs recorded the presence of an international cast of colorfully robed church leaders, from Anglican archbishops in gaiters to stovepipe-hatted and bemedalled Eastern Orthodox prelates to Asian and African delegates in vivid native garb. The presence of representatives from Iron Curtain countries, prepared to report and to enter into dialogue, was intriguing to many Americans in that cold-war year. Above all, in a time when spirituality was deemed important, Evanston seemed—at least for non–Roman Catholic Christians—a supreme celebration of its reality as a force in world affairs. Many no doubt hoped and prayed that somehow the assembly would truly change the course of human events for the better. All eyes turned toward the placid university city by the Great Lakes that hot summer. None other than President Eisenhower opened the session, calling faith "the mightiest force that man has at his command."[56]

Although far rightists had tried to prevent some East Europeans from entering the United States for the conference, leaders laboring under communist regimes were remarkably outspoken in Evanston. Dr. Guenter Jacobs of East Germany said, "It is impossible to believe both our Christian dogma and the communist dogma which reduces God to a product of a primitive mankind's anxieties and Jesus Christ, at best, to a revolutionary who tragically failed." Dr. Josef Hromadka of Czechoslovakia, on the other hand, affirmed that Christianity and communism could exist side by side. Bishop Janos Peter of the Reformed Church of Hungary declared the churches should proclaim their "independence . . . of all social systems more courageously . . . than heretofore." Many doubted his claim that the church in Hungary was free, but they applauded anyway.[57]

The World Council also produced an interesting and much commented-on debate between U.S. and European theologians on the theme of the conclave, hope. At the first plenary assembly, after the unifying experience of the opening worship service, opposing views on hope were presented by Professor Edmund Schlinck, Lutheran theologian and rector of the University of Heidelberg in Germany, and Professor Robert L. Calhoun, Congregationalist and professor of theology at Yale Divinity School. Schlinck declared that when people speak of Christ as the hope of the world, "they are always speaking of the end of the world." Perhaps with an eye on the "American way of life" all too visible around him, then considerably more affluent materially than Europe's and the rest of the world's, he declared that Christ is not a guarantee of the improvement of standards of living as assessed by worldly values. Nor is the Savior to be called upon to defend, or even sanctify as just or righteous, such material well-being. "The name of Christ is taken in vain if it is used as a slogan in this world's struggle for its own preservation."

Calhoun, in response, struck a note that reflected the characteristic greater optimism about hope in the present world of U.S. Christianity, with its tradition of Christian activism on behalf of the amelioration of the ills of this world. In the United States, he said, "when we think of hope, it is usually hope for a better life tomorrow for our children and for the increasing number of those who depend on us and for whom we feel responsible. In this context much of our theology has come to lay a special stress on ethics and to be far less confident about eschatology." Yet the Yale professor did warn against an American tendency "to confuse the will of God with our way of life," but he pointedly added that "it is surely right to keep our eyes on goals that seem to accord with God's will." Calhoun too was skeptical of any notion of automatic, secular "progress"—"there is no sign that earthly history is being progressively purged of evil and steadily nearing perfection."[58]

Did the World Council accomplish anything? The answer depends on how much stock one puts in the generation of words, sometimes very fine words, but words with no more armies behind them than had the pope. Clashes in theology displaying the dramatic gulf between Europe and America raised significant issues that foreshadowed the Sixties. A resolution was passed asking for the "elimination and prohibition of atomic, hydrogen, and all other weapons of mass destruction"—a call as politely ignored in the God-fearing host country as in all other world powers. As for communism, it was repeatedly condemned in speeches for its atheism and denial of human dignity and responsibility, yet the presence of Christian delegates from communist countries seated alongside their Western colleagues was evidence that the two worlds could conceivably engage in peaceful dialogue.[59]

In the end Evanston was remembered less for any accomplishments than simply for its happening. The reports unfortunately did not rise above the usual level of ecumenical bureaucratese. There were tensions, mostly surrounding the refusal of the Eastern Orthodox participants to cooperate on matters they regarded as not founded on a true concept of faith and church order. Little formal advance was made on social action, yet Evanston, very much in contrast to the surrounding U.S. society in those days, appeared entirely free of race or color barriers; perhaps on some level of national consciousness the media images of Christians of all hues dwelling together in harmony had a down-home impact, though many battles remained to be fought. Predictions had been made that the assembly would strengthen the cause of church unity in the United States; perhaps it did improve the ecumenical consciousness of some, though no concrete result in the form of a superchurch emerged.

Yet Evanston was significant. The sheer size of the event and the countless images remained etched on numerous minds. Many Americans no doubt had never before quite realized the scope and diversity of world Christianity. Whatever its ultimate world impact, Evanston was a part of an age of faith in the United States, its host country.[60]

Evangelicals, Billy Graham, and Christianity Today

Beside the façade of the "cooperative" denominations gathered in the National Council of Churches and at Evanston, evangelical Protestantism was gathering force for a new surge into U.S. life. In 1958, Arnold W. Hearn, in a *Christian Century* article, "Fundamentalist Renascence," called attention to a quiet, "respectable" version of conservative evangelical thought and life that was on the rise. It was certainly the fruit of energies set in motion in the early and middle years of the decade, notably the evangelism of Billy Graham and the 1956 launching of the journal *Christianity Today*. The new wave of evangelicalism was, Hearn said, not political, and unlike the fundamentalists of the "Monkey Trial" era had come to terms with science. The article began with these lines:

Students in many of this country's major seminaries today are likely to have heard that some years before they were born there was an ephemeral fracas called the "fundamentalist-modernist controversy." But, they will have been told, the controversy has long since been safely embalmed in the annals of American church history, and the only fundamentalists left are a semiliterate breed who continue to exist in certain cultural backwaters but need not be taken seriously.[61]

Even in mainline circles traces of an undertow drawing toward a fundamentalist renascence could be felt if not seen. It was definitely not fashionable to be liberal. One could be neoorthodox if Protestant, or if Anglican reasonably high church and "incarnational" in theology. In the outside world, an evangelical mood was rising, not so much within the cooperative churches as around them. In the Fifties, though Evanston and Niebuhr might be in the headlines, the Southern Baptists were the fastest growing denomination. During 1953 they built 631 new churches, increased giving by 12.4 percent, and baptized 361,835 persons.[62]

Further signs of the coming evangelical era included the popularity of Billy Graham; *Christianity Today*, intended to be the evangelical counterpart to the *Christian Century*; and even enthusiasm for C. S. Lewis, that perennial favorite of U.S. evangelicals despite his Oxford tone and his pipes and beer.

Hearn also directed attention to a new, sophisticated generation of evangelical thinkers, such as Bernard Ramm, Edward John Carnell, Dirk Jellema, Carl F. H. Henry (founding editor of *Christianity Today*), Warren C. Young, and Paul K. Jewett. Much more than their older counterparts, these writers reveal comprehensive theological concerns and awareness of current developments in theology and philosophy, deal honestly with the findings of natural science, and show more than just moralistic interest in social ethics. They are therefore entitled to a serious hearing even by those not disposed to agree with their premises. But the best-known evangelical was Graham.

Although he could hardly be called a sophisticated thinker and was not even considered respectable in some quarters, Billy Graham, born in 1918, was one of the founders of *Christianity Today*. The first issue of that periodical, October 15, 1956, led off with an article by the distinguished Dutch theologian G. C. Berkouwer, "The Changing Climate of European Theology." This conservative Calvinist noted the contemporary decline of nineteenth-century optimism and liberalism. But he did not consider the stylish neoorthodox theologians to be truly orthodox, noting for example that Rudolf Bultmann's existentialist demythologizing of the Scriptures still did not entail taking them as authoritative on their own terms.

Billy Graham then appeared as author of "Biblical Authority in Evangelism," an interesting and revealing piece. The great evangelist told of his early doubts about the full authority of the Bible, of his "wrestling with God" over apparent contradictions and difficult passages. Then he relates how, during the famous 1949 Los Angeles crusade that launched his celebrity career, "I discovered the secret that changed my ministry. I stopped trying to prove that the Bible was true. I had settled in my own mind that it was, and this faith was conveyed to my audience. . . . Authority creates faith" (6).

Carl H. Henry, the magazine's editor, in "Fragility of Freedom in the West," asserted that the West's defense of freedom and human dignity in the cold war was often too negative and merely anticommunist; it needed to go beyond "naturalism" to a perspective based on faith in the "Hebrew Christian God."

Addison H. Leitch, in "The Primary Task of the Church," outlined the perspective on individual salvation and social responsibility that has long been a hallmark of the *Christianity Today* ethos. The church has best been defined, he said, by two eras: the New Testament's apostolic age of Acts and the epistles, and the Reformation period; he thus unapologetically established the stoutly Protestant foundation of the magazine. Leitch then averred, "There is no salvation by way of the social gospel, but only in the individual's call to Christ" (13). But there is also no such thing as an "asocial Christian"; the Christian must live and minister in society. To aid the individually saved Christian in the social ethical expression of faith, the church can proclaim only values, not detailed prescriptions.

Finally, an editorial, "Why 'Christianity Today'?" declared that liberalism has failed to meet the needs of the day; the new magazine will stand for the authority of the Bible and traditional doctrines and will apply biblical revelation to "the contemporary social crisis" (20). That means, the editorial made clear, that social injustice is perceived not as an ultimate evil in itself but as a sign of humanity's falling away from God, and so can be thoroughly rectified only by striking at its roots in human disobedience, and only healed through conversion to Christ.

While liberals and even the reigning neoorthodox might continue to regard such a position as simplistic and fideistic, there is no doubt it indicated that evangelicalism—or, as many of its adherents would insist, plain Reformation Protestantism—could be presented in a challenging manner to a troubled age. Graham and *Christianity Today*, supported by the continuing growth of Baptist and other evangelical churches as they gained their share of the demographic explosion and population migrations, facilitated the crucial postwar intergenerational transmission of evangelicalism and lay the groundwork for its continuing vitality in the late twentieth century.

1955 and 1956 Events

The country and its religious communities were spared, in 1955 and 1956, single events as traumatic as those of 1954, the year of Bikini, Dienbienphu, Guatemala, McCarthy's fall, and *Brown*. But names and words appeared that would cast shadows down the corridors of the future, even as the religion boom continued.

In the last month of 1955 the name of Martin Luther King, Jr., first appeared widely in the news in connection with the burgeoning, newly hopeful post-*Brown v. Board of Education* civil-rights movement. It began with an event on a segregated bus in Montgomery, Alabama. On December 1, 1955, Rosa Parks, a woman of color, tired after a long day's work, had declined to surrender her seat to a white person when requested. She was arrested for violating the applicable Jim Crow ordinances.

Placing hope in the Supreme Court's outlawing of segregation two years earlier, black leaders, largely pastors, organized a protest boycott of Montgomery busses commencing December 5 under the aegis of a new organization called the Montgomery Improvement Association. King, who had been pastor of the Dexter Avenue Baptist Church in Montgomery for a little over a year, was selected as its leader. In his first speech in this capacity to a black audience, the young minister revealed the vibrant rhetoric that was to convey him to national prominence in the struggle: "We have no alternative but to protest. For many years we have shown an amazing patience. We have sometimes given our white brothers the feeling that we liked the way we were being treated. But we come here tonight to be saved from that patience that makes us patient with anything less than freedom and justice."[63]

The boycott lasted a few days beyond a year, until December 13, 1956, when the Supreme Court declared segregation in public transportation unconstitutional. After the victory, King and others formed the Southern Christian Leadership Council to continue and spread the work throughout the South, and in the process afford King a national platform. There would be more boycotts, more demonstrations, more memorable speeches—many more.

Unfortunately but inevitably, in the aftermath of Montgomery racial tensions heightened, especially in the South. In a widely publicized episode, in 1956 a black woman, Autherine Lucy, was finally admitted under court order to the University of Alabama in Tuscaloosa after a three-year legal battle, at the same time as the bus boycott in that state's capital. Her presence on campus induced steady violent and near violent protests from students and others, requiring the continual engagement of campus police in her protection. After only four days the new student was suspended "for her own good."[64]

Churches were often in the news as the South underwent its long and tortuous initiation into a new age. Both the white and the black South were religious, and churches were frequently the crucibles in which their passions were prepared. For example, in December 1956 Paul W. Turner, minister of the First Baptist Church of Clinton, Tennessee, intentionally walked to a newly integrated school with six black children after the local White Citizens Council had inflamed whites against them. On his way back home, Turner was assaulted by a half-dozen segregationists. His blood, splattered on a car that happened to be parked at the site, was photographed, and the picture appeared on TV news around the country. Though the events of Clinton were far from unique, that image shocked the nation, bringing home the simple courage on the part of persons of both races, as well as the violence, both of which seemed to be inseparable from the movement wrenching the country from one racial era into another.[65] (The possibility of change was evidenced in a follow-up story on Clinton a year later. A *Newsweek* reporter found that the schools were now peacefully integrated, and moreover that six of the seven convicted segregationists had since admitted they were wrong and sought to make amends. The Baptist minister, Paul Turner, believed that God had set Clinton on the right path. Many people in the town of 7,500 now just wanted out of the world news, to carry on their lives in peace.)[66]

A second 1956 event with religious linkages was the revolution by the Hungarian freedom fighters, bringing in the brief tenure of the liberal Imre Nagy government formed October 23, 1956, and suppressed by Soviet tanks November 4–6. During the window of freedom and its immediate aftermath, some two hundred thousand Hungarian refugees poured into Austria, more than thirty thousand of them eventually arriving in the United States. President Eisenhower had to "bend," as he put it, the Refugee Act of 1953, with its extreme McCarthyist security checks required for aliens, in order to handle the deluge. A large number of the Hungarians were sponsored and helped in their relocation by churches, many of which went to great lengths to improvise emergency housing, job placement, and English-instruction programs for the unexpected wave of newcomers.

During the few days of freedom, the Protestant churches in Hungary, a country about one-fourth Protestant, did some thorough housecleaning. Reformed bishop Albert Bereczky, whose entry into the United States to attend the World Council of Churches Assembly in Evanston two years earlier had been protested by the American Legion, and who was a holder of the Hungarian Communist Order of Labor, was immediately replaced by Ladislaus Ravasz as ministerial president of the Hungarian Reformed Church. Reformed clergy also demanded the resignation of Janos Peter, another Evanston attendee and a district bishop; he was now labeled "the worst kind of Stalinist" despite his calls at the World Council for freedom of the church from all social structures.[67]

Moreover, against the backdrop of those wonderful and terrible real-life events in Hungary, as the world swung giddily from hope to bitter despair, the Evanston confrontation between European and U.S. styles of theological hope was being reenacted with grim earnestness. The silence of Karl Barth, the world's most eminent theologian, who had been spiritual mentor of the anti-Nazi "Confessing Church" in Germany, and who had visited the Hungarian churches not long before the uprising, puzzled and infuriated observers, especially in the United States. Reinhold Niebuhr, now at the apex of his career as cold-war theologian, was particularly outraged. Calling Barth, because of his advisory role, "a kind of unofficial pope of the Hungarian Reformed Church," he considered this particular pontiff too "eschatological" and "transcendent"—in a word, other-worldly in his construction of hope—"to offer any guidelines for the discriminating choices that political responsibility challenges us to." When Barth claimed, for example, that communism was not as bad as Nazism because it was not anti-Semitic, citing the barbarism, nihilism, and anti-Semitism of the Nazis, Niebuhr reminded him of the fundamental totalitarian principle of both, pointing out that "some of the barbarism of nazism was derived from the same monopoly of irresponsible power from which the barbarism of communism is derived."[68]

Chapter 4

Ideas:
Beats and Books

Bᴀᴛᴛʟᴇs ᴀɢᴀɪɴsᴛ cold-war enemies continued on the home front. At the time of the 1954 meeting of the World Council of Churches in Evanston, the American Legion warned the State Department not to issue visas to Dr. J. L. Hromadka of Prague and Bishop Albert Bereczky of Hungary, considered collaborators with the communist regimes in their homelands. It also criticized WCC general secretary W. A. Visser t'Hooft for saying that some communist maxims stem from the teachings of Jesus.[1]

A characteristically popular book was Herbert Philbrick's *I Led Three Lives* (1952), chronicling the author's years of spying on communists for the FBI while serving as a top member of the Party's New England chapter, and while also maintaining an "ordinary" life as a family man working in advertising. Philbrick's book produced a syndicated TV series, fictional but with a documentary air, which aired from 1953 until 1956, possibly the most explicitly political popular drama series ever to appear on U.S. television. In it, communists engaged in nefarious activities ranging from drug smuggling to indoctrinating American youth to converting vacuum cleaners into bomb launchers.

At the same time, loyalty oaths everywhere, together with draconian punishments, were the preferred ways of purifying the country of subversives and communists. Not only teachers and government employees were affected. The Cal-Neva Casino, a Reno gambling house, required a loyalty oath of its 105 workers. The Disabled American Veterans called for the death penalty for "subversives." Nor was open discussion of such clear-cut issues desired. The University of Michigan refused to permit a debate on communism versus capitalism on campus, and in Toledo, the YMCA called off a scheduled debate titled "Is Communism a Threat to Christianity and Democracy?" when a group of businesspeople, church leaders, and American Legion representatives protested, as though the answer were so obvious the question should not even be asked.[2]

Typical attitudes toward communism were uncovered in the fascinating 1954 sociological study by Samuel A. Stouffer. At that time 19 percent of Americans considered that the danger from communism was "very great," 24 percent that it was "great," 38 percent that there was "some danger." Far more thought the danger from communists lay in the spreading of their ideas rather than in sabotage or espionage. "Many of our schools have communist teachers," said a bakery employee in Illinois. "If we let them go they'll try to turn everybody against religion and the way we live in this country," said a roofer in Alabama. "They're in our books, our movies, much more enmeshed in the life of the country than people realize," said a housewife in Connecticut.

Who were those insidious infiltrators? One in ten Americans said they knew somebody who acted suspiciously enough to make them think he might be a communist. "He was always talking about world peace," said a housewife in Oregon. "He didn't believe in Christ, heaven, or hell," said a building contractor in Mississippi. "I saw a map of Russia on a wall in his home," said a locomotive engineer in Michigan. "Avidly defends the underdog and explains the reasoning behind communist moves," said a business manager in Maryland.[3]

It is of course important to recall that, just as the Vatican of the 1950s was not that of John XXIII and the Vatican Council, so communism in those last years of Stalinism was not that of Gorbachev and *glasnost*. Many foolish and terrible things were done in the name of anticommunism, but one cannot doubt that communism itself was then generally a bloody and oppressive system from which there seemed no escape once it was imposed. Communist power came out of the barrel of a gun or the slogans of simplistic propaganda, subjected individuals totally to the system, and was spreading rapidly in the postwar world, having just seized China, the most populous nation on the face of the earth. It is not impossible to understand why numerous people still outside the communist orbit, including some liberals in the United States with its Niebuhrian tradition of "innocence" and exemption from world history, should feel bafflement akin to panic at this immense and sudden development.

What Christians and others were up against in communism as it was in the Fifties is well illustrated in the reports of F. Olin Stockwell.[4] When he was arrested and imprisoned by the communists after the revolution, Stockwell had been a Methodist missionary in China since 1929. He was a mainstream Protestant and neither then nor later a fanatical anticommunist. Yet the account he gave in the *Christian Century* in 1953 of his fourteen months of solitary confinement, followed by nine and a half months of interrogation in a special prison for counterrevolutionaries, offers a picture of one man's chilling confrontation with an impenetrable belief system.

If he protested that statements from communist scripts did not represent the whole truth—such as that half of U.S. laboring men were out of work, that thousands of Negroes are lynched each year, and that "six wealthy families" have a steel grip on U.S. life—he was, like his Chinese cellmates, berated and told he was wrong until he began to doubt himself. He was expected also to confess his own part, as a missionary/ foreign spy, in the suffering of China. Finally, he wrote,

> after I had been in this prison for counterrevolutionaries for more than eight months, had confessed my "crimes," and had had my case settled, I made a mistake that almost ended all chance of being released. We were discussing the progress that the new China had made in the past three years, and each one was setting forth his opinions in the terminology of newspaper editorials that we had been reading. I foolishly thought that I could put my ideas in somewhat different terms. So I said that I thought the new government had succeeded in many fields of mass education, health, and social reform where the missionaries and the church had failed.
>
> The reaction was immediate and violent. One after another my fellow prisoners condemned me because I did not see clearly that the missionary program had not helped China or even tried to help China, but had only been a tool of Western imperialism. Also, I had talked of Christianity, a useless superstition, in the same breath with communism, the glorious movement that was leading China to a new day of freedom and justice.[5]

In a later answer to charges that he should not have confessed in order to be released, Stockwell defended his actions, saying that by taking all blame on himself for certain accusations he saved his Chinese co-workers. He went on to state that his confessions were not all false, that missionaries had sometimes been implicated, if only passively, in evils of the old regime and of U.S. China policy; that he did have much to confess and confess openly even if certain charges were clearly frame-ups.[6]

The noncommunist mood, in its earnestness and perhaps also its naiveté, was well enough expressed in an October 4 article by Prentiss L. Pemberton, "Facing Communism Confidently." "The opponent of Communism," Pemberton writes, "if he is to use his superior understanding to gain victory in the ideological war, must treat the mental illness of the Marxist as critical, but not as fatal." Marxism will self-defeat because it fails to accept that people can vote or act for reasons other than economic self-interest, that is, for idealistic reasons, as does the Christian. "If Christians in all lands will act as Christians, Marxist communism will lose its power to act."[7]

Social Nonactivism

While the hounds were out after Reds, the *Christian Century* commented on a curious lack of interest among younger ministers and theological students in the type of social questions that had so preoccupied the previous generation, and a turning instead toward concern with the spiritual life. At an interseminary conference in Rock Island, a seminar on prayer led by the distinguished Quaker Douglas V. Steere was by far the most popular, and one on church and world order the least. Steere himself, a man strong in the conviction that prayer must find expression in practical good works, resisted the interpretation that students were rejecting social concerns. He proposed instead that the inner life was simply where they felt they needed most help. The *Century* too was hesitant to declare that students were "stampeding into lives of contemplative mysticism."[8]

Nonetheless, it is fair to say that the Fifties represented a relative recession from the social-gospel, activist thrust of the Thirties, under the impact of neoorthodoxy, anticommunism, and the almost desperate yearning for tranquillity and "normalcy" after World War II.[9] I can recall thinking two things in that decade, no doubt picking up on what countless other Americans also were thinking.

First, I reflected that nearly all the big battles for social justice had by now been won, especially in the huge but exhausting victory over evil that had occurred in 1945; it was now time to turn inward and see how people newly affluent, and freed from most of the burdens of the past, could live full and abundant spiritual lives. After all, the affluence of the Fifties, so much greater than so many had ever known before, must represent some sort of rough-and-ready social justice, but many had no more idea than the Rock Island seminarians how to correlate it with spiritual affluence. I saw too much as a pastor to be entirely comfortable with these comforting sentiments, but they were Fifties thoughts, reinforced by a sense there was little room for further progress except on the spiritual level. The remaining evil was just the sinful human condition the current theologians were always talking about, and too much social/political activism would be disruptive and destabilizing in the extremely delicate world situation.

Second, I considered that since we were locked in a life-or-death struggle against communism, even though some people were too fanatic about it, this was a time to close ranks rather than excessively criticize and destabilize the good side. During the war we had been forced to wait for many things, like new cars and TVs, till after victory; perhaps other things would have to wait until victory over communism.

Aging clergy of the old-style pacifist, Christian-socialist stamp still lingered, but the tigers of my generation looked at them with the usual condescension of the young. We knew from the much-talked-about neoorthodox theologians that the socialists and pacifists had no comprehension of how sinful the world and humanity really are. Somehow, without much sense of contradiction, that perception conjoined with the idea that the United States, at least, was already nearly perfect.

Together those notions confirmed a sense that there was little point in serious social action on the part of the church at the present time, just as it was not a time for radical liturgical experiments. If it's working and churches are growing, let it be. Our main Fifties mission was instead to minister to the individuals and the burgeoning families in our pews, and to build new pews for a growing population. We did serious preaching, counseling, and pastoral visiting. In effect, without realizing it, we turned Niebuhr on his head, thinking of the United States as a place not of moral man and immoral society, but of moral society and immoral man, who had to be dealt with one by one.

At the same time, we were reading a powerful genre of Fifties books that made much of the danger posed to society by intellectuals with ideas above their station, whose fancy-based blueprints for a better world are only likely to become bureaucratic paper traps and mazes. This was a wave closely related to the new intellectual conservatives, the Buckleys and their kin, of the last chapter. Some of us distrusted them when, like Buckley, they wore explicitly conservative or rightist labels but nodded approvingly if they presented themselves as pure intellectuals. I have already mentioned Eric Voegelin's forceful work on the modern gnostics: read intellectuals who take their dreams more seriously than reality. Karl Popper, in *The Open Society and Its Enemies*, traced Hitler not just back to Joachim of Flora but all the way to Plato. Eric Hoffer, the longshoreman philosopher whose *True Believer* was a best-seller and one of Dwight Eisenhower's favorite books, argued with Voegelin but more readably that the horrors of modern mass political movements, such as Nazism and communism, come from intellectuals who identify their own wishes with the course of history, then try to bend history to their will. They believe they can make history be what they want it to be because at heart they are nihilists, believing there is no knowledge or truth except as they define it, and so anything is permissible. The death camps can finally be blamed on "modernism"—on positivism, behaviorism, naturalism, and relativism. The Fifties intellectual and spiritual tone set cumulatively by such tomes from well-credentialed authors should not be underestimated.

Social action under the light of such suns meant to help people as individuals but to concede that, especially if one is an intellectual, one would do better to leave society alone. The deep thinker, gnostic as he probably is, is likely just to make it worse, like the communists with their iron dreams and slave paradises. Let history take its own course; don't force it. Voegelin, who himself had lived under the Third Reich and knew Europe's ideological wars at close hand, put it well enough when he alluded to "the massacres of the later humanitarians whose hearts are filled with compassion to the point that they are willing to slaughter one-half of mankind in order to make the other half happy."[10] Such sentiments may have been too one-sidedly pessimistic about progress and the quest for a better society. But they came from a generation that had heard a great deal of high-minded rhetoric about bettering society and had seen a good many massacres, and perhaps cannot be blamed for wondering if somehow the two went together.

So far as Christianity was concerned, though, the future looked bright. The great missionary historian Kenneth Scott Latourette, in *Christian World Missions in Our Day*, contended that despite talk of a post-Christian world, it was a great time for Christianity, which now for the first time was a truly global movement.[11] In most lands it was showing vitality and reaching out, making up in Asia and Africa for decline in Europe and superficiality in America.

There was much lamenting of "the lost churches of China"; in a book of that title, Leonard M. Outerbridge pointed out that over the last 1,300 years Christianity had seemed several times to have had a promising future in the vast Middle Kingdom, only to be nearly obliterated by the vicissitudes of history.[12] But it was a hard setback to accept, almost as much for mainstream Protestants as for evangelical and Roman Catholic missionaries who suffered so much, for China had long been a special preserve of the liberal vision of missions, educational and democratizing as well as soul saving, inspired by the "best" U.S. values. Not a few prominent figures were of China missionary stock, including Henry Luce of *Time* with his tormented cold-war liberal Republicanism; the U.S. missionary experience in China left many loose ends and difficult questions.

Religion and Youth

A serious concern of many Americans around 1954 was a rising crime rate, especially among the young people then called juvenile delinquents. A *Newsweek* article caught the concern in a title: "Our Vicious Young Hoodlums: Is There Any Hope?" It reported that nineteen million persons between ten and eighteen were now loose in the country—and that more than a million of them got into some kind of trouble with the police each year. The number of juveniles brought to court had doubled in thirteen years, reaching

435,000 in the last year. The crime rate for adults rose 1.9 percent in the same year, but for those under eighteen by an astonishing and disturbing 7.9 percent. Why? The article could only ruminate about parental authority disappearing too fast, about children growing up without love, about cars, about TV brutality and the need to deglamorize crime (this in the day of official "togetherness" and public piety).[13]

The *Christian Century* responded to the rise in criminality by pointing out that "[church] membership and attendance are reported at an all-time high" and asking, "What do the people, and particularly the young, learn from the churches?"

A good question, and one that deserved a very full answer. Unfortunately the *Century* had only this to say: "When the churches for their own gain break the law in various forms of mass gambling, what does this teach the young?" thereby reverting to a rather snide anti-Catholicism, since the use of games of chance as a means of fund-raising was primarily a Roman Catholic practice that Protestants loved to scorn.[14] But one suspects that a great deal more than parish-hall bingo lay behind the criminal upsurge of 1954.

The postwar prosperity was uneven, leaving behind inner cities thickly populated by African Americans and other minorities. It left numerous youth of all races unprepared for the new gray-flannel-suit jobs, youth who would never live in the bright new suburbs. But expectations had been raised, and confining social patterns and moral attitudes alike were shattered by wartime and postwar experiences. Even the left-out young people had heard the messages of self-fulfillment, of success and togetherness. But for some the only available means of success was through larceny, and the only togetherness in a gang.

Or perhaps the celebrated conformity of the era produced its own criminal rebellion. In 1954 I knew a young man, a university student and an officer in a campus religious group, of a good well-to-do family, who until he was caught and sent up robbed banks purely for the thrill of it.

What about religion on college campuses in the mid-Fifties? According to *Newsweek* in 1953, the current class was shrewd, mature, and cautious, wanting to conform and have security. A Northwestern coed said, "You want to be popular, so naturally you don't express any screwy ideas. To be popular you have to conform." The article said these students who had lived in the shadow of war in childhood now lived in the shadow of the draft. They had little urge to change the world much. They married young. They thought little about politics but were for the U.N.; wary of Reds, they accepted the goals of McCarthyism but questioned its methods. They had, we are told, a serious interest in religion. Few of the outspoken campus atheists and agnostics of the Thirties were still around, except in the professorate. Religious-studies courses were heavily enrolled.[15] (Those were also golden years for campus chaplaincies and ministries. The houses and chapels maintained by all the major denominations were popular social centers, holding dances and hayrides as well as services and nonstop bull sessions, and some of the chaplains were legendary campus figures.)

But youth and university campuses in the middle Fifties, though gradually emerging as problem, religious opportunity, and above all tremendous demographic presence, were nothing compared to the rising wind they would be in the last years of the decade, or the hurricane of the Sixties. In the meantime, conventional rather than youth religion or religious rebels held center stage in 1954.

The Spirituality Boom

One does not live by words alone. Alongside all the books and all the preaching, one senses in the Fifties a yearning for something more than sentimental I-and-God religion, or neoorthodox dialectics. That "more," for want of any other term, we may call *spirituality*. It was not the rough-and-ready faith inspired by Graham or Peale, not the theological and prophetic correctness of a Niebuhr, but a subtle, deeply-infused, wordless awareness of divine presence more akin to that known by the mystics. (In my Fifties parish, a young businessman, scion of a family wealthy by local standards, who attended church very regularly but otherwise did not seem especially devout, once surprised me a little by saying he often felt close to God but would like to "radiate" his faith more. This seems to me like an aspiration toward spirituality rather than toward either Niebuhrian prophetic theology or Pealean "success.")

Spirituality is suggested by the continued popularity of Thomas Merton, by the stream of postulants entering monasteries and convents (Episcopal and even Lutheran as well as Roman Catholic), and by the regular publication of books and articles reprinting or discussing the classics of Christian mysticism. It was an all-right thing to talk about; even *Time*, in its cover story on nuns, wrote knowingly of St. John of the Cross and the dark night of the soul.

A closely related theme was *glory*. Books like the ever popular C. S. Lewis's *Great Divorce* (1945) as well as his Narnia stories, or Chad Walsh's *Behold the Glory* (1956), told one that a light lay above the clouds that was brilliant as the sun. The theme suggested Christianity as not only a religion of peace and power or an alternative to communism, but a vision full of splendor and deep joy. Perhaps the mystical glory was some kind of deep-level preparation for the coming psychedelic vogue; it was contemporaneous with Aldous Huxley's mescaline experiment recounted in *The Doors of Perception* (1954) (to be discussed further in the next chapter), which described the vision induced by the drug in terms highly compatible with the world seen by the mystic's ecstatic eye.

Two persons from overseas associated with both spirituality and social action, Mohandas K. Gandhi and Albert Schweitzer, commanded something of a cult in the United States and were the subjects of a spate of books. Americans were aware that, however stable their own society, much of the rest of the world was changing rapidly. In the five years between the end of the war and 1950, the Communist sphere had advanced from one nation to a third of the world. Vast ex-colonial countries in Asia, like India and Indonesia, had attained independence, and Africa was restless. Words and phrases like "modernization," "westernization," and "rising expectations" were bruited about in relation to those tumultuous places, and the communists were thought to see them as ripe for the picking. Americans felt torn; they instinctively hated colonial empires and cheered on independence movements, but now suddenly it seemed that to do so might also be to cheer on the hated ideological enemy. In this situation it was good to find persons like Gandhi in India or Schweitzer in Africa who appeared entirely on the right side, both as to means and ends, and to make of them ideals.

Judaism in Fifties Midpassage

Jews and Judaism in the mid-Fifties were in a peculiar place. Certainly their position in American life was better than it was before the war. Jews were more affluent than ever before, they were moving out of inner-city ghettos to the new suburbs, the more noisy and blatant forms of anti-Semitism were silenced or marginalized by association with the horrors of Nazism and emerging diverse-heritage and "brotherhood" spirits in the land. The shining new state of Israel, for all its problems, gave most Jews a sense of pride and identity.

Their social situation was well represented in *The Jews*, a collection of sociological studies edited by Marshall Sklare.[16] Of particular interest from the present perspective is a paper by Herbert J. Gans on suburban Jews. Dealing with Park Forest, the same community as that studied by William Whyte, this article might almost be regarded as a Jewish *Organization Man*. The story of young Jewish families who moved to this Chicago suburb after the war, it described their organization of a temple in 1951 that was Reform but accommodating to Jews of other backgrounds. We are told that most of these young people, raised more or less Orthodox, had quietly given up strict kosher and other such observances after leaving home. Indeed, most did not attend synagogue or follow any religious practices at all after setting out on their own, unless for the sake of the parents. But almost as though to take the place of conscientious Orthodoxy and the tightly knit community it formed, they were very child-oriented; a major concern that engaged and divided the community was the formation of a Jewish Sabbath school. What was at issue was whether it should generally teach the children *about* Judaism or should emphasize the *practice* of "one kind of Judaism." The rabbi commented, "My primary interest is in the adults, and I am opposed to a child-centered Judaism. However, here the people seem to be mainly interested in the education of the children. . . . We hope, though, the children will bring the parents . . . perhaps they will return the parents to Jewish life."[17]

Judaism was, then undergoing a profound shift in emphasis. It was not yet losing its identity in the process, but questions remained as to what shape the new suburban identity would take, and how long it could last. Some were to suggest that pride and loyalty toward the state of Israel, to be powerfully reinforced by the Six Day War in 1967, was as much a symbol of Jewish identity for this generation of American Jews as anything.

But the transformation of Jewish life in the United States was far from complete. There remained, of course, Orthodox Jews, Jews in the inner city, new Jewish immigrants who had survived Hitler's Holocaust, and others. Rodger Kamenetz, commenting on the Judaism of the Fifties and Sixties when, as in the case of the new temple in Park Forest, liberal Reform Judaism looked to be on the rise, noted that

> Reform Judaism seemed the wave of the future. The Denomination
> had secure roots in the successful and wealthy German Jewish
> immigration of the 1830s. Baltimore was one of its strongholds and
> impressive Reform synagogues dominated Park Heights Avenue in the
> 1950s, where the successful children of immigrants had moved
> uptown. Reform Judaism was sleek and streamlined, discarding
> needless rituals and emphasizing the great moral heritage of Judaism.
> Its sophisticated, intelligent rabbis addressed current social issues in
> their sermons, and its cantors used choirs and organ music to create a
> stately, dignified service that any Gentile would feel comfortable with.
> That was important, because Reform Judaism was a way for Jews to
> remain both Jewish and American. And since that is what more of
> the children of the Eastern European immigration wanted, Reform
> Judaism was where the action was in the 1950s and 1960s. Some of
> that generation preferred more traditional prayer, and they found a
> home in Conservative Judaism. But it seemed likely that as the
> immigrant generation died out their residual Orthodoxy would also
> fade.[18]

Kamenetz points out that in fact this was not the way it happened. Since the 1970s Reform Judaism has been on the defensive against assimilation out of Judaism altogether on one hand, and resurgent Orthodoxy on the other, the latter reinforced by the immigration of prestigious "Modern Orthodox" and Hasidic rabbis from post-Holocaust Europe, and by a late Sixties and after move toward reaffirming Jewish distinctiveness and separateness. But in the Fifties the future of the Reform approach, ensconced in the new suburbs and supported by a new deghettoized Jewry, looked bright.

There were other Fifties Jewish concerns that, along with Israel, were frequently discussed in Jewish periodicals. As for everyone else, there was the issue of McCarthyism. Many Jews, because of a traditional commitment to liberal values and extremely unpleasant Old World experience with rightist demagogues, were viscerally opposed to McCarthy and all he represented. Yet at the same time, the longstanding Jewish identification with the left—sometimes the socialist or even communist left—was beginning to crack in the Fifties. On one hand, Jews were becoming aware of the extent of anti-Semitism in that supposed revolutionary paradise, the Soviet Union. On the other, increasing prosperity and suburban life, together with growing acceptance into the U.S. consortium of faiths and peoples, combined with traditional Jewish family and mercantile values to strengthen a relatively conservative and capitalist wing within Judaism. Jewish political neoconservatism was expressed in the journal *Commentary*. All this made for problems surrounding McCarthyism. Jews could sympathize with anticommunism in principle while cringing at the disproportionate number of Jewish-sounding names among the senator's victims, even though McCarthy very carefully avoided any hint of anti-Semitism in his rhetoric, and his investigative committee's counsel was a Jew named Roy Cohn. A 1954 article by Alan F. Westin, for example, sought evenhandedly to condemn Soviet totalitarianism and anti-Semitism, and the lingering anti-Semitism of the U.S. right now reenergized by the Wisconsin senator. That association was explored in two devastating pieces by James Rorty on the background of key McCarthy supporters with old right anti-Semitic antecedents.[19]

Another problem was the continuing discrimination against Jews in such areas as housing, hotel accommodations, and certain professions. Undoubtedly the situation was better than before the war. But it happened, legal recourse was still largely a thing of the future, and uncertainty about one's status in a land of "gentlemen's agreements" and stated preferences for "Christians of the white race" could be infuriating.[20]

Jews were also interested in the Fifties vogue for Freud because of the Jewish roots of the father of psychoanalysis and his problematically Jewish interest in such topics as Moses and monotheism.[21]

In the mid-Fifties, Judaism's relationship with the majority Christian churches was strengthened by the "brotherhood," heritage-honoring, three-faiths spirit so well articulated by Will Herberg in *Protestant, Catholic, Jew*.

Yet it was simultaneously weakened, at least in the perception of Jews, by growing theological conservatism in the churches, by the uncongenial growth of evangelicalism, and by Christian leaders who deplored the plight of Arab refugees from Israel; the complaint was that the same leaders had been silent before the Nazi Holocaust.[22] In short, Jews now felt a part of the United States but were uneasily conscious of being only a part, and of seeing many things, from McCarthy to Freud to Israel, from a unique angle.

Arthur A. Cohen, writing of Nathan Glazer's influential *American Judaism*, noted that "what baffles the non-Jew about Jews is the disinclination of the modern Jew to fulfill the mythic image which 2,000 years of Christendom have projected and secured."[23] That was not necessarily the stock anti-Semitic image; it may equally be a sympathetic but no less out-of-touch picture of a pious bearded gentleman wrapped in a prayer shawl and full of biblical quotations. But in fact Judaism in the United States has changed as much if not more in coming to the New World than Christianity; it had moreover participated in the ambiguous religious revival as much as Christianity, building its new synagogues and temples in the suburbs—yet Jews who do not conform to the image remain Jews. Their internal problem, however, remains the lack of a clear center of tradition without the traditional community or Torah way of life. Movements were afoot to redefine the core of Judaism in Zionism, the new suburban-style community life of a modern temple, or a Jewish tradition of art and culture.

Tillich, the Theologians, and the Books

Gradually, among the theological superstars, Paul Tillich grew more important as the Fifties advanced, and Niebuhr and Barth ever so slightly declined, despite—or maybe because of—the cold-war debate about Hungary. The world was turning. The radical sense of sin, so persuasive in the immediate aftermath of the Great War and the early-Fifties depths of the cold war, now seemed to be lightening a bit.

One could also borrow from another side of existentialism. One could affirm personal existence in the universe as a reality quite apart from and prior to one's involvement in sin—and even apart from and prior to one's relation to a personal God. All that could come later and separately, if it need come at all. One could still be Christian, acknowledging with Tillich the "transparency" of Christ to the ultimate reality that answers one's ultimate concern.

In the mid-Fifties all this, coming not from a homegrown American Unitarian or other liberal but from an evangelical German theologian with existentialist and neoorthodox connections, authentic anti-Nazi refugee credentials, and a rich appreciation of European culture, was exciting. The white-haired and heavily accented Paul Tillich was especially intriguing to younger theology students already finding the older "crisis theology" and its kin beginning to pall in a postwar world where hope, even secular hope, was starting to seem as viable as angst. They were, whether they realized it or not, the first fruits of the "secular theology" that was to become so potent in the next decade.

Tillich's 1953 book, *The Courage to Be*, emphasized the importance of self-affirmation, of letting oneself exist as a part of reality. "Faith is the state of being grasped by the power of being itself," and then experiencing that power as a ground for self-affirmation. Yet absolute faith transcended the subject-object relation, so in the end there was "the necessity of transcending theo-logical theism"—a radical statement for a mainline theologian, but theological radicalism was starting to become an exciting, driving religious force, with Tillich its grand old man.[24]

The Courage to Be was only one in a series of short books, based on ser-mons and popular lectures, that the renowned divine brought out in the Fif-ties. There was also *Love, Power, and Justice*, reviewing the eternal conundrums of social ethics as they endeavor to sort out the often entangled relationships of those three values. Tillich here argued that power must recede to make love possible; that is what God himself caused to happen upon creating the world. The three values are one in God, but not in us, for "man is estranged from the ground of his being, from himself and from his world."[25] In such typical Tillichian language, the theologian showed the metaphysical roots of a fun-damental moral dilemma of the decade, the same with which Niebuhr, in very different language, had wrestled in *The Irony of American History* and his much earlier *Moral Man and Immoral Society*: how a person or a people fated to ex-ercise great power is also to pursue justice, not to speak of love.

Another concise volume was the collection of sermons called *The New Being*. One of them, "Faith and Uncertainty," displayed a key theme. Tillich was always discovering God above God, God past all the lesser gods of cer-tainty and reason, the God who is past doubt and past the shaking of the foun-dations. "When we have left behind all objective probabilities about God and the Christ, when all preliminary certainties have disappeared, the ultimate certainty may appear to us."[26]

As the anatomist of spiritual doubt, doubt like that which must for some have crouched in the shadows of America's cold-war and religious-revival cer-tainties, Paul Tillich's star rose as the decade wore on. The German refugee theologian transferred from Union Theological Seminary to Harvard in 1955, as a major sign of President Nathan Pusey's drive to build up Harvard Divin-ity School to an institution of national stature, thus unintentionally helping to precipitate a religious crisis at the nation's oldest university (to be presented in the next chapter).[27] In those years Tillich was also working on the second volume of his *Systematic Theology, Existence and the Christ,* to be published in 1957.

Among other important theological books of the period was *Eternal Hope* by Emil Brunner, a Swiss neoorthodox theologian often associated with Barth, though not considered quite as great as the latter. Brunner had once differed with Barth by asserting that one can have knowledge of God, though not saving knowledge, apart from Christ; this drew forth Barth's thunderous *Nein!* Brunner's work on hope, prepared with Evanston in mind, continued in the same cautiously irenic vein. Brunner contended that hope is a Christian gift to the world; the majority of the other religions have little interest in history, and Christian hope is based in the faith's affirmation of history as an arena of God's action. However, Christian hope differs from scientific belief in progress, for it is based on faith in God. But Brunner's hope is also to be distinguished from that of Barth, who uses the term exclusively in a "resurrection of the dead" eschatological sense. Brunner affirmed that, with the help of God's grace and right use of the "orders of creation," Christians can structure occasions of hope in this world as well as in the new creation.[28]

An entire theological generation and more was evoked in Henry Sloan Coffin's *A Half Century of Union Theological Seminary,* by its president from 1926 to 1945; preeminently an institutional history, the book is enlivened by memoirs of the great names of Union's grandest era, the prewar and wartime years when Niebuhr, Tillich, and various refugee figures of legendary background and renown graced its halls at the heart of the nation's largest metropolis.[29]

Another now almost mythical world is evoked in the 1954 work *Spirit and Nature,* edited by Joseph Campbell, the latest in a distinguished series of papers from the Eranos conferences, fabled gatherings every summer since 1933 at the home of Frau Olga Froebe-Kapteyn near Ascona, Switzerland. Meeting with the blessing of a spectacular view of Lake Maggiore and its surrounding mountains, these conclaves brought together some of the greatest figures in the study of myth, art, and religion in a hall built especially for the purpose of generating a continual flow of ideas in the lofty realms of spiritual culture. The characteristic perspective was empathetic but undogmatic, in the spirit of such well-known frequent participants as Carl Jung, Heinrich Zimmer, Mircea Eliade, and Martin Buber. Campbell's volume only caught up with the end of the war, presenting documents from the 1945 and 1946 conferences— those dates suggesting that somehow the life of the mind and spirit went on in Europe amid the ruin and chaos of those years. This volume contains such treasures as "The Spirit of Science" by the Nobel Prize winner and scientific mystic Erwin Schrödinger; "Apollo Epiphanes" by the psychoanalytically aware mythologist C. Kerényi; Jung's "Phenomenology of the Spirit in Fairy Tales"; and the Catholic theologian Hugo Rahner's "Earth Spirit and Divine Spirit in Patristic Theology," amid much else.[30] This collection is significant because it embodies an alternative to the various Catholic, Protestant, and secular orthodoxies of the day, one linked to some of our underground Fifties spiritual themes. Like such writers as Aldous Huxley and Alan Watts, Eranos embraced an exploratory, wide-ranging, yet sympathetic approach to the planet's spiritualities.

The same flavor is sustained in Arnold Toynbee's *An Historian's Approach to Religion.* Virtually a cult figure among Fifties intellectuals, Toynbee took religion seriously, though in a way that, by the standards of the Fifties "return" to faith, was rather unorthodox. He contended that real history is religious history, and the events and civilizations of humankind ultimately nothing but stages on the path to deeper spiritual insight. But we have not arrived at the goal yet.

Still more provocatively for the times, Toynbee held that even more profound than the chasm between the communist and noncommunist (that is, mainly Christian) world is that between the "Judaic group of ideologies and religions" and the "Buddhaic group." The historian perceived, rightly, something in common in the two rival historicist and (as presently practiced) Eurocentric faiths founded by Christ and Marx, and a quite different Eastern way of viewing the human experience from the soul (or nonsoul) level up. But both these ways are currently in trouble. The historicist religions have rediscovered, in the history in which they live, original sin. It was evident in the bloodstained battlefields and smoking crematoria of the Forties, and a thousand other places. The Buddhistic religions, by discarding much of their culture for westernization, have bought into the evils of the West. What is needed instead is a synthesis of the best of both traditions.[31]

Religious synthesis was not an idea whose time had come in 1956, and for all his learning Toynbee may have held slightly naive ideas as to what is and is not religiously possible, as well as a tendency toward overgeneralization about East and West. But the book, much talked about, in some ways anticipated the spiritually more fluid Sixties.[32]

More Books

Among the important secular books published in the mid-Fifties, several provide incomparable insights into the religion and life of the times. Of these, foremost undoubtedly is William Whyte's *Organization Man.* This is the classic study of a new postwar generation in which not only factory workers but also the middle class lived as cogs in the system of a big organization—the corporation, the government, the university. Here Americans found security and a high standard of living, but at the cost of conformity to the organization's values. The new way of life was particularly displayed in the new middle-class suburbs, which imposed their own levels of conformism atop those of the corporation.

Whyte exemplifies what he means by conformism in a famous passage on the personality tests that were so much a part of corporate personnel policy. In taking these tests, he advises the aspirant to promotion always to "give the most conventional, run-of-the-mill, pedestrian answer possible." Then:

> When in doubt about the most beneficial answer to any question, repeat to yourself:
> I loved my father and my mother, but my father a little bit more.
> I like things pretty much the way they are.
> I never worry much about anything.
> I don't care for books or music much.
> I love my wife and children.
> I don't let them get in the way of company work.

Whyte adds, "If you were this kind of person you wouldn't get very far, but, unfortunately, you won't get very far unless you can seem to be this kind."[33]

In another celebrated passage, Whyte comments on essays written by students at a small preparatory school on Herman Wouk's *Caine Mutiny*, a World War II story of mutiny at sea. Whyte found that all but one essayist supported conformity to the demands of authority and felt Wouk had been too easy on the mutineers. Typical comments included, "We have to abide by the rules of our particular society to gain any end whatsoever," and "A subordinate should not have the power to question authority" (276). Clearly, these students feared anarchy far more than any possible abuse of authority—an attitude much in contrast with that of their confreres in the next decade, the Sixties.

Whyte's chapter on religion, "The Church of Suburbia," focuses on the Park Forest United Protestant Church, in a new planned suburb outside Chicago, an example of the spirit of the times. The organizer of the church, a former navy chaplain named Hugo Leinberger, held that denominationalism was not important; the church should be *useful,* and to that end should not offend anybody but rather meet people's needs for community and counseling. Leinberger said, "I think this is the basic need—the need to belong to a group. You find this fellowship in a church better than anywhere else." Also, "young people want a place to take their problems and someone to talk to about them. Put all these things together and you get what we're after—a sense of community. We pick out the more useful parts of the doctrine to that end"

(406–407). Even Judaism and Roman Catholicism as represented in Park Forest had tacitly moved some distance in the same direction, the latter through a "Christian Family Movement" that created a similar supportive community environment for young families, although some Catholics feared that in going "pragmatic" on a "group dynamics" course their church would sacrifice its "heavy moral and intellectual demands."

Finally, Whyte cites an ad from the *New York Herald Tribune* of May 20, 1955:

> Lots of acquaintances—not many friends. Is this increasingly true for you? Look at your life. You may find that it lacks those spiritual experiences which bring people together in understanding and friendship.
>
> Participation in the activities of the neighborhood church supplies the spiritual force to weld lasting friendships. Meet future friends in church this Sunday.
>
> A cordial welcome awaits you at
>
> YOUR NEIGHBORHOOD EPISCOPAL CHURCH. (418)

The message clearly is that what is truly important, at least for the organization man, is the church as community, in a society in which values emerge out of community. That was the message of an earlier important Fifties book, *The Lonely Crowd* by David Riesman. That work perceived a postwar change in American character from "inner-directed" to "other-directed" persons. The former internalize adult authority; the other-directeds are those whose character is chiefly formed by the example and values of their peers. To the authors other-directedness was an unfortunate trend that stifled creativity and could only offer pseudosolutions to the problems of loneliness, insecurity, and meaninglessness. "If the other-directed people should discover how much needless work they do, discover that their own thoughts and their own lives are quite as interesting as other people's; that, indeed, they no more assuage their loneliness in a crowd of peers that one can assuage one's thirst by drinking sea water, then we might expect them to become more attentive to their own feelings and aspirations."[34]

But inward feelings about what one was doing were just what other-directedness left out. Another sociological classic of the early Fifties, C. Wright Mills's *White Collar: The American Middle Class*, contains an interesting discussion of different views of work. For traditional Protestantism work has religious meaning, not intrinsic to the work itself, but because it is through work that one gains religious status and ultimate reward. The Renaissance view, on the other hand, is that work is intrinsically meaningful, as for a skilled artisan; and in the nineteenth century John Ruskin thought that work gave inner calm. But now, according to Mills, one sees a decline in the significance of work as such; it is done because one has to do it, for the sake of food or to buy what one does in one's leisure, or for the sake of "success."[35]

Whether this is really different from the motives of most people in other times and places I am not sure, but it is significant that someone in the Fifties, in an introspective moment, thought that work was now more servile to other ends and less an end in itself than heretofore. And to say that it is not the intrinsic reward or meaning of work as such that is important, but the fact that it is something one "has to do," is another way of saying that control is in the hands not of self but of society.

Yet though the group is important, it always leaves something to be desired. Whyte commented of those who were troubled in this way, "They sense that by their immersion in the group they are frustrating other urges, yet they feel that responding to the group is a moral duty—and so they continue, hesitant and unsure, imprisoned in brotherhood."[36]

The "brotherhood" and "togetherness" prisons of community and marriage were increasingly defied in several ways. One, as we shall see, was alternative spirituality. Another was a glamorized playboy life-style. Despite the Fifties sentimentalization of marriage, children, and family, the single life was gradually getting idealized too. Its vehicle was Hugh Hefner's *Playboy* magazine, which celebrated ways one could direct enjoyment of the new affluence toward other points of the compass than marriage, family, and a suburban home. In the first issue of his magazine, December 1953, Hefner wrote (using the papal "we," apparently as chief priest of his new faith), "We like our apartment. We enjoy mixing up cocktails and an hors d'oeuvre or two, putting a little mood music on the phonograph, and inviting in a female for a quiet discussion on Picasso, Nietzsche, jazz, sex."[37]

The Fifties, however, remained more concerned with the conflicting appeal and insidiousness of mass society. Robert Lekachman, reviewing *The Organization Man* in *Commentary*, criticized Whyte for the ambiguity, of his moral vision. Whyte, he thought, both undercut and endorsed the organization life, allegedly saying that one should be individualized and even a little eccentric, but only so one can work more effectively within an organization. Whyte was aware, we are told, that creativity and success, even within corporations, come not from people who score well on the personality inventories but from those with a touch of nonconformity; but instead of saying one should like music or read philosophy for their own sake, he wants it to be for the sake of organizational success, which Lekachman saw as a confusion of means and ends.[38]

Whyte can survive such criticism. The point is that the same conundrum was generally prevalent in Fifties society: people desperately wanted community, including other-directedness in establishing their values, yet they also had a dread of mass society and they retained a residual idealization of individualism. Much later Robert Wuthnow spoke of "the specter of mass society that was so much discussed in the 1950s: no identity stands between the atomized individual and the nation state. Everyone sinks into boring sameness."[39] We have noted ways religion tried to mediate this problem, whether through positive thinking or individual conversion or the prophetic voice within the community of the church.

But the problem remained. In 1957 William Kirkland, writing of both *The Organization Man* and *The Lonely Crowd*, remarked that though the new humanity may give lip-service to the "Protestant ethic," in reality these are its values: (1) the group is the source of all human creativity; (2) the ultimate need of "man" is "belongingness"; and (3) human and social engineering is the means by which the greatest adjustment of individual to group may be achieved.[40]

The trouble is that although no one really liked this philosophy when it was set down so starkly, very few organization males were yet ready to grow a beard or wear anything other than the famous gray-flannel suit and button-down collar, or women to give up home for law school. Even less were many prepared seriously to criticize the "American way of life" at home when it seemed so threatened from abroad—or from imagined, and perhaps a few real, "subversives" down the street.

Nor was the reluctance mere cravenness. Many Americans were quite aware, often on the basis of personal experience, of the destructive side of the old-fashioned individualism that destroyed not a few of those who fell short of clawing their way clear to the top. The new organizational way of life, together with government programs carried over from the New Deal, had brought more Americans than ever before to the threshold of a genuinely good life. The new Fifties way of life seemed actually more humane, more caring, even more loving than the old social Darwinism—if it were not for those nagging doubts, and the way a term like *mass society* has a nasty feel to it.

The tensions were more than a little alleviated by the new affluence. That was the subject of another important book of the decade, *The Affluent Society* by John Kenneth Galbraith, a significant document of the economic and moral climate within which Fifties and Sixties religion flourished. Galbraith documented what everyone knew: that more people were making more money than ever before. As the twentieth century advanced, income in the United States rose, and it was distributed more equitably in midcentury than before or after. In 1928 the top 1 percent received over 19 percent of all income, by 1946, 8 percent. Between 1941 and 1950 the income of the lowest fifth of all families had risen 42 percent, of the second lowest 37 percent, of the third lowest 24 percent, of the second highest 16 percent, of the highest 8 percent, while the income of the top 5 percent had declined by 2 percent. It was the poor, not the rich, who got richer in the war decade leading up to the Fifties, and now many of them were coming into their inheritance. Stark contrasts of wealth and poverty seemed to be becoming a thing of the past in this country. (Unfortunately, in the later decades of the twentieth century, the gulf between the richest and the poorest was to grow again.)

Galbraith, an unabashed liberal, attributed this change to the social and economic policies of the New Deal era. By making the working class more secure than in the days of unmitigated laissez-faire, they made it more productive than when workers were constantly on the edge of hunger and homelessness. Then, as workers won more disposable income, they became a better market for the products they themselves made. Well-paid, well-pensioned, well-organized workers ultimately benefit both labor and capital, and that happy mutual-support process was coming to fruition in the Fifties affluent society, according to Galbraith. Contrary to Marx, capital does not need to keep workers at the lowest wages for which they will (or can) work; it is to capital's own long-term benefit to pay them well instead.

The book heralds the arrival of large new working and middle classes with unprecedented money and leisure, holding up a mirror to most Fifties readers. But, as a moralist, Galbraith went on to admonish them of what must come next: investing less in goods and more in people through education and the general welfare, that is, through an enhanced public sector. Aware of remaining self-perpetuating pockets of poverty, he believed they could only be addressed through such governmental means. As is well known, *The Affluent Society* was a basic textbook of the next decade's New Frontier and Great Society.[41]

Will Herberg's *Protestant, Catholic, Jew: An Essay in American Religious Sociology,* was another blockbuster work of the time. It might have been subtitled "Organization Man and the Lonely Crowd Go to Church (or Synagogue) in the Affluent Society," for the basic theme of this thoughtful study was that religion was popular in America because it provided a means of identity that connected people both to their immigrant pasts and to their present common identity as Americans. The first, largely nineteenth-century generation of immigrants understandably clung to ethnic churches and synagogues as a means of maintaining contact with community and roots in a largely alien situation. The second generation reacted against them, desiring instead only American identity. But the third is comfortable with religion because it discovers that being different religiously is part of being American. That culture tacitly accepts that people can have different religions, and again tacitly recognizes that far from threatening a common Americanness, this diversity only reaffirms unity because Americans are *supposed* to be religiously diverse. "The only kind of separateness or diversity that America recognizes as permanent, and yet also as involving no status of inferiority, is the diversity or separateness of religious community."[42]

Therefore, according to Herberg, the major strands of U.S. religion really legitimated each other and provided their members with two different but important kinds of identity: a particular one, related to their specific roots; and a general one, as an American with a religion, something an American was expected to have. Together, all the religions amounted to a religion of America, the bedrock foundation of free-market, supply-side religion.

Herberg's work did much to create the "civil religion" discussion. Whether one liked it for its inclusive tolerance or disparaged it as "American Shinto," whether one saw it promoting "brotherhood" or fomenting a cold-war religious nationalism, civil religion or Americanism as a religion was a Fifties topic. Often this topic was not quite named or identified, but it was there. President Eisenhower reportedly said he thought all Americans should go to church, and he didn't care what church it was. If it was not quite true that "America" had no notions of social superiority and inferiority among religious communities, Herberg and the Fifties did much to level such as there were, at least among the big three groupings.

Much fun was had among religious sophisticates, especially in neoorthodox circles, about worshipping "the God of your choice," but in fact the pain of the decade's conflict between two "Gods"—the national God of brotherhood and tolerance, and the neoorthodox churchly God with a keen eye for sin and jealous of idolatry—was real. Both seemed to have something the society needed.

Then there was the problem of the inclusiveness of the three great faiths approach. As Herberg acknowledged (chiefly in footnotes) Eastern Orthodox and Buddhists might understandably have felt left out. But then, "not all [religions] are felt to be really American and therefore to be retained with Americanization. The Buddhism of Chinese and Japanese immigrants, for example, is definitely felt to be something foreign in a way that Lutheranism, or even Catholicism, never was; the Americanization of the Chinese or Japanese immigrant is usually felt by the immigrant himself, as well as by the surrounding American community, to involve dropping the non-American faith and becoming a Catholic or a Protestant, usually the latter" (44, n. 26).

In the same way, Euro-Americans drawn to "exotic" faiths could not escape the tripartite classification: "I know a distinguished professor in a New England college who is at once a Unitarian and a Buddhist (he was indeed initiated into one of the Buddhist sects); this is regarded by his friends as rather odd, but as in no way impugning his Protestantism. And his is not the only case of this kind that has come to my attention" (44, n. 27).

Still, however much one tried to bring the exotics into the Protestant-

Catholic-Jew tent, its fabric could not always be made to fit. Not all Euro-American Buddhists, however Wasp in background, were willing to be considered culturally Protestant like Herberg's Unitarian/ Buddhist, and in any case increasingly their background was Roman Catholic, like Jack Kerouac, or Jewish, like Alan Ginsberg. And the ethnic Buddhists (or Muslims, Hindus, Sikhs, and others) would not forever be content having to choose between converting and being indelibly "something foreign" and "not . . . really American."

Nonetheless, custodians of the great tradition found it very difficult in the Fifties to take Buddhists and other "aliens" seriously as intellectual or spiritual forces, though they might acknowledge with chagrin that such groups had been leading unwary Americans astray for a long time. Peter Fingesten in a 1959 article, "Beat and Buddhist," dilated on the "abandoning" of Christianity by "many of our young writers and artists"—the so-called Beats—in favor of "esoteric Buddhist practices." He said flatly, "This is a result of more than fifty years of effort on the part of Buddhist and Hindu missionaries in the metropolitan centers of America," and he referred to the Theosophical Society, founded in New York in 1875, the coming of Swami Vivekananda shortly before the turn of the century, D. T. Suzuki, and many others. Rather overemphasizing (and satirizing) the alleged incommunicability of Zen experience, and misunderstanding its alleged teaching that the world is illusion, Fingesten considered the East Asian doctrine ethically evasive and a "polar opposite to Christianity." But at least it was acknowledged to be there, and to have been there for a long time.[43]

But then, Alan Watts's *The Way of Zen* and Jack Kerouac's *The Dharma Bums* had already racked up impressive sales in the mid-Fifties. The paradox of a boom in conventional religion running alongside an upsurge of interest in exoticism is at the heart of the present book, as it endeavors to explore the peaks, plains, and underground currents of Fifties religion.

Notes from Underground

It was that experience of being, like William Whyte's suburbanites, "imprisoned in brotherhood"—and one might add incarcerated in the "togetherness" family—that left the way open for the spiritual underground. If the religious intellectuals on the peaks showed that all responsible choices involved compromise with evil, and the popular religion of the plains saw instead community and success blessed by God all around, a few turned aside from both vistas to see burning bushes in other directions. Disdaining both the pessimism of the elite Jeremiahs and the pabulum of mass religiosity, they sought in effect to gather cornerstones new and old with which to build new spiritual cultures for America. In the last chapter we briefly examined three very different examples of such alternative vision: the UFO prophet, George Adamski; the pacifist in a sterile season for his kind, A. J. Muste; and the most famous monk in the United States, Thomas Merton. Now we will look at two undergrounders who turned toward Zen and the East: the Beat chronicler, Jack Kerouac; and the Anglo-Catholic turned populist mystic, Alan Watts.

Some denizens of the underground, like Kerouac and his companions and like Watts, would find new spiritual foundations in Zen or other Eastern imports. Others, as we have seen, located them in UFOs or a Trappist monastery. Still others (to be discussed in the next chapter as they opened gateways to the Sixties) turned to mythology, psychedelics, or anticommunist extremism.

I wish now to propose that what really held the Fifties underground together most profoundly was its challenge to the fundamental, family-oriented, togetherness and brotherhood values of the mainstream. Sometimes that rejection was simply in favor of a life of the mind, or of mystical experience, or of an indefinable freedom, a wanderlust of the soul. Sometimes it was more explicitly in favor of male bonding—perhaps a legacy of the recent war—as it renounced the women-and-children world of the new suburbs and their religion, elite and populist alike. Such radical alternatives might require radically different symbols, from the East or the monastery or outer space.

A real though unstated tension in the Fifties not only lay between the often denounced mass society and the individual, or capitalism and communism, or the domestic and the exotic, but between family bonding and an alternative principle for human relationships, usually some form of male bonding that overtly or covertly rejected family and the male-female connection as the primary loyalty. It is not surprising that this tension should obtain in the decade after a great war. The disruption or postponement of family life caused by war, especially in the serving generation, inevitably produces a powerful burst of marriage and fertility among survivors after the armistice. This was clearly the case in the Fifties, years of the baby boom and of powerful idealization of the family.

But war can also leave different residues, both in veterans and in others fired by the wartime mystique: the passions of unhampered devotion to a great cause; the larger vision of the world divided between vast opposing forces representing good and evil; the intense band-of-brothers bonding of men in combat. Beyond doubt not a few Fifties males felt deep, probably almost inexpressible, tension between the postwar nesting instinct and those restless other drives. Expressed in religious or quasi-religious ways, the alternative impulses helped shape the spiritual underground.

How did it work? First let us look at the profamily side. Certainly one of the most ancient, if not *the* most primordial, function of religion in human society is to provide sanctions in support of family and the nurture of the young. That role asserted itself as powerful and basic in the mainline, above-ground religion of the decade. The Park Forest archetypal model of a new sub-urban church emphasized its role as a supportive fellowship of young parents, just as did the new Jewish temple in the same community. Peale's positive thinking, in its emphasis on success, really highlighted the breadwinning vir-tues of the family man. The new medium, TV, which featured Sheen and other prominent religious figures, was family oriented, the icon of the new family room.

Indeed, perhaps for the first time, the nation as a whole seemed to think of itself as an organic entity, like a family, rather than a group of individuals joined in some Lockean social contract. It was "group" in the sense that Mary Douglas uses the term as she contrasts "grid," or structure-based, societies with those that emphasize group or cohesive-bonding forces—and that seek with particular vehemence to expel "witches" and other pollutants.[44] That was what the wartime experience, and the cold-war trauma of facing a common enemy, had wrought. Civil religion and *brotherhood* (the common Fifties term may be significant) present the positive side of this national familism, while its more negative face is shown in the vociferousness with which dissidents were ejected like those disgraced family members one no longer sees or names. The great-est hatreds, like the greatest loves, are at home.

The underground was a little different. First, all on our varied list of un-derground figures—George Adamski, A. J. Muste, Thomas Merton, Jack Kerouac, Alan Watts, Joseph Campbell, Billy James Hargis, Aldous Huxley—were male. This is a rather striking anomaly, when one thinks about it, for a list of stars of alternative spirituality. The world of alternative altars, especially in the United States, has usually been illumined by clusters and even galax-ies of women in all ranks. One recalls nineteenth-century Spiritualism, founded by the Fox sisters and replete with many women mediums and ministers at a time when persons of their gender would have had very little opportunity for comparable roles in the major churches. One recalls Helena Blavatsky and Katherine Tingley of Theosophy, Mary Baker Eddy of Christian Science, and the numerous women mighty in the New Thought churches. As late as the Thirties, the news was full of Aimee Semple McPherson, and Edna Ballard of "I Am."

In the Fifties (overgeneralizing, of course) all of the women and most of the men apparently were engaged in bonding the "perfect universe" of the nuclear family, or in doing various mainstream things in church or on the job. But religion has other ancient roots than sanctioning family life: giving or in-terpreting solitary and individualistic visions and mystical raptures, bonding some persons in same-sex religious orders, providing roles for virtuosi shamans and magi, inspiring crusades. The mystical root of religion may, in the present context, be taken broadly to mean inner-directed religion, that which comes out of one's inner experience and perceived spiritual drives rather than those socially conditioned. The Fifties spiritual underground exalted that source of religion against the family and social sanctions side, then reified it through nonfamilial bonding, characteristically bands of brothers born of the Spirit out of comparable inner enlightenments. All the Fifties alternative commitments of that ilk, even though they might be pacifist, were broadly comparable in intensity, in life-or-death seriousness, to those of males in wartime submarines or foxholes, far from family and the fair sex. Some rather pointedly excluded women as coequals from their particular perfect universes.

In religion, that naturally meant a rejection of the Fifties mainstream churches, which were fundamentally oriented toward sanctioning family bonding. Take Jack Kerouac, the Beats, and their exotic Zen. Insofar as Beat religion was that fashionable oriental mysticism, it idealized the Beat Zen of Jack Kerouac's "dharma bums" for whom Buddhism meant utter freedom and spontaneity to meet personal rather than socially defined objectives. The Beats' flexible interpretation of Zen was criticized as little more than license for hedonism and irresponsibility, no doubt with some justice. Nonetheless it represented what critics thought the Fifties needed: an inner-directed life unafraid of nonconformity and unimpressed with "success." The cost was in a life-style legitimated, perhaps, by the inwardness of mysticism but expressed through a narrow, gender-based understanding of humanity and largely defined by what it rejected: family togetherness, conventional work and society, and women.

With Kerouac and the Beats as model, we can now look more briefly at other exponents of the Fifties spiritual underground. Thomas Merton inhabited a radically different but no less masculine world behind the monastery walls. George Adamski was primarily involved with his band of wise and mainly male "space brothers," speaking little of his wife, who was not present at any of his extraordinary encounters. While Alan Watts's mystical writings celebrated a joyous spiritual freedom, his own relations with wives and children were flawed to the point of serious neglect. He and Jack Kerouac both repeatedly failed at marriage and found solace in alcohol.

Billy James Hargis, though he presented himself as a Christian family man (an image weakened by post-Fifties scandals involving alleged sex with teenagers of both genders), clearly was most wholeheartedly committed to his anticommunist perpetuation of the mystic wartime spirit of devotion to a great crusade. A. J. Muste, Joseph Campbell, and Aldous Huxley were reasonably successful in marriage and cannot be associated at all with the misogynist attitudes of the Beats. Yet it is clear that in their lives, inner-directed mystical or spiritual experience, and the often peripatetic needs of their calling, took precedence.

Why were there no equally well-known female counterparts to these males bonding to each other and to some great cause in the Fifties? Good question.

No doubt, according to the fashionable Freudianism of the Fifties themselves, conscious or unconscious sexual antagonism would have to be presumed basic to the rebelliousness of the spiritual underground. It need not, however, be regarded as its sole dynamic. As we turn from time to time to the underground, we will also look at the two other themes that appear eminently in its rhetoric: mass society versus the individual, and domestic U.S. culture versus exotic alternatives. Finally, wherever it came from, the recovered treasures and strange imports of the underground added much to the color and diversity of the Fifties spiritual marketplace.

JACK KEROUAC AND THE BEATS

The Beats—poets, self-anointed philosophers, and intellectual rebels—raised a stir in the middle and late Fifties. Centering in such haunts as San Francisco's North Beach, Los Angeles's Venice district, and Greenwich Village in New York, like the slightly earlier European existentialists they sought to define a life based on unrestrained personal expression, setting aesthetic and spiritual values ahead of materialism, and proclaiming alienation from the square world. Sometimes, to the scandal of the same squares, all this entailed a grubby, non-working, hitchhiking way of life in which drink, drugs, and free sex were prominent. Beatdom articulated its separate space through distinctive dress, manner, and hip vocabulary. The word *Beat* was said to have originally meant "exhausted," later "beatific," and probably came from the argot of the jazz musician circles in which the movement had its roots.

There were significant ways in which the Beat wave was a spiritual movement, even if a muddled and underground one. It valued personal expression and illumination through heightened sensory awareness induced by such means as drugs, jazz, sex, or Zen. Its aesthetics were evangelical insofar as it attempted to liberate poetry from its academic shackles and bring it back to the streets. The Beats favored free, unstructured composition. Kerouac said that putting all his thoughts and feelings on paper, without premeditation or later correction, cleansed him as once had the regular confessions he made in the Catholic church.

Indeed, in a 1958 interview with Mike Wallace, Jack Kerouac—identified as at thirty-five the "patriarch and prophet" of the Beat Generation—and the equally Beat poet Philip Lamantia spoke of beatness as a religious movement. Kerouac claimed—it sounds as though through a haze of grass smoke so dense the reader can almost smell its tangy fumes—that the Beat evangel was nothing less than "a revival prophesied by Spengler. He said that in the late moments of Western civilization there would be a great revival of religious mysticism. It's happening." Yet also: "What I believe is that nothing is happening. . . . We're an empty vision—in one mind . . . [God] is the name we give it . We can give it any name. We can call it tangerine . . . god . . . tangerine. . . . But I do know we are empty phantoms. . . . And yet, all is well. . . . We're all in heaven, now, really." And Lamantia added, "You have to be pure. You gotta get throughout this life without getting hung up. . . . That's the whole question—not to get hung up."[45]

But the unhungup mystics were now outsiders, like countless saints and rebel-prophets of the religious past. About the same time Whyte was writing about people "imprisoned in brotherhood," Jack Kerouac, in *The Dharma Bums*, was celebrating his convention-defying Beat hero, Japhy Ryder, a character widely known to be based on the poet Gary Snyder, in this grand-slam sentence, set near the University of California at Berkeley:

> Japhy and I were kind of outlandish-looking on the campus in our old clothes in fact Japhy was considered an eccentric around the campus, which is the usual thing for campuses and college people to think whenever a real man appears on the scene—colleges being nothing but grooming schools for the middle-class non-identity which usually finds its perfect expression on the outskirts of the campus in rows of well-to-do houses with lawns and television sets in each living room with everybody looking at the same thing and thinking the same thing at the same time while the Japhies of the world go prowling in the wilderness to hear the voice crying in the wilderness, to find the ecstasy of the stars, to find the dark mysterious secret of the origin of faceless wonderless crapulous civilization.[46]

(It is mind-boggling to realize he is talking about *Berkeley*, of all places, which less than a decade later would be prowling with thousands of Japhies, or would-be Japhies.)

The Jack Kerouac who wrote these lines was born in Lowell, Massachusetts, in 1922. His family was of French-Canadian, ultimately Breton, ancestry; he spoke French before English, and there was not a little of Celtic romanticism in his perennial love of wandering, words, and wonders.

Kerouac's early years were unprepossessing. He dropped out of Columbia University, was dismissed from the navy during World War II for alleged mental instability, and took a number of jobs around the country in the immediate postwar years, hitchhiking to the West Coast in 1947. But he started writing and finally in 1957 published his first major book, *On the Road*.[47] Like all of his novels it is autobiographical, a formless epic recounting frenetic journeys across the United States by young men obsessed with, and in search of, life, love, jazz, mysticism, drugs, beauty, truth—and contemptuous of all conventional middle-class life. *On the Road* was read, talked about, and an immediate sensation: criticized, attacked, disdained, loved, emulated. The novel drew attention to a subculture (heretofore marginal, now where it was at) of poets, folksingers, jazz musicians, mystics, addicts, and their hipster hangers-on—the Beats. And Kerouac seemed to know them all. Persons like Allen Ginsberg, Gregory Corso, William Burroughs, Gary Snyder, Philip Whalen, themselves writers and poets, appeared in his works, often thinly veiled by pseudonyms.

The veiled names and the formless exuberance appear again in the dropout's next major novel, *The Dharma Bums* (1958), centering on Kerouac (as "Ray Smith") and Gary Snyder ("Japhy Ryder"). It was a book that presented the reverse side of the Fifties from the traditional view. Of it Seymour Krim wrote, "Kerouac, by throwing over the literary restraints, has succeeded in letting some of the real experience of our decade escape into his pages in crude, free-swinging, even shapeless form. . . . [He] doesn't apologize for his pursuit of pleasure," refusing to measure his experience against anyone else's ideal.[48] The picaresque novel begins with Ray hitchhiking and hopping freights to San Francisco, arriving at the fabulous City on the Bay just in time for the legendary Gallery Six poetry reading of October 6, 1955. Said to mark the formal opening of the Beat "poetry renaissance," that memorable evening first heard Ginsberg utter his famous "Howl!" and Snyder recite verses on the trickster Coyote, in the Native American genre that was ultimately to lead him to a Pulitzer Prize. Much impressed, Kerouac/Ray Smith took up with Snyder and others of the set, learning that along with poetry they were developing an interest in Buddhism, especially the Zen of those wonderful, whimsical old Chinese and Japanese masters of the puzzling koans and of seeing Buddha in the hedge at the bottom of the garden, or in hearing the sound of one hand clapping.

Above all, they liked the "Zen lunatics" of Eastern lore, those free spirits who lived by enlightened impulse, who drank when they felt like drinking and slept when they felt like sleeping, and who seemed to see all of life as an uproarious joke. It was a congenial philosophy for high-spirited young men exploring their world and seeking ecstasy through all its dimensions, and the book, for all its literary flaws, contains paragraphs in which all the flavor of youthful sensual and spiritual adventure on the part of males is wonderfully captured.

Japhy, though the younger, is portrayed as the ideal young orientalist, poet, outdoorsman, and Zennist, a twentieth-century Henry Thoreau, Walt Whitman, and Daniel Boone rolled into one, an American bodhisattva. And over all the revels of the Beat Zen set hung the knowledge that at the end of the year Japhy would be leaving their mountain-climbing expeditions and raucous parties to taste another distillation of life; he was going to Japan to study in a real Zen temple, as in fact did the real Gary Snyder. Japhy was indeed a special, set-apart being. He could be exuberant, noisy, a wild party giver, a mountaineer who ran shouting to the tops of peaks, a vigorous and much-desired lover of women; he was also a bespectacled scholar translating Chinese poets; and when compassion was called for he could be "tender as a mother," and he was always making little gifts to people (*dana*, giving, is one of the six *paramitas* or perfections of a bodhisattva). Alan Watts has nonetheless declared that Kerouac's Japhy "hardly begins to do . . . justice" to the real Gary Snyder. He paid Snyder what must be one of the most remarkable compliments in all literature: "I can only say that a universe which has manifested Gary Snyder could never be called a failure."[49]

The same could not quite be said of Kerouac, who paints himself in the novel as Snyder's immature but sensitive disciple in Zen. Jack was dependent on his mother and a failure in other relations with women, unsuccessful in anything but writing, helplessly compassionate toward the suffering of the world, already revealing the weakness for the bottle that was to lead to his early death in 1969. Clearly his set was a remarkable group in a distinguished American lineage, that of the Transcendentalists and of outsider, Orient-tinged poets like Walt Whitman and Ezra Pound. Yet the Beats were also products of their times, the middle Fifties, and so at least in part represent an obverse of those church and family togetherness years.

The Fifties underground meaning of all this is suggested by an innovative paper by Stephen Prothero, "'God Is a Masturbator': Religion, Gender, and Sexuality among the Beats." (The provocative title is from a controversial poem of that name by Gregory Corso, in which God becomes a sexual, vaguely masculine being emitting "wild joys.") Prothero points out that the Beat scene, like its literature, was "dominated by domineering men" to whom women were, in the title of Joyce Johnson's insightful book about her association with the Beats, "minor characters." In the novels of Jack Kerouac most women are troubled but ultimately inconsequential ornaments who appear when the loosely structured plot calls for sex or a party, then conveniently disappear when the menfolk get down to the serious business of drinking wine and talking philosophy. Writing at the time, Herbert Gold said caustically but, I think, relevantly, "The hipster's ideal is to smoke a cigar and study the *Daily News* while having immobile sexual intercourse. He has to carry out the act in order to refuse its meaning in vitality and refreshment and to debase the girl: he cannot simply refrain."[50]

Prothero interprets the Beats as grown-ups in the tradition of what E. Anthony Rotundo has called "boy culture," American boys growing up bonded to friendships of their own gender, doing "boys' things" like fishing and rough sports together, disdaining the matriarchal home and anything "effeminate."[51] When they grew up, they wanted to become a "man's man," meaning continuing to do the same kinds of things with other men most of the time, but having a wife, sex, and children to show they were real men in that respect too. Above all they wanted *freedom*, freedom in all its dimensions, freedom from home, mothers, schoolmarms, and "feminized" preachers, freedom to fight, freedom to wander with a band of brothers, sexual freedom. This mentality, Prothero argues, I think rightly, underlay the Beats. Ginsberg wrote significantly if a little awkwardly in 1954, "The social organization which is most true of itself to the artist is the boy gang." "Not," he added, "society's perfum'd marriage."[52]

Prothero points out that the Beats were Fifties men's men in many respects. Unlike the hippies of the Sixties, who took on an androgynous masculinity symbolized by long hair and long flowing garments, the Beats wore short hair and tight jeans and smoked and drank like "real men." Where they differed was in rejecting the role of the male as producer and provider, as well as rejecting the feminine. Thus they also rejected womanhood and family togetherness as they were particularly defined by the Fifties. They remained, in other words, in the boyhood and wartime male role, at odds with the overdrawn postwar family roles of the general culture.

ALAN WATTS

On the edge of the Beat culture though helping to define the Zen side of its ideology and a tutor to some of its principals was the English-accented voice of Alan Watts.[53] He also came out of a boy culture, though the rather different one of the British public school. It had left him, no less than the Beats, a rebel against conventional Christianity and no great shakes at family life, and like Kerouac he was in the end destroyed by drink. But he was never quite a beatnik. It took him a long time to get out of straight dress (in *The Dharma Bums* he makes a cameo appearance as Arthur Whane, where he appears smartly attired in coat and tie at a party where most of the guests are naked). One could always sense that Watts was from another time and place than the Beats and hipsters he admired, but they flocked to hear him as though he were a sympathetic uncle.

Alan Watts was born in England in 1916, went to a famous boarding school but, family finances diminished in the depression Thirties, was unable to attend a university. Instead, he lived and worked in London, making that great city, as he once said, his university. Haunting bookstores, he came in contact with people like Christmas Humphreys, leader of British Buddhists, and through him D. T. Suzuki, the premier apostle of Zen to the West. As early as 1935, when he was only nineteen, he published a short book on Zen.[54]

In 1938, as war clouds gathered over Europe, Watts married Eleanor Everett, daughter of a very wealthy Chicago businessman and of Ruth Fuller Everett, a leader in the First Zen Institute in New York. The promising young couple came to the New World, where Watts took up a life of writing, teaching, and lecturing.

Soon, however, Watts decided to seek holy orders in the Episcopal church. He was drawn by the aesthetic appeal of Anglo-Catholicism, and by a desire for a professional vocation in which he could fulfill within the context of his culture his main interest, spirituality. It was 1941, and possibly the prospect of clerical exemption from the draft was another motive. In any case, Watts began study at Seabury-Western Theological Seminary in Evanston, Illinois, and was ordained priest on Ascension Day, 1944. He promptly took up duties as Episcopal chaplain at Northwestern University.

Watts quickly became a campus legend. He was bearded and rode a bicycle around campus (both eccentric enough at the time), and his Canterbury House was the scene of nonstop bull sessions and unforgettable lectures in which Watts, as always, managed to make his listeners feel they were being let in on some wonderful cosmic secret. His Sunday liturgical enactments had the color of great theater and the mood of playful dance more than of courtly rite.

During these Episcopal years Alan Watts wrote a couple of successful books, *Behold the Spirit* and *The Supreme Identity*, which presented a richly mystical, incarnational, and sacramental vision of Christianity.[55] Drawing deeply from the Christian mystics, they were also enriched by frequent comparisons and quotations from their Eastern mystical colleagues, especially Taoist and Zen Buddhist. Uneven though sometimes brilliant, these books can, broadly speaking, be compared to Aldous Huxley's *Perennial Philosophy*, Thomas Merton's *Seven Storey Mountain*, and John Howard Northrop's *Meeting of East and West*, likewise popular in the immediate postwar period. All of them respond to a postwar yearning for what the mystics believed they had found, a timeless inner reality beyond the vicissitudes of the world. This reality was to be found, not as the Sixties was to have it, in radically extraorthodox spiritual adventures, but through recovering the rich mystical treasures already embedded in the major existing spiritual institutions, the churches, temples, monasteries, waiting to be found in their libraries and the annals of their canonized saints. That suited the mood of the late Forties and early Fifties, too exhausted and anxious to try anything new but eager to find some latent good in civilizations that had gone badly astray.

By 1950, however, Watts was ready to take the East directly from its source. His career as an Episcopal priest was over, and so was his marriage. Serious doubts concerning Christianity and his clerical calling, together with scandalous views (and practice) on sex and marriage, had ended both. He managed to land on his feet the next year, however, with a book that no doubt came out of the trauma of that transition, *The Wisdom of Insecurity*, a teaching position at the American Academy of Asian Studies in San Francisco, and a three-year fellowship from the Bollengen Foundation to do research for a book on Zen.[56]

That book, *The Way of Zen*, was published in 1957. A presentation of Zen in the D. T. Suzuki tradition, really as much or more Taoist as Buddhist, it emphasized the easygoing inner freedom and aesthetic spirit of the tradition more than the hard discipline of zazen meditation or brutal exchanges between student and master. But it had all the exoticism Watts could lend it with an opening line that read, "Zen Buddhism is a way and a view of life which does not belong to any of the formal categories of modern Western thought," and by Chinese characters Watts drew with his own hand.[57] The book, which came out just in time to catch the surge of curiosity about Zen piqued by the Beats and earlier lectures by Suzuki, made an impact.

Watts also wrote a notable essay, "Beat Zen, Square Zen, and Zen," saying some wise things about the two Zen paths now set before a candid public, that of the dharma bum Zen lunatics, and the "square" Zen of disciplined Japanese monks. After comments on the strengths and weaknesses of both, including remarks on Kerouac's novel that reveal Watts's lack of enthusiasm for what he considers its "anything goes" Beat Zen, Watts advocates a "no fuss" Zen without pretense either for "bohemian affectations" or for wanting "to run off to a monastery in Japan."[58] That left Watts at dead center, without having to do anything one way or the other except write, which was probably the way he wanted his own Zen.

Watts's essay and the periodical in which it appeared rated mention in *Time*, which gushed, "Zen Buddhism is growing more chic by the minute. Latest evidence: the summer issue of *Chicago Review*, which contains nine articles on the subject, a poem, and an excerpt from Zen-loving "beat" Novelist Jack (*On the Road*) Kerouac's forthcoming *The Dharma Bums*. Begins Kerouac: LET THERE BE BLOWING-OUT AND BLISS FOREVER MORE."[59]

Alan Watts also wrote *Nature, Man and Woman* (1958), suggesting that the Christian split between mind and body taken over from Greek dualism had affected attitudes of men toward women down to the present, and exploring with some tender wisdom new ways for the sexes to relate to each other. The spirit of this book, if not Watts's own example, may be considered a beginning shift from Beat manhood ideals toward the new paradigms of the Sixties and especially the Seventies on gender relations.

Overall, however, Alan Watts in the Fifties is important for epitomizing one response to two major themes and conundrums of the decade, individual versus mass society and the exotic versus the domestic. In his personal choice in 1950 no less than the burden of his books, he came down strongly for the value of the individual and the exotic. He was, as he liked to put it, a shaman rather than a priest, and he was forever favoring the gentle wisdom of the East over the follies of the West with its self-righteousness and its angry masculine God. That put him in the underground and made him one of its most eloquent voices, for though he tended toward repetitiousness he said what he had to say over and over very well; he was hardly capable of an awkward sentence. Perhaps he was too glib and facile, but what he spoke wanted to be heard in the Fifties. With Alan Watts around, America could not completely forget that there were other cultures in the world, and that they represented more than just places to fight communism and sell American goods. For all his flaws, he was a shaman, a prophet, a mystic, and, as he liked to call himself, a "philosophical entertainer."

Conclusions

The anxiety of 1950–1952, enhanced by the cold war, Korea, and McCarthyism, and also by Catholic-Protestant tensions on the religious front, was serious. Many now living still remember that in those days, as children or young people, they did not expect to live to full adulthood. They would die in a nuclear holocaust, or be sent to some far-off battlefield where the cold war had become hot, like Korea, and die there. Some of them did so die in Vietnam. In retrospect the anxieties look exaggerated, easy to caricature. But we must remember why they came about, and how they eased.

They came about fundamentally because citizens of the United States were in an unfamiliar position in the world, a state that inevitably generates anxiety. Never had the world been so polarized between only two powers, and never had the United States stood alone as unambiguously the dominant power on one side. Never had it been engaged in a world confrontation as clearly ideological and even religious as this one, though the engagement with fascism only a few years earlier was an obvious (though sometimes misleading) precedent. Never had weapons the magnitude of the new atomic devices hung as a continual threat over the heads of a nation's people, and the Soviet bomb had been tested only in 1949. This period was indeed a narrow trough through which U.S. history had to pass, and religion with it. Looking back, one almost feels it could have been worse and lasted longer; that it did not is a tribute to the collective sanity, and the spiritual traditions, of the majority.

Why did the anxiety ease a little in 1953 and after? On the political scene, the election of Dwight D. Eisenhower defused the appeal of McCarthy and his cohorts and promised an end to the Korean War. One can fault Ike on many scores, particularly for sins of omission, for all that he might have done with his gifts of leadership in such areas as civil rights and Latin American relations but that he let simmer till another day. But it must be acknowledged that his smiling, benign presence combined with his moderately conservative but civil-libertarian instincts were profoundly healthy for the United States of 1953 and after, as was his action to end war in Korea and his administration's eventual willingness to stand up to McCarthy.

At the same time, one senses a growing "anxiety fatigue" at home. The high-decibel rhetoric and the constant brinks of Armageddon had become a weariness. To take their place in the middle Fifties gradually arose something more positive: a sense of the common heritage—not ideology—of U.S. society. Religion contributed to this change in several ways. By 1953 and especially 1954 many important religious figures and periodicals were prepared to question extreme anticommunism on moral and spiritual as well as factual grounds. The growth of the brotherhood and heritage spirit, represented by the *Look* articles and subsequent books, helped form the new mood. Ike's own vague but affirmative religiosity, so civil-religious in tone, was constructive.

Although this spirit certainly did not extend to an increased appreciation of communism, it helped allay domestic religious feuds and created an atmosphere in which even the cold war could be taken more in stride. All this was a positive if indirect result, it seems, of the boom in church attendance and congregation building of the late Forties and early Fifties. While sometimes criticized as culture-religion or patriotic-religion, in the end the religion upswing helped defuse those compatriots who were only ideological, including some in churchly positions.

We must endeavor to understand Fifties religiosity in terms of U.S. religious history as a whole, including its relation to supposed secularization and the supposed "exceptionalism" of the United States to an otherwise secularizing world. (In Europe, for example, church attendance was declining in virtual free-fall during the same decade, the Fifties, that it was reaching all-time highs on the American side of the Atlantic. Why this discrepancy?) For now, it is sufficient to note what is special about religion in the mid-Fifties: its congruence with the needs of baby-boom families, its amelioration of domestic extremes, and its multilayered intellectual expression.

The mid-Fifties were a time of continuing tension between the supply-side, free-enterprise, unregulated religious-market ideal, and the lingering monopoly, state-church idea. Religious statism was represented by what still survived of the colonial Anglo-Protestant spiritual hegemony. That religious elite was ensconced in the real leadership of the National Council of Churches, apotheosized in the great event of the World Council's Evanston meeting and in the major interdenominational Protestant seminaries with their *gravitas*-holding theologians.

But that old leadership was challenged on one flank by populist Protestantism, whether Grahamite or Pealeite, and on the other by a Roman Catholic bid for national faith status, a cause close to the heart of Cardinal Spellman. It was also troubled by the rightist drive to make a sort of spiritual anticommunism a de facto national religion, with all the orthodoxy-proclaiming and heresy-hunting rights pertaining thereto. Sometimes seemingly endorsed by elites of Reinhold Niebuhr's stature, this movement in the end came much more naturally to the Protestant populists and the Catholic hegemonic hopefuls, for it was really as much a class and power realignment ploy as a policy question.

In this situation the Beats and the mystics also had a role. They kept alive the vitality of the United States as a free-enterprise religious market, ever expanding in clientele and diversity, even as there were those who tried to draw its circle closer and tighter. But in the end the ever widening spiritual pluralism always prevailed.

Signs Appearing in Heaven,

Part III   1957–1959

*And a great portent appeared in heaven, a woman clothed
with the sun, with the moon under her feet, and on her head
a crown of twelve stars; she was with child and she cried out
in her pangs of birth, in anguish for delivery. And another
portent appeared in heaven; behold a great red dragon.*

—REV. 12:1–3 RSV

Portents Old and New

THE DECADE began with the woman appearing in heaven, as the pope infallibly defined the dogma of the Assumption, reaffirming an ancient heritage of faith, myth, and mystical solidarity. Its last phase commenced with another sign in the sky, Sputnik, the Soviet artificial satellite whose appearance so confounded those who had trusted implicitly in God and the scientific superiority of the West. The makers of the metal moonlet mocked such pretensions, declaring the cosmic traveler had discovered nothing resembling God in the empty reaches of space.

The year of Sputnik, 1957, began with the classic Fifties still in full swing. Their supreme icon, President Eisenhower, was inaugurated for his second term. A representative of Eastern Orthodoxy was invited to participate in the ceremony in addition to clerics of the standard Protestant-Catholic-Jew troika; his tradition was thereupon hailed as "the fourth faith," and its presence was considered significant, for it suggested that the carefully balanced religious establishment could reconstellate, if ever so slightly.[1]

Indeed, some were even bold enough to suggest that, after the 1954 Supreme Court decision on school integration, there was a "renaissance of liberalism" in the United States. That fifth faith, liberalism, was tested and, to all appearances, reaffirmed in religion by several traumatic events of the late Fifties. Two came in late 1957. First, federal troops were sent into the capital of Arkansas, Little Rock, by President Eisenhower to enforce federal-court integration orders in the gravest domestic crisis since the Civil War. Then Little

Rock was pushed out of the headlines only ten days later by the great red dragon in the sky. But in fact liberalism was gathering force in the wake of those two compelling events, impelled by evidence from Arkansas that, however bloody the battles, integration and racial justice were coming to the United States, and by Sputnik's indirect insistence that science and education, rather than McCarthyism, were the straightest routes to cold-war victory. These were concerns of great importance to religionists, particularly liberals, and the confirmation of their beliefs and ethics they saw in the eventual outcomes was reinforced by the papal election of 1958, by the settlement of the great religious controversy at Harvard, and finally, of course, by the landmark U.S. presidential election of 1960.

Indeed, in the last half of 1957, while the first two of these dramatic events were filling the news, some observers seemed to intuit, rather than see, a spiritual turning in the nation. They sensed an invisible but palpable deflation of the Fifties religious revival despite continuing church attendance. It was as if the revival engine had been shut off, though the vehicle was continuing to roll on momentum. They felt a spreading weariness in the air toward the reigning religions, weariness and an inchoate yearning for something else to come over the spiritual horizon. The next year John XXIII, who was very much a new kind of pope, would be elected. The Sixties were getting closer.

Statistically, religious growth continued to be news into 1957. Church membership reached a high of 67 percent of the population, much of it in the suburbs, which had grown by 18 percent (as over against a national population increase of 11 percent) in 1950–1957, and according to the accountants those suburbs were strong in the areas of schools, liquor consumption, and church attendance. Religious-studies courses reportedly burgeoned on campuses, and Billy Graham's 1957 crusade in New York drew over a million to Madison Square Garden, breaking all records. Dial-a-prayer was invented.[2] Andrew Greeley, then as always the scoffer at egghead opinion, reassured Catholics in 1958 that the revival was still real. He pointed out that throughout the Fifties religious membership increased by 3 percent a year while the population by only 2 percent and went on to cast scorn on those "intellectuals" who scorned the revival.[3]

Yet doubts were rising. When the results were in for 1958, it was noted that for the first time since World War II the increase in U.S. church membership had failed to keep pace with the population increase.[4] By December 31 of 1958 the *Christian Century* was able to publish a much discussed editorial entitled "The Year the Revival Passed Crest." The vaunted religious upsurge of the Fifties was now history in that liberal periodical's eyes. Looking subtly at what was now not being said before getting to what was, it noted that "there has been a marked diminution in the criticism of Eisenhower's

Potomac piety, Peale's positive thinking, Sheen's pontificating preening, and Graham's latter-day crusades. An edge of ennui has set in."

So the public was getting a little tired of religion and its Fifties-type merchants. Opposition to religion among the "cultured despisers" was on the rise instead. Their disenchantment manifested itself in a number of ways, we were told by the *Century*: the Zen enthusiasm, the blasphemous "sick jokes" of 1957–1958, the vogue for the irreverent comedy of Mort Sahl, and the mocking songs of Tom Lehrer. "The pseudo-religious cult of togetherness was chided; a woman's magazine portrayed with approval a nonconformist suburban family, part of whose rebellion included staying away from church because the church merely represented a way of life." Faithless writers like Bertrand Russell, Julian Huxley, C. Wright Mills, and Alexander King appeared anew on publishers' lists. Beginning in the latter half of 1957, with dramatic suddenness, substantive liberal concerns about U.S. society—on education, civil rights, false religiosity—were serious issues. And as one might have expected, this news was not entirely unwelcome to a periodical with the critical perspective of the *Century*: "Religion always grows fat and vulgar and obscene when its strength is unquestioned."[5]

The shift away from high Fifties religiosity began amid the double shocks of the crisis-laden autumn of 1957, when the two quite different but equally traumatic blows to U.S. self-confidence, Little Rock and Sputnik, hit the TV screens. Both clearly demanded a serious rethinking of national priorities and values. It was plain that, though the middle Fifties of Eisenhower's first term had brought the Korean War to an end and left extreme McCarthyism behind, deep national and international fissures had been only plastered over, not filled in. A society that, for all its wealth and piety, still could not overcome racial bias or truly prioritize science and education over demagoguery fell painfully short of what the age or its own best ideals demanded.

At the same time, other less sharply focused but fundamental and persistent doubts about the Fifties revival were floating toward the surface. Even those well disposed toward conventional religion were beginning to wonder if something had gone wrong. The Fifties revival, with its crowded Sunday schools and program-rich suburban churches, was not entirely misguided. But it had sought first to build fortress walls around its nurseries, and around what was good, rather than to seek seriously to transform the bad. Now the children were growing up, and the world would have to change, as it does with every new generation.

And the bad was still present. Even apart from race and space, moral problems plagued the nation, and the religious revival seemed to have done little to prevent them. More and more was heard about juvenile delinquency, hoodlums running jukebox rackets, Charles van Doren and the quiz show scandals.

On the ecumenical scene the glamorous World Council of Evanston 1954 seemed gone three years later. At the World Council's Faith and Order Conference at Oberlin, September 3–10, 1957, some forty professors of theology debated revitalizing ecumenical Christianity at the local level, but one commented, "We are in a post-Evanston period. The romance of the ecumenical impact is over."[6]

Of course the burgeoning suburban churches, which had probably peaked as cultural phenomena by 1955, were still around. In January 1958 *Time* described the Glenview Community Church in Glenview, Illinois. This interdenominational "believe-as-you-like, worship-as-you-please fellowship of searchers" had, we were told, some two thousand members, hunting and fishing groups, a boys' hot-rod club, ten choirs, a church newspaper and radio program, and four ministers whose "language often sounds less religious than sociological," calling for a "relationship with God" through beliefs that are "anchored but open-ended."[7]

But perhaps this was one of the last such accounts. The critics of suburban religion were gathering under the aegis of the reigning neoorthodoxy and the growing social-activist faith inspired by Martin Luther King, Jr. A *Time* article on suburban religion in July said, "One of the surprising facts about the postwar surge of religion in the U.S. has been the caliber of its critics— the most telling jeers have not come from the village atheists but from the men of God."[8]

Out in the Chicago suburbs, in Elk Grove Village, dwelt "one of Protestantism's bright young men," Martin E. Marty. He was pastor of a Lutheran church and an associate editor of the *Christian Century*, and he characterized his life then as "typically gray flannel: station wagon, barbecue pit, and all that goes with it." But in a 1958 series of six articles for that periodical he declared that these are "post-Protestant times" in which the particularism that once typified U.S. church life has yielded to "religion-in-general." The best hope for authentic Christianity lay not in bigger and better revivals, but in local parishes that can act like the biblical remnant. While the implied vision of the country's Protestant past as mainly particularistic may be subject to qualification, the contemporary thrust of this message suggested that many religionists not only conceded the revival was past, they were glad that it was and now the church could get down to serious business.[9]

(In the last of these articles Marty pointed out that the ministers of Glenview Community Church took exception to *Time*'s portrait of the parish. Two weeks after the article, he said, all four ministers had responded with a letter to *Time*'s editor that dissociated them from "nontheological country clubbery." One of them had preached a sermon on January 26, 1958, extremely critical of the newsmagazine's analysis. On the same theme, Marty then took up the even more famous case of the United Protestant Church of Park Forest, Illinois, immortalized in William H. Whyte's classic, *The Organization Man*. While finding much of Whyte's portrait congenial, the ministers of that suburban megachurch also objected strenuously to the implication that they were party to the "nontheological packaging of religion to suit suburbia's social norms." Whatever the rights and wrongs of these cases, clearly the suburban apotheosis of U.S. religion was in for a rough passage, which would culminate in Gibson Winter's landmark work of the next decade, *The Suburban Captivity of the Churches*.)[10]

The passing of the limelight from suburban churches may have been missed by Methodism when, in late 1956, it launched a new magazine, *Together*, which took the place of the old *Christian Advocate*. (The latter was continued for a while as the *New Christian Advocate* in toothless digest format for clergy.) Colorfully illustrated but intellectually lightweight, *Together* was intended for the laity of the nation's then largest Protestant denomination, and it obviously envisioned them as mostly picture viewers rather than readers, no doubt suburban church types who might be enticed to spend a moment with photogenic spreads of cute, colorfully costumed children in foreign missions. But the new organ of Methodism clearly presumed its clientele unwilling to hold still for the comprehensive religious news coverage, insightful editorials unafraid to take a liberal stand, and sometimes provocative articles of the old *Christian Advocate*. The October 1956 launch issue of *Together* stated that the magazine sought "an editorial approach somewhat comparable to that used by Christ, who taught eternal truths through parables about people." Perhaps that was why, in late 1957, there was nothing about Little Rock or Sputnik—both of which would have stimulated excellent editorials in the old magazine—though much in the way of lovely portfolios on uncontroversial Methodist good works at home and abroad, country churches, and seasonal beauties.[11] (In regard to the last, the July 1957 issue of *Together* drew some letters-to-the-editor response. The magazine's cover had displayed, no doubt as an object lesson in togetherness, an attractive, casually dressed family at the beach, the very shapely young wife and mother clad in not only short shorts but also a thin summery blouse. There was amazed comment—such sights had never before been seen on or in a Methodist magazine.)

Events: Little Rock, Sputnik, John XXIII, and the
Chapter 5   Passing of the Fifties Mood

THE RACIAL mood at the beginning of 1957 might be characterized as all deliberate speed versus Jim Crow in the pew. Early in the year, *Time* did its first cover story on the Reverend Martin Luther King, Jr., "who in little more than a year has risen from nowhere to become one of the nation's remarkable leaders." In Montgomery, in the struggle that had caused his extraordinary rise, King had "struck where an attack was least expected, and where it hurt most: at the South's Christian conscience."[1] He had endured bombings, hate sheets, legal maneuvers against him and his cause, and he had prevailed. In the Fifties endgame, the domestic issue that more than anything else was to shape the moral climate of the tumultuous Sixties was being moved from the back burner where it had long simmered to the front of the stove.

Time was when it seemed race might be ignored for the sake of supposed national unity in the cold war. No longer; only by confronting race could true unity, not to mention the requisite moral stature, be realized. King more than anyone showed that race was a moral issue, a Christian issue; that it was going to be fought on moral and Christian grounds and by nonviolent means; and that it was not going to wait. *Time* quoted Baptist minister Will Campbell, "onetime chaplain at the University of Mississippi, now a Southern official of the National Council of Churches: 'I know of very few white Southern ministers who aren't troubled and don't have admiration for King. They've become tortured souls.'"[2]

In those years, church integration was still a remarkable event, supposedly calling for exceptional courage or foolhardiness on the part of the participants. Early in 1957 the Hennipin Avenue Methodist Church in

Minneapolis, called "the cathedral of Methodism," united with a small black Methodist church that had lost its property; this was news nationwide.[3]

Examples of foolhardiness—maybe of a fools-for-Christ sort—occurred too. A distinctly unpleasant racial note was struck as the Koinonia Farm near Americus, Georgia, was repeatedly attacked in February by unknown terrorists. Koinonia was a racially integrated Christian community founded by the Reverend Clarence Jordan, a Southern Baptist. The farm's roadside market was dynamited, an unoccupied house was burned, and shotguns were fired into the buildings on several occasions, once nearly hitting a ten-year-old girl. Finally a residence was raked with machine-gun fire. Answering to local hostility to the interracial community more than to his duty, the Sumter County sheriff provided little help.

The local ministerial association garnered county opposition with a relatively evenhanded statement that deplored "the use of violence in any form against property and/or persons because of their personal beliefs," while acknowledging the right to disagree with them. But the Americus clergy were in turn supported by the state Council of Churches. On the other hand, a Georgia grand jury, investigating the famed interracial community, revived the old charges and went on to claim that the farm was masquerading as a religious group to avoid taxes. Yet even it could find no specific law being violated. Nevertheless the attacks, including gunfire and a demonstration at the farm by 153 robed and hooded Klansmen, continued. Koinonia persevered, but the strain showed; more and more members were given leave for "battle fatigue."[4]

At the same time, some three hundred southern clergy attended the First Conference on Christian Faith and Human Relations in Nashville. In the edgy South "human relations" meant first and foremost race. In the sanctified world of the conference, the problem was well on the way to being resolved, as members of both races listened to each other and took communion together. They heard Martin Luther King say, speaking for black side, "We have the responsibility of freeing our white brothers from the bondage of crippling fear." But as one participant put it, "How do you preach Christ from the pulpit when Jim Crow sits in the pew?"[5]

About the same time, the General Assembly of the Southern Presbyterian Church, meeting in Birmingham, issued a very strong statement condemning discrimination in schools, defending Koinonia, and condemning the Klan and White Citizens Councils. The denomination's leadership clearly hoped to create a social climate within an influential southern church in which peaceful progress toward equality could be made.[6] But the promised land was not to be reached that easily.

That past would prove to be only prologue to the climactic race event—

and religious response event—of the year: Little Rock. The Arkansas capital was under federal court orders, pursuing the mandate of *Brown v. Board of Education*, to implement a plan for integration. The Little Rock board had produced an acceptable, though certainly very gradual, scheme that entailed the introduction of only nine black youths into Little Rock's Central High School that fall. Early on Tuesday, September 4, 1957, the day integration was to have begun, there was no evidence of any problem on the city's quiet streets. But the morning calm was broken as National Guard personnel carriers, under orders from Governor Orval Faubus, roared down the avenues toward Central High and disgorged troops who surrounded the building. Faubus claimed that the guard was necessary to "prevent violence," though no sign of violence had been visible before its arrival. Drawn by the excitement, however, a crowd of jeering segregationist protesters soon gathered before the building, vehemently trying to prevent entry by the nine children. The guard did nothing to restrain them, and indeed the mob was widely held to have been stirred up by the racist rhetoric of Governor Faubus.[7] (A contemporary article, however, contended that the mob was more aroused by the ultrasegregationist Governor Marvin Griffin of Georgia, who was in Little Rock only two days earlier to address a White Citizens Council, and whose presence and even more inflammatory language put great pressure on Faubus.)[8]

As an act of clear defiance of the federal courts by a state, it was a challenge of historical proportions. President Eisenhower felt he had no choice but to act. On September 24 he federalized the Arkansas National Guard and sent army troops into Little Rock to quell the mob and enforce the integration order.

The crisis sometimes seemed so dramatic as to be unreal, as lines hardened and rhetoric accelerated. "Some people say it's like a dream—it can't be happening here," said Presbyterian minister Dunbar H. Ogden, Jr., president of the Greater Little Rock Ministerial Association. "But I haven't felt like that. This is real."[9] It had to happen somewhere in the South, he added.

Little Rock was a headline story around the world, and one widely seen to give a bad impression of the United States, a matter of serious concern in those tense cold-war days. Communist newspapers played up U.S. racism and mob action for all it was worth, and even more friendly commentators found such a serious internal crisis arising in the leader of the free world disconcerting.[10] So did many Americans, their early Fifties confidence in democracy's redoubt sorely shaken. It remained to be seen how their confidence in Fifties religion would hold up.

The role of churches and the clergy in Little Rock—ostensibly as pious and churchgoing as any middle-American city—was under close observation. *Time* put it this way: "Little Rock's ministers, like ministers elsewhere in the

U.S., had been successful in building up their church memberships to new highs (103,224,954 nationwide). But no one knew whether this new strength could be translated into Christian action when it might be most needed and most uncomfortable."[11] In other words, now was the moment of truth regarding the moral worth of the late religion boom.

At least so far as mainline clergy were concerned, the answer was encouraging. It had been a white Presbyterian minister, the Reverend Dunbar H. Ogden, Jr., the previously cited president of the Ministerial Alliance, who had escorted black children to school the day the guard turned them away; he received a dozen threatening calls for his trouble. Led by Episcopal bishop Robert Raymond Brown, leading Protestant, Roman Catholic, and Jewish pastors met to support a day of prayer and efforts at reconciliation, including a breakfast meeting by Brown with Faubus. Billy Graham recorded a sermon for broadcast over stations in Little Rock, saying that "the violence, the hatred, the intolerance come from man's rebellion against the moral laws of God. We must love our fellow man . . . we must love him without even thinking about his race or the color of his skin."[12]

The significant news was not only that churches and churchpeople were working for civil calm and usually endorsed peaceful change in the direction of integration, but that this was considered important. As the *Christian Century* commented editorially, "Action is always ecumenicity's best vehicle."[13] Story after story on the crisis contained a sidebar on the role of the churches, presenting the opinions of southern church leaders. In the eyes of journalists, churches were expected to make a difference, and generally to be on the progressive side. Many white clergy in the South, touched by the leadership of Martin Luther King, Jr., were troubled by Little Rock, and by similar attitudes in their own bailiwicks. The handful of integrated churches across the South became newsworthy. Only a few anti-integration clergy were considered worth quoting, including a group of thirty-eight fundamentalist Little Rock ministers, mostly Baptist, who organized a prayer meeting to counter those of the liberals, asking for deliverance from federal dictatorship.

The Council of Church Women of Little Rock produced a resolution so impressive that the *Christian Century* printed it in full. The women forthrightly deplored the actions of Governor Faubus and of the "rabble-rousing crowds" and called for prayer, support of the school board, "treating every person as we would like to be treated," and refusing to spread or listen to "idle rumor" or "persons seeking to arouse hatred and setting group against group." The General Board of the National Council of Churches supported Eisenhower's action.[14]

However, a year later, after integration had been delayed in Little Rock and prosegregation religion had the opportunity to reassert itself, eighty Little

Rock ministers, though avowing their "abiding love for all people," asserted that "we believe the best interests of all races are served by segregation," and opposed its integrative opposite. When the (northern) Presbyterian Church USA gave $10,000 to the National Association for the Advancement of Colored People, the Ku Klux Klan responded with a statement to the effect that "few Americans and fewer Presbyterians ever thought they would see the day when the Presbyterian Church would sink so low in the mire of Social Gospel politics as to raise funds for the race-mixing activities of the Communist-dominated NAACP."[15]

The Jesuit periodical *America*, however, opined that Little Rock would ultimately help reintegrate the South with the rest of the nation. The new evangelical periodical *Christianity Today*, though commenting on social and political matters less frequently than its more liberal counterpart, the *Christian Century*, also rose to the issues presented by Little Rock. An editorial of September 30, 1957, noted that "America is in the throes of great sociological change" and went on to observe that "never has there been more need for Christian love and restraint. That the race issue has become political is to be deeply regretted. That the spiritual problem is ignored by some and stressed to the exclusion of sociological factors by others is equally regrettable." In this vein the periodical cited with "righteous indignation" the abuse and hatred vented upon blacks recently in Little Rock and elsewhere, noting with sadness the lack of "Christian love, sympathy, and common sense" this revealed, and calling for the church to lead in "Christian relations." Yet, while seeming to side more with the integrationists than the segregationists, *Christianity Today* carefully avoided calling for any particular judicial or legislative remedies to the crisis, thus remaining true to the vision of the church's role of its founding editor, Carl Henry.[16]

Little Rock was not the only scene of racial violence over school integration that tempestuous fall. Ugly events transpired elsewhere as well. They were most nightmarish in Nashville: rock throwing and a midnight dynamite explosion at the Hattie Cotton Elementary School, where a single five-year-old black girl had registered the day before. Only the greater drama of state versus federal authority in Little Rock overshadowed the Tennessee city's moment of infamy.

Nor were black or integrated churches the only places of worship affected by terror. On March 16, 1958, at 2:30 A.M., the school annex of Miami's Temple Beth El was bombed. Then at 8:07 P.M. on the same day, a Jewish community center in Nashville, which had been the scene of interracial meetings, was also destroyed. Shortly afterwards the wife of Rabbi William B. Silverman received a call from a man who identified himself as a "member of the Confederate Union." He added, "We have just dynamited the Jewish Community Center. Next will be the temple and next will be any other nigger-loving place or nigger-loving person in Nashville." On October 12 of the same year, the oldest and wealthiest Jewish temple in Atlanta was bombed as well. Again, a caller claiming responsibility identified himself as belonging to the "Confederate Union." In this case four suspects, all members of the National States' Rights Party or other racist groups, were arrested. However, in the end all were either acquitted or had charges dismissed in trials in which the defense employed unmistakably racist and anti-Semitic rhetoric. Bombs also went off at Jewish temples at Jacksonville and Peoria, and three more such bombings were attempted in the South.[17]

The Red Dragon

On Friday, October 4, 1957, St. Francis's day, the Russians launched the world's first successful artificial satellite. At twenty-three inches in diameter with extended antenna, weighing 184 pounds, the minuscule new moon contained nothing but a radio transmitter issuing a steady beep . . . beep . . . beep as it circled the earth again and again at eighteen thousand miles per hour. But that ominous beep changed the way the world looked as it entered countless U.S. living rooms that evening through radio and television news flashes. Sputnik, as the uninvited visitor now hurtling through U.S. as well as other skies was called, meant only one thing to most Americans: very unexpectedly, *they* were now ahead of us.

For while Sputnik itself was harmless, it was universally seen as a precursor to space travel, and so to the prospect that the first flag on the moon or Mars might be red. It could also be the forerunner of military satellites—and the launch told scientists that the Soviets already had ICBM rockets that with only small modification could send H-bombs as well as radios through the heavens. Senior officials of the Eisenhower administration played down the importance of Sputnik, calling it a "bauble," but those close to public opinion around the world knew better. It was a tremendous psychological coup for the Soviets, and the symbolic grand opening of the space era.

Worse was to come. On November 3 Sputnik II was launched, weighing 1,120 pounds and carrying a small dog, Laika. Then, on December 6, the U.S. Navy made a disastrous attempt to launch a satellite. The rocket exploded, leaving amid the rubble the small four-pound, grapefruit-sized sphere that was to have been America's answer to the Soviet triumphs. The Soviets, and much of the rest of the world, could not resist gloating at the humiliation of a nation all too ready until now to brag of its prowess as well as its righteousness. Not until January 31, 1958, did the Explorer I satellite put the United States back in the game. From then on, the space race would be run nonstop until the U.S. flag was first on the moon in 1969.

But in the intervening months, despite the holiday season, the country was seething. Fear, rage, and frustration in about equal measure are evident in letters to the editor and the posturings of politicians. Hatred of the Russians and their communist system inflamed many anew, this time suffused by teeth-clenching anxiety that they could really be about to win—and no one could think of the world except in winner/loser terms. There was plenty of searching for scapegoats, and no lack of plain fear. As the Jesuit publication *America* put it, everyone was saying to everyone else—Republicans to Democrats, Democrats to Republicans; scientists to educators and educators to scientists; ordinary citizens to Congress, schools, anyone supposed to be responsible—"Do something!"[18]

Christmas 1957 came at the depths of the dread, and *Newsweek* ran a holiday essay attempting to confront the anxiety entitled, "And the angel said unto them, Fear not . . . " It spoke of this as a "particularly troubled time," in which many are "beset with feelings of fear and anxiety," "perplexed and unsettled by sudden shifts of world power" and by "domestic uncertainties" (recall that Sputnik followed by only a week one of the greatest domestic crises of the century in Little Rock), all of which "threaten to blight the bright optimism of American life." The article offered the consolations of various leading clergy and theologians; they mostly presented variations on the theme that the antidote to fear is faith in God, but hinting that the lately popular peace-of-mind religion was not enough.[19]

That essay was paced by one in *Look* by Dr. Warren Weaver, vice president for the Natural and Medical Sciences in the Rockefeller Foundation, who asked why "a free Christian society appears less alert, less dedicated than a dictatorship." This authority spent less time than his clerical cohorts on pieties, however, moving fairly directly to what he saw as the practical solution: education. Anticipating and perhaps influencing the direction matters were to take in the Fifties endgame and the New Frontier early Sixties, Weaver declared that "all able young persons must have the opportunity—regardless of their financial, social or racial status—to obtain education up to the limit of their talents." The physical and intellectual resources necessary must be available to education, and ought to be in an affluent society. Then, hitting the obvious punchline to any such argument in 1957, Weaver affirmed that in Russia and elsewhere teachers are given good pay, and are respected and revered. How about here?[20]

It is safe to say that across the land at least fifty thousand Christmas sermons contrasted Sputnik and the star of Bethlehem, and contested the communist claim that, because the Creator had not been encountered by the whirling satellite, his existence was in doubt. On a deeper level, religious spokespersons endeavored to counter defeatism, while insisting the United

States must not surrender moral and spiritual values in an all-out weapons race with the Soviets.

Thus the *Living Church* said there is no guarantee that U.S. possession of a higher standard of living than that of the Russians is forever assured. Alluding to the temptations of Christ, it declared that material well-being does not necessarily demonstrate moral superiority or God's blessing. Americans have their faults. Raising themes that were later to crescendo, it linked desegregation and education to the post-Sputnik national introspection: "It is, for example, at least possible that the man [or woman?] who might have given us satellite priority is, in fact, shining shoes in a Philadelphia barber shop, because his black skin and poverty kept him out of a university. It is even possible that the question of whether the first pilot of a space ship to Mars will bear a Russian or American name is being settled on the streets of Little Rock this week."[21]

A remarkable change in the nature of the struggle was apparent in the wake of Sputnik, evidenced in the Weaver and *Living Church* comments. Though there were holdouts, a consensus was rapidly taking shape that McCarthy-type anticommunism, with its emphasis on supposed domestic infiltrators, was not the way to go. Not only was McCarthyism ethically dubious, it also weakened the United States where it counted, in the educational and scientific spheres, by undercutting and demoralizing the nation's best intellectual institutions and best minds. In view of the fact that the country had seriously underestimated the quality of Russian education, anything that weakened it further on that score could obviously be disastrous.

What was called for was not naming names and carrying out rites of inquisitorial purification, but larger defense budgets—a theme John F. Kennedy would exploit in the 1960 presidential race as he talked, fatuously, of a missile gap—and, in more long-range terms, better science with better education behind it. This was a theme enthusiastically taken up by the more liberal religious and educational opinion makers, visibly eager to open windows and clear out the fetid air of McCarthyism, which, in its attacks on numerous teachers and universities in the name of anticommunism, was now seen to have done more harm than good.[22] Ike's popularity declined after Sputnik, together with his health. As he sought spending cuts, Eisenhower had been able to offer only grudging aid to education. This and the talk of a missile gap by the opposition party were substantial factors in the post-Sputnik Democratic victories of 1958 and 1960.[23]

Despite the pessimism of the moment, the fresh emphasis on education, properly an open-ended enterprise, was actually the dawning of the new optimism that would characterize the Kennedy Camelot and the Great Society years of the first half of the next decade. That spirit was forged by the serendipitous coming together of the Sputnik imperative; the postwar, baby-boom demographic bulge, which made for an exploding college population and a new youth culture by the early Sixties as the children in the overflowing nurseries and schoolrooms of the Fifties matured; and the emergence of Galbraith's "affluent society" to pay for it all. In the end, the change was spiritual.

Sputnik was the sign in the heavens that, as it were, signaled divine judgment against the anticommunism state-church approach to the struggle, sustained by prayers and inquisitions. The day was instead to go to a mode of battle aligned with the world-come-of-age secular theology just beginning to emerge from the chrysalis of neoorthodoxy or Pian age Catholicism. That new religious consciousness was comfortable with education and educators, with social change and its makers, and with big budgets everywhere. The race for the moon was one that could be won. For faith was beginning to see the present moment not as apocalyptic but as eschatological in a positive sense—as a time when humanity was taking charge of its world, capable and prosperous as never before, and no longer needing to look for supernatural signs in the heavens. If in the end the open-minded, education option would lead some to question the pieties of anticommunism themselves, that is the sort of price faith always pays when it consorts with the educators rather than the bookburners of the age.

Of course religionists and nonreligionists still saw Sputnik differently. Speaking for the Vatican, L'Osservatore Romano claimed that the Soviet satellite had done nothing to change the church's views. It quoted Pius XII from a year before: "The more we explore into outer space, the nearer we get to the great idea of one family under the Mother-Father God." On the other hand, Joseph Lewis, of the Freethinkers of America, noted that "the new earth satellite . . . broadcast no discovery of God in the heavens" and added, "What a mockery does this great scientific achievement make of the petty religions of the earth."[24]

There were other kinds of caution from the religion side. Robert Fitch, dean of the Pacific School of Religion in Berkeley, warned of temptations that threatened a "new priesthood of science," with scientists as "a new sort of religious order," set apart from the rabble by "a discipline, a language, and an attitude" of contemptus mundi—disdain for the world of ordinary people—though their language was not Latin but the arcane hieroglyphics of mathematics. Their temptations, like that of any priestly class, were spiritual pride, and the desire to assume temporal authority, being ethical purists and devoutly believing that such power would be for the good of all—a prophecy of a great issue to come in the Sixties.[25]

Finally, the famous Anglican lay theologian C. S. Lewis, celebrated for his famous "space trilogy" of theological fiction, *Out of the Silent Planet,* *Perelandra,* and *That Hideous Strength,* was asked his views on life in space in light of the new developments. He responded judiciously by warning humankind against "all exploitation and all theological imperialism" toward the kindreds of other planets who may be under different divine plans than ours. "Our loyalty is not to our species but to God."[26] (It is interesting to compare the assumption that it is humans who might be guilty of imperialism with the grimmer alien scenarios rampant in some quarters in the late twentieth century, which say it is we who are being exploited.)

Evangelicalism on the Rise

The first big evidence of evangelical revival as the Fifties mainstream revival waned was Billy Graham's mammoth summer 1957 Crusade in Madison Square Garden, on the eve of Little Rock and Sputnik. The New York event was a statistical and logistical prodigy. Opening in May, it undoubtedly made evangelical Protestantism a presence in a city where it generally had little visibility: 1,941,200 attended the rallies over its ninety-seven evenings, and there were 56,526 decisions. The event retained thirty-five permanent staff members and two hundred volunteers; 1,510 churches and prayer groups were sponsors; there were 108,415 "prayer partners," and 2,143 trained "counselors" to handle converts.

Madison Square Garden, that site of many a raucous gladiatorial contest, was manifestly changed. Entry was free and ticketless for this quiet, well-dressed crowd. No haze of cigarette smoke clouded their vision, and strips of cardboard covered signs on refreshment stands that normally announced "*Beer.*" The climactic events were now the master evangelist's call to conversion— "You come on now"—and the lines of the born-again moving forward in their hundreds or thousands. That procession led to sometimes tearful meetings of the newly saved with counselors in the "Inquiry Tent," actually the basement of the Garden, as lives were reforged.[27]

Billy Graham himself, in a follow-up article about the crusade, affirmed that New York was particularly important to him because it was a strategic location. Like Antioch and Rome, to which Paul had directed his missions, the nation's largest city was a "crossroads" out of which influence could flow. Graham held that, apart from the prodigious statistics, the event had brought less quantifiable consequences: "The Crusade has been the talk of the city" in a town usually known for talk about anything but evangelical religion; New York's scattered and often demoralized Protestants have had new vision and a new sense of unity; a new surge of spiritual interest has swept across the country.[28]

Graham was especially proud of the crusade's impact on teenagers, above all in a place where they were too often identified with gangs and switchblades. One-third of the decisions were by teens, he said, and "Teen Week," the twelfth week, broke all records for attendance and decisions. The evangelist was himself profoundly moved by the testimonies of former gang members who had given up the switchblade for Christ.

Some perceived the intellectual girders of American theology being re-forged as well. A key article, "Fundamentalist Renascence," by Arnold W. Hearn observed that "away from the centers of ecclesiastical power and theo-logical education in the major denominations, there has been a remarkable renascence of intellectual activity among fundamentalist scholars, several of whom have studied in centers like Basel and Zurich and hold doctorates from places such as Harvard and Boston." Hearn went on to mention *Christianity Today*, "counting President Eisenhower's pastor among its contributing editors," as well as Fuller Theological Seminar, intellectual bastion of born-again fun-damentalism, and Billy Graham. In a review of *Contemporary Evangelical Thought*, edited by Carl F. H. Henry of *Christianity Today*, Martin E. Marty noted that this book puts itself at "dead center" in U.S. Christian theology. Looking at the range of religious thought from left to right, he noted that in the United States all theology claims to be strongly biblical, but that it gets quite a variety of different messages from the Bible.[29]

Another conservative theological statement was Edward John Carnell's *Christian Commitment: An Apologetic*. In reviewing it, William Hornden re-marked, "Signs are many that America is witnessing a revival of fundamen-talism." "Brilliant young theologians," like Edward Carnell of Fuller Theological Seminary in California, were appearing to defend conservative faith and shoring it up by means of a largely "rational" approach as they de-plored neoorthodoxy's existentialist "lack of reason."[30]

The best-known American name associated with neoorthodoxy, or some-thing like it, Reinhold Niebuhr, had entered the fray also. In 1958 he acknowl-edged that the term *neoorthodoxy* was by now virtually meaningless, being applied to theologians from Barth to Tillich. It originally indicated an approach that "took all the biblical concepts seriously without submitting to prescientific worldviews." But now the term extended so far as to embrace liberalism like that of Rudolf Bultmann, who introduced a novel existentialist tint to what amounted to plain humanism as he attempted to wash Scripture of "presci-entific" myth. He went about that purgative task in too flat and rationalist a way in Niebuhr's view, failing to recognize the rich complexity or historical significance of the Bible.[31]

Niebuhr also had something to say about Billy Graham. In a 1957 article on the deluge of mail he had received in response to his article in *Life* on

Billy Graham and his New York rally, the Union theologian conceded he had "damned with faint praise" the other in calling him an "honest and sincere exponent of . . . pietistic evangelism." Niebuhr insisted that his main criticism was not of Graham personally but of the support given him by "official Protestantism." He said he was especially concerned by letters from "almost masochistic" ministers who faulted themselves for not converting people at a Billy Graham rate. Those humble clerics therefore felt something must be wrong with them, it seemed to Niebuhr, as they declared one should not argue with Graham for doing their work for them. Reinhold Niebuhr pointed out that Graham, on the other hand, was not likely to convert people with intellectual concerns, and moreover that unlike the parish ministers Graham does not have to deal with ministry day in and day out in a "community of grace" wherein people are clearly in "different stages of grace."[32]

Religious liberals were less than enthusiastic about the "fundamentalist" resurgence. The bitter fundamentalist/modernist battles of the Twenties—the Scopes trial, the imbroglios involving H. E. Fosdick, feuds in countless local churches—were still traumatic living memories to some Fifties churchmen. Understandably, there was fear in that camp that the church would be recaptured by stern and divisive doctrines it had supposedly rejected a generation ago. Such a turn would, some thought, set back Protestant Christianity a half century. But while the new evangelicalism might still be narrow and divisive in some eyes, in important ways it was more mature and more solidly intellectual than before, as well as better meeting the yearnings of lonely souls in New York and in other cities' dark, gang-ridden streets. Presenting the case for a new evangelicalism before a candid world was the burden of new evangelical writers like Carnell, Henry, and above all those appearing in the movement's chief vehicle, *Christianity Today*.

The Remains of the Ecumenical Day

The Fourth General Assembly of the National Council of Churches met in St. Louis early in December 1957 and busily passed resolutions on several issues of the day, deploring corruption in trade unions and resolving that "racial segregation is contradictory to the teachings of Jesus." The latter issue was what most deeply stirred the delegates. The church representatives heard Martin Luther King, Jr., fresh from his victories in Montgomery, call for nonviolent action against the evil of racial injustice. "We must say to our white brothers over the South that we will match your capacity to inflict suffering with our capacity to endure suffering. We will match your physical force with our soul force. We will not hate you and yet we cannot obey your evil laws. Do to us what you will, and we will wear you down by our capacity to suffer and in earning our freedom we will so appeal to your hearts and consciences that we will win you in the process." Liston Pope, dean of Yale Divinity School, pointed out that the church is probably the most racially segregated major institution in U.S. society.[33]

The council ecumenists heard their outgoing president, Eugene Carson Blake, call the church to a new faith in Christian humanity as well as God: "Of all the failures and weaknesses of the Christian Church, there is none today more costly to our cause than lack of faith in one another." More provocatively, he predicted that the council would in time arrange visits between clergy of the United States and China.

The Sputnik crisis, together with race, was on everyone's mind in St. Louis, as throughout the nation and world. NCC speakers tended, however, to use the Soviet satellite as a mere launching missile for even loftier sentiments. Liston Pope said, "Sputnik's a big one, all right, but an even bigger one is the matter of defining what the church is and what Christian values are." The new president of the council was the Reverend Edwin T. Dahlberg, pastor of the Delmar Baptist church in St. Louis; in his inaugural address, he said, "It is not half so important that we send sputniks circling around the globe as that we should send more loaves of bread around the world." In calling, like many others in post-Sputnik America, for more emphasis on education, including scientific education, the council also asked for "increasing concern with the social sciences and the humanities for the education of the whole man to deal with the whole society." That resolution ended with a call for prayer that God's will may be done—"on earth and in the opening vistas of outer space."[34]

On another level of concern, however, it was to be feared that the influence of the National Council was already in decline, like that of the World Council. Ecumenicity on a practical level, as at Little Rock, was increasing and would take off at rocket speed in the civil rights and antiwar activities of the next decade. But the day of the stately national and world ecumenical gatherings, swarming with high-ranking and often colorfully robed prelates and "name" theologians of various respectable traditions, controlled behind the scenes by a "cooperative" old-line Protestant establishment, churning out endless resolutions and reports, seemed already to be well past high noon. Never again would such sacred gatherings seem as important, or so fill the news media, as at Cleveland in 1950 or Evanston in 1954. The ecumenically spirited *Christian Century* complained that NCC owed its decline to having a too restrictive geographical base in the Northeast, and to its being an agency of churches who have not given it much worthwhile work to do. *Christianity Today* complained that the NCC was out of touch with grass-roots members of its constituent churches, its programs and policies being determined instead by "a relatively small group of leaders—the General Board and staff members." In consequence, the Council's policies were often in accord with a "romantic" social gospel view of humanity and, this evangelical voice declared, at the St. Louis meeting "the biblical doctrine of Christ's vicarious atonement was not mentioned."[35] Some denominations, especially the Southern Presbyterians, went through lively internal debates on NCC membership in light of what they perceived to be its controversial social and theological drift.

Christ on Campus

Although the demographic explosion of the postwar boomers did not reach the campuses until the Sixties, youths whose lives had essentially been shaped by the world as it was after 1945 were already an important presence by the late Fifties. Compared to earlier generations, they were affluent, taking for granted a high standard of living and the open educational opportunities it afforded. They were tolerant, taking also for granted the premises of Fifties brotherhood and putative racial equality. Of whatever race or creed, they were prepared to brook no imposed limitations to their right to a full share of affluence or equality. At the same time they were anxious, having known little but war, the Bomb, and cold war as backdrop to their own brief lives. And they were definitely the next generation after the skeptical and Marxist, though of necessity self-disciplined, Thirties. Like all generations, they reacted against the one before and sought their own identity. For some, that meant spiritual questing and at least passing alignment with the religious revival. For others it meant delinquency.

The religious revival crested in the colleges. Responding to increased demand, two-thirds of state universities now offered credit courses in religious studies.[36] A *Newsweek* article claimed that "an astonishingly high number of the 3 million boys and girls now enrolled in American colleges and universities are on a great spontaneous quest, a search that may come as something of a surprise to their parents . . . they are seeking God."[37] They were coming out to hear Paul Tillich, Martin Buber, and their university chaplains, we were told; they were taking religious studies classes and attending services in their cumulative millions. Campus religious groups flourished, and the numbers going from college to seminary and the ministry were up.

Of course many Fifties students, perhaps the majority, were no more religious than students in most times. A survey of attitudes of Fifties college students by Philip E. Jacob found that they were definitely post-Thirties and post-Forties, conforming to the values of the day as defined by David Riesman's *Lonely Crowd* or William Whyte's *Organization Man*. They were "gloriously contented" with things as they are, and "unabashedly selfish" as they "cheerfully expect to conform to the economic status quo." "Social harmony" and "adjustment"—in other words, conformity—were of great importance, more so than honesty or courage. As for things of the spirit, Jacob perceived a "ghostly quality" about them; the students expressed a "need for religion" yet expected their real-life decisions to be "socially determined" rather than religiously guided. Like Reisman and Whyte, Jacob found that the ultimate source of meaning for this generation was the group, and the ultimate good "belongingness"; religion was of use insofar as it promoted those goods.[38]

Yet there was in the air a new seriousness about faith among the young. Significantly, it was not a turning toward fundamentalism, but—probably reflecting the mainline white Protestant background from which a substantial majority of students still came—the kind of earnest but liberal-toned wrestling with the issues represented by Buber and Tillich (now more than Niebuhr), by lectures and courses on the presence or absence of God in modern literature, or the smorgasbord of a campus Religion in Life Week. But by the end of the decade a skeptical undertow against those cresting new waves of the spirit was beginning to be felt.

The showplace of all this, particularly as characterized in the *Newsweek* article, was the oldest and the most prestigious of all U.S. universities, Harvard. Under the leadership of Nathan Marsh Pusey, president of Harvard since 1953, Fifties-type campus spirituality there reached its visible apogee and perhaps began its denouement.

Pusey, a devout Episcopalian, was determined that the spiritual life would not be neglected on his campus. He chose Harvard's then weak Unitarian-tinged Divinity School for his first campus address as a youthful president in 1953, and his words, iconoclastic in respect to Harvard's intellectual tradition, left no doubt that a new player was coming onto the field. He brashly took to task one of the icons of the old Harvard, the crusty Unitarian Charles William Eliot, his predecessor as president from 1869 to 1909. Eliot had declared in a 1909 Divinity School address, "The Religion of the Future," that the coming faith "will foster powerfully a virtue which is comparatively new in the world—the love of truth and the passion of seeking it. And the truth will progressively make men free. . . . When dwellers in a slum suffer the familiar evils caused by overcrowding, impure food and cheerless labor, the modern true believers contend against the sources of such misery by providing public baths, playgrounds, wider and cleaner streets, better dwellings and more effective schools—that is, they attack the sources of physical and moral evil." Of this sort of modernist social gospel Pusey said flatly in 1953, "This faith will no longer do."

"For President Eliot," the new president went on, "the enemies to his true faith were churches, creeds, priests, anything supernatural, any concern for a life after death, anything that professed to be sacramental. I suspect, for example—though I do not know this—that he would have considered the doctrine central to generations of believers—that Christ came into the world to save sinners—as so much twaddle." But the events of the twentieth century have shown, so Pusey believed, that nothing less than supernatural belief and "personal religion" can withstand the evils our day has revealed.

Interpreting Eliot's words as reflecting a too easy optimism, Pusey contended that the former's religion of good works, a "simple and rational faith" with no "metaphysical complexities or magical rites," was "at least wrong for our time, for it has now become frighteningly clear that if you try to ignore metaphysical considerations—I would say considerations of ultimate things—or cover them up in bursts of energy, they will rise up in perverted and distorted forms to mock one's thus too-circumscribed efforts." Set aside inner faith and participation in the life of the church, and one will become lost in "the all but universal adoration of the state, and in almost idolatrous preoccupation with the secular order, the accumulation of knowledge, and with good works. There is not and cannot be a quarrel with any of these things in themselves, but only with the notion that they are independently sufficient goods." What is needed instead, above all from the Divinity School, is "leadership in religious knowledge and, even more, in religious experience."[39]

Pusey put his own faith into action by building up the endowment of the Divinity School from $1 million to $7 million. He augmented its Unitarian tradition by importing a broadly ecumenical, though Protestant, array of stellar professors, including Paul Tillich, Richard R. Niebuhr (H. Richard's son), and Amos Wilder, overnight making it one of the four or five top interdenominational divinity schools in the nation.

The president not only favored the Divinity School, he also expanded undergraduate religious studies classes, contending that religion could be an underlying language for the common quest implied in all the curriculum. Pusey saw to it that the distinguished Presbyterian George A. Buttrick, for twenty-seven years minister of Madison Avenue Presbyterian Church in New York and once recognized by *Life* as one of the ten outstanding preachers in the United States, was appointed to Memorial Church, the Harvard chapel. Once thinly attended, this edifice now drew overflow crowds of religious revival college students.

Pusey reached the peak of his religious influence in the first half of 1957, the same season the nation's Fifties religious revival can probably be said to have crested. Those were the days of the *Newsweek* article featuring Pusey, and in a Harvard baccalaureate address that spring, the university president said:

It is true that today the climate within universities is more favorable toward religion than it has been for some time. There is more interest in religion, and less hostility toward it. If not all people view the change with favor, at least it is now widely recognized that religion is an acceptable subject of intellectual interest, and already one begins to wonder it could ever have been held that it was not. Discussion of religion is carried on with less frenzy and more tolerance than has been usual for some time. It seems that the mood of toleration, first learned in fierce struggles among religious sects, has now also taken hold of the aggressive secularists of a generation ago and of their irate opponents. In this changing climate many are coming again to speak up for religion in university and college communities as they have not for some time. I have myself been among this number.[40]

A little over a year later, Pusey reiterated the same theme even more force-fully (perhaps, as we shall see, in response to backlash), proclaiming that while old-time religious fundamentalism "worked to prevent a free play of mind," "at least in academic circles, [it] has long since been unmasked and put to flight." But a new and deadlier fundamentalism, "a secular variety," is now abroad. This new secularism, "which would forcibly eschew all attention to religion, unfortunately has scarcely as yet been identified, with the result that its noxious influence—noxious I believe to spirit, to imagination, and so also, in the long run, to mind—works among us almost unopposed, and at times indeed with approval," and its worst effect is not so much that it promotes atheism as that it implies that whether God exists doesn't matter. Disdaining such narrowness, we should instead work life through till we realize that "the final answer found through the enlightenment of joy and belief must . . . be God."[41]

By then, however, the intellectual revivalism of Harvard Yard's president-preacher did not go unchallenged. In a widely publicized 1958 article in the *Crimson*, a second-year philosophy graduate student, William Warren Bart-ley III, attacked what he called Harvard's "button-down hair shirt." Eliot's "minimum" faith of "love and service to one's neighbor" and war against "the evils which afflict humanity" was not really so bad as the creed of a large and pluralistic university, Bartley contended. Nor was emeritus president James B. Conant's call for faith in a "wide diversity of beliefs and the tolerance of this diversity." Against this, Pusey as read by Bartley seemed to want a religious unity centered on "only one kind of contemporary thinker: the flashy exis-tentialist or teutonic theologian who ministers to the 'Big Questions' with big answers and bigger 'systems.'" He was obviously alluding to Pusey's biggest catch at Harvard, Paul Tillich. But in fact, contended Bartley, Christianity is in no position to provide a ground for unity, given its bitter intellectual disputes between, say, the existentialist theologians and the Thomists. Let the university and the theologians go their own ways.[42]

This 1958 counterblast against the religious revival on campus, in the spirit of the religious revival's post-1957 sour aftertaste, was only exacerbated by the 1958 Memorial Church dispute. By late spring of that year no one was talking about anything in the Yard, it seemed, except the "religion issue" as defined by Pusey, the *Crimson* article, and Memorial Chapel, the university's quasi-official church. In the context it became clear that Pusey's Protestant paradise was itself sectarian, in fact beleaguered from all sides by others who felt left out: resurgent secularists, Jews, Roman Catholics, and Unitarians, not to mention orthodox Protestants of the *Christianity Today* sort who saw in Tillich's theology little more than smoke-and-mirrors doctrinal fidelity.

What happened was this. The Bartley article had claimed that Memorial's distinguished chief pastor, officially chair of the board of preachers and "preacher to the university," George A. Buttrick, under whom attendance has swelled to capacity and Christianity had been strongly emphasized, in 1955 had "refused to permit a Jewish student to be married in Memorial Church by a rabbi," contrary to longstanding tradition. Immediately, vocal representatives of Harvard's some two thousand Jewish students responded angrily, wondering if the tradition that they could be married in the church according to the rites of their own faith was being totally abrogated in light of the university's newborn Christianity. Some pointed out that the church was intended as a memorial to all of Harvard's war dead—Christian, Jewish, or other—and wondered sarcastically if the spirits of Jewish soldiers would now have to move out.

Pusey did not help matters with a response in the *Crimson* of April 9 declaring unequivocally that "Harvard's historical tradition has been a Christian tradition and although Memorial Church is not considered as affiliated with any one denomination, it has always been thought of as a house of Christian worship." This was indicated, he claimed, by the architecture of the building and by its dedication, which stated it was to be used "in the service of Christ." Regarding requests to hold weddings and funerals in the edifice, "the University preacher and his predecessors have made clear that the Corporation feels that the Memorial Church is a place for Christian worship. So far as I know, the only isolated exceptions to this rule occurred without authorization, or when there was no chairman of the board of preachers." He went on to point out that there were other locations on or near the Harvard campus where non-Christian ceremonies might be conducted.

Three days later a letter appeared from a professor of philosophy, Henry D. Aiken, who, as he referred to "my fellow Jews," questioned the validity of a revival of religion that had become "a source of discord." Aiken seemed twice to call on Pusey to resign, stating that "nothing more in this direction [the renewal of religion] seems possible or desirable. What remains for you to do?" and adding that he was "saddened that I will never again be able in conscience to attend any sort of service in Memorial Church."

Not long afterward the Unitarian contingent of faculty and students added their voices, asking whether—in view of the fact that some Unitarians decline to call themselves Christians—they could hereafter be married or buried from the church. Yet one Unitarian minister was a member of Memorial's board of preachers. Were the neighborhood of Boston's eminently respectable Unitarians still regarded as something like honorary Protestant Christians, like Will Herberg's Buddhist/Unitarian friend, though Jews were not?

The controversy was finally damped, though not forgotten, on April 22 when the Harvard Corporation, the governing body of the university, adopted a resolution acknowledging that Harvard is a "mixed society" within which "Harvard has a duty, while keeping its identity, to try to honor the convictions of each member of the Harvard community." It then permitted the use of the Memorial building for private ceremonies such as weddings performed by clergy of all religions, though reaffirming "the church's essentially Christian character." President Pusey mellowed sufficiently to say that, "if asked," he would answer that Harvard is a secular university, though "within it is a tradition of worship; one could wish that this were broad enough to include everyone in the community."[43]

After this one might have supposed that even a few old-fashioned campus atheists might have found their hallowed place, if that is the right expression. But word came early in 1957 from George Washington University that atheists could no longer hold faculty positions in that institution. Though university spokespersons subsequently claimed the item was quoted out of context, it was enough to permit the well-known gadfly Unitarian minister of All Souls Church in Washington, D.C., A. Powell Davies, to suggest that instead it might be a good idea to retain one or two nonbelievers on campuses to keep the theists on their toes.[44] The letters-to-the-editor response to the story in *Newsweek* on that affair at the peak of the revival was quite informative concerning the mood still prevalent in the hinterland. One reader queried whether, if the right to believe implies also the right to disbelieve, the right to protect one's country also implies the right to betray it. Another asked whether every business concern should perforce have a few dishonest employees to keep the honest ones on their toes.[45] The natural allusions to patriotism and capitalist institutions was interesting. A. Powell Davies died later the same year, before he could have appreciated the changes in mentality that the second half of 1957 were to bring.

It was that fall that the new president of Princeton, Robert F. Goheen, was to announce at his first faculty meeting that the university had withdrawn recognition from the Reverend Hugh Halton as chaplain to Roman Catholic students on campus. A Dominican priest, Halton had caused much controversy for making, from a highly conservative theological and social position, what were widely regarded as intemperate public comments about the university and particular faculty members.[46]

Juvenile Delinquency

What about youth at the other end of the social scale from famous Ivy League universities? And at the other end of virtue from their Christianized elites? As the decade wound down, "juvenile delinquency" was increasingly raised as a grave problem. A crescendo of urgent news stories told Americans that teenage crime was becoming more vicious. There were more and more killings, even in connection with petty theft. Nearly one child in ten was or had been "in trouble." The number of juvenile cases had doubled in the ten years between 1947 and 1957.

People who had once thought of gangs as run by the "Mob"—Al Capone and his ilk—now had to contend with districts of "urban jungles" in the big cities controlled by youth gangs that provided, for many members, their main family and identity, and that robbed and murdered as "a matter of social prestige." Even the police dared enter those "jungles" only in fully armed squadrons.[47]

Numerous writers tried sincerely to deal with the problem, though none seemed quite to engage whatever was at its core. Psychological explanations were in the air, and many tried to explain the distressing phenomenon through words about broken homes, overcrowding because of the postwar housing shortage, or the example of violence left over from World War II. David R. McCann, a clergyman, said that youth always want a model, an ideal hero, and the present-day delinquents lacked one.[48]

One of the best popular books on the problem was *The Shook-Up Generation*, by the distinguished journalist Harrison E. Salisbury. After a lurid portrayal of the gangs in several major cities, including accounts of neo-Nazi motifs, pure sadism for its own sake against gang victims, and sexual promiscuity involving very young girl members, Salisbury came to look at the role of churches in combating gangs. Although in his opening account of the sprawling, dismal, and gang-ridden Bedford-Stuyvesant area of Brooklyn he noted that those streets are "lined with liquor stores, Pentecostal churches, saloons and dimly lighted dives," the only church ministries he chose to discuss were those of respectable mainline churches, both Catholic and Protestant, who had the courage to reach into gangdom.[49]

He gave most attention to the admirable work of the Reverend C. Kilmer Myers of St. Augustine's, a chapel of the famous and very richly endowed Trinity Episcopal Church at the head of Wall Street. Trinity has used its wealth and its collection of dependent churches or "chapels" well for the promotion of social ministries and other good works, and "Kim" Myers was one of the best exemplars. The labor of gang redemption was slow going; Salisbury described the hours the priest spent talking and listening to just one young man before the "delinquent" could be led to give up his stubborn despondency, his loyalty to gang friends, and his fatalism about violence and endless cycles of provocation and revenge, to see the possibility of another kind of life.

Father Myers wrote a classic book about his work called *Light the Dark Streets*, in which he made a strong appeal for the special role of the church in dealing with delinquency. Without denigrating social agencies—but recognizing that tension between them and the church was a serious issue of the day—Myers made a clear distinction between their approach, or that of law enforcement, and that of religious institutions.

The view of social workers that community leadership must be "professionally trained" was, Myers contended, "a fundamental heresy from both the Christian and the democratic point of view."[50] On the other hand, the church has a certain "plus" in its ministry to young people that secular workers would have a hard time matching. Apart from any supernatural grace it may bring to bear, that institution and its ministers can also identify in a special way with a neighborhood when its edifice is an established presence and its clergy live nearby. At the same time the church presents an icon of a higher viewpoint on the passions and vicissitudes of life than those of the street.

Returning to Harrison Salisbury and his own conclusions about why gangs and delinquency had become a problem now and what to do about it, that reporter seemed as stymied as everyone else. On one level, he found the apparent cause of delinquency surprisingly simple. It lay in the way the youth culture was simply a twisted reflection of the culture of violence it saw all around, in war and cold war, in the "cheap tabloids, salacious magazines and brutal comic books" that pandered to the young, glorifying violence and dehumanizing humanity. The gangs seem, "as in a distorting glass, to mirror the conduct of nations" and the perverted society in which they live.[51] He carefully avoided blanket condemnation of the schools, the family, or any other too easy target, saying instead that we see writ large in the gangs what we are as a nation.

Then, evidencing what may be a left-over optimistic New Deal belief that planning and the right sort of programs can cure any social ills, he stated baldly that "violent juvenile delinquency can be reduced to modest proportions, rapidly, without staggering cost or titanic effort, simply by employing techniques which we very well know and institutions which already exist. The principal ingredients needed are common sense, civic leadership and community responsibility." The church ministries and other community programs he cites are examples of what can be done. Nothing new or different is required. They work; they need only to be multiplied many times over, and they could be if more people would get involved. "We have gangs not because we do not know how to prevent them but because we do not have enough interest or energy to do the things we already know will bring an end to delinquency. We do not lack knowledge. We lack the will" (167).

One motivation for finding that will lay conspicuously at hand. It was the usual Fifties motivation of ultimate appeal, the cold war. Mentioning Sputnik, Salisbury went on to say, "Despite all this few people have yet begun to correlate the wastage and deterioration of youth which we permit on the streets of the big cities, on the highways outside the suburbs and, I would suspect, in the quiet rural areas of the nation with our national defense potential. . . . The most rapid possible liquidation of adolescent delinquency and institution of a program to prevent its recurrence is thus becoming a matter of national security" (180).

Nonetheless delinquency was not attacked on anything like the scale of a defense buildup or the moon walk. Why not? Perhaps too many other Americans saw the delinquents only as "them" in contrast to "us"; while as Salisbury well perceived, they were too much "us," symptomatic not of a particular discrete cause that could be easily attacked but of a malaise inbred in U.S. society as a whole. There were, however, some religionists who tried to do what they could, often in the context of addressing the larger malaise as they understood it.

Billy Graham was one. During the celebrated August campaign in Madison Square Garden—the revival ran over schedule and continued all summer—he held special youth rallies during which former gang members would testify. A sixteen-year-old said, "I've seen broken heads, stabbings, black eyes, and broken bones that guys get in gang fights. But you guys, you teen-agers who think you're tough, you don't really know how tough it can get till you start witnessing for Christ." During Teen Week at the Graham rally about 60 percent of the audience were young people, some 17,500 a night, and all of them presumably heard testimony of this sort.[52]

On the Catholic side, the Catholic Youth Organization (CYO) also strove to combat delinquency. Founded in 1930 by the farseeing and relatively liberal Bernard Sheil, auxiliary bishop of Chicago (later to fall afoul of Cardinal Spellman on the issue of McCarthyism), it offered city sports and fellowship programs that its leaders claimed presented alternatives to gangs. But in the Fifties social approaches to juvenile delinquency often appeared in tension with another feature of the period's Catholicism, a strong identification with authoritarianism in the home and the law as well as in the church. Strengthening parental and police authority was time and again given as the real answer to delinquency.

A 1958 news item in *America* claimed that in Italy only 2 percent of sex crimes and 0.5 percent of all homicides were committed by youths under eighteen, compared to U.S. figures of 13 and 9 percent respectively. When a U.S. judge asked Italian officials the reason for this, "he got one consistent answer: the young people of Italy respect authority." The surest way to cure juvenile crime, he concluded—and the Jesuit magazine put this in caps—was PUT FATHER BACK AT THE HEAD OF THE FAMILY.[53]

(A subsequent letter to the editor of *America* by Estella M. Hughes questioned the report concerning the low rate of juvenile delinquency in Italy, asking how it squared with "the agonizing statements of American writers who have reported on their terrible findings with respect to the unsupervised children in Naples and vicinity.")[54]

However, in an item later the same year *America* damned with faint praise a U.N. report calling for more money for preventive and rehabilitative programs to combat juvenile delinquency. These programs were to be carried out by "specialists" who naturally wanted increased funding, and the whole document, the Jesuit magazine said, had a tone of "social adjustment." No reference was made to the spiritual aspect of the problem, or—more to the point that we are talking about—sin. "Perhaps the root therapy that alone will 'cure' juvenile lawbreaking is the inculcation of a sense of sin." A related article by Edward A. Connell argued that police need to do their job firmly and fairly, showing young delinquents the consequences of their acts, not muddling their image by trying to be social workers too.[55]

Despite such no-nonsense talk, a rather agonized article by a Catholic sociologist in *Commonweal* came to conclusions similar to Salisbury's, that there is no easy, one-shot solution because gang culture ultimately reflects, though it warps, the violent, hedonistic culture around it. A piece in the more popular *Sign* highlighted a Chicago policeman, Joseph Mildice (Catholic of course), who combined firm law enforcement on the job with effective Kim Myers–type after-hours sports and conversation with gang youths, winning their confidence and turning around more than one young life.[56]

Catholicism: From the Pian to the Johannine Age

The last full year of Pope Pius XII's pontificate, 1957 was—though none knew it then—virtually the last year of an age of Roman Catholicism reaching back at least to the Counter-Reformation. It was an age in which the church stood as unflinching bulwark, ready to do battle with the demons of atheism and modernity but never to change colors before them. Thus, in his own old age and that of the era, the pontiff in his 1956 Christmas message reportedly "lost patience" and called for a "crusade," stating bluntly that a Catholic cannot be a conscientious objector in a just war, calling the struggle against communism such a war, and alluding to the recent crushing of Hungary.[57] Closer to home, Cardinal Spellman maintained the same image of Catholic implacability in the face of the moral morass outside the church by condemning, to much media attention, the steamy but highly acclaimed movie "Baby Doll," even though he acknowledged he had not seen it.

But the age of Catholic confidence had a positive side as well, for which some remain understandably nostalgic. The novelist Whitley Strieber describes the summer of 1957, when he was twelve years old and caught between the faith and burgeoning scientific interests, this way:

> Still, my faith was a burning fire in me. I loved Christ and Mary especially, and used to pray with great fervor whenever I was trapped into going to church. . . .
> But when I brought up Einstein with my mother, she said, "We are Catholic. Catholics are absolutist." She and I would spend hours together sitting on the front-porch steps talking. We discussed everything from general relativity to the price of tennis shoes. I used to try to talk her out of her religiosity, but she was a Catholic intellectual in the heady days of the fifties, when the mass was still full of mystery and there were many fascinating and subtle potentials for sin.[58]

Catholic social teaching remained solid too, at least on the hottest issue of the moment, race. Despite some lapses in practice, in the days of Little Rock and Nashville Catholic spokespersons reminded the faithful that segregation was a sin. Father John La Farge, one of the founders of the National Catholic Conference for Interracial Justice back in 1934, said in 1958 that not only is segregation immoral as a system, but that any Catholic organization that rejected applicants on racial grounds would be "acting entirely contrary to the spirit of the Church" and to "true Catholicity."[59] Race relations was then one of the few areas of significant cooperation between Protestants and Catholics.

Intellectual surety was integrally interconnected with surety about leadership, and not only on the papal or archepiscopal level. The Fifties were the culminating decade of what Jay P. Dolan has called "the golden age of the American Catholic priesthood," when "the priest was the key figure in the Catholic subculture; he was put on a pedestal by a lofty theology of the office and kept there by the culture of clericalism."[60] The priest of the golden

age was idealized by Hollywood in movies like *Boys Town, Going My Way,*
and *On the Waterfront.* He was hardly less idealized by the great majority of
Catholics. Crowds would gather at railway stations to greet their pastor or see
him off, the poorest immigrant parishes took compensatory pride in the quality of the priest's residence and car, and he in turn was rarely if ever seen outside the role and the clerical collar required by it. The senior pastor ruled his
parish, and his subordinate priests, with unquestioned authority.[61] The Catholic subculture saw to it that appropriate lines between clergy and laity were
drawn, criticism of priests muted, and any hint of clerical scandal hushed. At
the same time, there were in this era not a few legendary priests—like Father
Flanagan of Boys Town—worthy of such exaltation.

That was the Catholicism of an era that climaxed in the Fifties, and that
seems now gone forever in that form: the Catholicism of the rock-solid doctrines, the famous converts, the Latin mass, the parochial schools staffed by
white-coifed nuns, the heroic priests, militant anticommunism, and (for intellectuals) a seemingly impregnable logical edifice based on Thomism. For
some who still remember it, the recollection brings a whiff of wistful nostalgia; for others, residual anger at its oppressive side. This was the Catholicism
that lasted through the time of the last pope named Pius.[62]

The pontiff born Eugenio Pacelli was perhaps more human than the popular image of those years allowed. Though Italian, he had spent long and tumultuous years in Germany as nuncio to Munich and Berlin, and his personal
style—precise, methodical, intellectually rigorous—suggested to many observers a temperament more German than Italian. There was also his peculiarly
close and longstanding (though undoubtedly chaste) relationship with his
housekeeper and confidante, the German nun Sister Pascalina.[63] She was not
called La Popessa for nothing and reportedly exercised much behind-the-scenes
influence on the Holy Father. None other than Francis Cardinal Spellman
allegedly owed the see of New York to her favor.

But the widely reprinted picture of Pius XII that lingered in one's mind—
and one also true to his nature—was of the spare, ascetic figure robed all in
white, arms outstretched as though to embrace the world, eyes lifted to heaven,
a saintly pontiff already looking more spirit than flesh. Such a man almost
demeaned himself, it seemed, to notice, much less combat, an evil like communism, but the battle was his duty and he was nothing if not conscientious
when duty called. Armed with many swords of the spirit, he did not shrink
from that battle, even though his course in the earlier titanic struggles against
fascism and Nazism had been seen by some as much more wavering.

Then, on October 9, 1958, Pope Pius XII died. He was mourned, but sor-
row soon turned to joy and even more to amazement as the personality of the
new pontiff, John XXIII, elected October 28, 1958, impressed itself on the

world. An elderly man, he was chosen as a compromise who it was thought might be little more than a timeserver as the church continued to search for new directions for itself. But he quickly showed himself his own man; he himself pointed out the new paths and started his flock walking down them, with himself at the head.

Within days of his election, all Rome and the world were astounded that the church had not only a new pope but a new kind of pope, a prelate as rotund, jovial, and innovative of mind as his predecessor had been lean and unbending. John's mental agility and above all his warmth took the ancient city by storm. The surprising sound of papal laughter, including laughter at himself, was heard ringing down the once hushed Vatican corridors. The new pope talked without notes or script, greeted visitors with hugs, and named new cardinals—including more non-Italians than before—only two weeks into office.

In January 1959 he issued his epoch-making call for a new ecumenical council. "We . . . open our heart and arms to all those who are separated from this Apostolic See," he declared, suggesting that the conclave would be concerned with the ancient dream of recovering Christian unity. John also let it be known that this council would look at the whole life of its own church— theology, canon law, discipline, the role of the laity in a secular world.[64] Thus in the last year of the Fifties, there was abundant evidence in Rome even more than anywhere else that the religious world was changing radically and would not again be what it had been heretofore.

	Ideas: Israel,
Chapter 6	Mescaline, and Zen

AN ASSORTMENT of interests that had some relation to religion seemed to en-gage the public these late Fifties years. They suggest a cornucopia of emer-gent spiritual enthusiasms bursting the seams of conventional Fifties piety: Zen, ghosts, the deepening from within of retreats, new theologies.

The fascination with Zen Buddhism, associated with Alan Watts and Beats like Jack Kerouac, continued apace, not having yet been overtaken by the psychedelic rainbows of the next decade. The lectures at Columbia Uni-versity of the octogenarian Japanese Zen teacher, D. T. Suzuki, continued to draw crowds, who then argued among themselves about Zen and psychoanaly-sis, Zen and existentialism, Zen and transcendentalism or Marxism—while Suzuki kept insisting that Zen was just Zen, not the same as or different from anything else.[1]

Another old/new interest was psychic phenomena and their relation to religion, especially in regard to the ministry of healing. The mainline religious bodies had long related in an ambivalent, and sometimes painful, way to such matters. On one hand, miraculous healings appeared to be often dubious and self-centered distractions from the main business of Judeo-Christian religion, justice, mercy, and community, not to mention rabbinical or ecclesiastical au-thority. On the other hand, psychic and miraculous phenomena were, none-theless important signs within the ministries of the founders of those traditions, Moses and Jesus, and people still yearned for them; when the major institu-tions neglected them too much, they showed up in alternative venues such as Spiritualism or Christian Science.

Interest in the psychic had something of an excitingly underground quality in the Fifties, since it was at odds with the temper of the reigning existentialism in philosophy, Freudian psychoanalysis in psychology, and neoorthodoxy in religion—all usually contemptuous of ghosts and the extrasensory on moral or epistemological grounds. Nevertheless, stimulated by the empirical work of J. B. Rhine on ESP, and by the subversive challenge of the much more sympathetic school of C. G. Jung, Freud's rebellious pupil who broke with his master partly over this issue, the psychic proved unwilling to die. Indeed, it seemed in lively and increasingly visible gestation, as though preparatory for its phoenixlike rebirth in the wide-open Sixties, when acceptance of everything from astrology to tarot cards would be the hallmark of a new culture.

One fruit of this interest was the founding of the Spiritual Frontiers Fellowship in March 1956, in Evanston, Illinois. The SFF was established by about seventy-five mostly Protestant religious leaders and laypersons, including Paul Higgins, a Methodist minister who became its first president, and Arthur Ford, the subsequently controversial Spiritualist medium who was also a Disciples of Christ minister. The stated purposes were to promote individual spiritual growth and to make the insights of Spiritualism and psychical research available to churchpersons. The SFF worked on the assumption that these findings were by no means demonic, but essentially natural and benign areas of phenomena that could help the faithful to understand miracles, life after death, the power of prayer, and ultimately the meaning of mystical experience. Meetings often included demonstrations of mediumship and spiritual healing. An important religious force in the late Fifties and the Sixties, the SFF subsequently experienced internal conflicts and went into decline.[2]

In the meantime a growing number of popular books indicated a burgeoning interest in ghosts, psychic phenomena, and the like. These even included some of Roman Catholic provenance, such as Shane Leslie's *Ghost Book*, reporting such Catholic ghost stories as a famous one of St. John Bosco, who in 1839 kept a preplanned midnight encounter with the spirit of a seminarian friend who had just died; the newly deceased assured the future saint that he was saved. In 1956 *The Search for Bridey Murphy*, an investigation of a reported reincarnation, was on the *New York Times* best-seller list for twelve weeks.[3]

Keeping pace with the SFF was a perceptible growing interest in the healing ministry in mainline churches. One example, along with the popular Roman Catholic pilgrimages to Lourdes or Fatima, was St. Stephen's Episcopal Church, Philadelphia, a historic parish of colonial background. The rector, the Reverend Alfred W. Price, was warden of the International Order of St. Luke the Physician, and past chaplain of the Military Order of the Purple Heart. The healing service at this church consisted of laying on of hands.[4] Healing services of the St. Stephen's type were introduced in many respectable mainline churches during the late Fifties.

All these manifestations clearly reflect a yearning for a greater supernatural element within mainline Protestant religion. Although the Sixties counter-culture, and Pentecostalism, were soon to outrageously outrun the mainline when it came to ghosts and miracles, in the Fifties the mainline looked in that direction and, with its usual decorum, tried.

Another sort of interest reflecting the heightening concern for the spiritual, if not the supernatural, was increased participation in retreats. The practice of retreats among devout Roman Catholics, often to monasteries and convents, had long been vital but was certainly enhanced by the popularity of Thomas Merton's evocation of the soul-renewing silence of the cloister. Some Episcopalians had also long since discovered the spiritual secrets of their own smaller quorum of religious houses. Many of both faiths came to visit, often on organized retreats, even if they could not stay. What was truly new was the multiplying number of Protestant retreat centers in the Fifties. Here too silence was kept, and residents maintained a regular schedule of devotion, work, and study. Here was another sign of the wide-ranging, sometimes (though not in this case) bewildered Fifties search for spiritual reality.[5]

A different sort of interest was piqued by the Dead Sea Scrolls, that fascinating collection of texts of the Hebrew Scriptures and of an ascetic Jewish community located at Qumran, in the Holy Land, around the time of John the Baptist and Jesus. The first of these scrolls were discovered accidentally in 1947; they and subsequent finds were the subjects of scholarly books and revelations throughout the Fifties. This archaeological treasure comported well with the Fifties liberal as well as conservative interest in religion, for the always intriguing results were not always supportive of conventional views. A *Time* article for Easter 1957 discussed Qumran in the background of John the Baptist, the role of the enigmatic "Teacher of Righteousness" and the "wicked priest," concluding that all this was a threat to the faith only of those Christians who do not recognize that Jesus was man as well as God, and so a person of his historical time and place.[6]

Interest continued in the German theologian and refugee from Nazism Paul Tillich, the headliner of Pusey's reordered Harvard Divinity School and the bête noire of conservative Protestants. We have noted that as the Fifties advanced the star of his benign cultural theology rose as that of the stern cold-war moralist Reinhold Niebuhr declined. By 1957, Tillich, now at Harvard, was "conceded to be the greatest Protestant theologian in the U.S.," according to *Newsweek*. His efforts seemed particularly well calculated to serve as a guide to the perplexed among the reasonably liberal and well educated who wanted to be part of the religious revival but were not sure if they honestly could, or if they wanted to pay the intellectual and moral price. Tillich's latest book, *Dynamics of Faith*, proposed that doubt is part of faith; without it faith moves toward idolatry and fanaticism. Faith itself, far from meaning commitment to objective propositions, meant a relation to that beyond all objective ideas or forms. It may reach beyond even God as a concrete notion but recognizes that this "Ultimate Concern" and "Ground of Being" may be expressed—though veiled under the name of God—in religion and life. A *Time* article on Tillich began, "What Is Sin?" and after rehearsing the fundamentalist, social gospel, and Niebuhrian neoorthodox answers ended with Tillich's existentialist-type view of it as a misplaced relation to one's Ultimate Concern.[7] Perhaps the popularity of Tillich in the mass media and around the cocktail-party circuit was a recognition that faith had by now reached the loftiest redoubts of U.S. intellectual life; perhaps it was a subtle hint that the simplistic Billy Graham or Norman Peale beliefs of the faith-filled earlier Fifties had now been opened to interrogation.

Around the same time, the Reverend Charles Leslie Kinsolving, of a distinguished Episcopal clerical family, had aroused controversy in the Episcopal church in Pasco, Washington, of which he was pastor, and also had drawn attacks by neighboring clergy, for a sermon in which he had expressed the view that hell is "a damnable doctrine—responsible for a large measure of the world's hatred."[8] This was apparently national news in 1957, though it was nothing compared to what was to come down in the Episcopal church and elsewhere in the next decade.

Judaism

As the late Fifties advanced, a sense continued to build in Judaism that an era was coming to a close, even as it was also, in different ways, within Protestantism and Catholicism. In the end, it was the demise of the world shaped by modernism, in all its variety.

One basic problem was still the adaptation of Judaism to the voluntaryism of American life, where one could be an American of Jewish background without being a Jew, at least in one's own eyes. In the premodern ghettoes of Europe that was impossible; ideally, the Jewish communities were separate, quasi-autonomous entities under their own law, but minutely regulated by it in a way of life that hardly distinguished between the religious and the secular, and whether or not one was a Jew was evident, and important, in countless secular as well as religious ways. Now, as Joseph Blau put it, "voluntaryism means that one's civil status, whether as a citizen or a wage-earner, has been made independent of his Jewish ties. He has political rights because he is a man, not because he is a Jew."[9]

But because Jews still knew, nonetheless, that they were Jews, they continued to explore ways of being Jewish in the new situation, where it depended on oneself to find a way. One way that fitted the mood of many in the modernist era was secularism.

Worldliness had its limits. An article by Herbert Panzen, "The Passing of Jewish Secularism in the United States," referred to the earlier creation of a secular Jewish culture. It had been formed by a generation of Jews deeply involved in progressivism and the labor movement, with all the secular socialist or Marxist perspectives that entailed; they may also have been secular Zionists. But now the next generation was becoming middle class, and Jewish optimism had been battered by the Holocaust; there was now a move to look again at Judaism as a religious identity, even to the extent of a new openness to Jewish mysticism and orthodoxy.[10] At the same time, however, the alternative vision of Reconstruction Judaism remained an option; its founder, Mordecai Kaplan, published *Judaism without Supernaturalism: The Only Alternative to Orthodoxy and Secularism.*[11] Reconstructionism, essentially based on a humanistic worldview, presented Judaism as a religious civilization. The majority of religious Jews remained in the Orthodox, Conservative, and Reform camps.

But whatever its strains Jewish identity seemed more and more to be larger than those sometimes shifting loyalties, especially as the conditions of Jewish life changed dramatically in postwar America. One thing that held most Jews together was the new state of Israel, which, if not identical with the whole people of Israel, gave them a new common focus despite the ambiguities of being Jewish in the secular U.S. state. Indeed, as Jakob J. Petuchowski remarked, "The secular State of Israel on the one hand, and the American citizen of Jewish faith on the other, are equally unprecedented in the history and tradition of pre-Emancipation Judaism."[12] But the times, with the memory of the Holocaust still fresh, were unprecedented too, and Jews and many others saw Israel as something new and hopeful in human affairs, almost transcendentally so. These were the days of Leon Uris's novel *Exodus*, which spent more than thirty weeks on the best-seller lists and became a hit movie. (Indeed, the novel was written with the screen version already under contract to Metro-Goldwyn-Mayer.)[13]

Joel Blocker, reviewing *Exodus* in *Commentary*, was rather caustic: "The book is perhaps the ultimate crystallization of the Western fantasy about Israel—a 'never-never land,'" fantasized as no less than "an idea incarnate, dynamic, brave, pure in its striving for goodness and serenity, unadulterated by the presence of evil or self-interest . . . [but] an impossible myth for the Israelis to live up to; it can only obscure their real problems and achievements."[14]

But that was the Israel many people wanted, perhaps needed, in those years of cold-war tensions and stressful social change. For Jews, it was an anchor to weigh against the aforementioned atomization of Jewish identity and dispersal to the suburbs, not to mention a token of redemption after the devastation of the Holocaust. But the Fifties were an era when, despite problems within the Jewish community, Jews and their achievements tended to be idealized by the larger community. Perhaps this was on some level unconscious atonement for earlier anti-Semitism and the Holocaust, as well as romanticization of the state of Israel, but the new attitude was largely genuine and contributed to the brotherhood spirit of the decade at its best. That mentality accompanied Judaism as it entered the tensions and prospects of the Sixties.

Notes from Underground

As the aboveground culture moved into the daylight of science and education, so its underground counterpart rediscovered mysticism, mythology, and the anticommunist true-believer religion of the decade's beginning. Here are three examples.

ALDOUS HUXLEY

The novelist and essayist Aldous Leonard Huxley (1894–1963) was born the scion of an English family that had done as much as any to create the mentality of the scientific modern world. His grandfather was that great Victorian popularizer of Darwin and modern science generally, T. H. Huxley; his older brother, Julian, author of books like *Religion without Revelation* and *Evolutionary Ethics*, was a distinguished biologist and advocate of scientific naturalism; his mother was a niece of Matthew Arnold.[15] Yet Aldous, while he retained the family brilliance and inquiring curiosity in full measure, frequently let them carry him in unexpected directions. His 1932 novel, *Brave New World*, one of the most celebrated dystopias of the modern era, characteristically explored possible human meanings and ends in the science-based society the twentieth century seemed hell-bent to construct, and found them ominous. Later, in the middle Thirties, influenced by a commitment to pacifism and friendship with the mystic Gerald Heard, Huxley turned increasingly toward undogmatic exploration of the world's religious and spiritual traditions. That move was only enhanced as war clouds darkened over Europe, for world consciousness as it was seemed capable of little but ill. Moving with Heard to California in 1937, enduring the grim war years there as an alien both nationally and, as a pacifist, ideologically, Huxley sought more and more urgently for some ultimate grounding of human life apart from the "rational" mind and its follies.

The quest finally produced his 1945 book, *The Perennial Philosophy*, a forceful quotation-studded study of common themes in world mysticism. Running his eyes from Buddhists, Chinese Taoists, and Plotinus to John of the Cross,

Eckhart, Jakob Böhme, George Fox, and William Law, Huxley concluded that there is one Reality manifesting in all that is, whose true nature is being, knowledge, and joy. Huxley called this underlying One the Ultimate Divine Ground, the Highest Common Factor, and Mind at Large, as well as God. In it all things and all persons find their unity, and toward knowledge of it we are striving.

But though we all seek that universal being at the deepest levels of our own being, the quest, though always worth undertaking after the right inner preparation, can go very much awry; for example, "the cult of unity on the political level is only an idolatrous ersatz for the genuine religion of unity on the personal and spiritual levels." For "only the pure in heart and poor in spirit can come to the unitive knowledge of God. Hence, the attempt to impose more unity upon societies than their individual members are ready for makes it psychologically almost impossible for those individuals to realize their unity with the Divine Ground and with one another."[16] This book had a remarkable appeal for a work of its type as the Great War wound down to an end, selling some 32,000 copies in its first few weeks. But more was to come; Huxley, though he had acknowledged that he himself was not a natural mystic, in the Fifties was not only to write about the Divine Ground, but also to see it before his eyes.

First, however, a characteristic early Fifties experience of alienation on a more worldly plane. In 1951 Aldous Huxley and his wife Maria (a Belgian) decided to apply for U.S. citizenship. They had lived in the country for fourteen years; their son, Matthew, had served in the U.S. Army Medical Corps during the war until invalided out and was a citizen. Preparation for the famous couple's citizenship petition took some two years. All went well until a judicial questioning in 1953 before the final swearing involved the applicant's willingness to serve in the U.S. armed forces, or to do alternative service. Huxley's pacifism came out. The judge explained that a 1946 Supreme Court decision had determined that a person refusing to bear arms could nonetheless be granted citizenship, but added, in what the Huxleys' friend Betty Wendel described as "regretful tones," that the decision was regarded by most lawyers as having been superseded by the McCarren Immigration Act of 1952, which denied citizenship to any person refusing to bear arms for any reason other than religious beliefs.

Huxley explained that his reasons for pacifism were philosophical rather than religious. The sympathetic jurist tried to persuade him to expand his definition of religion sufficiently to cover the present requirement, and to consider that at nearly sixty the issue was likely to be moot for him in any case, but these were matters about which the writer had firm and deep convictions, and he declined. The judge had no option but to adjourn the proceedings and help the Britisher prepare an appeal to Washington. According to notes taken by Betty Wendel, who accompanied the Huxleys to court, "When they left the building Aldous's face was white. He said with an entirely uncharacteristic show of feeling, 'They don't want us here!'" The appeal disappeared into Washington's bureaucratic maze, and eventually the Huxleys gave up and renewed their British passports and U.S. visas. No problem ever came from their continuing to the end of their lives to reside in California as resident aliens. As Sybille Bedford remarked of Aldous, "He remained what [naturally] he was, an evolved Victorian Englishman at home in the second part of the twentieth century, at home in Southern California, who walked alone."[17]

It was just after the unpleasant immigration court mishap that Aldous Huxley became, as it were, naturalized into a far stranger land than the United States or even California. In May of 1953 he took, under medical supervision, the four-tenths of a gram of mescaline dissolved in a glass of water that enabled him to see what he had only written about in *The Perennial Philosophy*, and that provided the raw material of his most controversial and influential book of the Fifties, the slim volume called *The Doors of Perception*.[18]

Now, Huxley wrote,

> I was seeing what Adam had seen on the morning of his creation—the miracle, moment by moment, of naked existence. . . . flowers shining with their own inner light and all but quivering under the pressure of the significance with which they were charged. . . . Words like "grace" and "transfiguration" came to my mind. . . .
>
> Being-Awareness-Bliss—for the first time I understood, not on the verbal level, not by inchoate hints . . . but precisely and completely what those prodigious syllables referred to.[19]

One could, of course, venture too deeply into that world:

> Confronted by a chair which looked like the Last Judgment . . . I felt myself all at once on the brink of panic. This, I suddenly felt, was going too far. Too far, even though the going was into intenser beauty, deeper significance. The fear, as I analyse it in retrospect, was of being overwhelmed, of disintegration under a pressure of reality greater than a mind, accustomed to living most of the time in a cozy world of symbols, could possibly bear. The literature of religious experience abounds in references to the pains and terrors overwhelming those who have come, too suddenly, face to face with some manifestation of the Mysterium tremendum.[20]

For Huxley, who had never been a visualizer, these prodigies of altered consciousness took the form, as these passages make evident, of the enhancement of ordinary reality, rather than of fantastic visions not otherwise viewed on land or sea reported by other psychedelic experiencers. However, Huxley was well aware of paradises and their opposites, and in 1956 he complemented *The Doors of Perception* with another short volume, *Heaven and Hell*, now often bound together with it.[21] This is a characteristically erudite yet luminous study of humankind's yearning for what he called "the antipodes of the mind," that realm of desire first suggested by our otherwise irrational fascination with jewels and flowers and fireworks, which expands into the full-blown heavens of the great religions, and which lies behind countless works of art and festival. Now, something of the real presence of that other side could be glimpsed all around through drugs that, like more traditional fasting, lower the inhibitions that ordinarily restrict consciousness to its practical uses. We can then see what the mystics have always known to be there, ultimate reality in each particular, for as William Blake had put it, "If the doors of perception were cleansed every thing would appear to man as it is, infinite."

Despite the charges of critics, Huxley did not claim that mescaline experience was exactly the same as mystical experience: "I am not so foolish as to equate what happens under the influence of mescalin or of any other drug . . . with the realization of the end and ultimate purpose of human life: Enlightenment, the Beatific Vision." But he did feel it could be spiritually helpful. Those pharmacies of heaven and hell could at least dispense the means to "what Catholic theologians call 'a gratuitous grace'" that could shake people out of the ruts of ordinary life into at least a preliminary realization that there is much, much more to reality than one drab day after another.[22] All people crave some kind of temporary separation from selfhood from time to time, Huxley believed, and seek it in alcohol, escapist entertainment, all sorts of indulgence—why not in a way that was, in contrast, harmless and spiritually uplifting?

Despite his enthusiasm, however, Huxley was not entirely unaware that drugs can produce negative effects. One of the principle points of *Heaven and Hell* was that drug-induced heavens can turn into hells. An article for the *Saturday Evening Post* took account of the devastation wrought by alcohol and opium addiction, though Huxley noted William James's observation that even in drunkenness there is a parallel to mystical experience and went on to comment that the then new drug LSD was being used by researchers in Europe and the United States to help subjects look deeply into the recesses of their own minds. Like peyote or mescaline, it "stimulates the mystical faculties" and could not be effectively outlawed any more than could practices like "yogic breathing techniques" which work to the same end.[23]

But the reaction to Huxley's natural mysticism was an interesting measure of Fifties spirituality as it confronted something very different indeed from Niebuhr, Peale, or Graham. The *Kirkus Review* said that "all this cannot be taken too seriously, but it makes amusing reading as well as a controversial commentary on current intellectual preoccupations." J. H. Jackson in the *San Francisco Chronicle* was tolerant enough to contend that "whether you agree that the experiment was worth trying or feel that the author is knocking on doors that 'should' be left untouched, you are likely to admit that a challenge is forcibly put, that ideas are freshly and prodigally presented, and that even to try to answer Mr. Huxley honestly might well be a valuable experience in itself for the hostile reader. But the *New Yorker* found only too much of the "old, weary dance of abstractions named Not-Self, Eternity, Mind At Large, Suchness, and the Absolute."[24]

Part of the problem for negative critics was that Huxley's present chemical mysticism was seen only as an extension of a larger mysticism based on such irritating abstractions as those just named, which seemed also to be involved with an unbalanced, though characteristically Fifties, cultural pessimism. William Esty, writing of Huxley's collection of essays, *Tomorrow and Tomorrow and Tomorrow*, saw in them a dialogue between two Huxleys, the likable rational humanist, discoursing pleasantly on art and culture, and the tiresome predicant of Pure Truth and Mind At Large, who was also "characterized by an incessant doom-crying, a caricature of our age's fashionable prophesying of disaster-just-around-the-corner. If the H-bomb doesn't get us, he appears to be saying, the end of civilization as we know it will." Marvin Barrett, though more tolerant of Huxley's "neo-mysticism," pointed out that it amounted to a turnaround for the prophet of mescalin, who in *Brave New World* had presented soma as a drug invented to "keep the regimented masses happy," but who held that "in its addiction to such anodynes as soma, modern materialism was to demonstrate its ultimate bankruptcy"; now drug-based awareness was the answer instead of the problem.[25]

But cultural pessimists seeking forgotten universals and lost trails back to the One did not need to deal only in such abstractions. They could also speak the language of myth.

THE MYTHOLOGICAL UNDERGROUND

Another inchoate but coalescing alternative to the above-ground religiosity of the Fifties was the interest in mythology in the tradition of scholars like Joseph Campbell, Mircea Eliade, and above all C. G. Jung and such disciples of his as Erich Neumann.

Important books for the new mythology begin with Campbell's *Hero with a Thousand Faces* (1949) and, at the other end of the decade, culminate in his *Masks of God: Primitive Mythology* (1959). In between, Campbell kept his influence alive through editing the distinguished German Indologist Heinrich Zimmer and the Eranos papers.[26] Also read were Jung's *Modern Man in Search of a Soul* and *Answer to Job*, and the first English editions of such works of Mircea Eliade as *The Sacred and the Profane*, *The Myth of the Eternal Return*, *Shamanism: Archaic Techniques of Ecstasy*, and *Yoga: Immortality and Freedom*.[27]

To the extent that these scholars reached a more than academic audience, it was certainly because they harmonized with the characteristic Fifties sense that the modern world had somehow gone terribly wrong, and that the answer could only be found through the recovery of some authoritative and viable tradition from out of a wiser past. We have noted how this yearning contributed to the revival of conventional religion in traditional, even nostalgic, forms. What the mythologists contributed to that quest was information that the golden-age past was even further back, and even more broadly based, than the religions of history allowed. It was in the universal primordial wisdom of humankind, now secreted only in the arcane language of myth and symbol. Although they were therefore, in a precise sense of the word, reactionaries, this brought them into conflict with even the most conservative of regular religions, for they were unwilling to grant exclusive title to the usable past to any one of them. The past they evoked was no subject of mere nostalgia, much less of material benefit, but a time when values and spirituality now almost forgotten reigned.

The loss of that kind of a past, well fused by mythology, was memorably outlined by Campbell:

> The rise and fall of civilization in the long, broad course of history can be seen to have been largely a function of the integrity and cogency of the supporting canons of myth. For not authority but aspiration is the motivater, builder, and transformer of civilization. A mythological canon is an organization of symbols, ineffable in import, by which the energies of aspiration are evoked and gathered toward a focus. The message leaps from heart to heart by way of the brain, and where the brain is unpersuaded the message cannot pass. The life is untouched. For those in whom a local mythology still works, there is an experience both of accord with the social order, and of harmony with the universe. For those, however, in whom the authorized signs no longer work—or, if working, produce deviant effects—there follows inevitably a sense both of dissociation from the local social nexus and of quest, within and without, for life which the brain will take to be for "meaning." Coerced to the social pattern, the individual can only harden to some figure of living death; and if any considerable number of the members of a civilization are in this predicament, a point of no return will have been passed.[28]

For the mythologist, those still living and workable pasts were in fact twofold in each case. On the one hand, there was the undated primordial golden age when myths were strong and human life meaningful under their aegis; on the other hand there was a more immediate secondary silver age within the last few hundred years, more fallen but also perhaps more accessible, for which they pined: Jung for a medieval harmony of symbol and life before it was fractured by the triple evils of the Reformation, the Enlightenment, and the Industrial Revolution; Campbell for an idealized early America of moral virtue and sturdy individualism. To put it another way, they were antimodern. While acknowledging that primal humanity was in some ways undeveloped, largely through the power of myth and ritual it was nonetheless better integrated spiritually and cosmically than moderns. They also held that enough recent examples obtain to suggest that primal integration can be recovered at least in part, though perhaps only on an individual basis.

In passing it may be observed that the Fifties were virtually the last decade in which continuity with the mythic and medieval past could be seen as a visible reality, or felt as a lingering living memory, in some places. Peasant and tribal cultures, interwoven with pre–Vatican II Roman Catholicism or comparable spiritualities, were still a presence, though diminishing, here and there in Europe, Asia, Africa, and Latin America. All too soon they would be caught up in the whirlwinds of reform, secularization, and political upheaval. Some would wish the best of that past might have tarried longer. But for moderns the mythic past was to be found only individually and within, in the form of retrieved atavistic memory, so to speak.

It was Carl Jung who then spoke of individuation, the harmonious inward integration of one's psyche and its symbols, as the way out. "Mass man," entrapped in the alienating modern world of impersonal cities and factories, is dangerously out of touch with true human nature and, for that matter, with natural nature; this was the profound-sounding contribution of analytic psychology to the great Fifties conundrum, already mentioned in connection with both existentialism and popular cultural analysis, of mass man and the individual.

All that could be done, Jung believed, was to awaken mass men from their dreams by individuation, and that is achieved by opening channels to the unconscious, including the archetypes and the collective unconscious. Myth and ritual can have a very important role in this awakening process, for they are able to penetrate mass man's amnesia and recall to some level of consciousness the archetypes and finally the mandala of full human/divine glory they embody when realized and in balanced harmony. Jungian works like *Archetypes and the Collective Unconscious* are full of studies of the Trickster, Kore, Fairy Tales, the Mother and Child archetypes, the last (as the marvelous child, the *puer aeternas*, the Christ Child) being the emblem of rebirth and new transformed selfhood.[29] So awakened, the archetypes can then fairly contend for the soul of the persona and forge it as with hammer and anvil. The way out can only be individual; there is little hope in mass movements or political action, for they are generally part of the problem instead, annealing mass man more than healing him.

The deep-thinking Jung was thus part of the Fifties mood that wanted to see the problems of the nation and world as spiritual in contrast to political and held that only inner renewal could make a true difference. To be sure, the Jungians and their kin were susceptible to the criticism that appeals only to inner conversion are politically conservative by default. Yet they were not content to deal with the inward on the level of a Peale or a Graham or even (so far as his Catholic exclusivism was concerned) a Merton. They brought to the soul's aid all the riches—the arts and rites, the myths and mandalas—of the world's great spiritual cultures. Their vision would to some extent be fulfilled in the Aquarian panorama of faiths revealed the next decade.

BILLY JAMES HARGIS AND SECTARIAN ANTICOMMUNISM

As the mythologists knew, the great myths of humanity afford priceless insights into the human condition, but one of the great perils of mythical thinking is the way it tends to deal with humans and issues in archetypal terms, reducing individuals in all their complexity to standardized roles as heroes or demons, and complicated confrontations to battles of light against dark. In the popular anticommunism of the Fifties, we often see mythology at work in the contemporary world. Communism was, to be sure, rightly perceived as a serious danger, for the fate of most humans would have been grim indeed had it prevailed worldwide in its Fifties form. But whether mythology, or science and liberal education, represented the best weapons of the mind for combat against the opiates emanating from the Kremlin was a basic Fifties issue no less potent because it was not always stated with the boldness it deserved.

Here is a late Fifties example of the mythological approach. Billy James Hargis and his Christian Crusade may be taken to represent the shape that anticommunism took after the fall of McCarthy and the semi-collapse of anticommunism as a putative state church, with its official mythology/ ideology and its purges of heretics. Like many another glorious cause after its hour of power had run out, it was reborn as sect among a dwindling number of true believers. Interestingly, in sectarian form it was less Roman Catholic than in the McCarthyist heyday and more fundamentalist Protestant in constituency and character. But as before, it combined anticommunism with anti-Washington attitudes and, more to the point, with obvious "grass-roots" resistance against a perceived national elite. These believers were not likely to resonate with the calls for education and science rather than preaching as answers to communism now being circulated around the loftier levels of national life. Their suspicions of godlessness in classroom and laboratory ran deep, but pulpitry was part of down-home culture and for them had not lost its power to save nations as well as souls.

Significantly, Hargis and his movement were born far out in the hinterland, he in Texarkana in 1925. He was ordained a minister in the Disciples of Christ in 1943. In 1948, while he was pastor of the First Christian Church in Supulpa, Oklahoma, a suburb of Tulsa, Hargis founded the Christian Crusade to oppose modernism, liberalism, and the social gospel, and to promote fundamentalism and premillennialism; by 1950 he was devoting full time to this cause. After hiring L. J. "Pete" White, Jr., as a public-relations expert in 1955, the crusade began to grow in national visibility, and to emphasize anticommunism. A recurrent theme in Hargis's rhetoric was an emphasis on the alleged uniqueness of the country's spiritual and political origins. The United States, in his eyes and those of his followers, was and had always been a Christian nation. It "began as a Christian nation, led by the spirit of God."[30]

Six feet tall, 270 pounds, baby faced, able to bellow and ooze emotion with the best of southern preachers, Hargis was an imposing figure on the lecture circuit as well as in the pulpit. He acknowledged to commentators that his flamboyant anticommunist language was mostly emotional but claimed that was the way to reach people. Hargis held "Anti-Communist Leadership Schools" at his headquarters in Tulsa, charging $100 tuition for weekends with a faculty that included many John Birch Society figures (Hargis was a director of that organization), several former communists, and other right-wingers. He also published articles in the far right *American Mercury*, gained widespread status in the same circles by a project to send Bibles by balloon behind the Iron Curtain, and took trips around the world to visit anticommunist leaders.

A glance at his *American Mercury* contributions will give some insight into the mentality of sectarian anticommunism. This once distinguished magazine had been bought in the fall of 1952 by J. Russell Maguire, a wealthy extreme rightist who had subsidized anti-Semitic as well as anticommunist authors. Maguire ousted the previous editor and made the periodical a vehicle for writers with views congenial to his own, such as Hargis and, as we have seen, J. B. Matthews.

In his first contribution, "Are We Opposed to Communism?" a one-page checklist in the February 1957 issue, Hargis asked, "If we *are* opposed to Communism, why do we . . . " do such things as "fellowship in the godless United Nationals Chambers with those Red devils?" "Send multiplied millions of dollars in foreign aid to Communist Yugoslavia?" "Spend taxpayers money on extravagant salaries for Communist professors in American Universities?" or support churches associated with the "World-National Council of Churches," with "Five (5) Communists from Iron Curtain Countries on its Executive Committee," and more in the same vein.[31]

In October 1957, in "A Christian Ambassador Surveys His Divided World," based on his travels as an "impartial and non-political observer," Hargis found anticommunist leaders overseas to be invariably virtuous, brilliant, and devoted Christians in beleaguered countries where the "common people" always looked to the United States. He highlighted three of those figures in East Asia—Chiang Kai-shek and Madame Chiang in Taiwan, and Syngman Rhee in Korea—noting that both the Chiangs and Rhee had been betrayed by Washington, which had refused them further military aid. A passage in a subsequent article should be underlined for the key it undoubtedly gives to Hargis's moral thinking: "To really fight Marxism-Leninism you must constantly keep in mind the fact that their doctrines were born of inordinate envy of others, of hatred, and of an uncompromising intent to create internecine strife and disintegration in every form of society other than their own cadres."[32]

Hargis's writings all reflect the view—mirroring that of the communist cadres—that the world is divided into black and white, the sphere of virtue and that of strife and evil. But the resolve on the good side is weakening. Certain *American Mercury* articles, such as "Patriotism—Once Revered, Now Smeared" and "The History of American Communist Fronts," revealed how important were the thankless and now reviled labors of Senator Joe McCarthy and J. Edgar Hoover. Communism, Hargis was persuaded, was continuing to infiltrate America through such influences as the "social gospel" in the churches; perhaps that made all the more important the symbol of counter-infiltration represented by his "Bibles from the Sky," the Word sent by balloons into the very heartland of the enemy.[33]

As to the appeal of this kind of sectarian and extreme anticommunism, perhaps no one put it better than Hargis himself. According to Mark Sherwin, the founder of the Christian Crusade once boasted that he had "the feel of the people" and went on to comment, "They wanted to join something. They wanted to belong to some united group. They loved Jesus, but they also had a great fear. When I told them that this fear was Communism, it was like a revelation. They knew I was right, but they had never known before what that fear was."[34]

(It remains to be pointed out that much later, in the mid-1970s, Hargis's work suffered a serious blow when he was accused of having had sexual relations with students of both sexes at American Christian College, an institution he had founded that was affiliated with his Christian Crusade Church. After they had presented their testimony to the college board, he was forced to retire from all his ministries in 1974. Six months later, however, he regained control of all of his former works except the college. In 1976, when the charges became public, he denied them and attributed his temporary disgrace to personnel and theological conflicts within the ministries.)[35]

Mention might also be made of one more or less equivalent Catholic anticommunist organization, the Cardinal Mindszenty Foundation. By and large the Roman Catholic hierarchy in those days opposed Catholic political-action groups as misleading and divisive, even for such an impeccable cause as anticommunism. This group, established in St. Louis in 1959, although not officially endorsed by the church, managed to maintain its Catholic identity, perhaps by providing in its bylaws that local pastors and bishops must be advised of its activities, and perhaps also by avoiding the word "anticommunist," adopting instead the more positive image of a cardinal who had suffered much at communist hands and was widely lauded as a conservative hero.

The foundation was founded by Father Stephen Dunker, for twenty years a missionary in China where he had witnessed the communist take-over. "I never gave up the idea," he said, "that a priest, who had heard and seen the things I had, should help others to hear and see these things." The inspiration for the organization came to Dunker after he had attended Dr. Fred Schwarz's Christian Anticommunist Crusade in a Baptist church in St. Louis in 1958. The board contained three former Catholic bishops in China, the bishop of Pusan, Korea, and ten priests; the executive secretary was Eleanor Schlafly, sister-in-law of right-wing activist Phyllis Schlafly.[36]

Books

At least for the religiously well read, the late Fifties was a season for combining psychology and spiritual introspection. Christian mysticism, as we have seen, was remarkably au courant in the age of Thomas Merton and retreats. So was psychoanalysis. The two were impressively brought together in the work of the psychologist Ira Progoff, author of *The Death and Rebirth of Psychology*, wherein Progoff claimed to be able to get behind Freud, Jung, Adler, and Otto Rank, the Olympian names of the regnant schools of analysis, to discover a deeper psychology that did not interpret humans just as waves of sexual or subconscious energies, but put them in harmony with the profoundest currents of the universe.[37] In *The Cloud of Unknowing*, Progoff "translated" that spiritual classic from fourteenth-century England into modern English laced with psychological terms. In the process, he pointed out that mysticism may lead to "a deliberate attrition of consciousness," which appears pathological to the secular mind, but which is actually a drawing back from all "attachments or projections, whether they are valid or false."[38] That liberation is also a requisite of psychological freedom, and likely greatly to increase the activity of the subconscious, with which all psychology wanted to get in touch. It was an age that wanted, among other things, to explore the mind, but to do so with the help of standard maps and to end up in a cathedral. Progoff's work, celebrated by religion-friendly journals like *Time* even as the wider Fifties revival appeared to be tapering off, appears a precursor of the humanistic and transpersonal psychology, or the psychedelic or Eastern-inspired mysticism, of the next decade.

Another late Fifties endeavor to get past orthodox psychoanalysis to something that put human life in a larger perspective, and one that resonated with the deeper philosophical and spiritual vibrations of the decade, was *Existence: A New Direction in Psychiatry and Psychology*, edited by Rollo May.[39] This work introduced existentialist psychology; the new point was that one need not just accept as normal such feelings as the oedipal but could, like the existentialists deciding what the universe was going to mean for them, face them and decide what to affirm as their truth and meaning for oneself. In these books, as in Leonard Gross's sympathetic presentation of psychoanalysis for religionists and religious counselors, *God and Freud*, one detects a trend toward the merging of psychology and religion for purposes of pastoral counseling; the two estranged friends of the spirit were finally becoming familiar enough to each other to shake hands, though warily, and to work together where they could.[40]

A different journey was that taken by Alexander King in the 1958 bestseller *Mine Enemy Grows Older*. Born in Austria in 1900, King came to New York where he made his way as an artist and writer, also finding time for drug addiction and four marriages. In this book, in large part about the addiction and its cure, and in *May This House Be Safe from Tigers* (1960), King, in high comic style, tells fragments of his life, along the way taking iconoclastic slants on all sorts of things, including religion. The Zen vogue was not immune; the title of the second book came from a mild-mannered Zen priest King claimed to have known who, upon leaving the writer's domicile, would always bless it with the words, "May this house be safe from tigers." King, growing tired of the rigmarole, finally curtly asked him what he thought that meant, to which the monk replied, "Well, you haven't been bothered by tigers lately, have you?"[41] Not bad for an age of conformity, when the underground often thought it had to be serious too; now many things were coming to an end.

Still better fun was made of religion in Peter De Vries's *Mackerel Plaza*, a satirical study of the Reverend Mackerel, pastor of People's Liberal Church, who advanced "the worship of a God free of outmoded theological definitions and palatable to a mind come of age in the era of Relativity." Mackerel, in a phrase almost anticipating the secular, death of God theology of the next decade, could preach that "it is the final proof of God's omnipotence that he need not exist in order to save us." [42]

One writer who certainly disbelieved in God's omnipotence, transferring it rather to humankind, was Ayn Rand, whose novel *Atlas Shrugged* was a late Fifties monument. One hero of this opus was a philosopher who became a pirate in order to prey on nonprofit commerce; he especially relished the looting of such ships as one loaded with food being sent as gifts to starving Europeans. "I'm the man," he declared, "who robs the thieving poor and gives back to the productive rich." The small, dark-eyed, intense woman behind such sentiments defined her philosophy, known as objectivism, as "the concept of man as a heroic being, with his own happiness as the moral purpose of his life, with productive achievement as his noblest achievement, and reason as his only absolute."[43]

As the 1,168-page novel staggers toward an end, several of the principals gather at a capitalist utopia in Colorado, where they think great thoughts and bide their time until the world has been made worthy of them. The dollar sign, raised up and made of gold, or traced in the air, is the community's supreme symbol, and those joining must take this oath: "I swear by my life and my love of it that I / Will never live for the sake of another / Man, nor ask another man to live for mine."[44] Some might assume that motifs like this could only be meant as broad satire. Such persons did not know Ayn Rand. Once she said: "The cross is the symbol of torture; I prefer the dollar sign, the symbol of free trade, therefore of the free mind."[45]

Born in St. Petersburg in 1905, Rand had seen the Bolshevik revolution as a child, going to university and working in the new communist society until 1926, and she hated communism with all the intense passion of which she was capable for its "collectivism" and its doctrine that the individual must exist for the state. But she rejected religion no less on the grounds of its departure from reason and its introduction of faith and charity, and indeed one gets a sense that her profoundest dislike was not for Marx but for Jesus, or at least for what he represents in such respects. This put her virtual cult status during the religious-revival decade, no less the great capitalist decade, in an interesting light. Behind the piety, was there a covert fantasy that maybe Ayn Rand's was the way the world really is, or ought to be?

Faith had its philosophers too. The modern traditionalism of Pius XII Fifties Catholicism received a final push in a book by one of the most distinguished advocates of neo-Thomism, Etienne Gilson, in *The Christian Philosophy of St. Thomas Aquinas.* Here Thomism, which had been the official philosophy of the Roman Catholic church since 1879 and was reaffirmed by the encyclical *Humani generis* in 1950, is vigorously defended against its current rival, existentialism. "The philosophy of St. Thomas is existential in the fullest sense of the word. . . . As a philosophy of the act-of-being, Thomism is not another existential philosophy, it is the only one."[46] As such, it vindicates Catholicism's medieval base as timelessly true, as appropriate to the twentieth century as the thirteenth. Yet in only a few years, as the church's self-image shifted from unchanging fortress to aggiornamento pilgrim under Pius's successor and the spirit of Vatican II, Thomism would be quietly demoted by such leading theologians of the conciliar era as Hans Küng or Karl Rahner. But to understand Fifties Catholicism fully, one must understand Thomas, and Gilson still makes him live.

Then there were the books related to the civil-rights crisis. One was Liston Pope's *Kingdom beyond Caste*, which contained the sometime dean of Yale Divinity School's previously mentioned and oft-quoted line, "The church is the most segregated major institution in American society."[47] Noting that the church has lagged behind the Supreme Court, trade unions, factories, schools, athletic teams, and department stores in regard to racial openness, Pope observed that this dismal reality was a de facto denial of freedom of worship, not to mention the church's proud claim to prefigure the Kingdom of God. He then proposed practical strategies for greater integration of churches and religious institutions.

Martin Luther King's *Stride toward Freedom* was the dramatic story of the Montgomery victory as only the indispensable leader could tell it. Though he was not at Little Rock, he remained in the background of civil-rights news even while that story was playing out, for the example of Montgomery lay behind everything else, giving hope and fear to the present moment beyond the steady medium tension between the races of generations. Montgomery was to remain a paradigm for a decade to come. King was stabbed in New York on September 20, 1958, when a deranged black woman attacked him with a letter opener as he autographed copies of *Stride toward Freedom*. She kept shouting he was "mixed up with the Communists," and King required a four-hour operation to remove the blade.[48]

The Fifties' passions for religion and psychological analysis came together powerfully in one of the most celebrated dramatic works of the decade, Archibald MacLeish's *J. B.*, a modernized interpretation of the story of Job. From the brilliant opening scene, in which God and Satan appear as sparring circus clowns, to the presentation of J. B. and his large family in their prosperity as typical Americans at Thanksgiving dinner, the timeless contemporaneity of the problem of theodicy, justifying the workings of God's justice or the lack thereof, is powerfully confronted.[49]

So it was also in another of the famous literary events that seemed to crowd those last years of the Fifties, the publication of Boris Pasternak's *Doc-*

tor Zhivago.[50] The maverick author, a Russian writer in the great tradition of epic scope combined with psychological vivisection molded by Dostoevsky and Tolstoy, was forced by his government to decline the Nobel Prize for this work on the era of the Russian revolution; it hinted at unorthodox political perspectives and, like its great predecessors, showed a profound though unsettling and very Russian sort of interest in Christianity. But that made Pasternak all the more a celebrity in the West. Zhivago's uncle Kolia, a kind of fellow traveler of Christianity, enunciates one of the book's major themes:

> What you don't understand is that . . . history as we know it now
> began with Christ, and that Christ's gospel is its foundation. Now
> what is history? It is the centuries of systematic exploration of the
> riddle of death, with a view to overcoming death. That's why people
> discover mathematical infinity and electromagnetic waves, that's why
> they write symphonies . . . the two basic ideals of modern man—
> without them he is unthinkable—[are] the idea of free personality and
> the idea of life as sacrifice.[51]

Here, perhaps in a more resonant and less overtly political octave, was a recovery of the big existentialist themes like history, freedom, and God with which the likes of Whittaker Chambers had wrestled in the early Fifties.

Finally, though the Fifties religious revival may have peaked, the books relevant to it continued to arrive. G. Bromley Oxnam's, *A Testament of Faith*, though it does not deal overtly with the celebrated Methodist bishop's ordeal before the House Un-American Activities Committee, is a simple and luminous expression of Oxnam's personal faith. Oxnam has, like most honest Christians, had questions and doubts; but he has known God in Christ: "I know so little about God, but what I know I have seen in the face of Jesus, and that is enough for the journey."[52]

Popular Religion: Inspirational Books in America, by Louis Schneider and Sanford Dornbusch, is an intriguing study based on a content analysis of popular religious writing from 1875 to the Fifties, including "New Thought" and positive-thinking classics, beginning with Henry Drummond's *Greatest Thing in the World*, Ralph W. Trine's *In Tune with the Infinite*, and Russell Conwell's *Acres of Diamonds*, and ending with Fulton Sheen and Norman Vincent Peale. It became apparent to Schneider and Dornbusch that such works generally idealized business and held that "positive" religion brought economic success; they spoke of "the mentalization of the Protestant ethic," meaning that the positive thinkers, broadly drawing from the mental world of popular U.S. Protestantism, turned such categories as faith and "clean living" into inner tools that could be redirected toward this-worldly ends.[53]

Much of that was going on in the Fifties, with respect both to positive thinking and to the spiritual sides of the cold war and civil rights. But now perhaps the Fifties mood was receding into the past and new kinds of mentalization were waiting behind the scenes. A. Roy Eckardt, in *The Surge of Piety in America*, an on-the-scene discussion of Fifties religion, told us, "There are, indeed, some signs that the crest of the recent flood of religious interest may already have passed. At this writing, the new piety is becoming a little old. It is not quite so vocal or manifest as it was as recently as one or two years ago."[54]

Please note that, despite Sputnik and Vietnam to come, the terms *cold war* and *communism* appear much less often in this chapter than in those on the early and middle Fifties. All in all, despite recession, the late Fifties were spiritually optimistic years. The worst was past, and a large new generation, with its cars and its new rock music, was getting ready to come into its own new world—the world of the Sixties. Already much was anticipated from it— it was expected to be the largest, best-educated, and most affluent generation in the history of the world. It might well go to the moon. Probably it would have new ideas on religion too, but these were not yet clear. Around the fall of 1963 the first of the boomers would hit college, and then the first faint outlines of the mystic future might begin to be visible. In 1959 the nation, and the world, waited with hope.

Conclusion: Quiet, Confident, and Troubled: The Fifties as the Last Modern Decade in Religion

Put in the sickle,
   for the harvest is ripe.
Go in, tread,
   for the wine press is full . . . .
Multitudes, multitudes,
   in the valley of decision!
For the day of the LORD is near
   in the valley of decision.
         —JOEL 3:13–14 RSV

Modernism and Its Contradictions

THE RELIGIOUS Fifties suggest a river, perhaps flowing toward a valley of decision. But first the river was forced through a narrow defile as the cold war went subzero: the harsh gateway year of 1950. That was the Holy Year and the year of the Assumption, those final glories of traditional Roman Catholicism; also the first annum of McCarthy and of Korea, of the blizzard beginnings of the National Council of Churches, of growing suburban churches, and of icy Catholic-Protestant relations.

From this strait gate the stream of Fifties religion passes over further rocky stretches, yet also widens and deepens, thawing and sometimes spreading out into fecund but stagnant marshes. Yet always in some places it continues to flow along with the years. At its best it provides a sociable and spiritual faith worthy of compare with any.

But Fifties faith does what it does within the riverbanks of certain sociological and historical parameters. These can best be defined, I believe, by speaking of the Fifties as the last modern decade in religion. (In *The Sixties Spiritual Awakening* I pursued what I mean by modern and postmodern religion, and why I perceive the Sixties as the moment of movement from the former to the latter.)

The qualities of modern religion particularly useful for understanding the Fifties can be summed up in the two metanarratives Jean-François Lyotard has offered as the essence of modernism: the metanarrative of the emancipation of humanity by progress and the metanarrative of the unity of knowledge.[1] The first means, briefly, that, since the effective beginning of modernism with the Enlightenment, the educated have believed themselves capable of freeing humanity from its shackles through more and better knowledge and its application; the second that this knowledge that emancipates is found through the generalized, abstract, rational ways of thinking characteristic of science and social science. The particular is subordinated to the abstract category; the old is generally inferior to the new; the local system submits to the universal.

A couple of important corollaries: although democracy was among the most deeply held ideals of modernism, the modern regimen also called for effective power by knowledge-holding elites, those who knew the universal/abstract as well the particularized knowledge: professionals, enlightened civil servants, teachers. Second, the unity of knowledge was paralleled in other modern unities: the unitary bureaucratic state able to implement the benefits of modern science and democracy on behalf of all, above all the modern university, the indispensable custodian and retailer of precisely the kinds of knowledge and application modernism most valued. It was the temple of universal knowledge, and the shaper of professionals, civil servants, and teachers. No wonder that, when the world of modernism was challenged in the Sixties as it had not been since the Enlightenment, it was at the great universities the challenge was first and most effectively mounted—and that the second point of challenge was the military draft on behalf of a mass army, that paradoxical product of the modern unitary, bureaucratic, "rational" state that so egregiously put its contradictions on display.

To be sure, this sort of modernism was not without challenge in the Fifties. Lyotard's two fundamentals of modernism have a great deal in common with Voegelin's gnosticism, the label that for him embraced more or less everything he disliked about modernity from the Puritans and the Enlightenment on. Indeed, antimodernism converges with certain prominent themes of Fifties mainstream religion generally: emphasis on human sinfulness and imperfectability, anticommunism and reaction against the social "dreams" of the recent past, traditional family and moral values. Should the Fifties then be considered "modern" after all?

My view is that the Fifties critique of modernism, though chic and important in many circles and related to the historical essence of the era, was basically antithesis—and therein lay its significance. Institutional religion and popular religion alike continued to work unflinchingly out of modernist presuppositions, with their structures of thought and organizational life unitary where it counted, viewing their burgeoning numbers and power as "progress." Even the antimodernists were unwittingly part of Fifties modernism, if they worked out of places like Harvard or Union Theological Seminary or showed themselves on television or wore a round collar in one of the prestige denominations. (Ironically, in the Fifties antimodernism was considered conservative; in the Sixties that cause was to become "radical" and anti-Fifties.)

Majority religion from the beginning of the modern era was heavily invested in modernism. That is no accident, for in fact the "great" religions, like Christianity, with their ancient founders and long histories are the world prototypes of what modernism really means. Before state or university went modern on anything like the same scale, they had their reasoned universal truths, their elites and bureaucratic institutions, their beliefs that history was, despite often dismal appearances, an arena of emancipation through progress: in this case through successive revelations of God or universal truth at specific historical moments, leading up to a supreme consummation. Beyond doubt, Western modernism, at least, is simply the secularization of Judaism and Christianity.

We are not surprised, then, that religious and secular modernism display common characteristics. Both moved more and more to define universal truth in modern modes; both moved to create typical modern institutions—schools, hospitals, centralized bureaucratic governance—whether in national capitals, at the Vatican, or in the headquarters of the major U.S. Protestant denominations. Of the latter two the local church became simply a local franchise; its administration (in Protestantism) took on trappings of democracy yet in all its ways was finally subordinated to a religious version of the modern meaning of universal truth. Finally, the missionary movement that was so much a part of the modern religious spirit paralleled belief in progress. It too insisted that in historical time changes can happen—can be made to happen—that improve people and bring them closer to absolute truth.

The religion of the Fifties spiritual marketplace climaxed all these qualities, yet at the same time pushed religion into modern conundrums that were to open it to the Sixties' radical challenges. A foundational problem was the ancient paradox of the one and the many, as applied to religious pluralism and U.S. unity. In the anxious cold-war years, Americans wanted spiritual unity desperately, yet the demands of the spiritual marketplace that lent religion its vitality called for diversity and competition. Will Herberg tried to smooth over the matter by insisting that to be religiously diverse *was* American; and talk of three (later four) faiths and of heritages also tried hard to make the many equal the one. The problem was finding a center that was not simply a vacuous abstraction.

Powerful forces wanted to make a sort of chic intellectual Protestantism the common faith that could unify essential spiritual knowledge. That was basically Henry Luce's purpose in pushing Niebuhrian "Christian realism," and later Tillichianism in his very influential publications, and what Nathan Pusey attempted at Harvard. But although those worthies and their venerable institutions might be laureled in a way latercomers could never quite hope to equal, too much was left out: Jews, Catholics, even Eastern Orthodox, not to mention skeptics of all religion, were no longer content quietly to let an ivy-covered Protestant elite hold center stage.

The Roman Catholicism of Cardinal Spellman and Bishop Sheen and of the bulging seminaries, monasteries, and convents was determined that its claims and its power be recognized, whether in the corridors of power or on the new medium of television—and they were. An attempt was made to establish what amounted to a national anticommunist state church, with McCarthy as its high priest, supported by Cardinal Spellman and at one time by a goodly number of Catholic spokespersons and Protestant legislators. But that faith fizzled with the collapse of McCarthyism, and decisively after the post-sputnik education and science thrust; moreover its essentially rightist worldview had nothing to offer a burgeoning civil-rights movement with a very different rhetoric, now honed by the traumas of Montgomery and Little Rock. Yet religion and religious talk soldiered on.

The One and the Many in Modern Times

A key token of the Fifties as the last modern decade in religion is the way religious discourse could still be taken as normative for understanding, and criticizing, the political process or society generally. (We are not thinking here of the political/social role of the so-called fundamentalists very much with us still, whose ideologies and verities patently suggest the perspective of one self-identified as an outsider to some supposed mainstream; that outsider-against-the-center mentality does not abandon them however strong they are, however many elections they win, for they know that au fond they are of some other time and place.) In the Fifties the religious antitheses could be very closely related to the cultural synthesis. Persons like Reinhold Niebuhr, Paul Tillich, C. S. Lewis, Martin Luther King, Jr., Etienne Gilson, even Norman Vincent Peale and Fulton Sheen if not Billy Graham, were very much men of the center of their time and place, critics from within who accepted the normative institutional and intellectual canons of the day, turning them to religious use no less well than others employed them in the service of psychoanalysis or cold war; and not only as critic, but also as purveyor of maps of the whole human terrain. It was thought in some of the best intellectual circles that the right religious map could box the intellectual and social compass once and for all, as the brief reign of the Puseyites at Harvard shows.

Yet there were many such maps, and they did not always overlap one with another. For despite its supposed intellectual blandness and talk of the "end of ideology," in retrospect (from a time when even less seems to be believed in, except by the "fundamentalists"), the Fifties present themselves as still an age of faith in competing totalistic belief systems.[2] One could live one's whole life, not just as a fundamentalist, but also as an existentialist, Freudian, Jungian, neoorthodox Protestant, Thomistic Catholic, Jew, scientific humanist, even Marxist—talking, working, and taking recreation only with those of the same persuasion. Even being a Methodist, Baptist, or Episcopalian was taken a bit more seriously than later from both ecclesiological and social-status points of view. The Fifties were still a season of belief, an age of faith; paradoxical as it may seem, that is what marks the decade as modern. For the key to the modern, as Voegelin realized, is belief—not necessarily in creeds outworn, but in its own modern credenda, as Nathan Pusey pointed out—in science, political ideologies, psychology, and the rest. The common ground of all these was that they could become total explanations of the significant world and could offer an esoteric wisdom that, if fully discovered and applied, could improve the world to the point of paradise.

Nonetheless the deadly power of ideologies was coming home to a people who had seen a surfeit of blood spilled on the altars of creed and party, and so began to swell the at first conservative and then radical undertow against the dreams. Though the churches still worked institutionally in the Fifties, the abundant churchly and secular seamless ideological coats of many colors were beginning to fray along the edges and, for younger people especially, to feel tight and outgrown. The Great War against fascism was just behind them, and now came cold war against another implacable set of Voegelin's "humanitarians" willing to massacre half the human race to give happiness to the other half. In the red light of the atomic era it was now possible to see most all of them as gnosticisms, in that political philosopher's sense, promising a new heaven and earth, or a new humanity, through some esoteric wisdom. The secret price in the end would be no doubt more holocausts of victims before what was left of the human race could enter singing into the long-awaited earthly paradise.

It is always easier to perceive the myth, the gnosticism, or the blind dogmatism in someone else's eye than to recognize a beam of the same in one's own. For a time the Christian critics of the gnosticisms fared rather well, especially against the iron dreams of the communists' dogmatic slumbers. Christian views of original sin comported well with the commonsense realism of the Anglo-American enlightenment out of which came the "American proposition" to deflate the dialectical cant of the other side. Undoubtedly the

Marxist paradise was beyond real human capability, or the revolutionary frenzy to create it by godless human housecleaning likely to cast out more demons than it let in.

The once serious McCarthyist anticommunist state church was clearly a contradiction in original-sin terms, since it presupposed a preternatural insight into the evil lurking in the hearts of others on the part of the witch finders. While the benign messianic vision of America's historic role contemplated by thinkers in the Luce stable and others may also fall short of the self-reflexiveness a sin-conscious decade might have had to offer, its critique need not detain us here. Fifties ideologies were to expand to world-devouring girth in the Sixties, then dramatically implode; enough was said then.

Religion, in a free-market bazaar of beliefs such as Fifties America presented, could then refurbish what was outworn and change as much coin as any of the others. The ordinary customers understood quite well that in their social setting and their cold-war world religion was not only a faith choice but a rational choice; it could defend togetherness better than the psychoanalysts or the communists, and struck the right note between the dreaded "mass man" and existentialist aloneness.

The spiritual problems of the Fifties came down to the ancient conundrum of reality as one and as many. In seeking the One through religion, Fifties people could, with Aldous Huxley, often recognize the false oneness proffered by political or intellectual pseudo-faiths. Yet, also like the mystic novelist, they could see that at its best the yearning for social oneness—call it togetherness, belongingness, brotherhood, Americanism—might be, instead of an idol, a step up the great chain of being toward ultimate unity. In the face of immense external pressures and growing racial and demographic divides at home, U.S. society tried to find middle-level as well as ultimate unities that would at least do more good than harm. In the end, religious unities, made here below but in awareness of the Ultimate, probably worked best.

The idea of national religious unity—call it civil religion—remained alive to the end of the decade, a notion hovering in the air that was always trying to bring about democratic unity, always trying to do so by means of an elite who, by the very nature of their credentials, left many out who might have been included. Here is one example, an attempt to make a kind of covert national religion on far more sophisticated and less ultra grounds than the McCarthyist effort.

The National Purpose

An interesting closing perspective on the Fifties can be had in a collection of essays that appeared in 1960, *The National Purpose*, edited by John K. Jessup, chief editorial writer for Luce's *Life* magazine.[3] The series of articles first appeared in that magazine and offer the late Fifties national reflections of Adlai Stevenson, Archibald MacLeish, David Sarnoff, Billy Graham, John W. Gardner, Clinton Rossiter, Albert Wohlstetter, James Reston, and Walter Lippman. The enterprise was undoubtedly inspired by Luce and his views of nation and world, views that were usually tinged with a high-minded evangelistic zeal rooted in his missionary upbringing in China.

Thus the volume clearly presupposes that the United States must have some overarching national purpose, some reason for existing as a people and an organized nation. It would be unworthy of such a mighty land not to have a high vision of what it could achieve, one that saw beyond the present years and past its own boundaries. Now, at the end of the Fifties, it appeared to the eyes of several writers in this volume that the sense of national purpose, required as never before, was becoming rusty and needed to be reforged.

The idea of a national purpose is itself an interesting one. Some nations, like Switzerland and Sweden, have had little concern with such a transcendent world-historical perspective on their significance, being content merely to meet the day-to-day needs of their citizens for practical governmental services, and to meet them very well. Others, like Britain and France at certain periods, have cloaked an empire-building impulse in the rhetoric of spreading the benefits of civilization around the globe, and have done so to both the weal and woe of their multiracial subjects. Still others, like the former Papal States and the former Soviet Union, have bestowed upon their peoples the immense privilege and burden of living in the pied-à-terre of a vast extraterritorial ideological/ spiritual cause and the sprawling worldwide institutions supporting it. To those interests merely national concerns often had to take second or last place.

Certainly, for one of the Luce sort of missionary mentality, the national purpose of the United States reached to the ends of the earth, and its definition veered toward the papal/Soviet end of the scale, always with the understanding that the United States was wholly benign and so very different from the empire-building, domination-minded national purposes of others across the water. For the nation's reason for being, it was argued, can only be the preservation and expansion of the same freedom and democracy first essayed as a national vision on U.S. shores. Of those excellent ideals the United States was now the chief exponent and bulwark. Indeed, in forthright affirmations of what is now called "American exceptionalism," these writers of 1959 or 1960, like many others, could not help concluding that America's common morality in the great political and international issues was somehow of a different order than that of the rest, and could lead the country to unprecedented "greatness." In *The National Purpose*, Jessup, amid much else in the same vein, spoke ringingly of "America's public love affair with righteousness" (p. 17). Stevenson no less grandly proclaimed that we must "extend our vision . . . to all mankind" (p. 21).

Thinkers like these, with the cold war never far from mind, esteemed it too easy merely to justify the United States by such obvious criteria as supermarket shopping carts much fuller than the pitiful baskets carried by babushkas in Russia's dismal state stores, or by the armory of bombs and missiles in freedom's U.S. fortress. Some larger, less material vision ought to pull that purpose forward. Yet the panelists seemed surprisingly unsure exactly how to phrase the purpose beyond the basic rhetoric. Perhaps that was because, as several recognized, freedom is a process rather than a benchmark; as Archibald MacLeish noted, it is "infinite in its possibilities—as infinite as the human soul which it enfranchises" (p. 39).

At the same time, it seemed to these late Fifties spokesmen that too many in the country now thought that freedom had in fact been already realized, after the two world wars and at least in the United States. The goals had been reached, and there was nothing now to do but enjoy them. The problem then was nothing more to look forward to either—and, patriotic rhetoric aside, no place on the sublunar earth, the United States included, is truly the earthly paradise. People still hurt in late Fifties America, where Jim Crow was the law in some places and urban jungledom in others, and where gender and class barriers lay athwart the corporate high-rises. The writers in *The National Purpose* were aware of all this, though not as much as they might have been. So they perceived 1960 as actually a kind of stasis. There was then no past to which the country really wanted to return, but the present was muddled, and nothing seemed to lie ahead but more of the same.

They were certainly aware of the cold war, and the pall it cast across the land. They did opine that the strange conflict, though far from won, had reached a new and relatively more mature phase by the end of the decade. As MacLeish put it, harking back to the McCarthyist early Fifties, "We have outgrown the adolescent time when everything that was wrong with America was the fault of the Russians and all we needed to do to be saved was to close the State Department and keep the Communists out of motion pictures. It isn't just the Russians now: it's ourselves. It's the way we feel about ourselves as Americans. We feel we've lost our way in the woods, that we don't know where we are going—if anywhere" (p. 38).

And problems remained that had to be cut away before that woods could be exited. One was race. Clinton Rossiter commented acidly that "always we have known that every claim for the fairness of our social order had to be footnoted 'except for the Negroes'" (p. 86). But now, in 1960, "the Negroes" were no longer a footnote, he observed, and could no longer be treated merely as an exception.

For most other writers, though, the full impact of Montgomery and Little Rock had apparently not set in. Albert Wohlstetter, while recognizing the innate justice of reducing racism, seemed mainly interested in the fact that "race prejudice at home is an enormous handicap to any nation aspiring to lead a non-Communist world that is largely colored" (p. 101). What the civil-rights movement was to mean in the next decade, not to mention the even less anticipated New Left and antiwar movements, was not really foreseen by these pundits. What social problems remained in the citadel of liberty often appeared more like final scrub that had to be cleared before the nation could enter the empyrean of eternal "greatness": they were somehow not serious compared to the cold-war issues or ideological "freedom."

Perhaps the lacunae were related to another feature of this work that strikes a later reviewer: all the writers were white males, to the best of my knowledge all Protestant in background save one who was Jewish. For all their newsworthiness, apparently not Martin Luther King, Jr., not John Courtney Murray or Fulton Sheen or Margaret Mead (perhaps the best-known wise woman of the time) was considered worthy to participate in a symposium on the level of this one.

And so what was seen by those prophets was a world whose truly important people were white males of a comfortable, educated class; they perceived a world of global challenge and a nation with some residual problems, but one that needed above all to be stirred to some great purpose. The stirring and the purposes would come, but not only because of the cold war or national-purpose speeches like John F. Kennedy's inaugural and his going-to-the-moon talk, both of which may have been partly inspired by this book. Causes mounting into national purposes and excited by real passions would arise, at southern lunch counters and on Berkeley commons, out of the life concerns of nonelites and fired by the politics of the Holy Ghost rather than of the knowledge holders.

The National Purpose indicates that the metanarratives of progress and unification of knowledge about what the United States meant were still operative in public intellectual discourse, at least those related to the Luce publications: the "American proposition," the "national purpose." Yet this Fifties nationalistic way of thinking was in deep tension with the religious pluralism that was expanding in the free-enterprise religious marketplace, and with the increasingly visible social/intellectual contradictions of modernism. So did the spirit of religious free enterprise strain against the Fifties "modern" denominational bureaucracy and centralization, paralleling that of a modern government or supermarket chain, with the desperate energy of a street peddler turned rival entrepreneur. The potential tension was hinted at by Sheen's Catholic converts and Graham's rallies, disturbing traditional denominational and demographic polities. It was more forcefully exacerbated by civil rights, a spiritual movement neither denominational nor centralized.

Above all, the early Fifties hegemonies of the spirit were thrown off-balance by the education thrust after 1957, serendipitously mixed as it was with the baby-boom demographic bulge and Galbraith's affluent society to create megauniversities teeming with restless young. All that was enough to shrivel the roots of classical modernism in education, ideology, and faith; in religion it meant challenges to received thought on matters from denominational centralization to Christian nationalism. From Berkeley to Selma, from Vatican II to the Haight-Ashbury, those interlocking systems were set upon in the Sixties and would never again be what they were in the Fifties and before.

But that is another and later story. Our purpose here has been to see Fifties religion primarily as a reality in itself, with its own distinctive quality, experiences, and motifs. Certainly Fifties faith in the United States had a distinctive "feel" comprised of several strands: full churches, many children and young people, relatively uncritical cold-war religious nationalism, traditionalist assumptions combined with growing intellectual curiosity about faith, a peculiar combination of underlying confidence and anxiety.

There was the theme of recovery of the best of the past, including theological awareness of sin and the fallibility of all human institutions, yet it was also a time of church building and family bonding. All that was, however, under challenge by a differently bonded "underground" and, more broadly, by existentialist individualism and excoriation of "mass man." It was a time of denominational and institutional prestige, including a significant rise in the power and status of Roman Catholicism on the national scene, yet also of a deep split between popular and "elite" forms of religiosity as well as of interreligious tensions. It was a time of great interest in psychology and spirituality, and of gnawing unease about the direction of personal and national life.

And religion was powerful in American life. That was partly because most people believed they needed it, and there was nothing to discredit it in the eyes of most. It was also because the varied spiritual marketplace provided dynamic and competition enough to keep it going. It was an age of affluence—sometimes a spendthrift age—in things of the spirit as well as of this world.

Notes

Introduction

1. Cited in David Halberstam, *The Fifties* (New York: Random House, 1993), p. 591.
2. Ibid.
3. William H. Whyte, Jr., "The Wife Problem," *Life*, Jan. 7, 1952, pp. 32–48.
4. See, for example, R. Stephen Warner, "Work in Progress: Toward a New Paradigm for the Sociological Study of Religion in the United States," *American Journal of Sociology* 98,5 (Mar. 1993): 1044–1093; Roger Finke and Rodney Stark, *The Churching of America, 1776–1990: Winners and Losers in Our Religious Economy* (New Brunswick, N.J.: Rutgers University Press, 1992); and Rodney Stark and Laurence R. Iannoccone, "A Supply-Side Reinterpretation of the 'Secularization' of Europe," *Journal for the Scientific Study of Religion* 33,3 (Sept. 1994): 130–152.
5. Stark and Iannoccone, "A Supply-Side Reinterpretation," p. 321; Bryan Wilson, *Religion in Secular Society* (London: Watts, 1960), p. 126. See Samuel H. Reimer, "A Look at Cultural Effects on Religiosity: A Comparison between the United States and Canada," *Journal for the Scientific Study of Religion* 34,4 (Dec. 1995): 458–469.
6. For these and other examples see James Hudnut-Beumler, *Looking for God in the Suburbs: The Religion of the American Dream and Its Critics, 1945–1965* (New Brunswick, N.J.: Rutgers University Press, 1994), especially pp. 38–53.
7. "Protestant Architect," *Time*, Apr. 19, 1954, pp. 62–66.
8. David A. Roozen, "Denominations Grow as Individuals Join Congregations," in *Church and Denominational Growth*, ed. David A. Roozen and C. Kirk Hadaway (Nashville: Abingdon, 1993), p. 16, fig. 1.1, "Membership of Selected Denominational Families as a Percent of 1950 Membership."
9. Wade Clark Roof and William McKinney, *American Mainline Religion* (New Brunswick, N.J.: Rutgers University Press, 1987).
10. William Lee Miller, "The 'Religious Revival' and American Politics," in *Piety along the Potomac: Notes on Politics and Morals in the Fifties* (Boston: Houghton Mifflin, 1964), pp. 125–126.
11. "Protestant Architect." See also "Resurgent Protestantism," *Newsweek*, Mar. 28, 1955, pp. 55–59.
12. *Christian Century*, Mar. 23, 1955, p. 370.
13. Sherwood Eliot Wirt, *Crusade at the Golden Gate* (New York: Harper, 1959), p. 176.
14. Michael S. Sherry, *In the Shadow of War: The United States since the 1930s* (New Haven, Conn.: Yale University Press, 1995).
15. Ibid., p. 153.

16. William H. Whyte, *The Organization Man* (New York: Simon and Schuster, 1956), p. 404.
17. J. Ronald Oakley, *God's Country: America in the Fifties* (New York: Dembner, 1986).

Part I   The Years of Dark and Dreaming

1. "The Younger Generation," *Time*, Nov. 8, 1951, pp. 46–51.

Chapter 1   Events: Korea, Catholics, Protestants, and Anticommunism

1. See Ellen V. Schrecker, *No Ivory Tower: McCarthyism and the Universities* (New York: Oxford University Press, 1986), pp. 165–166; and Robert Newman, *Owen Lattimore and the "Loss" of China* (Berkeley and Los Angeles: University of California Press, 1992).
2. "The Cultivation of Fear," *Christian Century*, Apr. 5, 1950, pp. 423–424; "What Should We Fear?" *Christian Century*, Apr. 12, 1950, pp. 455–456.
3. David Halberstam, *The Fifties* (New York: Villard, 1993), p. 53.
4. Edmund A. Walsh, *Total Empire: The Roots and Progress of World Communism* (Milwaukee: Bruce, 1951).
5. John Cooney, *The American Pope: The Life and Times of Francis Cardinal Spellman* (New York: Times Books, 1984), pp. 219–220.
6. Donald F. Crosby, *God, Church, and Flag: Senator Joseph R. McCarthy and the Catholic Church, 1950–1957* (Chapel Hill: University of North Carolina Press, 1978), pp. 47–52. Crosby notes that the senator has begun harping on the communists-in-government theme even before Wheeling, though to less media attention than his notorious list afforded. The *Christian Century* pointed out at the time that Pearson was "not always a reliable authority, but often informed on doings in Washington" (Apr. 5, 1950, p. 424).
7. Crosby, *God, Church, and Flag*, pp. 22–23.
8. Thomas A. Dooley, *Deliver Us from Evil* (New York: Farrar, Straus and Cudahy, 1956).
9. James Terence Fisher, *The Catholic Counterculture in America, 1933–1962* (Chapel Hill: University of North Carolina Press, 1989), p. 149.
10. On Dooley and his role in Catholic consciousness see ibid., chaps. 5 and 6. Dooley died of cancer in 1961 at the age of thirty-four.
11. Editorial, "The Fourth of July and McCarthy," *The Sign*, July 1950, p. 5.
12. Editorial, "Senator McCarthy's Charges," *America*, Apr. 1, 1950, p. 737.
13. Doris Grumbach, "The Lost Liberals," *Commonweal*, Mar. 28, 1952, pp. 609–610; and see, e.g., "Enough's Enough," editorial, *Commonweal*, Aug. 4, 1950, p. 406. Dorothy Day, *The Long Loneliness* (New York: Harper & Row, 1952).
14. Cooney, *The American Pope*, p. 221; Crosby, *God, Church, and Flag*, pp. 167–169.
15. Crosby, *God, Church, and Flag*, pp. 83–87.
16. "Current Fact and Comment," editorial, *The Sign*, Mar. 1952, p. 9.
17. Cited in Cooney, *The American Pope*, p. 226.
18. Crosby, *God, Church, and Flag*, p. 41.
19. Fisher, *Catholic Counterculture*, p. 152.
20. "Out of Darkness, Hope," editorial, the *Christian Century*, July 12, 1950; letter by A. J. Muste, p. 952, and "Revolution in Foreign Policy," editorial, p. 941, both in *Christian Century*, Aug. 9, 1950.
21. Robert Root, "All in the Name of Peace," *Christian Century*, Sept. 27, 1950, pp. 1130–31.
22. Samuel A. Stouffer, *Communism, Conformity, and Civil Liberties: A Cross-Section*

of the Nation Speaks Its Mind (Garden City, N.Y.: Doubleday, 1955), pp. 42–43. The survey reported in this work was taken in the summer of 1954 and included 6,000 Americans in "all walks of life" and 1,500 "local community leaders."

23. John C. Cort, "The Case of the Agnostic Teacher," *Commonweal*, Mar. 7, 1942, p. 541.
24. Ibid., p. 542.
25. William Lee Miller, *Piety along the Potomac* (Boston: Houghton Mifflin, 1964), pp. 46–47.
26. The *Commonweal* article by John C. Cort pointed out that the West Virginia constitution states, "No religious or political test oath shall be required as a prerequisite or qualification to vote, serve as a juror, sue, plead, appeal, or pursue any profession or employment." Cort, "Case of the Agnostic Teachers," p. 542.
27. "Fighting Fire with Gasoline," *Christian Century*, Sept. 27, 1950, p. 1126.
28. "World in Revolution," editorial, *Christian Advocate*, May 4, 1950, p. 12.
29. "Great Churches of America: XI, Collegiate Church, Ames, Iowa," *Christian Century*, Nov. 29, 1950, pp. 1418–1423.
30. "The Church and the Churches," *Time*, Mar. 26, 1951, pp. 68–75.
31. "NCC's Two Years," *Newsweek*, Dec. 22, 1952, p. 68.
32. "Mount Olivet Lutheran Church," *Christian Century*, Jan. 25, 1950, pp. 105–111.
33. "This Is How Churches Are Born," *The Lutheran*, Apr. 26, 1950, pp. 18–20.
34. "Great Churches of America: XII, First Community Church, Columbus, Ohio," *Christian Century*, Dec. 20, 1950, p. 1515.
35. Eugene Carson Blake, "The American Churches and the Ecumenical Mission," in *The Ecumenical Era in Church and Society*, ed. E. J. Jurji (New York: Macmillan, 1959), pp. 77–78. Cited in Rodney Stark and Roger Finke, "A Rational Approach to the History of American Cults and Sects," in *Handbook on Cults and Sects in America, Part A*, vol. 3 of *Religion and the Social Order*, ed. David G. Bromley and Jeffrey K. Hadden (Greenwich, Conn.: JAI, 1993), p. 111.
36. "Billy and His Beacon," *Newsweek*, May 1, 1950, pp. 66–67.
37. "Wheaton Repents," *Newsweek*, Feb. 20, 1950, p. 82.
38. Wynn Boliek, "Estimate of an Evangelist," *The Lutheran*, July 5, 1950, pp. 13–18.
39. Arthur Lester Frederick, "Billy Graham's Seattle Campaign," *Christian Century*, Apr. 23, 1952, pp. 494–496.
40. W. E. Garrison, "Propaganda—But Good," *Christian Century*, Apr. 12, 1950, p. 648.
41. Harold C. Gardiner, "Prelate in Technicolor," *America*, Apr. 1, 1950, pp. 754–55.
42. Paul Blanshard, *Communism, Democracy, and Catholic Power* (Boston: Beacon, 1951) and *American Freedom and Catholic Power* (Boston: Beacon, 1949).
43. "Lopsided Liberalism," editorial, *America*, July 1, 1950, p. 349. For a substantial Catholic rebuttal of Blanshard's *American Freedom and Catholic Power*, presenting alleged examples of his misuse of sources, see the review by Francis J. Connell in *Cornell Law Quarterly* 35, 3 (Spring 1950): 678–684. See also Blanshard's reply, "Father Connell and Mr. Blanshard," *Cornell Law Quarterly* 36, 2 (Winter 1951): 406–415.
44. Robert A. Vogeler, *I Was Stalin's Prisoner* (New York: Harcourt, Brace, 1952). Nicholas Prychodko, *One of The Fifteen Million* (New York: Little, Brown, 1952). The figure refers to the number of Stalin's political prisoners, most of whom were in unspeakable gulags.
45. "Religious Tensions Deplored," editorial, *America*, Jan. 13, 1952, p. 417. *America*, a Jesuit periodical, claimed that its own record was much better.
46. Will Herberg, *Protestant, Catholic, Jew: An Essay in American Religious Sociology* (Garden City, N.Y.: Doubleday, 1955).
47. William Norman Pittenger, "What Is an Episcopalian?" May 19, 1953, p. 6+; Ralph Sockman, "What Is a Methodist?" Oct. 6, 1953, pp. 116–118+; Morris N. Kertzner,

"What Is a Jew?" June 17, 1952, pp. 120–128: John Cogley, "What Is a Catholic?" Oct. 21, 1952. pp. 74–81, all in *Look*. All seventeen articles in this series, including "What Is an Agnostic?" by Bertrand Russell, were reprinted in *A Guide to the Religions of America*, ed. Leo Rosten (New York: Simon and Schuster, 1955).

48. William Norman Pittenger, *The Episcopalian Way of Life* (1957), Gerald Kennedy, *The Methodist Way of Life* (1958), Abraham O. Karp, *The Jewish Way of Life*, (1962), all published in Englewood Cliffs, N.J., by Prentice-Hall.

49. Louis Finkelstein, ed., *Jews: Their History, Culture, and Religion*, 2 vols. (New York: Harper, 1949; 2d ed., 1955).

50. Bernard Iddings Bell, *Crowd Culture: An Examination of the American Way of Life* (New York: Harper, 1952).

51. "Year of Pardon," *Newsweek*, Jan. 2, 1950, p. 32.

52. "War over Holy Year," *Newsweek*, Jan. 2, 1950, p. 41.

53. Particularly the encyclical *Aeterni Patris* of Pope Leo XIII in 1879, and the "Twenty-four Theses" published by the Sacred Congregation of Studies in 1914 with the approval of Pope Pius X; the latter represent a rigid and conservative distillation of Thomas's thought. They describe the body as form made up of primal matter and substance, and capable of being separated from and reunited with the soul, an immortal animating entity without constituent parts.

54. Juniper B. Carol, "The Recent Marian Congress at Le Puy-en-Velay," *American Ecclesiastical Review*, Oct. 1950, pp. 273–283. The views cited are those of such relatively prominent French theologians of the day as Charles Boyer, S.J., Jean-F. Bonnefoy, OFM, and Father Réginald Garrigou-Lagrange.

55. "Urbi et Orbi," *Time*, Dec. 14, 1953, p. 70.

56. See C. G. Jung, *Answer to Job*, trans. R.F.C. Hull (London: Routledge and Kegan Paul, 1954; German original, Zurich, 1952), p. 169. Jung emphasizes the dogma as "a slap in the face for the historical and rationalistic view of the world" (p. 175). See also Jung's "Psychological Approach to the Trinity," especially part 5, "The Problem of the Fourth," in *Collected Works of C. G. Jung*, vol. 11, *Psychology and Religion West and East* (New York: Pantheon, 1958), pp. 170–172. This material, originally written in German in 1948, includes a note suggesting that because of the pressing need for a "consistent and logical restoration of the archetypal situation," the "exalted status" of Mary represented by the Assumption "must therefore become a 'conclusion certa' in the course of time." An editorial note in the English *Collected Works* adds that this indeed happened only two years later, in November 1950.

Jung's enthusiasm was not entirely reciprocated. The Reverend Victor White, O.P., leading Catholic authority on Jungianism, well perceiving that the analytic psychologist's identification of religious symbols with intrapsychic dynamics was not at all the same as the orthodox view, remarked that "the friendliness of Jung presents a far more serious and radical challenge to religion than ever did the hostility of Freud." Victor White, "Jung and the Supernatural," *Commonweal*, Mar. 14, 1952, p. 561. In this connection see Ann Conrad Lammers, *In God's Shadow: The Collaboration of Victor White and C. G. Jung* (Mahwah, N.J.: Paulist, 1994). The sometimes troubled relationship of Jung and his chief Catholic interpreter and friend, the Dominican White, is a fascinating and significant one.

Interest in myth was reviving; not only was there Jung, but also growing literary investigation of writers like William Blake and Sir James Frazer, not surprising in such a myth-consumed world. But the whole matter seemed to raise profound anxieties on the part of Roman Catholics. Michael F. Moloney, discussing the problematic in "The Return to the Myth" (*America*, Mar. 11, 1950, pp. 669–671), would only concede that the desire for "myth" is there, noting that if deprived of a "true" myth like the gospels, moderns will turn to false contenders, such as the myths of Nazism or communism.

57. "Assumption Dogma to be Announced," editorial, *Christianity Century*, Aug. 30, 1950, p. 1012.
58. "Fast-Traveling Cardinal, His Fast-Growing Church," *Newsweek*, May 24, 1954, pp. 54–57. "Laborare Est Orare," *Time*, Apr. 11, 1955, pp. 76–84.
59. See Patricia Wittberg, *The Rise and Fall of Catholic Religious Orders* (Albany: SUNY Press, 1994).
60. See Philip Gleason, *Contending with Modernity: Catholic Higher Education in Twentieth Century America* (New York: Oxford University Press, 1995).
61. See Fulton J. Sheen, *Treasure in Clay: The Autobiography of Fulton J. Sheen* (Garden City, N.Y.: Doubleday, 1980).
62. Kathleen Riley Fields, "Bishop Fulton J. Sheen: An American Catholic Response to the Twentieth Century" (Ph.D. diss., University of Notre Dame, 1988), p. 166.
63. Ralph E. Pyle, "Religion and Eminence: A Study of Who's Who, 1950 and 1992" (paper presented at annual meeting of the American Academy of Religion, Nov. 1994).
64. Joseph Fichter, *Southern Parish* (Chicago: University of Chicago Press, 1951).

Chapter 2   Ideas: UFOs, Existentialists, and Double Lives

1. The Rosenberg case produced numerous appeals for mercy, some by religious figures, as well as considerable review and reflection in subsequent decades. Ironically, for all the hysteria, the Rosenbergs were virtually the only Americans actually executed for alleged Communist espionage or other activities, and they were by all accounts fairly unimportant personages. Fuchs and Alan Nunn May, far more significant spies, got lesser sentences. The Rosenberg case was not as convoluted with religious issues as others, though of course the simple question of whether justice was done entails religious values. In commenting on it in "Reflections on the Rosenberg Case," the *Christian Century* (Jan. 14, 1953, p. 36) remarked that the execution will be looked back on ten years hence as unnecessarily severe, but added, "To be sure, the communists themselves have done their utmost to mess up the Rosenberg case and to insure that they get the martyrs out of it which their propaganda is eager to exploit. . . . The Rosenbergs, as disciplined party members, must have understood and accepted this."
   On the final evening, the execution was rushed hours ahead of the customary time so as not to desecrate the Jewish Sabbath. A rabbi walked beside the pair on their way to the electric chair, and after death their bodies were draped in Jewish prayer shawls, though in life they had regarded their ancestral religion with communist contempt, according to the *Christian Century*, in "The Rosenbergs Are Executed" (July 1, 1953, p. 763).
2. Peter Viereck, "Symbols: Hiss and Pound," *Commonweal*, Mar. 28, 1952, pp. 607–608. In the same vein, see also Doris Grumbach, "The Lost Liberals," in the same issue, pp. 609–610.
3. Larry Miller, "Clarence Pickett and the Alger Hiss Case," *Friends Journal*, November 1994, pp. 9–13; December 1994, pp. 12–15. The December article documents the 1953 application of Priscilla Hiss and their son Tony for membership in Twentieth Street Friends Meeting in New York, and the decision of the Pastoral Committee to hold the request under advisement indefinitely. Although Priscilla Hiss is often identified as a Quaker and was described by Chambers as "a birthright Quaker," Meyer Zeligs, citing Alger Hiss, states that she was actually raised a Presbyterian but, though not a member of a Quaker meeting, came under substantial

Quaker influence while in college at Bryn Mawr and was involved in Quaker activities. Zeligs cites this discrepancy as an example of Chambers's inaccuracy and tendency to jump to conclusions, though he quotes Alger Hiss as saying, "Anyone who had heard her talk in her own house as Chambers had, and who did not know otherwise, might readily have concluded that she was a Quaker or of Quaker persuasion." *Friendship and Fratricide* (New York: Viking, 1967), pp. 220–221. However, another writer sympathetic to Hiss, John Chabot Smith, states that when Priscilla was interviewed by Nixon on behalf of HUAC, "Mrs. Hiss asked if she had to swear to the oath, and Nixon, remembering that Chambers had said she was a Quaker, told her she could affirm instead, which she did." *Alger Hiss: The True Story* (New York: Holt, Rinehart and Winston, 1976), p. 229.

4. These two wings of American Quakerism are in fact expressed through several independent Quaker meetings or denominations. The more liberal, politically and theologically, tend to center around Philadelphia Yearly Meeting and to have silent, nonministerial worship; the more conservative, based in the rural or small-town West and Midwest, tend to form "Friends churches" with ministers and formal worship, like the Friends church in Whittier, California, in which Nixon grew up.

5. A. J. Muste, the famous minister, Quaker, pacifist, and director of the Fellowship of Reconciliation (FOR) in the Forties and Fifties, had been a radical labor organizer earlier. In this capacity he had espoused Marxism and worked with Trotskyites and Communists, especially in the "United Front" days of the Thirties. But he was never a member of the Communist Party, and indeed "Musteism," meaning being on the right side but with an idealistic, pacifist thrust rather than Party commitment, was a prominent heresy in the communist lexicon. Muste knew Hiss in those years, and thus it is of interest to note that, in a long, quite perceptive, and often critical review of Chambers's book *Witness* in the FOR magazine, based on a more intimate knowledge of the Thirties people and milieu than most readers probably had, Muste writes, "Though I have no recollection that anyone ever told me this, I had a distinct recollection that in the non-Stalinist radical circles in which I once moved Alger Hiss had been regarded as a 'Stalinist.'" A. J. Muste, "Chambers, God, and the Communists." *Fellowship*, July 1952, p. 7. (Coming across this testimony from such a highly unexpected, utterly honest, and far from right-wing source led me personally to look more favorably than before on Chambers's reliability. He may be a less appealing character in some ways than Hiss, but that does not mean he may not also be telling the essential truth about Hiss. How one then judges Hiss in terms of motive and consequence, of course, is another matter.)

6. "Faith for a Lenten Age," *Time*, Mar. 8, 1948, pp. 70–71.

7. Whittaker Chambers, *Witness* (Chicago: Regnery, 1952), p. 482. See Zeligs, *Friendship and Fratricide*, and Smith, *Alger Hiss: The True Story*, for pro-Hiss treatments of the drama that unearth alleged errors in *Witness*.

8. Chambers, *Witness*, p. 9.

9. Elizabeth T. Bentley, "The Appeal of Communism," *The Sign*, Dec. 1950, pp. 11–14.

10. Cited in Rebecca West, *The New Meaning of Treason* (New York: Viking, 1967), p. 187.

11. Bernard Iddings Bell, *Crowd Culture* (New York: Harper, 1952), p. 71. Peter Viereck, *Conservatism Revisited*, rev. ed. (New York: Scribners, 1949; New York: Free Press, 1965), p. 47.

12. Eric Voegelin, *The New Science of Politics* (Chicago: University of Chicago Press, 1952), pp. 147, 172.

13. Russell Kirk, *The Conservative Mind* (Chicago: Regnery, 1953), pp. 7–8.

14. Ibid., p. 130.

15. George H. Nash, *The Conservative Intellectual Movement* (New York: Basic, 1976), p. 81.
16. L. Brent Bozell, "Freedom or Virtue?" *National Review*, Sept. 11, 1962, pp. 181–187, 206. Cited in ibid., p. 176.
17. William F. Buckley, Jr., and L. Brent Bozell, *McCarthy and His Enemies* (Chicago: Regnery, 1954), pp. 323–324. Cited in Nash, *Conservative Intellectual Movement*, pp. 119–120.
18. See Patrick Allitt, *Catholic Intellectuals and Conservative Politics in America, 1950–1985* (Ithaca, N.Y.: Cornell University Press, 1993).
19. Eva J. Ross, review of *God and Man at Yale, The Sign*, Feb. 1952, p. 70.
20. William F. Buckley, Jr., *God and Man at Yale* (Chicago: Henry Regnery, 1951). Reprint, 1971, pp. lx–lxi.
21. T. S. Eliot, *The Cocktail Party: A Comedy* (New York: Harcourt, Brace, 1950), p. 141, 163.
22. Thomas G. V. O'Connell, "T. S. Eliot's 'The Cocktail Party,'" *America*, Mar. 25, 1950, pp. 724–725.
23. T. S. Eliot and George Hoellering, *The Film of "Murder in the Cathedral"* (New York: Harcourt, 1952).
24. W. E. Garrison, "Church Law, God's Law," *Christian Century*, June 9, 1952, p. 804.
25. Reinhold Niebuhr, *The Irony of American History* (New York: Scribners, 1952), p. 3.
26. Karl Barth, *Against the Stream* (New York: Philosophical Library, 1954), p. 116.
27. Ibid., p. 129
28. "Words for the Spirit," *Newsweek*, Apr. 19, 1954, p. 111.
29. Cited in Miller, *Piety along the Potomac*, p. 151. Barth and Niebuhr had long sparred with each other on various issues. See Richard Fox, *Reinhold Niebuhr: A Biography* (San Francisco: Harper and Row, 1985), especially p. 265. See also Reinhold Niebuhr, "Why Is Barth Silent on Hungary?" *Christian Century*, Jan. 23, 1957, pp. 108–110; and James C. Cox and others, with reply by Reinhold Niebuhr, "Barth on Hungary: An Exchange," *Christian Century*, Apr. 10, 1957, pp. 454–455. There was another fracas in 1959, in regard to a forty-five-page letter by Barth "to an East German pastor" that was published by a Swiss publisher, and that raised hackles because of reported anti-American remarks contained in it, together with failure to condemn the communist regime outright, though when substantial portions of the text finally reached America in English they seemed more innocuous than anticipated. See "Barth Assails the U.S," editorial, Feb. 4, pp. 123–124; Reinhold Niebuhr, "Barth's East German Letter," Feb. 11, pp. 167–168; and "Karl Barth's Own Words" (excerpts from the East German letter translated by RoseMary Barth), Mar. 25, pp. 352–355, all in *Christian Century*, 1959.
30. See Carol V. R. George, *God's Salesman: Norman Vincent Peale and the Power of Positive Thinking* (New York: Oxford University Press, 1993).
31. James Collins, "The Appeal of Existentialism," *Commonweal*, Oct. 8, 1954, pp. 7–9.
32. "Fighting Sartrism," *Newsweek*, Jan. 7, 1952, p. 35.
33. "Far-out Mission: Bread and Wine Mission," *Time*, June 29, 1959, p. 38; "Minister for the 'Beatniks,'" *Newsweek*, Mar. 16, 1959, p. 88. For a somewhat fictionalized memoir see Pierre Delattre, *Episodes* (St. Paul: Graywolf, 1993).
34. Charles Clayton Morrison, "The Liberalism of Neo-Orthodoxy, Part III," *Christian Century*, June 21, 1950, p. 760.
35. James Collins, *The Existentialists* (Chicago: Regnery, 1952).
36. Nicolas Berdyaev, *Dream and Reality* (New York: Collier, 1962), p. 178. First English publication, London: Bles, 1950.

37. Thomas Merton, *The Seven Storey Mountain* (New York: Harcourt, Brace, 1948).
38. Thomas Merton, *Seeds of Contemplation* (New York: New Directions, 1949) and *The Waters of Siloe* (New York: Harcourt, Brace, 1949).
39. Thomas Merton, *The Sign of Jonas* (New York: Harcourt, Brace, 1953), pp. 256, 346.
40. In 1950 even *Commonweal*, the liberal Catholic periodical in which Merton published devotional articles, also presented strong cold-war articles like James Burnham, "The Nature of Modern War" (Feb. 10, 1950, pp. 480–483; excerpted from his book, *The Coming Defeat of Communism* [New York: Day, 1950]), which declares that modern war makes no distinction between military and civilians, pointing to the millions dead at communist hands in China, the Baltic States, and so on, and states that the struggle against Stalinism is already such a war.
41. Merton, *The Waters of Siloe*, pp. 251–261. See also Michael Mott, *The Seven Mountains of Thomas Merton* (Boston: Houghton Mifflin, 1984), p. 256.
42. Merton, *The Sign of Jonas*, p. 243.
43. Thomas Merton, "Self-Denial and the Christian," *Commonweal*, Mar. 31, 1950, pp. 649–653.
44. Merton, *The Sign of Jonas*, p. 5.
45. Jean Canu, *Religious Orders of Men*, trans. P. J. Hepbourne-Scott (New York: Hawthorne, 1960), p. 134.
46. Thomas Merton, *The Ascent to Truth* (New York: Harcourt, Brace, 1951). Review of *Ascent to Truth*, *New York Herald Tribune Book Review*, Sept. 23, 1951, p. 7.
47. Cited in Nat Hentoff, *Peace Agitator: The Story of A. J. Muste* (New York: Macmillan, 1963), p. 12.
48. A. J. Muste, "Nehru Walks a Thin Wire," *Christian Century*, Sept. 3, 1952, pp. 996–998, and "Neo-Gandhian India," *Christian Century*, Aug. 12, 1953, pp. 914–916.
49. "Flying Saucers Again," *Newsweek*, Apr. 17, 1950, p. 29.
50. C. G. Jung, *Flying Saucers: A Modern Myth of Things Seen in the Skies* (New York: Harcourt, Brace, 1959).
51. Desmond Leslie and George Adamski, *Flying Saucers Have Landed* (New York: British Book Centre, 1953). Desmond Leslie was a British esotericist who appended Adamski's account to a learned study of UFO encounters in ancient legend and throughout history. George Adamski, *Inside the Space Ships* (New York: Abelard-Schuman, 1955). For information on Adamski, see Jerome Clark, *The UFO Encyclopedia*, vol. 2: *The Emergence of a Phenomenon: UFOs from the Beginning through 1959* (Detroit: Omnigraphics, 1992), pp. 1–12. For the entire UFO phenomenon, see David M. Jacobs, *The UFO Controversy in America* (Bloomington: Indiana University Press, 1975).
52. Roland H. Bainton, *Here I Stand: A Life of Martin Luther* (New York: Abingdon-Cokesbury, 1950). Wilhelm Pauck, *Heritage of the Reformation* (Boston: Beacon, 1950). H. Richard Niebuhr, *Christ and Culture* (New York: Harper, 1951).
53. Paul Tillich, *Systematic Theology*, vol. 1 (Chicago: University of Chicago Press, 1951).
54. J. D. Salinger, *The Catcher in the Rye* (Boston: Little, Brown, 1951). Herman Wouk, *The Caine Mutiny* (Garden City, N.Y.: Doubleday, 1951). Ernest Hemingway, *The Old Man and the Sea* (New York: Scribners, 1952).
55. Harry Overstreet, *The Mature Mind* (New York: Norton, 1950). Immanuel Velikovsky, *Worlds in Collision* (New York: Macmillan, 1950).
56. Division of Christian Education of the National Council of the Churches of Christ in the United States of America, *The Holy Bible, Revised Standard Version* (New York: Nelson, 1952).

57. John Baillie, John T. McNeill, Henry P. Van Dusen, gen. eds., *The Library of Christian Classics*, 26 vols. (Philadelphia: Westminster, 1953–1969). Ludwig Schopp, gen. ed., *The Fathers of the Church*, 90 vols. (various publishers, 1947–1994). George Arthur Buttrick et al., eds. *The Interpreters Bible*, 12 vols. (New York: Abingdon-Cokesbury, 1951–1957).
58. Robert Maynard Hutchins, ed. in chief, *Great Books of the Western World*, 54 vols. (Chicago: Encyclopedia Britannica, 1952).
59. Christopher Isherwood, ed., *Vedanta for Modern Man* (New York: Harper, 1951). Swami Akhilananda, *Mental Health and Hindu Psychology* (New York: Harper, 1951).
60. Daisetz Teitaro Suzuki, *Essays in Zen Buddhism*, 2d ser. (New York: Harper, 1952).
61. Homer A. Jack, "The Gandhi Literature," *Christian Century*, Apr. 2, 1952, pp. 398–399, and *The Wit and Wisdom of Gandhi* (Boston: Beacon, 1951). Louis Fischer, *The Life of Mahatma Gandhi* (New York: Harper, 1950).
62. R. S. Lee, *Freud and Christianity* (New York: Wyn, 1949), p. 193.

Part II   Shadows at High Noon

1. "The Four Girls," *Newsweek*, June 28, 1954, p. 80.
2. R. D. Heldenfels, *Television's Greatest Year, 1954* (New York: Continuum, 1994).
3. "For Your Information," *Newsweek*, May 24, 1954, p. 13
4. "Words & Works," *Time*, Jan. 11, 1954, p. 62.
5. "Journalism and Joachim's Children," *Time*, Mar. 9, 1953, pp. 57, 59. The Joachim of the title refers to Joachim of Flora, the medieval seer who predicted a coming "age of the Spirit" and was regarded by Voegelin (and *Time*) as the prototype of the modern progressive eschatologist.
6. Eric Voegelin, *The New Science of Politics* (Chicago: University of Chicago Press, 1952), pp. 166–167.
7. Ibid., p. 125. See also Eric Voegelin, *Science, Politics, and Gnosticism* (Chicago: Regnery, 1968), p. 83.
8. Voegelin, *Science, Politics and Gnosticism*, pp. 86–88.
9. See Arthur Verluis, *American Transcendentalism and Asian Religions* (New York: Oxford University Press, 1993), pp. 119–129.
10. See Robert A. Segal, "Gnosticism, Ancient and Modern," *Christian Century*, Nov. 8, 1995, pp. 1053–1056.

Chapter 3   Events: Bikini, the World Council, and the McCarthy Endgame

1. "No Christian Peace in Korea?" *Christian Century*, Feb. 4, 1953, pp. 126–127.
2. "What Can Christians Contribute to Peace in Korea? A Symposium," *Christian Century*, Feb. 18, 1953, pp. 190–193.
3. "Chastened Nation Is Grateful for Truce," editorial, *Christian Century*, Aug. 5, 1953, p. 883.
4. See Robert S. Hunting, "'For Me, War Is Good,'" *Christian Century*, Oct. 14, 1953, pp. 1162–1163.
5. The two were currently under fire from anti-McCarthyites for a whirlwind tour inspecting the holdings of U.S. overseas libraries. Far from pleased with what they saw in those outposts of literary America, they demanded the removal of books by communists, communist sympathizers, and "controversial" authors. The U.S. Information Service had caved in to these demands and issued the appropriate instructions; in one place the offending volumes were incinerated. But cries of book

burning arose, State was increasingly concerned about the bad image such antics were creating internationally, and Ike himself obliquely criticized attempts at "censorship."

6. J. B. Matthews, "Reds and Our Churches," *American Mercury*, July 1953, pp. 3–14. The cover of the issue displayed a reclining cross against a red background. Matthews went on to write "Red Infiltration of Theological Seminaries" (*American Mercury*, Nov. 1953, pp. 31–36), and inquiries into other fields, published in the same journal: "Communism and the Colleges," May 1953, pp. 111–114, and "Moscow's Medicine Men," Oct. 1953, pp. 58–62.

7. "McCarthy Appointment Raises a Storm," editorial, *Christian Century*, July 15, 1953, p. 811. See also "Mr. Matthews Is Not a Communist" (editorial, *Christian Advocate*, July 13, 1953, p. 6), a tongue-in-cheek argument that he was not, despite his past and "despite the aid and comfort he has given the Communist cause" by weakening the faith of Protestant laypeople in their church and its leaders.

8. Reinhold Niebuhr, "Communism and the Clergy," *Christian Century*, Aug. 19, 1953, pp. 936–937.

9. See, for example, "Velde Threatens the Churches," editorial, *Christian Century*, Mar. 25, 1953, p. 341.

10. Cited in "Joe's Bloody Nose," *Time*, July 20, 1953, p. 15.

11. "O'Brien Defends Stand," *Christian Century*, Sept. 16, 1953, p. 1062.

12. J. B. Matthews and R. E. Shallocross, *Partners in Plunder: The Cost of Business Dictatorship* (New York: Gossett & Dunlop, 1935).

13. Paul Hutchinson, "The J. B. Matthews Story," *Christian Century*, July 29, 1953, pp. 864–866; "Matthews, J(oseph) B(rown)," in *Political Profiles: The Eisenhower Years*, ed. Eleanora W. Schoenbaum (New York: Facts on File, 1977), pp. 417–418.

14. "Joe's Bloody Nose," p. 15.

15. Donald F. Crosby, *God, Church, and Flag: Senator Joseph R. McCarthy and the Catholic Church, 1950–1957* (Chapel Hill: University of North Carolina Press, 1978), pp. 129–132.

16. "Winner: The Bishop," *Time*, Aug. 3, 1953, p. 11.

17. H.E.F. [Harold E. Fey], "Bishop Oxnam's Challenge," *Christian Century*, Aug. 5, 1953, pp. 885–887. See also Mary Elizabeth Fox, "Clear Oxnam of Red Ties," *Christian Advocate*, Aug. 6, 1953, pp. 3+, and "The Record Is Clear," editorial, *Christian Advocate*, Aug. 6, 1953, p. 6. The Methodist magazine held Oxnam completely vindicated and declared that, "more solidly than ever before, the Methodist church supports him." See also the bishop's own book giving his account of the two days: G. Bromley Oxnam, *I Protest* (New York: Harper, 1954).

18. Niebuhr, "Communism and the Clergy."

19. Richard Fox, *Reinhold Niebuhr: A Biography* (San Francisco: Harper and Row, 1987), p. 155.

20. Reinhold Niebuhr, "Editorial Notes," *Christian and Crisis*, Mar. 16, 1953, p. 26.

21. Reinhold Niebuhr, "Communism and the Protestant Clergy," *Look*, Nov. 1953, p. 17.

22. Fox, *Reinhold Niebuhr*, p. 254.

23. "God's Country," *Time*, May 4, 1953, pp. 57–58.

24. As it happens, the dean's sermon which I heard has been preserved in print: "Servants without Masters," in Hewlett Johnson, *Christians and Communism* (London: Putnam, 1956), pp.101–109. See also, on this intriguing clergyman, Hewlett Johnson, *Searching for Light: An Autobiography* (London: Joseph, 1968).

25. Reinhold Niebuhr, "Coronation Afterthoughts," *Christian Century*, July 1, 1953, p. 771.

26. "America the Unloved," *Christian Century*, June 3, 1953, p. 651.

27. Paul Blanshard, "The Case of Archbishop O'Hara," *Christian Century*, May 6, 1953, p. 539. See also "Are Catholics Different?" *Time*, Mar. 2, 1953, pp. 53–54, and a letter from Blanshard in *Newsweek*, June 21, 1954, pp. 9–10.

28. "The Hearings," editorial, *Commonweal*, May 14, 1954, pp. 133–134.

29. "'Peaceful Overthrow' of the U.S. Presidency," *America*, May 22, 1954, pp. 210–211.

30. "Freedom of Catholic Opinion," *America*, June 5, 1954, p. 261.

31. Crosby, *God, Church, and Flag*, pp. 178–185.

32. "Roman Catholics and McCarthy," *The Lutheran*, June 16, 1954, pp. 7–8.

33. On Sheil, "A Bishop Speaks Out," *Commonweal,,* Apr. 23, 1954, p. 56. See also a letter from Ed Marciniak in *Commonweal*, May 14, 1954, pp. 146–149, documenting the spotty handling of Bishop Sheil's remarks in the Catholic press. On the NCC protest, "Church and Controversy," *Newsweek*, Mar. 29, 1954; "Investigation of Investigators: Text of NCC Statement," *Living Church*, Apr. 4, 1954, p. 9. On the Methodists, "The Church and Subversion," editorial, *Christian Advocate*, Mar. 18, 1954, p. 11. On Oxnam's defense, Charles C. Perlin, "Cleaning Up Our Investigations," *Christian Advocate*, Apr. 22, 1954, pp. 6–7. The critique was supported by an editorial in the same issue, "Investigations, American Plan," pp. 12–13.

34. "The Secret," editorial, *Living Church*, Apr. 4, 1954, p. 15.

35. "America Is for Everybody," editorial, *Living Church*, May 30, 1954, pp. 10–11.

36. "Leaven in the South," news column, *Living Church*, June 6, 1954, pp. 7–8.

37. Woodrow A. Grier, "Church Colleges and Integration," *Christian Advocate*, Feb. 11, 1954, pp. 6–7+.

38. "As Jim Crow Fades Away," editorial, *Christian Advocate*, May 27, 1954, p. 12. The reaction of Methodist leaders to the decision was presented in "Call Courts Race Ruling a Milestone," June 3, 1954, p. 15.

39. "Pacific Inferno," editorial, *Christian Century*, Mar. 31, 1954, pp. 391–392.

40. Ibid.

41. "In the Wake of the Bomb Blast," editorial, *Christian Advocate*, Apr. 22, 1954, p. 12.

42. "H-Bomb Reactions," *Commonweal*, Apr. 16, 1954, p. 27.

43. "The Nemesis of Power," *Christian Century*, Apr. 21, 1954, p. 485.

44. "The Bomb," editorial, *Living Church*, Apr. 25, 1954, p. 9.

45. Fox, *Reinhold Niebuhr*, p. 240.

46. Allan M. Winkler, *Life under a Cloud: American Anxiety about the Atom* (New York: Oxford University Press, 1993), p. 98.

47. Ibid., p. 105.

48. "Views in Brief," *The Sign*, May 1954, p. 6.

49. "Defeat in Asia," editorial, *Commonweal*, May 14, 1954, p. 134.

50. David Halberstam, *The Fifties* (New York: Villard, 1993), p. 387.

51. "Armament Race in Central America," *Christian Century*, June 9, 1954, p. 691.

52. "Is Tension Easing in Guatemala?" *Christian Century*, June 23, 1954, pp. 756–757. On conditions in the country, see Carleton Beals, "Guatemala's Land Reform," *Christian Century*, June 23, 1954, pp. 762–764. See also Carleton Beals, "Second Thoughts on Guatemala," *Christian Century*, Dec., 8, 1954, pp. 1490–1491.

53. "Guatemala Changes Governments," *Christian Century*, July 7, 1954, p. 811. "After Guatemala," editorial, *Commonweal*, July 7, 1954, pp. 331–332.

54. "Guatemala Takes Land from Peasants," editorial, *Christian Century*, Sept. 8, 1954, pp. 1060–1061.

55. "Assembly in America," *Christian Century*, Sept. 1, 1954, p. 1031.

56. "Faith, Hope, Unity," *Newsweek*, Aug. 30, 1954, pp. 56–57.

57. Ibid.

58. "First Session Dives into Hope Debate," *Christian Advocate*, Aug. 26, 1954, p. 7.
59. "What Did the World Council Do?" *Christian Advocate*, Sept. 9, 1954, pp. 10–11; "Evanston Retrospect," editorial, *Christian Century*, Sept. 22, 1954, pp. 1124–1125. Books on Evanston include John Marsh, *The Significance of Evanston* (London: Independent Press, 1954); John Hasting Nichols, *Evanston: An Interpretation* (New York: Harper, 1954), a conventional treatment; and James W. Kennedy, *Evanston Scrapbook* (Lebanon, Pa.: Sowers, 1954), a more personal description.
60. Assemblies of the World Council of Churches are held approximately every six years. The roster to date is (1) Amsterdam, 1948; (2) Evanston, 1954; (3) Delhi, 1961; (4) Uppsala, 1968; (5) Nairobi, 1975; (6) Vancouver, BC, 1983; (7) Canberra, 1991. But no later assembly received the public and media attention of Evanston.
61. Arnold W. Hearn, "Fundamentalist Renascence," *Christian Century*, Apr. 30, 1958, pp. 528–530.
62. "Words and Works" *Time*, Feb. 22, 1954, p. 59.
63. Cited in Stephen B. Oates, *Let the Trumpet Sound: The Life of Martin Luther King, Jr.* (New York: Harper and Row, 1982), pp. 70–71.
64. See Nora Sayre, *Previous Convictions: A Journey through the 1950s* (New Brunswick, N.J.: Rutgers University Press, 1995), pp. 157–171 for the full Autherine Lucy saga.
65. "Clinton Minister Lives His Faith," *Christian Century*, Dec. 19, 1956, p. 1470.
66. "Return to Integrated Clinton," *Newsweek*, Oct. 7, 1957, p. 37.
67. "Freedom Blooms Briefly for Hungarian Church," *Christian Century*, Nov. 14, 1956, p. 1317.
68. Reinhold Niebuhr, "Why Is Barth Silent on Hungary?" *Christian Century*, Jan. 23, 1957, pp. 108–109.

Chapter 4   *Ideas: Beats and Books*

1. "Periscoping Religion," *Newsweek*, May 10, 1954, p. 67.
2. "Surfeit," editorial comment, *Fellowship*, Dec. 1950, pp. 1–3.
3. Samuel A. Stouffer, *Communism, Conformity, and Civil Liberties: A Cross-Section of the Nation Speaks Its Mind* (Garden City, N.Y.: Doubleday, 1955), pp. 156, 161, 176–177.
4. F. Olin Stockwell, "What Is Brainwashing? Part I—The Communist View of Man and His World," *Christian Century*, Jan. 21, 1953, pp. 73–74, and "Part II—How China's Communists Apply Social Pressure to 'Counterrevolutionaries,'" Jan. 28, 1953, pp. 104–106. See also "The Missionary Who Lied," *Time*, May 18, 1953, pp. 78–81, on the Stockwell case, and Stockwell's book, *Meditations from a Prison Cell* (Nashville: The Upper Room, 1954), quite a fine devotional work from his time of internment.
5. Stockwell, "Part II," p. 105.
6. "A More Excellent Way," *Christian Century*, May 6, 1953, pp. 537–538.
7. Prentiss L. Pemberton, "Facing Communism Confidently," *Christian Century*, Oct. 4, 1950, pp. 1163–1165.
8. "Theological Emphasis Is Shifting," *Christian Century*, Jan. 11, 1950, p. 37. See also Robert G. Middleton, "Yogi, Commissar, and Christian," *Christian Century*, Apr. 12, 1950, p. 396.
9. Sydney Ahlstrom listed some major themes of Fifties religion as "home missions" to the suburbs; enlivened civil religion, or a sense of the religious character of the nation as a whole transcending denominationalism; the quest for "peace of mind"; the "revival of revivalism"; the movement for parish renewal and the liturgical movement; and the continuation of neoorthodox theology. Political social activ-

ism is not among them, as it would have been in the Thirties or Sixties. Sydney Ahlstrom, *Religious History of the American People* (New Haven, Conn.: Yale University Press, 1972), pp. 951–963.

10. Eric Voegelin, *From Enlightenment to Revolution* (Durham, N.C.: Duke University Press, 1975), pp. 28–29.

11. Kenneth Scott Latourette, *Christian World Missions in Our Day* (New York: Harper, 1954).

12. Leonard M. Outerbridge, *The Lost Churches of China* (Philadelphia: Westminster, 1953).

13. "Our Vicious Young Hoodlums: Is There Any Hope?" *Newsweek*, Sept. 6, 1954, pp. 43–44.

14. "Why Is Crime Increasing?" *Christian Century*, Oct. 6, 1954, p. 1196.

15. "U.S. Campus Kids of 1953: Unkiddable and Unbeatable," *Newsweek*, Nov. 2, 1953, pp. 52–55.

16. Marshall Sklare, ed., *The Jews: Social Patterns of an American Group* (New York: Free Press, 1958).

17. Herbert J. Gans, "The Origin and Growth of a Jewish Community in the Suburbs: A Study of the Jews of Park Forest," in ibid., pp. 205–248. Citations p. 238.

18. Rodger Kamenetz, *The Jew in the Lotus* (San Francisco: HarperCollins, 1994), p. 20.

19. Alan F. Westin, "Winning the Fight against McCarthy," *Commentary*, July 1954, pp. 10–15. James Rorty, "The Native Anti-Semite's 'New Look,'" *Commentary*, Nov. 1954, pp. 413–421, and "What Price McCarthy Now?" *Commentary*, Jan. 1955, pp. 30–35.

20. See, for example, Charles Abrams, " . . . Only the Best Christian Clientele," *Commentary*, Jan. 1955, pp. 10–17, a discussion of racial and religious discrimination in hotels and resorts.

21. See Lillian Blumberg McCall, "The Hidden Springs of Sigmund Freud," *Commentary*, Aug. 1954, pp. 102–110; and David Bakan, "Freud's Jewishness and His Psychoanalysis," *Judaism* 3,1 (Winter 1954): 20–26. Bakan later published *Sigmund Freud and the Jewish Mystical Tradition* (Princeton, N.J.: Van Norstand, 1958).

22. See Morris N. Kertzer, "Interfaith Relations in the United States," *Judaism* 3,4 (Fall 1954): 456–468 (special issue on Judaism in America).

23. Arthur A. Cohen, "Revival in Judaism, Too," *Christian Century*, Oct. 16, 1957, p. 1232. Nathan Glazer, *American Judaism* (Chicago: University of Chicago Press, 1957).

24. Paul Tillich, *The Courage to Be* (New Haven, Conn.: Yale University Press, 1952), p. 173.

25. Paul Tillich, *Love, Power, and Justice* (New York: Oxford University Press, 1954), p. 115.

26. Paul Tillich, *The New Being* (New York: Scribner's, 1955), p. 78.

27. "Harvard's Theologian," *Newsweek*, May 17, 1954, p. 66.

28. Emil Brunner, *Eternal Hope*, trans. Harold Knight (Philadelphia: Westminster, 1954); Karl Barth, *Nein! Antwort an Emil Brunner* (Munich: Kaiser, 1934).

29. Henry Sloan Coffin, *A Half Century of Union Theological Seminary, 1896–1945* (New York: Scribner's, 1954). For a more recent account see also Robert T. Handy, *A History of Union Theological Seminary in New York* (New York: Columbia University Press, 1987).

30. Joseph Campbell, ed., *Spirit and Nature* (New York: Pantheon, 1954).

31. Arnold Toynbee, *An Historian's Approach to Religion* (New York: Oxford University Press, 1956).

32. See "The Professor's Ark," *Time*, Sept. 10, 1956, pp. 734–736. See also "Of

Religion's Mission, *Newsweek*, Sept. 17, 1956, pp. 107–108. An even earlier book on a comparable theme, often discussed in the Fifties, was F.S.C. Northrop, *The Meeting of East and West* (New York: Macmillan, 1946).

33. William H. Whyte, Jr., *The Organization Man* (New York: Simon and Schuster, 1956), p. 217.

34. David Riesman, with Nathan Glazer and Reuel Denney, *The Lonely Crowd: A Study of the Changing American Character* (New Haven: Yale University Press, 1950), p. 373.

35. C. Wright Mills, *White Collar: The American Middle Class* (New York: Oxford University Press, 1952), pp. 216–217.

36. Whyte, *Organization Man*, p. 404.

37. Cited in Halberstam, *The Fifties*, p. 573.

38. Robert Lekachman, "Organization Men: The Erosion of Individuality," *Commentary*, Mar. 1957, pp. 270–276.

39. Robert Wuthnow, "Christian Identity, Church Reality," *Christian Century*, May 12, 1993, pp. 520–523.

40. William H. Kirkland, "Fellowship and/or Freedom," *Christian Century*, Apr. 17, 1957, pp. 490–492.

41. John Kenneth Galbraith, *The Affluent Society* (Boston: Houghton Mifflin, 1958).

42. Will Herberg, *Protestant, Catholic, Jew: An Essay in American Religious Sociology* (Garden City, N.Y.: Doubleday, 1955), p. 38.

43. Peter Fingesten, "Beat and Buddhist," *Christian Century*, Feb. 25, 1959, pp. 226–227.

44. Mary Douglas, *Natural Symbols* (New York: Vintage, 1973). See also my book *Alternative Altars* (Chicago: University of Chicago Press, 1979), pp. 22–25, in which I outline the salient features of strong and weak grid and group societies, and apply the model to different aspects of U.S. society, from the weak grid and group of the early Republic to the strong-group, weak-grid pattern of U.S. evangelicalism; the Fifties surely brought basic features of that pattern to national life as a whole, such as strong concern for purity within the social body, rituals focused upon group boundaries and expelling pollutants (witches) from the social body, and a dualistic cosmology featuring warring forces of good and evil.

45. "Beat Mystics," *Time*, Feb. 3, 1958, p. 56.

46. Jack Kerouac, *The Dharma Bums* (New York: Viking, 1958), pp. 38–39.

47. Jack Kerouac, *On the Road* (New York: Viking, 1957).

48. Seymour Krim, "King of the Beats," *Commonweal*, Jan. 2, 1959, pp. 359–360.

49. Alan Watts, *In My Own Way: An Autobiography, 1916–1965* (New York: Vintage, 1973), p. 309.

50. Stephen Prothero, "'God Is a Masturbator': Religion, Gender, and Sexuality among the Beats" (paper presented at annual meeting of the American Academy of Religion, Nov. 1992). Joyce Johnson, *Minor Characters* (Boston: Houghton Mifflin, 1983). Herbert Gold, "Hip, Cool, Beat—and Frantic," *The Nation*, Nov. 16, 1957, p. 351.

51. E. Anthony Rotundo, "Boy Culture: Middle-Class Boyhood in Nineteenth-Century America," in *Meanings for Manhood: Constructions of Masculinity in Victorian America*, ed. Mark C. Carnes and Clyde Griffen (Chicago: University of Chicago Press, 1990), pp. 15–36. See also E. Anthony Rotundo, *American Manhood* (New York: Basic, 1993).

52. William S. Burroughs, "The Wild Boys," in *The Faber Book of Gay Short Fiction*, ed. Edmund White (London and Boston: Faber and Faber, 1991), p. 165. Burroughs, like Ginsberg, was bisexual but primarily homosexual.

53. The best biography is Monica Furlong, *Zen Effects: The Life of Alan Watts* (Boston: Houghton Mifflin, 1986). See also Watts, *In My Own Way*.

54. Alan Watts, *The Spirit of Zen* (London: Murray, 1935).
55. Alan Watts, *Behold the Spirit: A Study in the Necessity of Mystical Religion* (New York: Random House/Pantheon, 1947), and *The Supreme Identity* (New York: Random House/Pantheon, 1950).
56. Alan Watts, *The Wisdom of Insecurity: A Message for an Age of Anxiety* (New York: Random House/Pantheon, 1951). Watts may also have exorcised some surviving remnants of his high-church ritualism, as well as provided a book of great interest to those still concerned with traditional liturgical spirituality, in a meditation on the mythical/mystical inner meanings of the traditional Western rite, Eucharist, and other liturgical practices, in *Myth and Ritual in Christianity* (London: Thames and Hudson; New York: Vanguard, 1953).
57. Alan Watts, *The Way of Zen* (New York: Random House/Pantheon, 1957), p. 3.
58. Alan Watts, *Beat Zen, Square Zen, and Zen* (San Francisco: City Lights, 1959). Reprinted in Alan Watts, *This Is It* (New York: Pantheon, 1960).
59. "Zen: Beat & Square," *Time*, July 21, 1958, p. 49.

Part III Signs Appearing in Heaven

1. "The Fourth Faith," *Newsweek*, Feb. 4, 1957, p. 86.
2. James E. Sellers, "Religion by Telephone," *Christian Century*, Aug. 7, 1957, pp. 939–941.
3. Andrew Greeley, "The Religious Revival: Fact or Fiction." *The Sign*, July 1958, pp. 25–27.
4. "Downgrade," *Time*, Sept. 8, 1958, p. 74.
5. "The Year the Revival Passed Crest," *Christian Century*, Dec. 31, 1958, pp. 499–501.
6. "Romance Over," *Christianity Today*, Sept. 16, 1957, p. 28. The *Living Church* noted moreover that, though Oberlin brought no agreement, it seemed to have put behind it "watered-down" Christianity of the old liberal sort. "Faith and Order at Oberlin," editorial, *Living Church*, Sept. 29, 1957, pp. 20–21.
7. "Church in Suburbia," *Time*, Jan. 27, 1958, p. 52.
8. "Suburban Religion," *Time*, July 15, 1957, p. 78.
9. Martin E. Marty, "The Triumph of Religion-in-General," Sept. 10, pp. 1016–1019; "The New Man in Religionized America," Sept. 24, pp. 1072–1075; "The New Establishment," Oct. 13, pp. 1176–1179; "Protestantism in Panuria," Oct. 29, pp. 1232–1235; "A Revival of Interest," Nov. 12, pp. 1296–1299; "The Remnant: Retreat and Renewal," Nov. 26, pp. 1361–1365, all in *Christian Century*, 1958. See also "Spiritual Slenderella?" *Time*, Dec. 8, 1958, p. 78.
10. Marty, "The Remnant," p. 1363. Gibson Winter, *The Suburban Captivity of the Churches* (New York: Macmillan, 1962).
11. There was a short news item: "Sputniks Stir New Thinking on World Peace," *Together*, January 1958, p. 66.

Chapter 5 Events: Little Rock, Sputnik, John XXIII, and the Passing of the Fifties Mood

1. "Attack on the Conscience," *Time*, Feb. 18, 1957, p. 17.
2. Ibid.
3. "Methodist Integration," *Newsweek*, Jan. 7, 1957, p. 50.
4. "Embattled Koinonia," *Time*, Apr. 29, 1957, pp. 44–46.
5. "Christianity v. Jim Crow," *Time*, May 6, 1957, pp. 86–89.
6. "Presbyterians v. Jim Crow," *Time*, May 13, 1957, p. 68. For the saga of Southern Presbyterians generally on race matters, see Joel L. Alvis, Jr., *Religion and Race:*

Southern Presbyterians, 1946–1983 (Tuscaloosa: University of Alabama Press, 1994).

7. Making a Crisis in Arkansas," *Time*, Sept. 16, 1957, pp. 23–25, and "What Orval Hath Wrought," *Time*, Sept. 23, 1957, pp. 11–14.

8. Fletcher Knebel, "The Real Little Rock Story," *Look*, Nov. 12, 1957, pp. 31+.

9. "The Meaning of Little Rock," *Time*, Oct. 7, 1957, p. 21.

10. "As Others See Us: U.S. and Little Rock," *Newsweek*, Oct. 7, 1957, p. 34.

11. "Religion in Action: Little Rock's Clergy Leads the Way," *Time*, Oct. 14, 1957, p. 30.

12. Cited in "South's Churchmen: Integration and Religion," *Newsweek*, Oct. 7, 1957, p. 37.

13. "All Prayers for Little Rock," *Christian Century*, Oct. 23, 1957, p. 1251.

14. "Hats Off to the Women of Little Rock," *Christian Century*, Oct. 2, 1957, pp. 1155–1156. "NCC General Board Lauds Eisenhower's Little Rock Action," *Living Church*, Oct. 20, 1957, p. 7.

15. "Integration & the Churches," *Time*, Oct. 6, 1958, p. 70. "The Most Vigorous," *Newsweek*, May 13, 1957, p. 112.

16. "Current Comment," editorial, *America*, Oct. 5, 1957, p. 2. "Race Relations and Christian Duty," editorial, *Christianity Today*, Sept. 30, 1957, p. 23.

17. Jackson Toby, "Bombing in Nashville," *Commentary*, May, 1958. pp. 385–389; Nathan Perlmutter, "Bombing in Miami," *Commentary*, June 1958, pp. 498–501; *American Jewish Year Book*, vol. 60, ed. Morris Fine and Milton Himmelfarb (New York: American Jewish Committee, and Philadelphia: Jewish Publication Society of America, 1959), pp. 44–47; Melissa Fay Greene, *The Temple Bombing* (Reading, Mass.: Addison–Wesley, 1996).

18. "Sputnik's Wake," editorial, *America*, Oct. 26, 1957, p. 94.

19. "And the Angel Said Unto Them, Fear Not . . . " *Newsweek*, Dec. 23, 1957, pp. 52–53.

20. Warren Weaver, "Christmas 1957 . . . and a World Encircled," *Look*, Dec. 24, 1957, pp. 21–23. See also Warren Weaver, "A Scientist Ponders Faith," *Saturday Review of Literature*, Jan. 3, 1959, pp. 8–10+, for a conventional but perhaps significant treatment by the same writer on the limitations of science and the notion that scientists leave room for God.

21. "Man's Moon," editorial, *Living Church*, Oct. 20, 1957, p. 14.

22. See, for example, "Dare We Admit the Truth?" *Christian Century*, Oct. 23, 1957, pp. 1251–1252.

23. Robert A. Divine, *The Sputnik Challenge* (New York: Oxford University Press, 1993), pp. 196–199.

24. "Religion and Space," *Newsweek*, Oct. 21, 1957, p. 98.

25. "In All Persons Alike," *Time*, Apr. 7, 1958, p. 57.

26. "Faith and Outer Space," *Time*, Mar. 31, 1958, p. 37.

27. "God in the Garden," *Time*, May 27, 1957, pp. 46–48.

28. Billy Graham, "New York and I," *Look*, Oct. 15, 1957, pp. 35–39.

29. Arnold W. Hearn, "Fundamentalist Renascence," *Christian Century*, Apr. 30, 1958, pp. 528–530. Martin E. Marty, "Intruder in the Crowded Center: A Review Article," *Christian Century*, July 3, 1957, pp. 820–821. Carl F. H. Henry, ed., *Contemporary Evangelical Thought* (Great Neck, N.Y.: Channel, 1957).

30. Edward John Carnell, *Christian Commitment: An Apologetic* (New York: Macmillan, 1957). William Hornden, "Uncritical Conservative," *Christian Century*, Sept. 4, 1957, pp. 1041–1042.

31. Reinhold Niebuhr, "The Gospel in Future America," *Christian Century*, June 18, 1958, p. 712.

32. Reinhold Niebuhr, "After Comment, the Deluge," *Christian Century*, Sept. 4, 1957, pp. 1034–1035. Reinhold Niebuhr, "Differing Views on Billy Graham: A Theolo-

gian Says Evangelist Is Oversimplifying the Issues of Life," *Life*, July 1, 1957, p. 92. A "pro" view of Graham was given by another mainline Protestant, Dr. John Sutherland Bonnell of Fifth Avenue Presbyterian Church in New York, on the same page under the same head.

33. "Fourth General Assembly of NCC," *Christianity Today*, Dec. 23, 1957, p. 28.
34. "Protestants at Work," *Newsweek*, Dec. 16, 1957, p. 70.
35. "The State of the Council," *Christian Century*, Dec. 4, 1957, pp. 1437–1439. "NCC Re-Examines Its Organization and Message," editorial comment, *Christianity Today*, Dec. 23, 1957, pp. 24–25.
36. "More Colleges Offer Religion Courses," *Christian Century*, July 3, 1957, p. 812.
37. "Religion in Our Colleges," *Newsweek*, Apr. 22, 1957, p. 115.
38. Philip E. Jacob, *Changing Values in College* (New York: Harper, 1957). See also a review article on this book, William H. Kirkland, "Fellowship and/or Freedom," *Christian Century*, Apr. 17, 1957, pp. 490–492.
39. "Knowing by Faith," *Time*, Oct. 5, 1953, p. 68.
40. Nathan M. Pusey, "Spiritual Odyssey," *Christian Century*, July 24, 1957, pp. 888–890.
41. Nathan M. Pusey, "Secularism and Religion," *Christian Century*, Oct. 8, 1958, p. 1143.
42. "The Button-Down Hair Shirt," *Time*, Apr. 14, 1958, p. 63.
43. "What Religion at Harvard?" *Christian Century*, May 14, 1958, pp. 579–582.
44. "What of the Godless?" *Newsweek*, Mar. 18, 1957, p. 89.
45. Letters to the Editor, *Newsweek*, Apr. 8, 1957, pp. 12–16.
46. "Princeton Withdraws Recognition of Roman Catholic Chaplain," *Christian Century*, Oct. 30, 1957, pp. 1293–1294.
47. See, for example, "Why the Young Kill: Prowling the Juvenile Jungles of the Big Cities," *Newsweek*, Aug. 19, 1957, pp. 25–28.
48. David R. McCann, *Delinquency: Sickness or Sin* (New York: Harper, 1957).
49. Harrison E. Salisbury, *The Shook-Up Generation* (New York: Harper, 1958; New York: Crest, 1959), p. 141.
50. F. Kilmer Myers, *Light the Dark Streets* (Greenwich, Conn.: Seabury, 1957), p. 137.
51. Salisbury, *The Shook-Up Generation*, pp. 164, 163.
52. "A Count—and Conduct," *Newsweek*, Sept. 9, 1957, p. 96.
53. "Put Father Back," *America*, Mar. 15, 1958, p. 682.
54. "Correspondence," *America*, Apr. 12, 1958, p. 35.
55. "U.N. Report on Delinquency," *America*, Aug. 16, 1958, pp. 503–504. Edward A. Connell, "Policemen Mean Law and Order," *America*, Mar. 15, 1958, pp. 692–694.
56. Gordon C. Zahn, "In Our Image," *Commonweal*, June 17, 1959, pp. 302–304. Dan Herr and Joel Wells, "'Cop' with a Cause," *The Sign*, Feb. 1958, pp. 17–20.
57. "The Pope Loses Patience: A Call to Crusaders," *Newsweek*, Jan. 7, 1957, p. 50.
58. Whitley Strieber, *Communion* (New York: Morrow, 1987), p. 115.
59. James O'Gara, "Integration—Why? An Interview with Father John La Farge, S.J.," *The Sign*, Nov. 1958, pp. 19–21.
60. Jay P. Dolan, "Patterns of Leadership in the Congregation," in *American Congregations*, vol. 2, *New Perspectives in the Study of Congregations*, ed. James P. Wind and James W. Lewis (Chicago: University of Chicago Press, 1994), p. 248.
61. Save for the occasional upheaval, often occasioned by rivalry between different Catholic immigrant groups; the desire for a pastor of their own language and nationality was not seldom a flashpoint. But such conflicts had subsided by the Fifties as Catholic immigration became increasingly assimilated.
62. One of the last popular documents of this era is perhaps the second of *Look's* series of articles on U.S. religious traditions, Hartzell Spence, "The Story of Religion in America: Roman Catholics" (Nov. 12, 1957, pp. 117–29). After a summary

of the history of Catholicism in America and reference to controversial issues such as censorship and parochial schools, in which the Catholic case is fairly presented, Spence suggested that Catholics had put a "self-imposed shell" around themselves and need now to take a more active part in all aspects of the nation's life. That perception indicates how U.S. Catholicism was still viewed in the Fifties; the situation was rather suddenly to become quite different in the activist Sixties.

63. See Paul I. Murphy, *La Popessa* (New York: Warner, 1983).

64. "To Warm Hearts . . . " *Newsweek*, Feb. 9, 1959, p. 82.

Chapter 6   Ideas: Israel, Mescaline, and Zen

1. "Zen," *Time*, Feb. 4, 1957, pp. 65–67.

2. See W. E. Mann, "Spiritual Frontiers Fellowship," *Christian Century*, Mar. 12, 1958, pp. 309–311. The major independent study of the group is Melinda Bollar Wagner, *Metaphysics in Midwestern America* (Columbus: Ohio State University Press, 1983).

3. Shane Leslie, *Ghost Book* (New York: Sheed and Ward, 1956). See also "Ghost Stories," *Time*, Feb. 18, 1957, p. 69. Morey Bernstein, *The Search for Bridey Murphy* (Garden City, N.Y.: Doubleday, 1956). For an assessment of this book see C. J. Ducasse, *A Critical Examination of the Belief in Life after Death* (Springfield, Ill.: Thomas, 1961), chap. 25, "The Case of 'The Search for Bridey Murphy,'" pp. 276–299.

4. Martin E. Marty, "Healing Ministry—Historic Church: St. Stephen's Episcopal Church, Philadelphia," *Christian Century*, Aug. 28, 1957, pp. 1010–1013. This was the seventh in a series on creative churches.

5. "On Retreat," *Time*, June 24, 1957, pp. 52–54.

6. "Out of the Desert," *Time*, Apr. 15, 1957, pp. 60–68.

7. "The New Being," *Time*, June 10, 1957, pp. 51–54. See also "Three Cheers for Doubt?" *Newsweek*, Jan. 14, 1957. Paul Tillich, *The Dynamics of Faith* (New York: Harper, 1957).

8. "Is Hell Necessary?" *Time*, Dec. 30, 1957, pp. 30–31.

9. Joseph Blau, "What's American about American Jewry?" *Judaism* 7,3 (Summer 1958): 218.

10. Herbert Panzen, "The Passing of Jewish Secularism in the United States," *Judaism* 8,5 (Summer 1959): 195–205.

11. Mordecai M. Kaplan, *Judaism without Supernaturalism: The Only Alternative to Orthodoxy and Secularism* (New York: Reconstructionist, 1958).

12. Jakob J. Petuchowski, "The Limits of 'People-Centered' Judaism," *Commentary*, May 1959, p. 387.

13. Leon Uris, *Exodus* (Garden City, N.Y.: Doubleday, 1958).

14. Joel Blocker, "Fantasy of Israel," *Commentary*, June 1959, p. 539.

15. Julian Huxley, *Religion without Revelation* (New York: Harper, 1927); *Evolutionary Ethics* (London: Oxford University Press, 1943).

16. Aldous Huxley, *The Perennial Philosophy*, reprint (New York: Harper, 1945; New York: Harper and Row Colophon ed., 1970), p. 11.

17. Sybille Bedford, *Aldous Huxley: A Biography* (New York: Harper and Row, 1974), pp. 543–546, 558. Quotes from pp. 546, 558. See also, for this period, David King Dunaway, *Huxley in Hollywood* (New York: Harper and Row, 1989), and the memoirs of Huxley's second wife, Laura Archera Huxley, *This Timeless Moment: A Personal View of Aldous Huxley* (New York: Farrar, Straus and Giroux, 1968).

18. Aldous Huxley, *The Doors of Perception* (New York: Harper and Row, 1954). Other Fifties works of religious interest by Huxley include *The Devils of Loudun* (1962), the fictionalized history of demonic possession in a seventeenth-century French convent, with McCarthy-era overtones; *The Genius and the Goddess* (1955), a con-

versation-based novel about art, not considered one of Huxley most successful works; and a collection of essays, *Tomorrow and Tomorrow and Tomorrow* (1956).

19. Aldous Huxley, *The Doors of Perception and Heaven and Hell* (New York: Harper Colophon ed., 1990), pp. 17, 18.

20. Ibid., p. 35.

21. Aldous Huxley, *Heaven and Hell* (New York: Harper and Row, 1956). See, e.g., Aldous Huxley, *The Doors of Perception and Heaven and Hell* (New York: Harper Colophon ed., 1990).

22. Huxley, *Doors of Perception*, 1990 ed., p. 73.

23. Aldous Huxley, "Drugs That Shape Men's Minds," *Saturday Evening Post*, Oct. 18, 1958, pp. 28–29+.

24. *Kirkus Reviews*, Dec. 1, 1953, p. 779. J. H. Jackson, review, *San Francisco Chronicle*, Feb. 18, 1954, p. 13. *New Yorker*, review, Mar. 13, 1954, p. 133.

25. Aldous Huxley, *Tomorrow and Tomorrow and Tomorrow* (New York: Harper, 1956). William Esty, "Competitive Co-Existence in Aldous Huxley," *New Republic*, Nov. 26, 1956, pp. 18–19. Marvin Barrett, "Aldous Huxley, Merchant of Mescalin," review of *The Doors of Perception*, *Reporter*, Mar. 2, 1954, pp. 46–47.

26. Joseph Campbell, *The Hero with a Thousand Faces* (New York: Pantheon, 1949); Heinrich R. Zimmer, *Philosophies of India*, ed. Joseph Campbell (New York: Pantheon, 1951); *The Art of Indian Asia*, ed. Joseph Campbell, 2 vols. (New York: Pantheon, 1955); Joseph Campbell, ed., *Papers from the Eranos Yearbooks*, trans. Ralph Manheim and R.F.C. Hull, vol. 1, *Spirit and Nature*, 1954, vol. 2, *The Mysteries*, 1955, vol. 3, *Man and Time*, 1957 (New York: Pantheon).

27. Carl G. Jung, *Modern Man in Search of a Soul* (London: K. Paul, Trench, Trubner, 1933); *Answer to Job* (London: Routledge and Paul, 1954). Mircea Eliade, *The Sacred and the Profane* (New York: Harcourt, Brace, 1959); *The Myth of the Eternal Return* (New York: Pantheon, 1954); *Shamanism: Archaic Techniques of Ecstasy* (New York: Bollengen, 1964); *Yoga: Immortality and Freedom* (New York: Pantheon, 1958).

28. Joseph Campbell, *Creative Mythology: The Masks of God* (New York: Viking, 1968), pp. 5–6.

29. C. G. Jung, *The Archetypes and the Collective Unconscious*, vol. 9, pt. 1 of the *Collected Works* (New York: Pantheon, 1959).

30. John Harold Redekop, *The American Far Right: A Case Study of Billy James Hargis and Christian Crusade* (Grand Rapids, Mich.: Eerdmans, 1968), p. 27.

31. Billy Jim Hargis, "Are We Opposed to Communism?" *American Mercury*, Feb. 27, 1957, p. 28.

32. Billy Jim Hargis, "A Christian Ambassador Surveys His Divided World," *American Mercury*, Oct. 1957, pp. 141–145, and "Three Christian Giants in a World of Dwarfs," *American Mercury*, Dec. 1957, p. 16.

33. Billy Jim Hargis, "Patriotism—Once Revered, Now Smeared," *American Mercury*, Dec. 1958, pp. 137–147, and "The History of American Communist Fronts," pp. 26–33. Pete White, "Bibles from the Sky!" *American Mercury*, Apr. 1957, pp. 89–91. This article also contains biographical data on Hargis.

34. Mark Sherwin, *The Extremists* (New York: St Martin's, 1963), p. 110.

35. J. Gordon Melton, *Encyclopedia of American Religions*, 4th ed. (Detroit: Gale, 1993), pp. 1009–1010.

36. Edward Cain, *They'd Rather Be Right* (New York: Macmillan, 1963), p. 218.

37. Ira Progoff, *The Death and Rebirth of Psychology* (New York: Julian, 1956). "'A Soul without Psychology,'" *Time*, Dec. 24, 1956, pp. 51–52.

38. Ira Progoff, trans., *The Cloud of Unknowing* (New York; Delta, 1957).

39. Rollo May, ed., *Existence: A New Direction in Psychiatry and Psychology* (New York: Basic, 1958).

40. Leonard Gross, *God and Freud* (New York: McKay, 1959). See also "Mind and Spirit," *Time*, Dec. 29, 1958, pp. 26–27.
41. Alexander King, *Mine Enemy Grows Older* (New York: Simon and Schuster, 1958), and *May This House Be Safe from Tigers* (New York: Simon and Schuster, 1960).
42. Peter De Vries, *The Mackerel Plaza* (Boston: Little, Brown, 1958), pp. 7–8.
43. Ayn Rand, *Atlas Shrugged* (New York: Random House, 1957). "No Walls Will Fall," review of *Atlas Shrugged*, *Newsweek*, Oct. 14, 1957, pp. 130–133 (quotes from this source).
44. Rand, *Atlas Shrugged*, p. 731.
45. "Down with Altruism," *Time*, Feb. 29, 1960, p. 94. Cited in James T. Barker, *Ayn Rand* (Boston: Hall, 1987), p. 28. Rand was later to deny having made that statement, but according to Barker it seems very likely she did.
46. Etienne Gilson, *The Christian Philosophy of St. Thomas Aquinas* (New York: Random House, 1956), pp. 367–368.
47. Liston Pope, *The Kingdom beyond Caste* (New York: Friendship, 1957), p. 105.
48. Martin Luther King, Jr., *Stride toward Freedom: The Montgomery Story* (New York: Harper, 1958). "King Is Stabbed in New York," *Christian Century*, Sept. 20, 1958, p. 1101.
49. Archibald MacLeish, *J. B.: A Play in Verse* (Boston: Houghton Mifflin, 1958).
50. Boris Pasternak, *Doctor Zhivago* (New York: Pantheon, 1958).
51. Cited in "The Passion of Yuri Zhivago," *Time*, Dec. 15, 1958, p. 81.
52. G. Bromley Oxnam, *A Testament of Faith* (Boston: Little, Brown, 1958), p. ix.
53. Louis Schneider and Sanford Dornbusch, *Popular Religion: Inspirational Books in America* (Chicago: University of Chicago Press, 1958).
54. A. Roy Eckardt, *The Surge of Piety in America* (New York: Association Press, 1958), p. 19.

Conclusion

1. Jean-François Lyotard, *The Postmodern Condition: A Report on Knowledge*, trans. Geoff Bennington and Brian Massumi (Minneapolis: University of Minnesota Press, 1984), p. ix.
2. Daniel Bell, *The End of Ideology* (New York: Colliers, 1961).
3. John K. Jessup, ed., *The National Purpose* (New York: Holt, Rinehart and Winston, 1960). See also Michael Novak, "Anatomy of a Debate," *Christian Century*, Dec. 7, 1960, pp. 1432–1434.

Index

About the Author

Robert Ellwood is professor in the School of Religion at the University of Southern California. He has published over a dozen books including *Islands of the Dawn* and *The Sixties Spiritual Awakening* (Rutgers University Press).